THE
THIRD WORLD
HANDBOOK

THE
THIRD WORLD
HANDBOOK

SECOND EDITION

Guy Arnold

CASSELL

FITZROY
DEARBORN
FD
PUBLISHERS

Cassell
Wellington House, 125 Strand, London WC2R 0BB

127 West 24th St., New York NY 10011

First published 1989
This revised second edition published 1994

Reprinted 1996

Published in the United States of America by
Fitzroy Dearborn Publishers
70 East Walton Street, Chicago, Illinois 60611

© Guy Arnold 1989, 1994

British Library Cataloguing-in-Publication Data
A catalogue record for this book is available from the British Library.

ISBN 0-304-32837-5 (hardback)
0-304-32835-9 (paperback)

Library of Congress Cataloging-in-Publication Data

A catalog record for this book is available from the Library of Congress

ISBN 1-884-964-12-5

Typeset by Litho Link Ltd, Welshpool, Powys, Wales
Printed and bound in Great Britain by Redwood Books, Trowbridge, Wiltshire

Contents

91953

Preface

In this Handbook, I have tried to describe what we have come to call the Third World, although since the mid-1980s the term 'South' has been used increasingly in place of Third World and the two are now interchangeable. The term Third World has been with us for nearly 40 years, but most people are vague as to just what it means. How many countries belong to it? What individual and collective policies do its members pursue? What are the problems common to the Third World? What is it that allows countries as different as Brazil or India, Kuwait or Grenada, Nigeria or Fiji each to claim membership of this huge group?

Developments in Africa during the 1980s focused much attention upon the problems of the Third World because the continent experienced an appalling decade of falling income and living standards, natural disasters and civil wars, which between them came to be seen in the North as the norm for much of the South. Too often, however, the public response to the Third World is only in terms of a disaster and there is little understanding of how the Third World came into being and why so many countries see themselves as belonging to it.

This Handbook is concerned with three broad areas: the emergence of the Third World; membership and regional collaboration; and the problems faced by its members.

The emergence of the Third World is covered under End of Empires; the United Nations; and the Third World and Non-Alignment. Membership and regional groupings are dealt with in the central part of the Handbook, while the final chapters (5 to 9) deal with problems, predominantly economic, which are common to Third World countries. Finally there are Biographical Notes and a Country Gazetteer.

Omissions are inevitable when covering so wide a subject. Volumes could be written about the activities of transnational corporations, the arms business, liberation movements or the emancipation of women. One form of liberation leads to another. Political independence has brought in its wake all the other demands. Nonetheless, I have tried to encapsulate in one volume the chief developments, achievements, problems and attitudes which between them have produced what we call the Third World.

This second edition of the Handbook has been revised and updated in the light of the momentous events of 1989-92, which saw the end of the Cold War and the collapse of the Soviet Union. One result of these cataclysmic events has been the emergence of a number of successor states to the former USSR – Azerbaijan, Armenia, Georgia, Kazakhstan, Kyrgyzstan, Tajikistan, Turkmenistan and Uzbekistan – which, in terms of their stages of development, qualify as Third World countries and have been included in this new edition of the Handbook as a result.

Guy Arnold
London, 1994

Introduction

The genesis of the Third World, or the South as it is increasingly called, lies in the fear of domination. The age of the 'end of empires' through which our world has only recently come represents, at least superficially, an end to domination of the weak by the strong. This development, more apparent than real, is greatly reinforced by the fact that almost all members of the Third World, except for the countries of Latin America, were until recently colonies of the major imperial powers. But exhilaration at political independence was quickly replaced by a grim awareness of the South's vulnerability to the manipulations of the developed North at almost every level of economic and most levels of political life.

Today when we discuss the Third World – now that the Cold War has ended – we will no longer do so in terms of its capacity to stand aside from Cold War confrontations or its ability to mediate between the big powers – a discussion that might have taken place in the 1950s during the political ascendancy of India's first prime minister, Jawaharlal Nehru. Now such a discussion will be confined to Third World problems: poor economic perfomance, an apparently insatiable and never-ending need for aid, mounting debts or political instability characterized by coups, small wars, revolutions or guerrilla movements fighting against the central government. The North sees the South as unable to solve its own problems and when any form of North–South dialogue takes place it always degenerates into a one-way petition: the South asking for yet further concessions, acting as a suppliant, and demanding favours over the terms of trade, aid, or debt. This is not a healthy relationship.

The Third World has emerged out of years of exploitation. As much as anything, it arose out of frustrations with the world's power structures. The world community as a whole has the capacity to solve most of its problems. We can produce enough food so that no one need starve. Distribution and the ability to pay for what is produced are the problems, not lack of land or ability to grow what is needed.

Although it is now relatively less important, the nuclear question long focused attention upon power inequalities better than anything else. It was the stark realities of a Cold War confrontation backed by nuclear weapons with all their potentially frightful consequences that led Nehru and other leaders to create a Third Force concept in the 1950s. Arguments about the bomb have always been one-sided, weighted in favour of the maintenance of the old political order. Countries of the North first produced and used nuclear weapons. These same countries subsequently built up huge arsenals of nuclear weapons and based their military policies upon their possession and the means to deliver them on such a scale that any nuclear war would spell the end of our world. Only at this stage did the terrifying nature of the weapons appear to register with the nuclear powers. They then proceeded to lecture the rest of the world upon the frightfulness of the weapons and insist – for the sake of humanity – that no one else should produce such weapons. At the same time they refused to stop making more of them or to eliminate existing stocks. The monopoly must remain with the power brokers of the North. India's explosion of its first nuclear device in 1974 provoked much anger that the leading nation of the Non-Aligned Movement should want to create its own nuclear arsenal. Yet much of the moral indignation which ensued was in fact outrage that India had dared to break the monopoly of the North and was not prepared to behave according to the North's dictates. (In this regard China was seen as belonging to the North rather than the South.) This attitude goes to the root of the North–South relationship. As yet we have hardly begun to move away from a situation in which the North knows how the world ought to conduct its affairs and is prepared to help the South only on sufferance, when it behaves as the North requires. The sin of Nehru and other non-aligned or Third

World leaders has been their refusal to accept this arrogant assumption.

Many strands go to make up the Third World. All of them have their origins in the relationship between South and North. They are the reactions of the weak to the strong, of those with little or no power to those with a great deal. Historically this is hardly new. What is new in our age is the extent to which the relationship between weak and strong, poor and rich or South and North has been so clearly documented, discussed and exposed. It was once taken for granted that the powerful would oppress the weak – they usually did (and do) – but today we pretend to abhor this assumption.

In 1945, when the victors of World War II created the United Nations, they saw it as an instrument (which they would control) to maintain peace or a status quo largely favourable to their dominant position. They did not envisage the United Nations which has emerged: the champion of the rights of all people to have a voice in the running of their world. This is a novel idea, unique to the twentieth century. And whatever the failings of the world body, this single accomplishment justifies its existence.

In power terms, not much changes. The big powers interfere in the name of a current ideology or to sustain a 'friendly' government, but in reality they are buttressing their own interests. The Nigerians learnt a good deal about such motives during their civil war in the late 1960s, as did the countries of the Horn of Africa in the mid-1970s, or Afghanistan in the 1980s.

Broadly there are three reasons for such interference. The first, least complex motive is simply the desire to safeguard interests – investment, trade and strategic bases. The second is less precise, but comes to the same thing in the end: the determination to keep a Third World country within one's sphere of influence. And third, an arrogant assumption arising out of power and its long exercise, is that the powerful of the North *know* what is best for the development of the South. Those in the North who are basically unsympathetic to the aspirations of the South wish, nonetheless, to interfere in order to promote their own advantage. And those in the North who are sympathetic still wish to interfere because they almost always assume that the South cannot solve its problems on its on. The North knows best.

The determination of the major powers to continue interfering after their colonies had become independent was a primary reason for the emergence of Third Force politics in the 1950s. The fear among the leaders of the big powers that India under Nehru (1947-64), Egypt under Nasser (1954-70), or Yugoslavia under Tito (1945-80) would go their own ways immeasurably strengthened the resolve of such leaders to do just that. And so the Third World was born.

Yet if the Third World refused to join sides in the Cold War, economic weakness did not allow it to do much else of an independent nature. Sensing this vulnerability the North substituted aid for colonialism and the aid age was born. Aid in its various forms has become the North's most potent weapon in its dealings with the South. Not that aid solves development problems. What it does is create ongoing dependency and open up endless opportunities for interference in the economic and political affairs of the South. Development assistance, military interventions, management of markets, and the reports of Canada's Lester Pearson (1969) and West Germany's Willi Brandt (1980) are part of the same equation: a Northern finger in the Southern pie = control.

Fashions change and the fashion of the late 1980s, for example, was to ask whether aid assists development, or at least (for options must be kept open) whether aid of the *kind* dispensed so far assists development. One can be quite certain that aid in some form will continue. The correct question to ask is whether aid was ever intended to help development, as opposed to providing the donors with an entry into the countries where they have interests to defend or wish to extend their influence.

President Julius Nyerere of Tanzania was correct to insist in the Arusha Declaration (1967) that aid ought only to be used as a catalyst, while the main thrust of development should come from within. But the difficulty about such a proposition advanced on behalf of any poor country is at once obvious. Once a Third World country turns to the international aid agencies, it surrenders control over part of its development. The donors decide what is needed, how much they will provide, on what terms, when they will come and go. This has now been the pattern for many Third World countries for more than a generation.

If it is objected that such major donors as the USA or Britain have cut back their aid severely during the latter part of the 1980s and the early 1990s, this does not invalidate the above arguments.

Nor are reductions of aid the result of any lessening of guilt feelings in the North about former imperial activities (another fashionable argument of the 1980s). Rather, such cutbacks have taken place because, in a time of recession, the North finds it can manipulate the South by other means. In 1984 the total flow of world aid from both bilateral and multilateral sources came to approximately $36 billion, while world expenditure on arms exceeded $450 billion. Ten years later the end of the Cold War might have reduced the pressures to spend vast sums on arms but it had also lessened commensurately the pressures to provide aid and though the aid flow had increased to $54 billion, arms expenditure had risen to more than $1,000,000 million.

The formidable array of institutions concerned with the South established in countries of the North over the last 40 years offers a revelation of the North's determination to be involved in the Third World. These institutions range from the World Bank (technically a world institution, though in fact controlled by the North) through government aid ministries in the countries of the North (Moscow's aid abruptly terminated with the end of the Cold War), university departments and independent research bodies, missionary bodies, churches and numerous other non-government organizations, all of which are busy in the Third World. Such a spread of organizations requires careful study: who controls them, what are their objectives, what do they achieve for the Third World, and whose interests do they serve?

One of the most familiar arguments to pinpoint North–South antagonisms concerns the activities of the International Monetary Fund (IMF). Does it really exist to help economies in trouble? Or is it prepared to help only if they conform to a pattern of economic behaviour laid down by the North? In the South the IMF has become a bogeyman and is seen as a policeman acting on behalf of western capitalist interests. The IMF is hardly alone in this perceived role even if it is one of the most exposed international institutions. The World Bank, the IMF and the transnationals in particular are all viewed in a similar light from the South. They are seen as institutions designed to buttress western capitalism whose end result (whatever explanations are offered along the way) is to keep firmly within the capitalist camp all Third World recipients of their funds or investments and, at least for the immediate future, in the aftermath of the

Cold War there is nowhere else for countries of the South to go.

The fashionable argument now carefully fostered in the North is that the time for guilt about colonial exploitation has passed. This is a lie in the simple sense that there never was much guilt. The colonial powers fought hard and long to hold on. If finally they relinquished political control, they did so because it would have proved too costly to attempt to hold on any longer. Individuals may feel guilt, but there is little evidence in the post-imperial age that either Britain or France have any sense of remorse. Indeed the contrary appears to be the case. A wave of nostalgia about imperial achievements is now under way.

And if the rhetoric about colonialism and imperialism of Third World leaders has now become purely ritualistic, this is no more than to acknowledge a hard political truth: that guilt among nations is a rarity and that policy is always based upon self-interest. The North involves itself in Third World problems not in order to find solutions to those problems, but so as to further its own interests.

The converse is the argument, often advanced but rarely acted upon, that the Third World would do best if left to its own devices. Third World self-reliance which rejects interference from the North may be an answer in theory. In practice Third World countries are simply too weak and, as a rule, either unwilling or unable to opt for genuine policies of self-reliance. In any case they are generally far too much in debt to the North to be able to break free of its controls.

It is easy to take the North to task for its endless opportunism at the expense of the South. At the same time it is important to ask how many countries of the South – or more accurately how many of the governments and ruling élites – wish to break the ties which bind them to the North. How many would choose policies of self-reliance if these demand greater local effort and a longer period before wealth objectives are obtained, and if they create political hazards for the ruling élites?

Almost all the organizations of the South, such as the Group of 77,* are concerned primarily to bargain with the North: to obtain more aid, better terms of trade, greater investment, easier access to

*The Group of 77 (now numbering 124) includes virtually all the developing countries. The group (and name) came into being following the first United Nations Conference on Trade and Development (UNCTAD) which was held in 1964.

markets, and so on. Every international meeting of the UN, the United Nations Conference on Trade and Development (UNCTAD), the World Bank or those bodies concerned with such special topics as the Law of the Sea follows the same course. Battle lines are drawn up with the Rich determined to defend a status quo which works to their advantage (whose ground rules were anyway drawn up decades ago by the rich) and the Poor concerned to wring more concessions from them. That is the pattern of North-South dialogue in so far as it exists.

And sadly much Third World development is characterized by violence. In 1992-93, a rough count showed that about 35 wars, civil wars or insurrections were taking their toll around the Third World. Of these 12 were in Africa, 16 in Asia (including the civil wars in the southern tier of successor states to the Soviet Union such as Armenia and Azerbaijan) and six in Latin America. In certain cases, most notably Somalia, the extent of the fighting and subsequent suffering brought a new dimension to Third World conflicts with the intervention on a major scale of the United Nations (now released from the stalemate of inactivity that had been imposed upon it during the Cold War). Whether such UN interventions will actually curtail conflicts is another question entirely. The Gulf War of 1991 between Iraq (which had invaded and seized Kuwait in 1990) and the US-led, UN-sponsored coalition possibly set a new pattern for North–South relations: the concept of the North (through the United Nations) acting as a policeman in the South now that the end of the Cold War also meant the effective disappearance of the USSR as a counterweight, or brake, on American action. Many of these wars have been with us for years and some, such as the civil war in Angola which was renewed in 1992, are brutal in the extreme.

Festering leftovers of empire still erupt from time to time and will continue to do so until the problems are solved: the Falklands and New Caledonia. One such problem, however, was finally solved in 1990: after a quarter of a century of guerrilla activity against the occupying South Africans, Namibia achieved its independence in the new climate then prevailing in southern Africa and at least one Third World struggle was brought to a satisfactory conclusion. But all too often, big power interventions, including the Russians in Afghanistan and the Americans bombing Tripoli

to teach 'terrorist' Gaddafi a lesson, demonstrate how little, if anything, has changed. What the North refuses to do is bring its power to bear upon the problems which cause the bloodshed. Thus, if the western nations which do so much business with South Africa had brought to bear upon that country the awesome economic levers at their disposal, the world would have forced Pretoria to end the injustice of apartheid years before a developing revolutionary situation inside South Africa forced President de Klerk to reverse 40 years of National Party policy to release Nelson Mandela in 1990 and begin talking with the African National Congress (ANC). Similarly, if the Americans had insisted (using the threat to withhold their economic and military aid) that Israel talked with the Palestine Liberation Organization (PLO) until a solution to the Palestine problem was reached there would have been no call to bomb Libya in 1986. But those who are driven to violence by deprivation, such as the PLO and the ANC, are dubbed terrorists, while those whose policies have forced them to behave in such a manner are supported by the North through thick and thin.

The Third World, then, has come into being in reaction to the arrogant, omnipresent power of the North. Even its collective power is small and puny and when we consider that there are now about 157 members of the Third World it is hardly surprising that they do not often achieve a consensus. In terms of its total gross national product (GNP), Britain ranks seventh in the world after the USA, Japan, Russia, Germany, France and Italy. Yet nonetheless Britain has a GNP equivalent to two and one third times the combined GNPs of all the countries on the African continent. American power – its GNP is about six times that of Britain – is truly awesome in relation to the South (for figures see Gazetteer).

The main concern of the Third World is to assert its collective and individual identity in relation to the powerful North. What is startling – given the normal patterns of history – is the extent to which the Third World has managed to maintain its independence, its Non-Alignment and its ability to pursue its own policies despite aid, debt, transnationals and all the other mechanisms of control which are exerted from the North. The Third World owes this achievement at least in part to the media. The spread of information, the fact that arguments and events are instantly publicized through television has provided the Third World with a platform unimaginable even a generation ago. And that is true even though the North overwhelmingly controls the media.

The ending of the Cold War followed by the dissolution of the Soviet Empire has meant, if anything, that Third World problems have become greater rather than less: for just as the Third World grew out of the original Cold War as the newly independent countries determined not to be drawn into the confrontation of the big powers, so they gained from that confrontation because they had two 'courts of appeal' to whom they could apply for assistance. The end of the Cold War and the determination of Russia to join the western-dominated world community has meant that the Third World's two courts of appeal have been replaced at a stroke by a single North that no longer feels it has to involve itelf in the affairs of the South through fear that by neglect its rivals will gain an advantage while, at the same time, a number of new Third World countries clamouring and competing for the attention and aid of the North have emerged on the international stage. What many Third World countries sensed in the early 1990s was a dwindling interest on the part of the North in their problems – the interest was in any case never very great without the compulsions of Cold War politics to act as a spur – and now it had become even less. At the same time there was growing fear that American involvement in the Gulf in 1991 and Somalia in 1992 represented a new approach by the North to the South: that involvement when it did occur would increasingly be in the form of 'Big Brother' policing actions. The prospects for the South in 1993, therefore, were far from encouraging while its problems of poverty, debt and violence were as great as ever.

The title of the radical writer Frantz Fanon's book *Wretched of the Earth* highlights the most important single difference between North and South – poverty. If the South can overcome poverty, then its other aspirations – for greater equality and a bigger say in the ordering of the world – will follow. But poverty remains the key. That is why almost all North–South dialogue concerns aid, trade and the transfer of resources. Once Third World countries achieve economic breakthroughs which enable them to improve the condition of their people and become self-sustaining economies, then other political objectives will come within reach.

1 End of Empires

When in 1940 Winston Churchill said 'I have not become the first minister of the Crown in order to preside over the liquidation of the British Empire', he was employing political rhetoric at a time of high drama. Even so, few then could have believed that the end of the European-ruled empires was so near. When World War II ended in 1945, the British Empire was intact (though it had been a close thing) and the other imperial powers, most notably France and the Netherlands, which had been occupied by Germany, hastened to regain control of their overseas possessions. The assumption was a return to 'business as usual'.

But this was not to be. In French Indo-China and Malaya, the Communists who had fought the Japanese from the jungle now became the spearhead of the nationalists fighting against the returning imperial powers. As Britain disbanded its wartime armies and sent the troops home, about 250,000 soldiers recruited from its African colonies returned home. As soldiers, they had been taught that they were fighting for liberty against tyranny, but at home they discovered that they were second-class citizens without any voice in government. One such young soldier from Kenya, Waruhiu Itote, later became famous as 'General China' during the nationalist Mau Mau uprising in the 1950s.

Then the United Nations came into being. Its Charter proclaimed equal freedom for all people and naturally, therefore, it exercised a particular attraction for the subject peoples of the old empires. Increasingly it became a forum in which imperialism could be denounced.

Still more important as a factor for change was the emergence of the two superpowers – the USA and USSR. Neither was an imperial power like Britain or France, although the USSR was in fact an empire as events at the beginning of the 1990s were to demonstrate, despite Moscow's constant denials of such a status over the years. Each of the superpowers, for historic reasons, was fundamentally opposed to the idea of empire. Both, there-

fore, began to exert major pressures upon the old imperial powers to hasten the end of empires. The confrontation between their rival ideologies, which rapidly developed into the Cold War, made the process of their pressures all the more insistent.

Then, too, the colonial powers were exhausted by the war in Europe. The fact that they accepted American Marshall Aid to assist their economic recovery made them more susceptible to other American pressures. When confronted by prolonged resistance by determined nationalists, as the Dutch discovered in Indonesia and the French in Indo-China, the will to hold on no longer existed.

Even more important, however, was the simple demand for independence, for freedom, for an end of empires. The strength of this demand gathered ground every year after the end of World War II. Nothing is more powerful than an idea whose time has come. And the time to end empires and allow the emergence of independent states throughout the old colonial dependencies had indeed arrived.

A key to the break-up of empires was India. This huge subcontinent had long been regarded by Britain as the centrepiece of its empire. Quite simply, while Britain held India it was in the superpower bracket, but ceased to be so when India went. Indian demands for independence had been growing ever since 1919 and by 1945 were focused in the extraordinary figure of Mahatma Gandhi. During the war, the British had, however reluctantly, promised independence in return for India's support. When the Labour Party under Clement Attlee swept to power in Britain in 1945, the new government, unlike its Tory opponents, was committed to Indian independence. Two years later, the British Indian Empire ceased to exist. Two new nations, India and Pakistan, emerged instead and Burma (now Myanmar) and Ceylon (now Sri Lanka) became independent soon afterwards. The key dates in the advance of India and other former colonies towards independence are set out below.

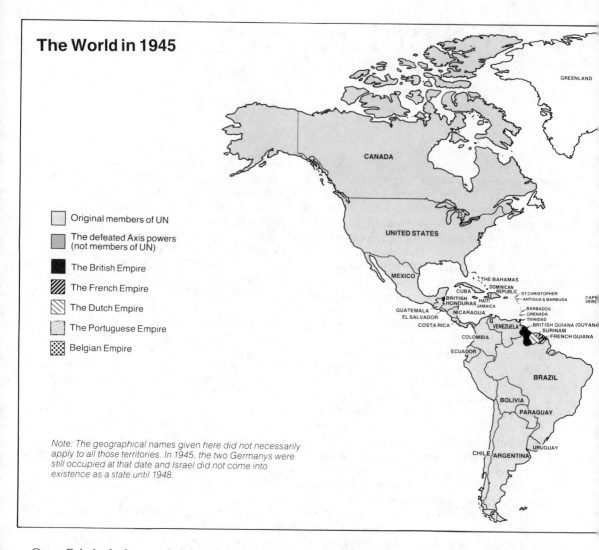

The World in 1945

Original members of UN

The defeated Axis powers (not members of UN)

The British Empire

The French Empire

The Dutch Empire

The Portuguese Empire

Belgian Empire

Note: The geographical names given here did not necessarily apply to all those territories. In 1945, the two Germanys were still occupied at that date and Israel did not come into existence as a state until 1948.

Once Britain had conceded independence to India, the process of decolonization was bound to speed up. It was a matter of logic. Having admitted the right of Indians to govern themselves, Britain could not easily argue that Malays, Africans or West Indians should not enjoy the same right. The only argument left (though many were used to delay independence elsewhere) was that of timing. Moreover, the effect of Indian independence was immense throughout the remaining empires.

Then in 1949 Mao Zedong (Mao Tse-tung) and the Communists triumphed in China and that huge country became menacingly united (as the western world saw it) for the first time in the twentieth century. Cold War considerations at once became of even greater importance. For example, an independent India was seen in the West more as a counterbalance to China in Asia than simply a non-aligned country (despite Nehru's insistence that it should be so).

Meanwhile independence struggles were growing in intensity. The Dutch failed to regain control of their East Indian Empire and in 1949 the United States of Indonesia were proclaimed. The French found themselves fighting an increasingly bitter and apparently endless war in Indo-China. The British were fighting Communist insurgents in the Malayan jungle. In French Madagascar (1947) an almost unheard-of uprising took place and some 10,000 people were killed. In British East Africa the 1950s were dominated by the Mau Mau struggle in Kenya. And in Algeria a long and

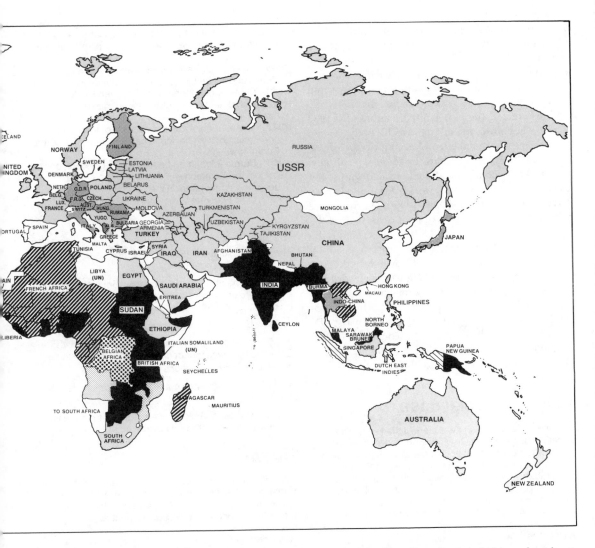

brutal struggle between the French settlers (*colons*) backed by France and the Algerian nationalists resulted in independence in 1962. These and other struggles had consequences far beyond the borders of the territories where they were fought. On the one hand they encouraged general opposition to the imperial powers throughout the colonial empires. On the other hand they helped persuade the imperial powers that the time had come for them to quit. If one colony after another was only to be held by force and costly wars, then empire had ceased to be a paying proposition. It made more sense to grant independence and work for good subsequent relations.

It was not an easy process. The humiliating 'defeat' of the Anglo-French intervention in Suez in 1956 helped to discredit the old idea of gunboat diplomacy with the imperial powers policing lesser nations. Then in 1960 when Britain's prime minister Harold Macmillan made his famous 'Wind of Change' speech in Cape Town, South Africa, he effectively signalled that Britain had accepted decolonization as the policy for the remainder of its empire. Indeed, 1960 was to be called the *annus mirabilis* of African independence. Seventeen African countries, including Britain's largest African colony, Nigeria, the Belgian Congo (now Zaïre) and France's West and Equatorial African possessions, Somalia and Madagascar, became independent. Problems remained. For example, white-dominated Southern Rhodesia did not become independent as Zimbabwe until 1980 after

15 years of illegal white minority government and bitter guerrilla warfare. But 1960 may be taken as the year when the old colonial powers accepted that the end of their empires was in sight.

The results of this (historically) incredibly rapid process were almost incalculable. In 1945, 50 nations created the new United Nations. By 1980 when Zimbabwe joined the world body it had more than 150 members and a majority belonged to the Third World. This large group of new nations has become one of the key factors affecting the policies of our present world. Not only do they have a majority in the United Nations, they have also created organizations of their own, such as the Organization of African Unity (OAU) and the Non-Aligned Movement. They were wooed by both sides as long as the Cold War lasted. And they now present the rich North with awkward but compelling questions of how our world should be run: the aid debate; the idea of a New International Economic Order (NIEO) advocated by the UN General Assembly in 1974; the concept of Non-Alignment; and the North–South dialogue. All are the direct outcome of the end of empires.

India: a special case

The sheer size of British India made it the key to Britain's imperial policies. It was an empire on its own. Had the British attempted to hold on to India after 1945, the story of world decolonization would have been very different – and probably far more violent – than in fact was the case. The decision of the British Labour government to agree to Indian independence immediately after World War II had immense consequences for the whole Third World.

Key dates

1885 First meeting of the Indian National Congress.
1919 Punjab riots; the Amritsar Massacre; constitutional reforms introduce limited democracy.
1920 Gandhi begins civil disobedience campaign.
1922 Gandhi arrested (for civil disobedience) for first time.
1931 London Round Table Conference: Gandhi insists upon all India government but is opposed by Muslims.
1935 Government of India Act: a reshaping of the Indian Constitution, Burma is separated from India.
1939 By the outbreak of World War II, it is no longer a question of whether or not India should have independence but only of when it will gain it.
1941 Britain offers Congress autonomy after the war, but is met with a demand for immediate independence; unrest follows.
1942 Widespread unrest; Congress leaders arrested; Britain maintains full control. The fall of Singapore is

followed by the Japanese invasion of Burma; both events contribute to a collapse of British and western prestige in Asia.
1945 The Labour Party wins the general election in Britain and is committed to independence for India.
1946 Growing communal strife between Hindus and Muslims; Britain offers full independence and sets a timetable.
1947 Independence and the partition of India into India and Pakistan; both decide to become members of the Commonwealth.
1948 Burma (Myanmar) becomes independent, does not join the Commonwealth; Ceylon (Sri Lanka) becomes independent in the Commonwealth.
1950 India becomes a republic within the Commonwealth.

Results

The break-up of the British Indian Empire had momentous consequences:

1. It led to the partition of the subcontinent and the emergence of four independent Asian nations – India, Pakistan, Burma (Myanmar) and Ceylon (Sri Lanka).

2. India became the world's largest democracy.

3. Modern aid programmes came into operation: the Colombo Plan was founded in 1950 in response to the development needs of these new countries.

4. Indian independence made decolonization elsewhere inevitable.

5. Indian independence relegated Britain from the first to the second rank of world powers.

Egypt

Although technically fully independent since 1922, Egypt remained subject to British political interference and sometimes control. It was used as a British base throughout World War II despite its 'neutrality'.

Key dates

1951 The Egyptian government abrogates the 1936 Treaty with Britain; British troops occupy the Canal Zone.
1952 General Muhammed Neguib and Colonel Abdel Nasser seize power in a coup and force King Farouk to abdicate.
1954 Nasser takes full control; an Anglo-Egyptian agreement on the Canal Zone stipulates that the British base is to be evacuated within 20 months.
1956 Britain gives independence to Sudan (1 January) in part as a move to pre-empt any union between Egypt and Sudan. Egypt in an arms deal with Czechoslovakia; the World Bank, the USA and Britain withdraw their preferred aid for the Aswan High Dam; the Russians offer to build it.
The Suez Crisis In retaliation for the withdrawal of western aid Nasser nationalizes the Suez Canal; Britain, France and Israel in secret agreement; Israel

invades Sinai and reaches the Canal providing the excuse for an Anglo-French military invasion; the two superpowers oppose; the UN calls for a cease-fire and its forces replace the British and French who withdraw. This last major use of gunboat diplomacy by the old colonial powers backfires disastrously and Britain is humiliated; Nasser becomes an immensely popular figure in the Third World; his subsequent influence and the impact of the *Voice of Cairo* radio play a vital role in the next 10 years of African and Arab independence struggles.

1957 Suez Canal reopened to international shipping.

1958 Revolution spreads in Arab Middle East: the pro-British monarchy of Faisal in Iraq is overthrown; American intervention in Lebanon and British intervention in Jordan; the formation of the United Arab Republic (UAR) between Egypt and Syria (to 1961).

1967 The Six Day War between the Arab nations and Israel: Egypt loses Sinai to Israel; the Canal is again blocked (until 1975).

1970 The completion (with massive Soviet aid) of the Aswan High Dam.
The death of Nasser.

Indonesia

The early and spectacular successes of Japan in World War II brought closer the end of the European empires in Asia. This was especially true of the Dutch East Indies.

Key dates

1942 The surrender of 100,000 British troops in Singapore destroyed the myth of western (white) superiority in Asia which had long been fostered as a justification of empire.
Prior to 1939 the Dutch had granted various representative institutions in their East Indian Empire but these had not prevented nationalist demands for independence or stopped the rise of a Communist party.
Some of the nationalists, including Achmed Sukarno, collaborated with the Japanese when they occupied the Dutch Indies in 1942.

1945 The Indonesian nationalists proclaim an independent republic with Sukarno as President before the Dutch return and establish control.

1945-49 The Dutch attempt but fail to regain full control of the Indies: a period of fighting and negotiations; a tentative agreement is made to establish an Indonesian republic linked to the Netherlands. External pressures are mounted upon the Netherlands: it comes under attack in the UN; newly independent India and Australia (coming to terms with the political realities which exist on its doorstep) take the question of the Dutch East Indies to the Security Council.

1949 The Dutch finally admit defeat and withdraw; a United States of Indonesia is proclaimed; the vague union with the Netherlands lasts for five years and is then dissolved.

French Indo-China

Key dates

1940 Japan invades French Indo-China.

1945 The Japanese formally displace French suzerainty, but following the defeat of Japan the French return and at first appear to have regained full control.
The Japanese had amalgamated Annam, Cochin China and Tonkin to form the new state of Vietnam. Ho Chi Minh, leader of the local Communist party, proclaims a Republic of Vietnam in defiance of the returning French; the nationalist revolution which he sparks off spreads quickly; Ho Chi Minh had spent years in Paris and was well acquainted with French as well as Communist ideology.
Substantial French military forces are sent to the country and France attempts to forestall full independence by recognizing Vietnam as an autonomous region in the French Union; the compromise fails; there is growing violence and French troops are attacked.

1946 French residents in Hanoi are attacked; French relief forces arrive; Ho Chi Minh is forced to flee but a major struggle now gets underway; Ho Chi Minh identifies himself with the nationalist aim of independence.

1949 France recognizes Cambodia (Kampuchea) and Laos as associate nations of the French Union. Moscow and Beijing (Peking) recognize the government of Ho Chi Minh.

1953 Following the end of the Korean war, China begins to supply arms to the Communist guerrillas in South Vietnam; France finally relinquishes control of Cambodia; French forces occupy Dien Bien Phu in North Vietnam.

1954 *Dien Bien Phu* Crushing defeat of the French destroys their will to continue the war.
Geneva Conference Divides Vietnam along the 17th parallel of latitude creating two independent nations: North Vietnam (Communist-backed) and South Vietnam (western-backed).
At this point Cold War considerations become of paramount importance yet despite them the struggle in Vietnam which continues for many years remains in essence an anti-colonial struggle; that is, one of its principal objectives is to free an area of Asia from western interference.

1962 President Kennedy sends 4000 American military advisers to South Vietnam and for the next 10 years the USA is increasingly deeply involved; before the American withdrawal in 1973 more than 50,000 US soldiers are killed; the effects of the war upon home politics in the USA are traumatic.

1973 The USA withdraws from South Vietnam.

1975 The North Vietnamese (Communist) army takes over South Vietnam and the two Vietnams become a single nation.

Algeria

Key dates

1945   Fighting (by nationalists) breaks out in Algeria; ruthless suppression and 15,000 killed; the nationalists at that stage only asked for autonomy in a federation with France.

1947   Concessions and constitutional reforms made by France anxious not to abandon the 1 million *colons* (white settlers).

1952   Ahmed Ben Bella forms the Algerian Revolutionary Committee in Cairo.

1954   The nationalists form the FLN (National Liberation Front) and the National Liberation Army. The war begins as France is drawn into the fighting on behalf of the 1 million *colons* who refuse to recognize the possibility of change.

1956   Suez: French collusion with Britain and Israel is aimed at toppling Nasser whose support sustains the FLN; the failure of Suez is followed by a growth of support for the FLN among the newly independent non-aligned countries.

1958   The *colons* set up Committees of Public Safety in Algerian towns and Algerian unrest leads to the collapse of the Fourth Republic in France where General Charles de Gaulle comes to power.
By this time, at the height of the bitter fighting, there are 500,000 French troops in Algeria.

1960   The *colons* rebel (January) against de Gaulle as it becomes clear that he is coming to recognize the strength of nationalist claims; the *colon* rebellion lasts 9 days.
De Gaulle begins secret negotiations with the FLN provisional government in Cairo.
The discovery of oil in the Sahara desert leads meanwhile to the suggestion that France should grant independence to northern Algeria but hold on to the oil-rich desert region.

1962   Negotiations reach a climax: France is to retain its naval base at Mers-el-Kebir for 15 years and be allowed a further 5 years for nuclear testing in the Sahara.
General Salan leads a final *colon* insurrection which fails.

1962   Referendum (1 July) is held; 91 per cent vote for independence which is proclaimed on 3 July.
The great majority of the *colons* return to France.

Kenya

Key dates

1945   The Sixth Pan-African Conference is held at Manchester attended by the Kenyan Jomo Kenyatta, the Ghanaian Kwame Nkrumah and other nationalists; they set targets for independence.

1946   Kenyatta returns to Kenya after 16 years in Britain and begins to organize nationalist demands for independence.

1950   The Kenya government proscribes the secret (nationalist) society – Mau Mau.

1952   Following growing violence against the settler-dominated colonial government, a state of emergency is declared; the principal Kikuyu (nationalist) leaders (100 including Kenyatta) are arrested and British troops are flown into the colony from the Canal Zone in Egypt.

1952-59   The state of emergency lasts for 7 years, although the rebellion has been brought under control by 1955.

1953   The trial of Jomo Kenyatta (with other leaders) on charges of managing Mau Mau; he is sentenced to 7 years in prison; it is the last of the great stage-managed colonial trials.

1959   When the state of emergency ends, about 13,500 people (mainly Kikuyu) have been killed; at its height Britain had 10,000 troops in the colony and the emergency cost her £55 million.
Mau Mau plays a vital role in persuading Britain to decolonize: the government does not wish to face comparable rebellions in other African possessions.

1960   Demands for Kenyatta's release grow but the Governor of Kenya (Sir Patrick Renison) describes him as the leader 'to darkness and death'.

1961   Kenyatta is finally released: he becomes the leader of the Kenya African National Union (KANU), the Premier and then first prime minister of an independent Kenya (December 1963).

1964   Kenya becomes a republic within the Commonwealth and Kenyatta its first president, a position he retains until his death in 1978.

Portugal's African wars

Despite being one of the smallest and poorest countries in Europe, Portugal nonetheless held on to its African colonial possessions – Angola, Guinea-Bissau, Cape Verde, Mozambique, São Tomé and Príncipe – almost longer than any of the major imperial powers. To do so it committed most of its armed forces to fighting long and costly colonial wars during the 1960s and 1970s. As a result it almost crippled itself economically and in the end brought about a political revolution at home. Portugal created the fiction that its overseas possessions were an integral part of the country.

Key dates

1951   Portugal transforms its colonies into Overseas Provinces: this makes them integral parts of Portugal.

1956   Amilcar Cabral founds the resistance movement (PAIGC) in Guinea-Bissau.

1961   The liberation struggle is launched in Angola.

1962   Eduardo Mondlane unites the different Mozambique liberation groups in Frelimo (the Mozambique Liberation Front).
The United Nations bans the sale of arms to Portugal although its NATO allies continue to keep it supplied for NATO purposes only.

1963   Cabral launches an all-out independence struggle in Guinea-Bissau.

1964   Frelimo launches war against the Portuguese in Mozambique.

1967   PAIGC has its own Radio Liberation in operation. Portugal is now deploying 60,000 troops in Mozambique.

1969   Assassination of Mondlane; power passes to a triumvirate of Uriah Simanga, Marcelino dos Santos and Samora Machel who soon emerges as the effective leader of Frelimo.

1970   Portugal increases military service to 4 years; it can only carry on its African wars because it is sustained by NATO allies.
By the beginning of the decade the PAIGC controls most of the interior of Guinea-Bissau away from the towns.

1971   The Portuguese claim that after 10 years of war in Angola 10,000 guerrillas and 1071 soldiers have been killed in the fighting.

1972   The PAIGC hold elections in the areas of Guinea-Bissau they control.
Portugal now has around 150,000 troops (out of a total army of 204,000) deployed in its African territories fighting three separate and very hard wars – and losing them; there are approximately 60,000 men in both Angola and Mozambique and 30,000 in Guinea-Bissau.

1973   The PAIGC proclaim the independence of Guinea-Bissau; Cabral is assassinated in Conakry.

1974   The Caetano regime in Portugal is overthrown by the army: General Spinola takes over as head of state; he announces that Portugal recognizes the right to independence of its African territories. The Lusaka Agreement (September) between Portugal and Frelimo sets June 1975 for Mozambique's independence; the whites of Lourenço Marques (Maputo) briefly seize power but the revolt does not succeed.
Portugal recognizes the independence of Guinea-Bissau.

1975   Mozambique (June), São Tomé & Príncipe (July), Cape Verde (September), Angola (November) become independent; the Portuguese Empire has finally come to an end.

Zimbabwe

Key dates

1953   Britain forms the Central African Federation (CAF) of Northern Rhodesia, Southern Rhodesia and Nyasaland under white control.

1958-63   African opposition to the CAF escalates accompanied by increasing violence and demands for independence.

1963   The CAF is dissolved.

1964   Nyasaland becomes independent as Malawi; Northern Rhodesia becomes independent as Zambia; the white minority government of Southern Rhodesia, now simply called Rhodesia, demands independence under its control; Ian Smith becomes the leader of the Rhodesia Front and prime minister.

1965   The white government in Rhodesia makes a Unilateral Declaration of Independence (UDI), which Britain and the UN condemn as illegal.

1966   The UN imposes sanctions on Rhodesia; no agreement is reached in British-Rhodesian negotiations.

1968   Further negotiations between Britain and Rhodesia fail.

1970   Rhodesia proclaims itself a republic.

1971   The British Pearson Commission visits Rhodesia: the Africans who are allowed to make representations to it overwhelmingly reject the proposed constitution which would have left control in white hands.

1972   The commencement of sustained guerrilla warfare in the north-east of the country by forces of the Zimbabwe African National Union (ZANU).

1973   Rhodesia closes the border with Zambia.

1974   South Africa sponsors détente to ease tensions in the region; this follows the collapse of the Caetano government in Portugal and South Africa's realization of its growing isolation.

1976   An attempt by US Secretary of State Henry Kissinger to resolve Southern Africa's deadlock shows that Rhodesia has become a significant international problem.
Robert Mugabe, leader of ZANU, and Joshua Nkomo, leader of the rival Zimbabwe African People's Union (ZAPU), form the Patriotic Front.

1978   The Smith government arranges an 'internal settlement', but the Patriotic Front vows to continue the struggle.

1979   The Lusaka Commonwealth Conference: Britain convenes a constitutional conference in London and a settlement is finally reached at the end of that year.

1980   Zimbabwe becomes independent and Robert Mugabe becomes prime minister. UDI had lasted nearly 15 years; official figures show 30,000 to have been killed during the guerrilla war.

Other independence struggles

There were many other independence struggles: some were less well publicized than Algeria or Kenya and some were token struggles. Others, such as that in Malaya, were inextricably bound up with the East–West ideological struggle. Four examples are summarized below.

Aden   An increasingly bitter guerrilla war was waged against Britain in Aden before independence was finally granted in 1967. The successor government of what became the People's Democratic Republic of Yemen (it finally united with the Yemen Arab Republic in May 1990 to form the single state of Yemen) was Marxist oriented and Aden did not become a member of the Commonwealth.

Cyprus   The independence struggle in Cyprus lasted throughout the 1950s. By 1956 Britain had removed its huge military base from the Suez Canal Zone to Cyprus and this became an added reason for it to hold on to the colony. The nationalist struggle in Cyprus was complicated by the demand for *enosis* (union with Greece) and the bitter communal strife between Greek and Turk. In the end Cyprus achieved independence in 1960 and Archbishop Makarios became the island's first president. It remained in the Commonwealth but in 1974 Turkey invaded the north of Cyprus (the predominantly Turkish area) and effectively partitioned the island.

Madagascar   A major but little publicized uprising against the French took place in 1947. This was brutally suppressed with an estimated 10,000 killed. Madagascar became independent in 1960.

Malaya   In 1948 Britain proclaimed a state of emergency; this was the prelude to a long jungle war against Chinese Communist guerrillas. This war – part nationalist, part ideological – seemed less clear cut in its nationalist aims because of the Cold War overtones. When Britain granted independence to Malaya in 1957, the Communist insurgents had already been defeated and a basically conservative government took power.

Latin America

Unlike the other regions which make up the Third World (including most of the Caribbean), Latin America alone achieved independence in the first half of the nineteenth century with the break-up of the Spanish and Portuguese empires in the Americas. Thus in 1945 20 Latin American countries were among the 50 founder members of the UN at a time when most of the other countries which now make up the Third World were still colonies.

This huge region on the doorstep of the USA is more cohesive than the other areas of the Third World since its members shared a more uniform common history of Spanish and Portuguese colonialism. In the early post-war period (1945-60) Latin American pressures for economic change played a crucial role in determining what became the North's response to calls for a fairer distribution of world wealth and the growth of aid. Inevitably the USA, which had no historic involvement in the empires of Africa and Asia, paid particular attention to development in the region on its doorstep.

The size of the leading Latin American countries – Argentina, Brazil, Chile, Mexico, Peru, Venezuela – as well as the level of development they had achieved by 1945 put them in a different category from the countries of Africa or the smaller states of Asia and the Pacific. Some of the Third World's problems, such as the population explosion or the rapid growth of urban sprawl and slums, are to be found in this region in their acutest form.

Independence dates

1804	Haiti
1811	Paraguay
1816	Argentina
1818	Chile
1819	Gran Colombia (including Ecuador and Venezuela) until 1830
1821	El Salvador
	Mexico
	Peru
1822	Brazil
1825	Bolivia
1828	Uruguay
1830	Colombia
	Ecuador
	Venezuela
1838	Costa Rica
	Guatemala
	Honduras
	Nicaragua
1844	Dominican Republic
1898	Cuba
1903	Panama
1945	These 20 Latin American countries became founder members of the UN.

Britain: Empire into Commonwealth

In just 40 years (1945-85) the British Empire, the most powerful as well as the most extensive of the European colonial empires, was almost entirely dismantled, though a few small dependent territories, mainly islands, remained under British control. Most newly independent successor nations joined the Commonwealth. The following table shows the sequence of events in the break-up of the British Empire. Asterisks indicate countries which are not members of the Commonwealth.

Independence Year	Countries
1947	India, Pakistan
1948	Burma* (now Myanmar); Ceylon (now Sri Lanka)
1956	Sudan*
1957	Ghana; Malaya (Federation of Malaysia since 1963)
1960	Nigeria; British Somaliland* (with Italian Somaliland, it formed Somalia); Cyprus
1961	Sierra Leone; Tanganyika (part of Tanzania since 1964)
1962	Jamaica; Trinidad and Tobago; Uganda; Western Samoa (joined the Commonwealth in 1970)
1963	Kenya; Zanzibar (united with Tanganyika in 1964 to form Tanzania)
1964	Malawi; Malta; Zambia
1965	Gambia; Maldives (became a special member of the Commonwealth in 1982 and a full member in 1985); Singapore (formerly part of Malaysia)
1966	Barbados; Botswana; Guyana; Lesotho
1967	Aden* (the People's Democratic Republic of Yemen which united with the Yemen Arab Republic in 1990)
1968	Mauritius; Nauru; Swaziland
1970	Fiji; Tonga
1971	Bangladesh (formerly East Pakistan; joined Commonwealth in 1972)
1972	Pakistan leaves the Commonwealth
1973	Bahamas
1974	Grenada
1975	Papua New Guinea
1976	Seychelles
1978	Dominica; Solomon Is.; Tuvalu

1979	Kiribati; St Lucia; St Vincent and the Grenadines
1980	Vanuatu; Zimbabwe
1981	Antigua and Barbuda; Belize
1983	St Christopher-Nevis
1984	Brunei
1987	Fiji leaves the Commonwealth
1989	Pakistan rejoins the Commonwealth
1990	Namibia

In 1993 Britain still had a number of colonial possessions as follows:

Anguilla	Gibraltar
Bermuda	Hong Kong
British Antarctic Territory	Montserrat
British Indian Ocean	Pitcairn Is. group
Territory	St Helena and
British Virgin Is.	Dependencies
Cayman Is.	Turks and Caicos Is.
Falkland Is.	

Most of these territories are so small that at present they prefer to maintain the colonial links with Britain. Three have created special problems:

Hong Kong After several years of difficult negotiations, Britain agreed with China in 1985 that Hong Kong would revert to China according to treaty in 1997.

Gibraltar Spain lays claim to Gibraltar; the resident population (by referendum) have voted overwhelmingly to remain British; the problem remains.

Falkland Is. In April 1982 Argentina which has long claimed the Falkland Is. (as the Islas Malvinas) invaded them; contrary to Argentina's calculations, Britain mounted a Sea Task Force and after a two-month war retook the islands from the Argentinians whose occupying forces surrendered. One result of this defeat for the military régime of General Galtieri was a return to democracy in Argentina.

Argentina continues to claim the Falklands. However, in 1985 the British prime minister, Margaret Thatcher, said the islands were British and there was no question of sovereignty to discuss with Argentina.

In 1993 both Australia and New Zealand remained responsible for a number of small colonial territories as follows:

Australia	**New Zealand**
Australian Antarctic Territory	Cook Is.
Norfolk Is.	Niue
Heard and McDonald Is.	Tokelau Is.
Cocos (Keeling) Is.	Ross Dependency
Christmas Is.	
Ashmore and Cartier Is.	
Coral Sea Is.	

(NB. For a map of Commonwealth see Chapter 4, part 5, **The Commonwealth**, page 108.)

France

Apart from Indo-China and a number of Caribbean and Pacific territories (mainly islands), the French Empire was overwhelmingly concentrated in Africa.

Independence Year	Countries
1949	Laos
1953	Cambodia (later Democratic Kampuchea)

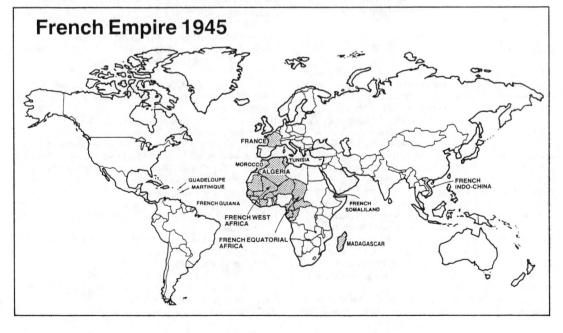

French Empire 1945

1954	North and South Vietnam (the two Vietnams emerged as a result of the Geneva Conference of that year)
1956	Morocco (including Spanish Morocco and the international zone of Tangier); Tunisia
1958	Guinea
1960	Cameroon (including an area formerly ruled by Britain); Central African Republic; Chad; Congo; Dahomey (later renamed Benin); Gabon; Côte d'Ivoire; Madagascar; Mali; Mauritania; Niger; Senegal; Togo; Upper Volta (later renamed Burkina Faso)
1962	Algeria
1975	Comoros
1977	Djibouti

In 1993 France still had a number of overseas possessions as follows:

Country	Status
French Guiana	Overseas department
French Polynesia	Overseas territory
Guadeloupe	Overseas department
Martinique	Overseas department
Mayotte	Collectivité territoriale*
New Caledonia	Overseas territory
Réunion	Overseas department
Saint Pierre and Miquelon	Overseas department
Southern and Antarctic territories	Overseas territory
Wallis and Futuna	Overseas territory

*Status between a territory and a department

New Caledonia From 1984 onwards, growing violence between French settlers and the indigenous inhabitants presented France with one of her final colonial problems.

China

China was never colonized but internal conflict for more than a century before 1949 made it weak and the prey of imperial exploitation and manipulation. Its position since the Communist revolution of 1949 has been unique.

The unification of China in 1949 under Mao Zedong (Mao Tse-tung) and the Chinese Communist Party is arguably the most important single event of the twentieth century. Today this huge country, containing more than a fifth (more than 1100 million) of the world's population, occupies a unique position. In terms of its potential, it is regarded as a future superpower; in terms of its politics it still proclaimed itself to be Communist in 1993; in terms of its poverty and development needs, it is a part of the Third World. Furthermore, the achievement of unity in 1949 and the subsequent experiments during Mao's rule (1949-76) – the Great Leap Forward, the Red Guard, the Cultural Revolution (whatever their successes or failures) – had the effect of providing an alternative way for newly emerging nations to follow.

China's revolutionary example, its determination to pull itself up by its own efforts, and the lead it took in the formation of the Non-Aligned Movement at the time of the Bandung Conference (1955) gave it an influence in the Third World which was doubly reinforced by its own history. Few peoples had been more exploited than the Chinese and the fact that under the Communists they at last threw off the endless oppressions from inside and outside that had burdened them for so long lent to the Communism of Mao an attraction and gave it a dignity (whatever its real shortcomings and brutalities) which no ideological opposition from the West could undermine.

Mao reversed the ideology of Marx and Lenin and based his revolution upon the peasants of the countryside instead of the industrial workers of the towns. The peasants were his strength. The great achievement of Mao's Communism was not material improvement, important though that may be, but the attainment of human dignity which had been too long denied to millions of people. China's example was of incalculable importance to the rest of the Third World at a time when it was struggling first to obtain independence and then to survive for the most part as small, weak and often hardly viable independent states.

Mao's successors may change the orientation of China towards greater materialism. But they are fortunate to lead 1100 million people who have discovered a level of self-confidence and dignity unknown through the previous century.

Key dates

1842 Cession of Hong Kong to Britain after China's defeat in the first 'Opium War'; Chinese ports are opened to foreign trade. This was the first of a series of what China came to call unequal treaties because they were imposed upon her by more powerful nations.

1860 British forces occupy Peking; China is forced to open new ports for western trade.

1894-95 War between China and Japan which takes Port Arthur (now Lushun), Formosa and Korea.

1900 Boxer (nationalist) rebellion: foreign embassies in Peking besieged; foreign intervention ends the rebellion.

1905 Several revolutionary organizations combine to form the United League and Sun Yat-sen becomes the leader.

1912 Fall of the Manchu Dynasty: a republic is proclaimed under Sun Yat-sen.
In the following two decades China was torn by civil war between war lords and political factions until the Kuomintang (Nationalists) under Chiang Kai-shek and the Communists under Mao Zedong emerged as the two contenders for power.

1931 Japan occupies Manchuria.

1932 Japan establishes the puppet state of Manchukuo.

1934-35 Mao leads the Communists on the Long March from Jianxi to Shaanxi Province where they establish themselves.

1937 Japan begins its rapid conquest of China, takes Shanghai and Peking; Mao and Chiang Kai-shek co-operate against the Japanese.

1945 The collapse and defeat of Japan.

1946   Civil war is renewed as the wartime anti-Japanese collaboration (between Nationalists and Communists) is abandoned.

1949   The Chinese Communist Party establishes control over mainland China and the People's Republic of China is established; the Nationalist rump escapes to Formosa (Taiwan).

1950-53   Korean War: China intervenes on the side of the North.

1950-51   China invades and conquers Tibet.

1955   Zhou Enlai (Chou En-lai) plays a leading role at the Bandung Conference which proclaims the idea of Non-Alignment.

1962   China in border clashes with India.

1971   China is admitted to the UN after the USA withdraws its longstanding objection; Taiwan is expelled.

1975   Completion of the TANZAM (Chinese-built) Railway from Tanzania to Zambia represents a high point of Chinese influence in the Third World.

1976   The deaths of first Zhou Enlai and then Mao Zedong end an era of Chinese history.

1980   Trial of the Gang of Four, including Mao's widow, Jiang Qing. They are condemned to death in 1981, but her sentence is reduced to life imprisonment in 1983.

1989   The massacre of Tiananmen Square: about 1000 unarmed student protesters are killed; the event does great damage to China's international image.

The collapse of the Soviet Empire

Over the years 1989-92 the world's last major empire was dismantled during an astonishing period of rapid change that also saw the Cold War, which had divided the world into opposing camps for more than 40 years, come to an end. In a process initiated by Soviet President Mikhail Gorbachev (who came to supreme power in the USSR in 1985), the Soviet Union signalled its readiness to withdraw its troops from Europe, allow the two Germanies to reunite and end the Cold War. Gorbachev's theme words were *glasnost* (openness) and *perestroika* (restructuring) but in the course of ending the Cold War (which was essential if the USSR was to tackle its appalling economic problems), Gorbachev also initiated a process of change inside the USSR whose end results had not been intended: the rapid disintegration of the Soviet Empire.

Thus, in 1990 the issue of nationality came to dominate Soviet politics as its various peoples used *perestroika* first to air the problem of language, and then (passing rapidly through several stages of distancing themselves from the centre) to demand autonomy, followed by sovereignty and finally independence; it became an unstoppable process. In 1990, the three Baltic republics – Estonia, Latvia and Lithuania which had been incorporated into the USSR at the beginning of World War II – declared their independence while the other twelve component parts of the USSR, including Russia itself, opted for sovereignty and claimed that their

laws should take precedence over laws emanating from the centre. By the end of 1990 it was clear (despite Gorbachev's refusal to discuss independence with the individual Soviet republics) that independence was the goal of all twelve. At the same time there was an escalation of bloodshed and fighting between ethnic groups, particularly in or between the republics of the southern tier such as Armenia, Azerbaijan, Georgia and Tadjikistan where ancient ethnic quarrels and bitter border disputes erupted in fighting which the centre was no longer remotely capable of controlling.

During 1991 it became clear that the process of break-up was irreversible. The abortive coup of hardliners against Gorbachev in August served to weaken his hold on the central government and though he struggled all year to preserve the Union it was not to be. In November 1991 seven republics led by Russia agreed to form a new Union of Sovereign States but on 1 December Ukraine voted for independence. On 8 December Russia, Ukraine and Belarus agreed that the USSR no longer existed but proclaimed a Commonwealth of Independent States (CIS). On 21 December the presidents of eleven of the republics signed an agreement to create the Commonwealth of Independent States. On 25 December Gorbachev resigned as President of the now defunct USSR which ceased to exist.

Results

1. The end of the Cold War deprived the countries of the Third World of two courts of appeal: as a result they must deal with a single North which, without the compulsions of Cold War rivalries, is likely to prove less amenable to their pressures and less ready to provide economic assistance that does not also lead to an immediate return for the North.

2. The break-up of the USSR has replaced a single superpower with 15 sovereign states, half of which in terms of their development needs and poverty qualify to join the ranks of the Third World.

3. There is now only one superpower – the USA – and the future politics of North–South are likely to be increasingly dependent upon US initiatives.

The successor states to the USSR

Russia remains a major world power (though no longer a superpower) while the Ukraine (in terms of resources and population) will be a leading European nation; Belarus and Moldova will also be treated as European states as will the three Baltic republics – Estonia, Latvia and Lithuania.

But the former Soviet republics of the southern tier – certainly in terms of their state of economic development and general poverty – qualify to join the ranks of the Third World. This process may be further encouraged because of the size of their Muslim populations and the attraction of links southwards to the Islamic countries of southern Asia (such as Iran), and because of their ethnic links especially with Turkey.

These eight republics are:

Armenia	Kyrgyzstan
Azerbaijan	Tajikistan
Georgia	Turkmenistan
Kazakhstan	Uzbekistan

– and they have now been listed in the Gazetteer.

The break-up of Yugoslavia

The civil war that destroyed Yugoslavia at the beginning of the 1990s and the confused and inadequate response to it from the main European powers and the USA sent warning signals to the world that a period of instability was likely to dominate the remaining years of the twentieth century. Should this prove to be the case the problems of the Third World will be accorded even less priority by the North than was already the case at the beginning of the 1990s.

End of Empires: date chart

1945 The United Nations is established.
1946 Civil war in Indo-China between the French and the Vietminh led by Ho Chi Minh, a Vietnamese Communist.
1947 Independence for British India which is partitioned to form India and Pakistan.
1948 State of emergency declared in Malaya. Assassination of Gandhi.
The National Party under Daniel Malan comes to power in South Africa: the word *apartheid* comes into currency as the official explanation of South Africa's racial policy.
Burma and Ceylon become independent.
British Nationality Act: dissolves common citizenship of old Commonwealth and Empire and replaces with Commonwealth citizenship.
1949 Indonesia is formed; the end of the Dutch East Indian Empire.
Mao Zedong and the Chinese Communist Party establish full control over mainland China and proclaim the People's Republic of China.
India becomes a republic and by its decision to remain in the Commonwealth alters the nature of that association.
1951 Egypt abrogates the 1936 Treaty with Britain and British troops occupy the Canal Zone.
1952 Ahmed Ben Bella forms the Algerian Revolutionary Committee in Cairo.
1952-56 Moroccan revolts against France.
1952-59 Mau Mau revolt and state of emergency in Kenya.
1952 King Farouk of Egypt overthrown in military coup led by General Neguib and Colonel Nasser.
1953 French forces occupy Dien Bien Phu in North Vietnam.
Britain creates the Central African Federation of Northern and Southern Rhodesia and Nyasaland.
Trial of Jomo Kenyatta in Kenya: the last great colonial trial which misfires and helps create the myth of Kenyatta, the nationalist leader.
1954 Defeat of French at Dien Bien Phu; Geneva Conference recognizes two Vietnams divided by 17th parallel of latitude: North Vietnam (Communist), South Vietnam (western-backed).

Nasser takes full control in Egypt; Anglo-Egyptian agreement on Suez Canal.
The beginning of the Algerian War of Independence which lasts to 1962.
1955-59 State of emergency in Cyprus.
1956 Sudan, Morocco and Tunisia become independent.
Terrorism in Cyprus reaches its peak: Archbishop Makarios is deported to the Seychelles.
Suez crisis: following the withrawal of western aid for the Aswan High Dam, Nasser nationalizes the Suez Canal; Israel invades Sinai; Britain and France invade Egypt; the UN replaces their forces and they withdraw; this is the last major example of old style imperial gunboat diplomacy; a watershed in the emergence of the Third World.
1957 Suez Canal is reopened to all shipping.
Gold Coast becomes independent as Ghana and Kwame Nkrumah becomes a figure of major influence in the politics of Africa and decolonization.
1958 The British West Indies Federation, comprising ten British colonies, is established; an attempt to come to grips with the problems of the small states, but it is dissolved in 1962.
Guinea turns down association with France and votes for total independence under Sekou Touré.
1960 Harold Macmillan gives his 'Wind of Change' speech in Cape Town, South Africa.
The Sharpeville massacre in South Africa heightens world condemnation of apartheid.
De Gaulle abandons the idea of a special community; 17 African countries become independent; the *annus mirabilis* of African independence.
Cyprus independent.
Belgian Congo independent; mutiny of *Force Publique* signals the beginning of a major international crisis; Moise Tshombe attempts to take the mineral rich Katanga (now Shaba) Province out of the Congo (now Zaïre).
1961 Assassination of Patrice Lumumba, Congo's first prime minister, and Dag Hammarskjöld (UN Secretary-General) on a Congo Peace Mission.
South Africa becomes a republic and leaves the

Commonwealth; it becomes increasingly isolated and a focus of Third World condemnation.

Tanganyika independent.

1962   Algeria becomes independent after 8 years' war.

Britain passes Commonwealth Immigration Act to control entry into Britain: its object was to restrict entry of non-white Commonwealth citizens into Britain.

1963   The Addis Ababa conference of independent African nations establishes the Organization of African Unity (OAU).

Kenya and Zanzibar independent.

Britain dissolves the Central African Federation.

1964   Tanganyika and Zanzibar form the United Republic of Tanzania.

Malawi and Zambia become independent.

1965   Unilateral Declaration of Independence (UDI) by the white minority government in Rhodesia.

1966   United Nations sanctions against Rhodesia.

1967   Britain cuts back its forces and reduces its Far East (Singapore) commitment.

1968   Britain withdraws from East of Suez.

Britain passes Commonwealth Immigration Act further restricting immigration.

Enoch Powell, leading British politician on the right, proposes the repatriation of Commonwealth (i.e. non-white) immigrants.

1974   Army coup in Portugal overthrows Caetano government and opens the way to end Portuguese empire in Africa.

India becomes the sixth nation after the USA, the USSR, Britain, China and France to explode a nuclear device.

Guinea-Bissau independent.

1975   Angola, Mozambique, Cape Verde and São Tomé and Príncipe independent.

1979   Lusaka Commonwealth Conference produces a formula to restore legal rule in Rhodesia and Britain resumes 'control'.

1980   Robert Mugabe and his party, ZANU, win elections in Rhodesia which becomes independent as Zimbabwe so ending 15 years of UDI.

1982   The Falklands War: British force defeats the Argentinians who had seized the islands which they claim belong to Argentina.

1990   Namibia independent.

1992   The dissolution of the USSR resulting in the emergence of 15 independent states half of which qualify for Third World status.

1993   Eritrea independent of Ethiopia.

2 The United Nations

Birth of the United Nations

When in 1985 the United Nations celebrated 40 years of existence, the mere fact of its survival for that long could be seen as a major achievement. The great powers, too often, have regarded the UN either as ineffectual (dismissing it as a talking shop) or as an irritant to be ignored or bypassed. Such attitudes are understandable if the role of the UN as a catalyst for change is properly understood, especially change which promotes the interests of Third World countries. Such a role was hardly foreseen when the world body was created at the end of World War II. Yet this role was logical once the ideas embodied in the UN Charter – that all member nations are to be treated as equal and that colonial peoples should become independent – were (even partially) put into practice.

The United Nations represents the world's second attempt to create the structures of world government. The failure of the League of Nations and most particularly its failure in the face of fascism during the 1930s induced a degree of cynicism about the concept of world government which, in the long run, may have worked in favour of the United Nations. No one has expected too much of it.

The ability of the big powers to obstruct the wishes of the UN majority – formally embodied in the existence of the veto – is easier to understand when it is realized that even today most of the world's really important decisions are still taken by only a handful of nations and until 1990 led by the two superpowers. Ever since 1945 the major powers have rejected the idea that collective decisions of the UN as a whole should become the practice of the world body.

On the other hand, weak nations – which provide the greater part of UN membership – see collective action as the best way for them to influence events. The persistence of the majority in pushing their views in the General Assembly bore fruit in 1985, when there were distinct signs that both the USA and the USSR were revising their estimates of the usefulness of the UN and were preparing to work through the world body to a greater extent than they had done for some years. This did not represent a sudden superpower conversion to the idea of world government, but rather a growing awareness of the effective uses which could be made of collective pressures. For example, despite its overwhelming military power, the USSR had discovered that it could not ignore Islamic opinion backed by solid Third World support over its intervention in Afghanistan. And there were already indications prior to the end of the Cold War that the USA might find it more productive to work through the UN, lobbying intensely among its members, rather than ignoring the world body. Persistent Third World lobbying in the United Nations does produce results.

The end of the Cold War followed by the disintegration of the Soviet Union at the beginning of the 1990s had a profound impact upon the United Nations. Almost overnight, the United Nations found that it was no longer hampered by superpower rivalries; instead, it was expected to intervene in every crisis and from being unable to take effective action, except in a handful of cases, it was called upon to make massive interventions wherever a crisis had arisen. It was an astonishing turnround with dangerous implications for the world body: from being regarded as ineffectual the UN now found that it was overstretched and too much was demanded of it. On the other hand, the USA which had always been deeply suspicious of UN initiatives now took the lead in using the United Nations as it did in the Gulf confrontation and conflict of 1990-91 and Somalia in 1992, acting in the unfamiliar role of spearhead of UN interventions. As it became clear that the 1990s were likely to be one of the most unstable decades of the century the United Nations was given a new lease of life. The danger now was that too much would be expected of it and that when it was unable to meet such expectations the resulting disillusion could do the world body lasting and perhaps fatal damage.

United Nations: history and structure

When it came into being in 1945, the UN had 51 original members – 50 of them had participated in a conference in San Francisco in April 1945 and Poland joined them after the big powers had finally agreed to recognize its government. Since then the membership of the world body has more than tripled and the organization has become enormously more complex with the addition of many new agencies, a majority of which are mainly concerned with aspects of development in the Third World.

The Charter of the United Nations was signed on 26 June 1945. It had been drawn up over the previous two months according to proposals worked out by Britain, China, the USA and the USSR during the previous year (August to October) at Dumbarton Oaks, an estate in Washington DC. The UN came into formal existence on 24 October 1945 after the Big Five – the USA, the USSR, Britain, China and France – had ratified the Charter. As the successor to the defunct League of Nations, the UN was seen to be a new attempt at world government. Its primary task, in the aftermath of World War II, was to keep the peace.

A major problem which has remained central to the working of the UN ever since – the power of veto by any of the Big Five over actions of the Security Council (see below) – came to the fore at the very beginning of the deliberations of the San Francisco Conference which created the world body. The main argument then resolved itself into a confrontation between the Big Five and the 'Little Forty-Five' about the powers of veto.

The small and middle powers, like Australia and Canada, resisted the idea that the Five should have a veto. They objected to this concentration of power in the hands of a few nations and argued that the General Assembly should have wider powers. On the other hand, the Big Five powers maintained their solidarity on this issue (if over little else), arguing that responsibility should be given to those who had the capacity to enforce decisions. They won the day.

As a result of the San Francisco Conference, the United Nations Charter became the basis for the new world body. The Statute of the International Court of Justice was also agreed at the same time. The UN was at first regarded primarily as an intrument for maintaining world peace.

Its two principal purposes as defined in the Charter were to maintain international peace and security and develop friendly relations among nations. Its principles included the recognition of the sovereign equality of all its members; of the need to settle disputes by peaceful means; and acceptance of the principle that the UN may not intervene in matters of domestic jurisdiction.

Membership of the UN was open to all 'peace-loving' nations which accepted the obligations of the Charter. Amendments to the Charter required a two-thirds majority in the General Assembly. The official languages of the UN were English, French, Chinese, Russian and Spanish; Arabic was added later.

The structure of the United Nations

Six bodies constitute the main working structure of the world body: the General Assembly; the Security Council; the Economic and Social Council; the Trusteeship Council; the International Court of Justice; the Secretariat.

The General Assembly is the central organization in which every member sits and has a vote. The Security Council originally had 11 members, but this was later increased to 15, of whom five are permanent and the others serve two-year terms on a rotating basis. The Security Council has responsibility for peace and because its five permanent members have a veto it remains the focus of UN power. The Economic and Social Council with 54 members (who serve for three years) exists to coordinate the economic and social work of the United Nations and oversee its many organizations – 'the UN family of organizations'. By 1993 most of the work of the Trusteeship Council concerned with decolonization had been completed, especially following the achievement of independence by Namibia in 1990. The International Court of Justice is primarily concerned with arbitration.

The Secretariat is responsible for running the UN and the Secretary-General has great power as the world's leading international civil servant. There have been six secretaries-general: Trygve Lie (Norway) 1946-53; Dag Hammarskjöld (Sweden) 1953-61; U Thant (Burma) 1961-71; Kurt Waldheim (Austria) 1972-81; Javier Pérez de Cuéllar (Peru) 1982-91; and Boutros Boutros-Ghali (Egypt) 1992 – the first African but also the first Arab to hold the post. Three secretaries-general have come from Europe, a reflection of UN power structures, and one each from Asia, Latin America and Africa.

The United Nations budget is assessed according to the capacity of individual members to pay. For the biennium of 1992-93 the budget came to $2,389,234,900. Other UN programmes, namely those of the United Nations Development Programme (UNDP), the World Food Programme (WFP) and the Office of the United Nations High Commissioner for Refugees (UNHCR), are funded by additional voluntary contributions from members.

The way in which the UN was originally established with the Big Five veto built into its structure ensured Big Five control. Given the background to its creation and the nature of the Big Power rivalries which then existed, it is unlikely that any other structure would have been acceptable. Be that as it may, much of the subsequent UN story has concerned the struggle by the General Assembly to wrest more and more decision-making power from the Security Council so as to offset the powers of veto vested in that body. Moreover, the UN has grown in numbers largely as a result of the decolonization of empires which it has done so much to accelerate. The result is that the great majority of the new members from 1946 onwards almost automatically saw themselves as belonging to the Third World. In consequence they have worked to strengthen Third World influences in the UN and, wherever practicable, to reduce the big power ascendancy.

Thus, right from the beginning, there has been a division between the interests of the great powers and the interests of the rest. The great powers have often regarded the UN as irrelevant or as an irritant to be overruled or ignored when they were unable to control its decisions.

On the other hand the majority of weaker countries have seen the UN in a very different light. For these nations, the majority of whom consider themselves to belong to the Third World, the advantages which they can derive from the world body may be listed under three general headings:

1. The UN provides a forum in which they can jointly advance their views to ensure an international hearing which otherwise they would not be able to obtain.
2. It enables them to exert pressures upon the big powers: for example, this has been particularly important over questions of decolonization.
3. It is a major source of development assistance: this comes mainly through the work of the UN specialized agencies, most of which – and certainly the better known ones – are designed primarily to assist with economic and social developments.

Since 1945 the United Nations has experienced many ups and downs. It has often been the target of derision, usually by major powers whose interests were being questioned through the General Assembly. It has also been blamed for its inability to solve problems even when it was clear that it had been denied the means to solve them. Yet by the mid-1980s even the superpowers found they could not ignore its activities and by the early 1990s it had been given a new lease of life following the end of the Cold War.

One of the main lessons to be learnt from its history has been how effective group pressures can be, especially if such groups persist in pursuing a particular objective year after year. The story of decolonization, of UDI in Rhodesia, and of apartheid in South Africa would be very different had it not been for the constant exercise of pressures in the UN upon countries such as Britain and France. And the UN provided both Britain and France with a face-saving escape mechanism in the aftermath of the 1956 Suez Crisis.

Some of the UN's most consistent and ultimately successful work has been in the field of decolonization, an area of activity which has helped create the Third World. And despite its faults – and these are easy enough to criticize – the UN has now become a part of our international structure. Third World countries regard it as their principal means of exerting pressures upon the major powers. They also obtain through its many specialized agencies a great deal of assistance with their development. Understandably, therefore, the United Nations has great significance for the Third World.

Membership of the United Nations

Between 1945 and 1985, the membership of the United Nations grew from an original 51 to 158, a three-fold increase in numbers. As can be seen from the accompanying maps, most of these new members – especially since 1955 – are countries of the South who would consider themselves to be part of the Third World.

Thus after 1955 (the end of the first decade of the UN) the great majority of the world body's new members were newly independent nations of

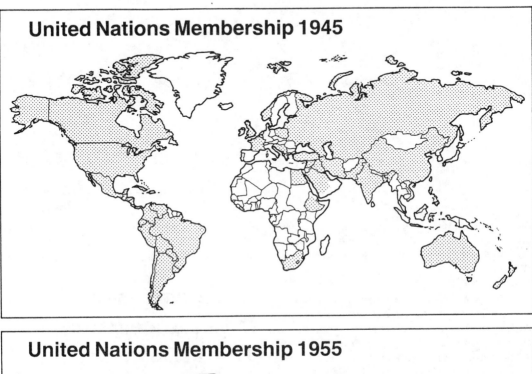

United Nations Membership 1945

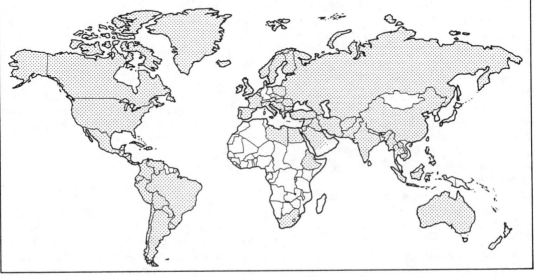

United Nations Membership 1955

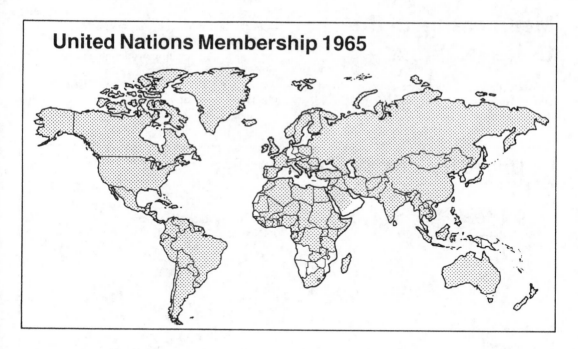

United Nations Membership 1965

the former empires. Increasingly towards 1985, these nations were small, often island groups, and were to regard themselves as members of the Third World.

After 1985, however, the pattern changes. By 1990 the number of members had increased to 160 with Liechtenstein from Europe and Namibia from Africa joining. In 1991 there was a jump in membership from 160 to 167 when new members joining included the two Koreas, Estonia, Latvia and Lithuania and the Federated States of Micronesia and the Marshall Islands. Apart from the three Baltic states, the other five were members of the Third World, though the two Koreas fall uneasily in middle ground.

Then in 1992, following the collapse of the Soviet Union and the break-up of Yugoslavia, 12 new members joined to bring total membership up to 179. The new members were: Armenia, Azerbaijan, Bosnia and Herzegovina, Croatia, Georgia, Kazakhstan, Kyrgyzstan, Republic of Moldova, San Marino, Tajikistan, Turkmenistan and Uzbekistan. Russia, meanwhile, had assumed the permanent seat on the Security Council formerly belonging to the USSR.

In 1993 membership increased to 183: Czechoslovakia's single seat was replaced by two for the new Czech and Slovak republics; they were followed by the admission of Macedonia from the former

Yugoslav Republic; then Monaco and the newly independent state of Eritrea were admitted to bring total membership to 183 by mid-year.

UN agencies of importance to the Third World

A wide range of activities are embraced by the UN special committees and agencies and the work of many of these agencies has particular relevance for Third World countries.

First come special political activities, such as those concerned with decolonization. These activities have played a significant part in bringing many countries to independence and hence to membership of the UN in the first place.

Second are the economic institutions headed by the autonomous World Bank and including the United Nations Development Programme (UNDP) and the Food and Agricultural Organization (FAO), whose main activities lie in the field of aid and development (see Chapter Five of this book on Aid and Its Agencies).

Third come those agencies which are mainly concerned to improve living or social conditions.

These include the International Labour Organiza- tion (ILO), United Nations Educational, Scientific and Cultural Organization (UNESCO) and the World Health Organization (WHO).

It has to be understood why UN agencies, which are at the disposal of *all* the organization's members, are much more important to Third World countries than to others. Much of the history of the UN concerns the way its poor, least developed members have used its mechanisms either to assist their development process directly or, through them, to persuade the rich, more

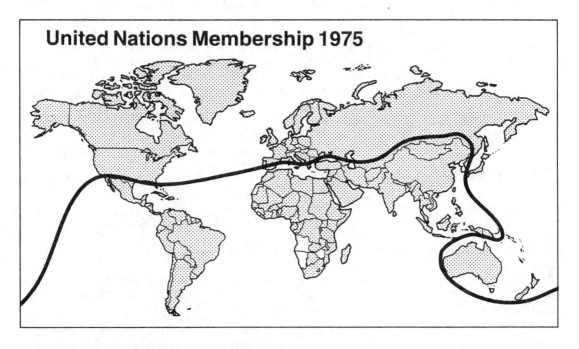

United Nations Membership 1975

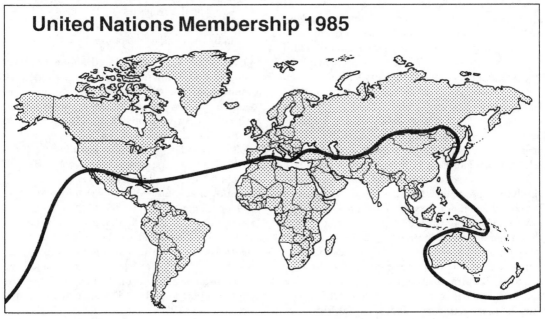

United Nations Membership 1985

economically developed members to help in this process.

At the time of joining the UN, the majority of Third World countries were underdeveloped both as to institutions and laws, such as those relating to labour, and economically. UN agencies such as the ILO or WHO have been able to provide structures or assist in the eradication of disease in countries otherwise too poor and with too few trained personnel to enable them to tackle these tasks unaided. Often, therefore, while countries like the USA or Britain see only marginal use in such bodies, because they already have the capacity to deal with the problems the agencies address, Third World countries urgently require the services which these agencies can provide.

Decolonization

Pressures exerted through the special committees of the United Nations on decolonization have greatly assisted the growth of the Third World. The General Assembly has also acted as a form of brake upon the colonial powers. For example, it is quite possible that without the constant pressures exercised through the General Assembly over UDI in Rhodesia, Britain might well have allowed the illegal regime headed by Ian Smith to become independent by default.

In the case of South Africa, whose policy of apartheid has, in theory, been universally condemned, the General Assembly has provided the principal world forum through which the Third World countries, in this case spearheaded by African members, have at the very least prevented the major western powers, such as the USA and Britain, from allowing their sympathy for white South Africa to become more than a negative insistence upon the status quo. Thus, while for years vetoing such positive steps as sanctions they felt, at the same time, obliged to condemn South Africa's policies and demand changes. Very slowly, yet positively, world opinion as expressed through the General Assembly did move the great powers inexorably towards a position from which they began to take steps to end apartheid and from 1985 onwards sanctions were applied to South Africa, despite the extreme reluctance to do so by countries like Britain. In the end, however, it was collaboration between the USA and USSR over Angola (1988-89) which led to a settlement in Namibia, and the fact that the white minority was simply losing control of the situation inside South Africa, which combined to bring about major changes. These were initiated by President F. W. de Klerk with his speech of 2 February 1990 when he unbanned the ANC and other banned political parties and organizations and then, 9 days later, released Nelson Mandela.

Over 100 nations – former colonies – have joined the UN as newly independent states since 1945. The UN has played a vital role, now largely fulfilled, in encouraging dependent peoples in their aspirations for independence by setting deadlines for the colonial powers to meet. Understandably such a role has endeared the UN to the new countries of the Third World. The UN Charter advances the principle of 'equal rights and self-determination of peoples' and this became the cornerstone of the independence struggles which have taken place since 1945.

The Trusteeship Council

The Trusteeship Council was established under the UN Charter to supervise Trust Territories which fell under three headings:

1. Mandates of the former League of Nations;
2. Territories taken from the defeated Axis powers by the Allies during World War II;
3. Territories voluntarily placed under the system by the responsible powers.

Of 11 Trust Territories placed under the Trusteeship system at the time the UN was formed, 10 became independent as follows:

Togoland under British administration: United with the British colony of the Gold Coast to become jointly independent as Ghana in 1957.

Somaliland under Italian administration: United with British Somaliland Protectorate to form independent Somalia in 1960.

Togoland under French administration: Became independent as Togo in 1960.

Cameroons under French administration: Became independent as Cameroon in 1960.

Cameroons under British administration: The northern part of the Trust Territory joined the Federation of Nigeria on 1 June 1961 and the southern part joined the Republic of Cameroon on 1 October 1961.

Tanganyika under British administration: Became independent in 1961.

Ruanda-Urundi under Belgian administration: Voted to divide into two states of Rwanda and Burundi in 1962.

Western Samoa under New Zealand administration: Became independent in 1962.

Nauru, administered by Australia on behalf of Australia, New Zealand and the United Kingdom: became independent in 1968.

Northeastern New Guinea, administered by Australia: United with the non-self-governing territory of Papua, also administered by Australia, to become the independent Papua New Guinea in 1975.

The Trust Territory of the Pacific Islands (Micronesia), comprising the former Japanese mandated islands of the Marshalls, the Marianas (except Guam) and the Carolines, was a strategic Trust Territory administered by the United States since 1947. In 1991, the **Federated States of Micronesia** and the **Marshall Islands** joined the United Nations as independent states.

Most colonial powers agreed to transmit information to the United Nations concerning their non-self-governing territories. However, the slow rate of decolonization led the General Assembly in 1960 to produce its *Declaration on the Granting of Independence to Colonial Countries and Peoples* and the Assembly established a 17-member Special Committee in 1961 (enlarged to 24 members in 1962 and 25 in 1979) to examine on a regular basis the application of the Declaration. Between 1960 and 1980, 40 former non-self-governing territories became independent. By 1992 (after Namibia had become independent) the number of territories with which the Special Committee was still concerned had fallen to 17.

Territories with which the Special Committee on Decolonization is concerned (as at 30 June 1992)

Territory	Administering authority
Africa	
Western Sahara	Spain*
Asia and the Pacific	
American Samoa	United States
East Timor	Portugal*
Guam	United States
Pitcairn	United Kingdom
Tokelau	New Zealand
Atlantic Ocean, Caribbean and Mediterranean	
Anguilla	United Kingdom
Bermuda	United Kingdom
British Virgin Is.	United Kingdom
Cayman Is.	United Kingdom
Falkland Is. (Malvinas)	United Kingdom
Gibraltar	United Kingdom
Montserrat	United Kingdom
St Helena	United Kingdom
Turks and Caicos Is.	United Kingdom
United States Virgin Is.	United States

*Spain and Portugal have effectively relinquished any responsibility for these territories. Western Sahara is now largely occupied and controlled by Morocco which is in dispute with the OAU over its policy. East Timor was incorporated in Indonesia as the 27th province in June 1976.

The United Nations specialized agencies

Apart from its various peace-keeping bodies, such as UNFICYP (United Nations Peace-Keeping Force in Cyprus), the most important UN agencies include UNCTAD, UNICEF, UNHCR, UNDP, UNFPA, ILO, FAO, UNESCO, WHO, IMF, IBRD, IDA, IFAD (see Chart showing the structure of the UN). These intergovernmental agencies are autonomous bodies. They work with the UN and each other through the Economic and Social Council. Some 15 agencies are known as 'specialized agencies' and report to the Council. These include of the above ILO, FAO, UNESCO, WHO, IMF, IBRD, IDA, and IFAD. These various bodies have had widely differing histories and they vary enormously in terms of their impact. Some, like UNCTAD, are highly political and have achieved comparatively little. Others, such as the UNDP and FAO as well as the financial institutions (the World Bank and IMF), have become of vital importance to most aspects of development in the Third World.

UNESCO

The United Nations Educational, Scientific and Cultural Organization (UNESCO) was formed in 1946 with the primary aim of contributing to peace and security in the world by promoting collaboration among nations through education, science, culture and communication.

Growing controversy surrounded UNESCO in the early 1980s and a classic confrontation took place between its Third World members (in this case supported by the USSR) and the major western powers. There were several reasons for the confrontation, but the principal factor was the demand of a majority of UNESCO members for a new 'information order': a news service providing information supplied by Third World governments. This was bitterly opposed by the West which opposed any curtailment of the liberties of the press in favour of government-censored news. The row which took the form of demands by western nations for UNESCO to reform itself culminated in the withdrawal of the USA at the end of 1984 followed by Britain at the end of 1985.

Leaving aside the rights and wrongs of the various arguments, this confrontation in UNESCO highlighted problems endemic to all North–South arguments whether within the UN family or outside it. In this case the western powers were heavily outvoted by the majority of UNESCO members, yet they provide the greater part of the organization's funds. Thus in 1984 the USA was responsible for 25 per cent of the total budget. As so often happens, therefore, the argument resolved itself into one of power: the Third World countries have the votes; the rich countries of the North the power (in the form of finance). Though no veto was built into the UNESCO structure, the withdrawal of the USA and Britain effectively deprived UNESCO of 30 per cent of its budget.

This particular controversy served to emphasize what is a constant factor in all Third World-North relations: the Third World has the numbers and the needs; it does not possess the finances required to pay for the programmes it desires to implement.

IMF

The International Monetary Fund (IMF) whose articles of agreement were drawn up at the 1944 Bretton Woods Conference came into being on 27 December 1945 and began operations on 1 March 1947. The Fund aims to promote international monetary co-operation and to facilitate the expansion of trade. It makes available financing to members when they face balance of payments difficulties and provides technical assistance to enable them to improve their financial management. Of all UN specialized agencies, the IMF is arguably the most controversial, at least in the eyes of the Third World. (For a fuller discussion of its impact, see Chapter Five of this book on Aid and its Agencies.)

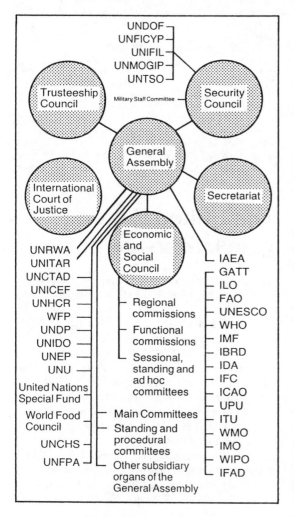

Geography of Exile – the Refugee Problem

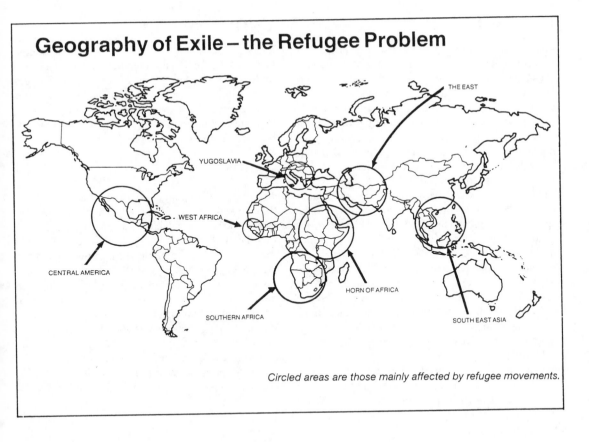

Circled areas are those mainly affected by refugee movements.

UNHCR

The Office of the United Nations High Commissioner for Refugees (UNHCR) was established in 1950 to protect refugees and promote durable solutions to their problems. The UNHCR depends entirely upon voluntary contributions from governments or private sources. There were in 1985 approximately 10 million refugees under its care and the great majority of these were located in Third World countries. By 1992, however, the number had risen to 17 million and the main areas affected by refugee movements (see map) were: Central America, although here a majority of refugees were being voluntarily repatriated (Costa Rica to Nicaragua, Mexico to Guatemala, and from several countries to El Salvador); West Africa (as a result of the civil war in Liberia and the border war betwen Liberia and Sierra Leone – 175,000 in Guinea, others in Côte d'Ivoire and Liberia); Southern Africa (as a result of the civil wars in Angola and Mozambique millions in those countries have become refugees and Malawi alone is host to 1 million refugees from Mozambique); the Horn of Africa (the chaotic situation in Somalia produced huge refugee movements in 1991-92 which include the return to Ethiopia of 450,000 refugees from Somalia, an influx of 280,000 refugees into Kenya, and 91,000 into Djibouti, while 200,000 refugees from Sudan in Ethiopia were obliged to return (unwillingly) to Sudan). In Asia there remain 5,200,000 refugees from Afghanistan in Iran and Pakistan, although in 1992 an estimated 1 million of these returned home. In South and Southeast Asia movement included: the voluntary repatriation of 370,000 Cambodians from Thailand; 190,000 refugees from Myanmar to Bangladesh, 30,000 from Bhutan to Nepal. Europe, however, provided the greatest new refugee upheaval with an estimated 2 million refugees from the various parts of former Yugoslavia either moving into neighbouring countries or becoming refugees in their own.

UNCTAD

The United Nations Conference on Trade and Development (UNCTAD) first met at Geneva in 1964. Subsequent UNCTAD conferences were held in Delhi (1968), Santiago (1972), Nairobi (1976), Manila (1979), Belgrade (1983), Geneva (1987). The 1992 Cartagena meeting produced the 'Cartagena Commitment' which emphasized 'good management'. The main task of UNCTAD is seen as negotiating multilateral legal instruments to govern international trade. UNCTAD seeks to set stable prices especially for commodities produced by Third World countries. Under its auspices specific agreements have been reached covering rubber (1979), cocoa (1980) and tin (1981), which have been attempts to stabilize trade in those products so as to protect producers from wild market fluctuations. Thus the rubber and tin agreements provide for the mandatory financing of buffer stocks by both producers and consumers. Other agreements have been reached over shipping and restrictive business practices.

Unfortunately UNCTAD meetings usually degenerate into confrontations between North and South with the Third World countries of the South demanding trade liberalization from the North which the advanced economies are as a rule unwilling to concede.

UNICEF

The United Nations International Children's Emergency Fund (UNICEF) was originally created in 1946 to meet the needs of children in post-war Europe and China. But in 1950 the emphasis was changed and its main task became the long-range benefit of children in developing countries. Although the name was changed to the United Nation's Children's Fund in 1953, the acronym UNICEF was kept.

UNICEF's main activities in developing countries are: to assist in the planning and extension of services which benefit children; to provide funds for training of national personnel especially of health workers, teachers, nutritionists and child welfare specialists; to supply technical equipment and other aids ranging from educational and health supplies to piping for clean water to villages.

UNDP

The United Nations Development Programme (UNDP) is the largest channel in the world for multilateral technical and pre-investment co-operation. It has programmes in over 150 countries and covers almost every aspect of development. (For further information see Chapter Five of this book on Aid and its Agencies.)

UNFPA

The Population Commission was set up in 1947. In the 1960s the very rapid rate of world population growth became the focus of attention and in 1969 the Trust Fund for Population Activities was renamed the United Nations Fund for Population Activities (UNFPA). UNFPA provides technical assistance in population activities. Its role is to build up the capacity to respond to needs in population and family planning, to promote understanding of population factors and assist governments to achieve population goals. It has become the largest internationally funded source of assistance to population programmes in developing countries (see Chapter Eight of this book on Population).

ILO

The International Labour Organization (ILO) was established in 1919 in association with the League of Nations. In 1946 it became the first specialized agency associated with the United Nations. The ILO works to promote social justice for working people. Its programme of technical co-operation provides experts to assist with vocational training, management techniques, manpower planning, employment policies.

FAO

The Food and Agricultural Organization of the United Nations (FAO) was founded in 1945. Its aims are to raise levels of nutrition and living standards; to improve the production, processing and marketing of food and agricultural products; to promote rural development and to eliminate hunger. It is a principal source of technical assistance for developing countries (see Chapter Five of this book on Aid and its Agencies).

WHO

Established in 1948 the World Health Organization has as its objective 'the attainment of all peoples of the highest possible level of health'. The Organization is now mainly concerned with primary health care. WHO reinforces national health systems by building up infrastructures and promoting research. It takes a lead in promoting campaigns: for example, the provision of safe drinking water, or the provision of immunization (a principal objective through the 1980s) to prevent the six major communicable diseases of childhood – diphtheria, measles, poliomyelitis, tetanus, tuberculosis and whooping cough. Among its campaigns has been the successful worldwide elimination of smallpox. The 1993 *World Development Report* of the World Bank was devoted to the issue of health.

The World Bank group

The International Bank for Reconstruction and Development (IBRD), generally referred to as the World Bank, began operations in 1946 and, like the IMF, came from the Bretton Woods deliberations. The International Finance Corporation (IFC) was set up in 1956; and the International Development Association (IDA), the 'soft' arm of the World Bank (providing finance on easy terms as opposed to hard loans at the full market rate), in 1960. The World Bank has become the largest source of development finance for Third World countries. (See Chapter Five of this book on Aid and Its Agencies.)

Between them the agencies of the UN provide a huge range of expertise across most aspects of development. They are a vital source of assistance for Third World countries over and above what these countries receive on a bilateral basis from individual donor nations. And many programmes in developing countries rely upon UN specialized agency inputs to be effective.

Other UN bodies whose activities assist the development process include UNITAR (United Nations Institute for Training and Research), WFP (World Food Programme – a joint UN/FAO exercise), UNIDO (United Nations Industrial Development Organization), UNEP (United Nations Environment Programme) and UNCHS (Habitat) (United Nations Centre for Human Settlements).

Third World countries also benefit from the expertise provided through such UN agencies as the UPU (Universal Postal Union) and ITU (International Telecommunications Union).

Location of United Nations bodies and organizations

City	Organization
New York City	United Nations Headquarters; General Assembly, Security Council, Secretariat. All UN bodies not listed as being located elsewhere are also in New York.
Geneva	ILO, WHO, ITU, WMO, WIPO, GATT, UNHCR, UNCTAD
Washington DC	The World Bank Group: IBRD, IFC, IDA, IMF
The Hague	International Court of Justice
Rome	FAO, IFAD, WFP, World Food Council
Vienna	IAEA, UNIDO, UNWRA
Paris	UNESCO
London	IMO
Montreal	ICAO
Berne	UPU
Nairobi	UNEP, UNCHS (Habitat)
Tokyo	UNU

There are UN Information Centres in 22 African cities, in 13 cities in the Americas, in 18 in Asia and Oceania and in 14 in Europe.

The location of so many agencies in North America and Europe merely serves to emphasize the power realities when the United Nations was established as well as the fact that a majority of qualified personnel would also be recruited from these countries. The siting of UNEP and UNCHS (Habitat) in Nairobi represents a conscious later attempt to redress the balance in favour of the Third World.

How UN structures work for the Third World

In the General Assembly, the absolute majority of Third World countries means that if they work together they can, at least in theory, win their point. As a result, the General Assembly has adopted many resolutions favourable to Third World aspirations both in the field of development and in decolonization.

An example of this occurred on 1 May 1974, when a special session on development adopted (in the General Assembly) the *Declaration and Programme of Action on the Establishment of a New International Economic Order*. Member nations declared their determination to work for 'the establishment of a new international economic order based on equity, sovereignty, interdependence, common interest and co-operation among states, irrespective of their economic and social systems' so as to 'correct inequalities and redress existing injustices, make it possible to eliminate the widening gap between the developed and developing countries and ensure steadily accelerating economic and social development in peace and justice for present and future generations'.

Such statements illustrate both the strengths and weaknesses of the United Nations. The resolution accords with the economic desires of the developing countries of the Third World; at present the economic climate is controlled largely by the advanced economies of the West, whose interests often work to the detriment of those of the Third World.

Understandably the Third World majority in the General Assembly passes resolutions of a kind favourable to its aspirations. Yet the implementation of such resolutions is not in the power of the Third World countries, despite their voting majority in the General Assembly. Implementation depends on the willingness of the major economic powers to accept changes which they are likely to see as working to their detriment. The leading economic powers – the USA, the EC and Japan (and, no doubt, Russia once it has sorted out its post-USSR problems) – will not alter the thrust of their economic policies because of such a resolution, whatever lip service they may pay to its general principles.

In political terms, however, the major powers do not wish too often or too obviously to be seen to go against the Third World. In consequence they may not oppose such declarations even if they have no intention of doing anything to implement them. As a result such declarations often become dead letters. And yet, not quite...

In the case of the demand for a new international economic order, the pressures were sufficiently strong that two consequences ensued. The first was a series of meetings held in Paris during 1975 which produced the new concept of North and South. And second, arising in part out of the Paris meetings, the Brandt Commission was set up. Its subsequent report, under the title *North–South: A Programme for Survival*, represented another small victory for the Third World.

It is Third World strategy to get such declarations approved and, as it were, on the UN statute book. Later these can be used as points of reference in the ongoing struggle between North and South to bring about adjustments and changes in a world system which is still dominated overwhelmingly by the North.

Thus, the Third World carries resolutions in the General Assembly which have as their object a readjustment of world structures, especially economic structures, so as to bring about a more equitable world, less subject to big power control. In themselves such declarations neither persuade the big powers to change their ways nor alter the balance in any material sense. Yet they are not without point. They become 'weapons' in a propaganda war between North and South, reference points which, with skill, can be brought into play at a later date to persuade the major powers to make concessions. And bit by bit, some of their points – the least radical at first – do eventually get adopted.

When the UN was established in 1945, only a small number of its members could be classified as belonging to the Third World. And the views of the Big Five which established the world body – the USA, the USSR, Britain, China and France – almost always prevailed. They were concerned at that time to create an organization which would reinforce the world system they controlled. Moreover, the concept of the Third World had not then been born. Much United Nations activity today, however, consists of Third World actions designed to change the very order which the UN was supposedly created to uphold. And, ironically, the UN has become the most important instrument for bringing about such changes in the world order. It is mainly through the UN and its various affiliated bodies that Third World countries have the opportunity, collectively, to exert pressures of this kind, which explains the importance they attach to it.

The United Nations and apartheid

Few policies anywhere have been so much debated or produced so much hostility as has apartheid. It became official policy in South Africa following the victory of the National Party under Dr Daniel Malan in 1948, although racial segregation and discrimination had been practised in South Africa for far longer. Apartheid had particular significance for the Third World. It was inaugurated and formalized in a series of laws passed during the 1950s and 1960s just when the colonial empires in Africa were being dismantled. It was seen as a direct racial insult to the black peoples of newly independent Africa and by extension to all other black or brown people. And because it was seen to depend upon huge British and other western investments, the West was regarded as providing the economic means to enable South Africa's government to defy world opinion.

The struggle against apartheid, therefore, became symbolic: and its final demise will be seen as the end of colonial exploitation in Africa. The fact that the great powers in the UN, particularly the old colonial powers, always blocked attempted international action against South Africa, including sanctions, has given added point to the colonial nature of apartheid. The racist white minority in South Africa came to be regarded (as were the Rhodesian whites in 1965) as a final colonial rearguard action, and western support for South Africa's government and reluctance to exert meaningful pressures upon it confirmed Third World suspicions of the North's motives.

Apartheid became a focus of the great differences which divide North and South. The apparent determination shown by both the British and American governments over many years to resist any moves against South Africa (including sanctions) emphasized – for the Third World – their lingering sympathies with colonialism and exploitation. Nonetheless, between 1985 – following President P. W. Botha's 'Rubicon' speech in which he made no concessions – and 1990 first the USA, then the EC and finally an extremely reluctant Britain (giving minimal ground to pressures from her Commonwealth colleagues) did apply a variety of limited sanctions to South Africa.

The collapse of the rand in the latter half of 1985, the growth of violence and the deteriorating security situation inside South Africa, as well as international pressures which were greatly strengthened by the ending of the Cold War, combined to produce the circumstances needed to usher in change. Thus, in February 1990, South Africa's new President F. W. de Klerk began the process of dismantling apartheid and working towards real power sharing with the black majority whose logical outcome must be majority rule.

Important dates in the struggle against apartheid

1946 From this year onwards the subject of race discrimination in South Africa has been regularly discussed in the General Assembly of the United Nations.

1960 The Security Council meets following the Sharpeville massacre and calls upon South Africa to abandon apartheid.

1962 The General Assembly calls upon member states to break diplomatic relations with South Africa, boycott its goods and refrain from exports including arms to South Africa. The Special Committee against Apartheid is established.

1963 The Security Council institutes a voluntary arms embargo against South Africa.

1965 The General Assembly establishes a UN Trust Fund for South Africa.

1966 The General Assembly proclaims 21 March (Sharpeville Day) as International Day for the Elimination of Racial Discrimination (to be observed annually).

1967 A UN Educational and Training Programme for Southern Africa is established: it provides scholarships for students from Namibia, South Africa and Rhodesia (now Zimbabwe) and the Portuguese territories; by 1980 the scholarships are confined to students from South Africa and Namibia.

1970   The UN strengthens the arms embargo against South Africa and urges member states to terminate diplomatic and other official relations with South Africa.

1971   The International Court of Justice rules that South Africa's presence in Namibia is illegal.

1972   The Security Council meeting in Addis Ababa recognizes the legitimacy of the anti-apartheid struggle and requests all nations to adhere strictly to the arms embargo.

1973   The General Assembly adopts the International Convention on the Suppression and Punishment of the Crime of Apartheid and establishes a Trust Fund for Publicity against Apartheid.

1974   The General Assembly invites representatives of South African Liberation Movements recognized by the OAU to participate as observers in its debates on apartheid; the General Assembly rejects South Africa's credentials and, from 1974, South Africa ceased to participate in the deliberations of the General Assembly.

1975   The General Assembly proclaims that the UN and the international community have a special responsibility towards the oppressed people of South Africa.

1976   The General Assembly condemns South African aggression in Angola; the Assembly rejects the independence of the Transkei (a *Bantustan* or Homeland) as spurious.

1977   The Security Council makes the arms embargo against South Africa mandatory.

1978   The General Assembly proclaims an international Anti-Apartheid Year.

1982   The General Assembly proclaims 1982 International Year of Mobilization of Sanctions against South Africa.

1984   The General Assembly rejects the new South African racially segregated tricameral constitution.

1985   The Security Council condemns the Pretoria regime for the killing of defenceless Africans.

1989   The General Assembly adopts a Declaration which lists the steps the South African government should take to create the necessary climate for negotiations.

1990   The UN Secretary-General sends a mission to South Africa to report on progress in the implementation of the Declaration.

1992   Nelson Mandela addresses the United Nations and calls upon it to lift sanctions as a result of progress made inside South Africa.

Special dates in the history of the United Nations

1945   26 June Signing of the United Nations Charter. 24 October The United Nations is born.

1946   Inauguration of the International Court of Justice. UNICEF is formed.

1948   Birth of Israel endorsed by the United Nations. GATT is formed. Universal Declaration of Human Rights approved.

1949   UNWRA is formed.

1950   27 June The Security Council approves sending a UN Force to Korea under US command; the UN Commission for the Unification and Rehabilitation of Korea remained in South Korea until 1973. UNHCR is formed.

1956   UN Emergency Force (UNEF) for Suez; this is the first UN Peacekeeping Force.

1957   IAEA is formed.

1958   First UN Conference on the Law of the Sea.

1960   United Nations intervention in the Congo (now Zaire). Declaration of the Granting of Independence to Colonial Countries and Peoples.

1963   Declaration on the Elimination of All Forms of Racial Discrimination.

1964   UN Force withdrawn from Congo. UN Peacekeeping Force in Cyprus (UNFICYP) established. UNCTAD is formed.

1965   Membership of the Security Council is increased from 11 to 15.

1966   Trust Fund for Population Activities is formed; renamed UNFPA in 1969. The General Assembly terminates South Africa's Mandate over South West Africa. UNIDO is formed, becomes operational in 1967.

1967   UNEF is withdrawn from Suez at Egypt's request. UN Security Council adopts Resolution 242 on Israel which defines principles for a just and lasting peace in the Middle East.

1968   The General Assembly renames South West Africa as Namibia.

1972   UNEP is formed.

1973   UNEF II is established between Egypt and Israel; remains until 1979.

1974   The General Assembly adopts Declaration and Programme of Action on the Establishment of a New International Economic Order.

World Food Council is formed.
First World Population Conference, Bucharest.
1975   International Women's Year.
1977   IFAD is formed.
1978   UNCHS (Habitat) is formed.
1982   Manila Declaration on the Peaceful Settlement of International Disputes.
1984   Declaration on the Right of Peoples to Peace.

(The end of the Cold War gave the UN a new lease of life and the world came to expect far more of it.)

1988-92   Thirteen new peace-keeping operations are mounted round the world; by 1992 the number of military and police personnel deployed on these missions is 52,000.
1992   January UN Summit of 15 heads of government (Security Council representatives) pledge to strengthen UN peace-keeping.
June The UN Conference on Environment and Development (UNCED) at Rio de Janeiro.

Note: The growth of demands for the UN to take action (in the wake of the end of the Cold War) brought new problems to the world body: the first was simply that of capacity – how much could it undertake at any given time; the second was that of expense – what could it afford to do (especially since certain members led by the USA continued to withhold funds); and third was the problem of expectations: there is the real danger that the UN will be asked to undertake too much, will be unable to do what is demanded of it and as a result will cause disillusion among its supporters. Finally, the world body faced insistent demands that it should tackle the question of corruption among its officials.

3 The Third World and Non-Alignment

Membership of the Third World

Prior to 1990 it was possible to divide the countries of the world according to three main groups: the West (or First World); the Communist bloc (or Second World); and the Third World (or Non-Aligned). The end of the Cold War has effectively replaced the first two groups (the First and Second worlds) with a single North while, if anything, the Third World or South has increased its total membership as a result of the break-up of the Soviet Empire. The Non-Aligned Movement grew out of the Cold War confrontation and an understanding of how this happened is vital if we are now to readjust our thinking to a world essentially divided into two: the rich North; and the poor South.

By 1992 there were a number of disturbing signs that the West, deprived of its traditional Soviet antagonist, was seeking to cast the South (with its voracious demands for economic assistance and its threatening numbers) in the new demon role of enemy. And if, with the passing of the Cold War, the Non-Aligned Movement no longer had any ideologies about which to be non-aligned, its members faced an even more difficult future as the North gave unmistakable signs of withdrawing into a 'laager' or fortress as its members became increasingly wary of the Third World and the problems they associated with it.

All members of the Non-Aligned Movement are members of the Third World, but not all members of the Third World are non-aligned. The Non-Aligned Movement covers the entire spectrum of Third World politics. At one end of the scale is Cuba with its Marxist politics that Fidel Castro seems determined to maintain even after Moscow has abandoned him and given up Communism. At the other end of the scale countries such as Kenya and Côte d'Ivoire in Africa always maintained close ties with Britain and France respectively and made clear that their political sympathies lay with the West.

Such countries, at either end of the Third World's range, were not non-aligned in any meaningful sense, because their interests were overwhelmingly tied to the fortunes of one or other side in the Cold War confrontation. They would reply, however, that their interests did not preclude them from membership of a group whose principal aim is to lessen any form of world confrontation. A number of countries which do see themselves as belonging to the Third World – Brazil, Chile and Venezuela – are not members of the Non-Aligned Movement.

Since the 1980s the term South has come increasingly to be used for the Third World. Attempts at definition and arguments about the origins of the term Third World are complex. For the purpose of this book, the term Third World is applied to all those countries shown on the map (The North–South Divide, see below). These countries share certain basic characteristics. They all suffer from poverty and lack of development; most of them have been subjected until recently to colonial exploitation; and they all desired to stand aside from the confrontations of the Cold War.

All members of the Third World face problems of poverty – sometimes extreme poverty – and regard development as their first priority. Yet there are huge variations. In terms of its low per capita income, the vast numbers of very poor and uneducated, the lack of services, Brazil is a Third World country. Yet at the same time some Brazilians enjoy enormous wealth and the country is on the verge of major industrial breakthroughs.

Saudi Arabia and other oil-producing Gulf states now have the wealth they need to promote their development. They lack the technical expertise, which they purchase from the North in the form of massive technical assistance and know-how. Such countries present stark contrasts. There are immensely wealthy cliques at the top end of the scale and great poverty elsewhere even if, as in most of the Gulf states, determined efforts have

The North-South Divide during the Cold War

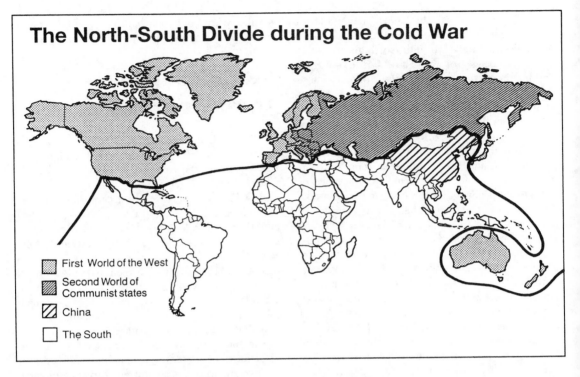

First World of the West

Second World of Communist states

China

The South

been made to spread some of the wealth downwards. Other developing countries without benefit of major mineral resources, such as Ethiopia or Lesotho, face almost insuperable problems of poverty so that sometimes their very survival is dependent upon international assistance.

The Third World is sometimes divided into groups according to region. There are such major differences between these regions that, though we speak of the Third World as an entity, it is in fact nothing of the sort. The most obvious division is as follows:

1. The Latin American countries which achieved their independence early in the nineteenth century and are generally far more Euro-centred in their cultures than the rest of the Third World.
2. Africa whose more than 50 nations almost all came to independence since 1945 and generally are among the world's poorest countries.
3. The huge new nations of Asia whose ancient cultures differ radically from those of the recently dominant western imperial powers.
4. The Arab World of the Middle East whose oil wealth has transformed its economic position.
5. The numerous small territories, mainly islands,

in the Caribbean Sea and in the Pacific and Indian Oceans which face special development problems related to size.

6. Finally China, which in terms of development needs is a Third World member. In terms of its long-term superpower potential, however, it is already a great power. In the 1960s and early 1970s it demonstrated this potential when it provided substantial aid for a number of Third World countries.

In economic terms, at least as far as development is concerned, the Third World consists of the 'have-nots', even though many Third World countries are rich in resources. They need development at almost every level and, in consequence, have a vested interest in changing the present world economic status quo.

The term Third World is sometimes seen by its members as a derogatory term, implying less importance or worth than the First or Second Worlds of the capitalist West, and (formerly) the Communist East. This is not the case. If the origins of the term are taken into account – a Third Force consciously developed to hold the ring and attempt to prevent the Cold War escalating into a hot war – then it is an honourable description. But unfortunately, in later years, the sheer magnitude of development problems set against declining world economic conditions led both North and South to think increasingly of the Third World not as a Third Force, but only as the 'poor', whose principal relationship with the North is that of suppliant for economic concessions.

Indeed, in the world of the 1980s, the economic factors which Third World countries had in common were their most binding characteristics. A majority of Third World countries remain exporters of raw materials – whether minerals or agricultural products. With only a few exceptions, they lack anything more than the beginnings of industrialization. They are deficient in technical skills and suffer from poor infrastructure at almost every level. And because of their poverty, they are able to exert only minimal pressures upon the powerful nations of the North. As a result they can almost never argue from strength, but instead appear constantly in the role of suppliants for favours whether in the councils of UNCTAD or the many other forums where dialogue between North and South supposedly takes place. Yet despite this depressing picture, the changes which have taken place over the last 40 years and the relative power residing in the hands of Third World countries today as opposed to 1955 (at the time of the Bandung Conference, see below) is very great indeed.

Nonetheless, the countries of the Third World or South still find that in most things they are obliged to follow a set of international rules laid down by the North in the era before the Third World came into being. The South is determined to break this pattern. For example, its determination to change the old ways of doing things emerged in the demand made through UNESCO for a new 'information order'. Such assaults upon the status quo are bitterly resisted by the North. For a brief period in the 1970s, the Organization of Oil-Exporting Countries (OPEC) threatened the western capitalist economic system and as a result produced demands for a New International Economic Order and the North–South Dialogue. This process – a continuing assault upon the bastions of the North – will continue.

Nothing in international politics remains static. Those Third World countries able to improve their economic conditions will move upwards to join the so-called advanced economies. They are then unlikely to see themselves as part of the Third World. A few could achieve this economic transition by the year 2000. A majority will not.

Attitudes to the Third World

Dealing with the arrogance of power has always been a major task for Third World leaders; this was especially the case in the early years of the Cold War when neither the West nor the Communist bloc was prepared to accept the notion of non-alignment. The fact that a growing group of countries simply did not wish or intend to join sides in a struggle which both East and West regarded as central to world politics appeared inconceivable to such statesmen as the American Secretary of State, John Foster Dulles. Such an attitude was even more marked in the West, which for so long had dominated international affairs, than in the Communist countries.

The end of World War II witnessed a succession of extraordinary political events: the emergence of the two superpowers as centres of rival ideological systems; the decline of Europe; and the rapid break-up of the European empires which introduced an unprecedented number of new nations on the world stage. These new nations brought to international politics perspectives which were almost always resented by the old powers and the latter were to find that their approach to world problems was now to be regularly questioned.

When on 15 August 1947 British India became independent, the sub-continent was detached from the Cold War line-up whose main demarcations had by then already been drawn. In 1960, when 17 African countries became independent, membership of the United Nations reached 100 and for the first time the African and Asian group was in a position to command an absolute majority in the UN Assembly.

In December 1961, in a reference to the troubles in the newly independent Congo (later Zaïre) and the beginning of armed resistance to the Portuguese in Angola, India's prime minister, Nehru, said: 'Something we consider as a great sin is looked upon (by the Western countries) as a minor misdemeanour which can be passed by, and something which we consider a minor misdemeanour is perhaps considered a great sin. So our values differ. Apparently, our standards differ.'*

Nehru's studiedly bland language nonetheless went to the root of the problem. In the early 1960s the West and the Communist bloc did come to accept, though grudgingly, that Non-Alignment represented a genuine political stand and was not simply fence-sitting. By the end of the 1960s the two sides in the Cold War appeared to believe that Non-Alignment had been tamed or at least that they had got its measure. This belief was reinforced because the emphasis of the Third World countries had switched by then from questions of world peace to economics. When Yugoslavia's Marshal Tito died in 1980, depriving the Non-Aligned Movement of one of its founding fathers, world depression and the emergence of new hard rightwing attitudes in the North meant that the Third World had become more embattled and, economically, in deeper trouble than at any time since its emergence in international politics. But many crucial developments had occurred before this point was reached.

The position of China in relation to the Third World has always been ambivalent. Although it took an uncompromising ideological stand during the Mao years, China had also, under Zhou Enlai's expert manipulation, played a significant role at the time of his meeting with Nehru in 1954 (see below), and at the Bandung Conference in 1955. Both these events advanced the concept of Non-Alignment. Then and now China remains among the world's poorest nations and on that count alone qualifies for membership of the Third World.

In 1948, the year before the Chinese Communists took control of the mainland, Mao Zedong said: 'It is impossible to sit on the fence; there is no third road.' The unification of China under Mao was a matter of pride to Asians who had long suffered from western exploitation. This was the case no matter what their attitides to Communism might be. The new China was neither beholden to any outside power nor in any sense subservient to a western mentor (as had been the Nationalists of Chiang Kai-shek). At last the greatest nation in Asia was seen to take control of its own destiny. That fact alone gave Communist China immense prestige, which Zhou Enlai used to maximum effect.

On a visit to New Delhi in 1954, Zhou agreed with his host, Jawaharlal Nehru, that the two great

*Against the Cold War by Chanakya Sen, Asia Publishing House, 1962.

Asian nations should adopt *Panchsila* or the Five Principles of Peaceful Co-existence. The next year Zhou attended the Bandung Conference where he made a major impact. Peaceful Co-existence was accepted by countries determined to be non-aligned even though they were completely opposed to Communist ideology. The acceptance of the concept of Peaceful Co-existence represented a breakthrough for China in the Third World where Zhou managed to project an image of a China prepared to accept ideologies other than Communism. Yet in 1959 in his pamphlet 'People's Democratic Dictatorship', Mao Zedong again attacked the idea of a third way: 'Neutrality is merely a camouflage; a third road does not exist.'

Should the new, more open China which Mao's successor, Chairman Deng Xiaoping, appeared to be encouraging in the mid-1980s (at least prior to the Tiananmen massacre) make the technological breakthroughs it seeks and achieve rapid industrialization, then China could move out of the Third World altogether. By 1993, although it was achieving quite remarkable industrial and commercial growth, China's leadership continued to insist that China remained a Communist state.

The *Free World*, as the western democracies referred to themselves in the early stages of the Cold War, contained all the old colonial powers. This fact caused deep suspicion in the Third World especially when the West argued that the new nations should adhere to its ideology rather than to that of the Communist bloc. Thus in 1951 (18 January), when the UN Secretary-General Trygve Lie met Nehru in Paris, he attempted to persuade him that the new countries of Asia should line up with the western democracies. But Nehru's reaction was that the peoples of Asia themselves would have to decide the future of Asia.

The West saw the early days of the Cold War as an ideological struggle and one that demanded a choice beteen the 'Free West' and 'godless Communism'. This attitude was to be the hallmark of the American Secretary of State, John Foster Dulles. He found it impossible to accept Non-Alignment as a positive force, a view that most of his successors in the United States have in fact shared whatever public postures they may have adopted. Dulles dominated American policy from 1953 until his death in 1959. The United States in particular but also the European powers regarded Non-Alignment with deep suspicion as 'fence-sitting'. In essence the western approach of those

Military Alliances at the Height of the Cold War

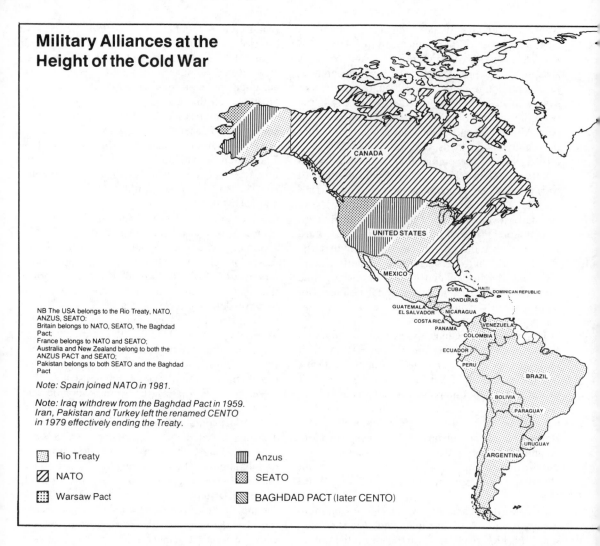

NB The USA belongs to the Rio Treaty, NATO,
ANZUS, SEATO;
Britain belongs to NATO, SEATO, The Baghdad
Pact;
France belongs to NATO and SEATO;
Australia and New Zealand belong to both the
ANZUS PACT and SEATO;
Pakistan belongs to both SEATO and the Baghdad
Pact

Note: Spain joined NATO in 1981.

*Note: Iraq withdrew from the Baghdad Pact in 1959.
Iran, Pakistan and Turkey left the renamed CENTO
in 1979 effectively ending the Treaty.*

▨ Rio Treaty		▥ Anzus	
▨ NATO		▨ SEATO	
▦ Warsaw Pact		▨ BAGHDAD PACT (later CENTO)	

years was: 'Either you are with us or against us.' This was not how the new nations of Asia in particular saw the Cold War and such an attitude was counter-productive. If anything it strengthened the determination of Third World countries to adopt Non-Alignment. Indeed, the anger that Non-Alignment generated in the West reinforced its impact in what was then a dangerously divided world.

The Korean War (1950-53) saw the first Third World effort to mediate between the two power blocs. A major breakthrough came with the UN vote of 27 August 1953 on the question of whether or not India (the acknowledged leader of the Non-Aligned Movement) should be invited to attend the Korean Political Conference. In the First Political Committee of the General Assembly it

The main military alliances of the Cold War

Rio Treaty (1947) The United States and 20 Latin American countries: it was a treaty of collective security, the USA to assist if aggression was committed against any member of the group.

NATO (North Atlantic Treaty Organization) (1949) There were 12 original members: the USA, Britain, France, Canada, Belgium, the Netherlands, Luxembourg, Norway, Denmark, Iceland, Italy and Portugal. They agreed mutual security arrangements against possible aggression. Turkey and Greece joined NATO in 1951, West Germany in 1955, and Spain in 1982.

ANZUS Pact (Australia, New Zealand and USA) (1951) The three countries were to go to one another's

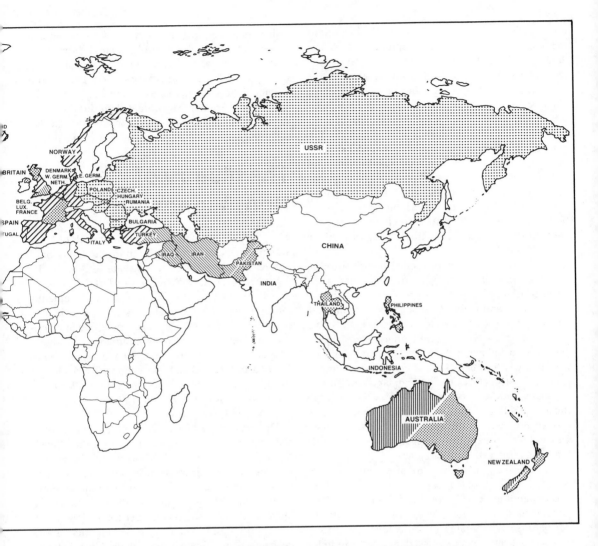

assistance in the event of aggression. In the mid-1980s the USA suspended New Zealand from ANZUS because of its non-nuclear policy.

SEATO (South East Asia Treaty Organization) (1954) The USA, Britain, France, Australia, New Zealand, Thailand, the Philippines and Pakistan joined in a mutual defence pact which in effect was part of the creation of a southern tier of allies against possible Soviet or Chinese aggression. Pakistan withdrew in 1973 and SEATO was dissolved in 1977.

The Baghdad Pact (1955) Britain, Pakistan, Iraq, Iran and Turkey joined together in what was the second of the southern tier treaties aimed at containing possible Soviet expansion southwards. Although the USA was not a member, it provided massive financial support for Pact members. Following its revolution of 1958, Iraq left the Pact in 1959, so that the organization was renamed *CENTO (Central Treaty Organization)* (1959).

In 1979, following the withdrawal of Iran, Pakistan and Turkey, the alliance was dissolved.

The Warsaw Pact (1955) The Pact was a military-political alliance. It was formed in 1955 between the USSR and Albania, Bulgaria, Czechoslovakia, East Germany, Hungary, Poland and Romania. Albania left the Pact in 1968. The Pact was only committed to the defence of the European territories of member states and was primarily the Communist response to NATO. The Warsaw Pact was formally dissolved on 1 April 1991.

Note: Pakistan's membership of SEATO, to which it already belonged when the Bandung Conference was held, and its subsequent decision to become a member of the Baghdad Pact (after Bandung), as well as its strong pro-western stance during this crucial phase of the Cold War meant that it could not be regarded as truly non-aligned.

was agreed by 27 votes to 21 with 11 abstentions that India should attend the conference. This was a defeat for Foster Dulles and a major victory for the Non-Aligned countries. India did not vote in the proceedings. Thus 2 years before the Bandung Conference, the idea gained ground that Non-Alignment could make contributions to peace.

The 1950s saw the Cold War confrontation extend into every corner of the globe and expand into economic as well as military and ideological rivalry. This global rivalry proved of immense value to the Third World during its formative stages (1955-65), because it was during these years that both sides decided to woo the new nations with offers of economic assistance with their development.

The Cold War proved of special significance for two countries which in their different ways were destined to play immensely important Third World roles: Egypt and Cuba. Colonel Nasser, who had come to power as a result of the coup of 1952 which overthrew King Farouk, emerged as a Third World hero following the Suez Crisis of 1956. In March 1961, he said: 'The struggle against imperialism is a struggle for the African land and for the African mines; for national wealth is the mast of the national flag.' Egypt was already playing a vital propaganda role in the African nationalist struggles and Nasser himself was regarded as one of the founding fathers of Non-Alignment.

And speaking in April 1961 after the abortive Bay of Pigs invasion of Cuba, Che Guevara who became another Third World folk hero said: 'The Americans hate us not because of our intentions but because we threaten their economic interests and because our revolution is a dangerous example for all Latin America.'

Yet despite such statements the concept of Non-Alignment was gaining acceptance, however grudging. In 1959 the UN General Assembly passed a unanimous resolution endorsing the philosophy of Peaceful Co-existence. In January 1961 the new American Ambassador to the UN, Adlai Stevenson, said that the American government (of President John F. Kennedy) would make no distinctions between aligned and non-aligned nations. Further, the United States would use the UN as a forum not for conducting the Cold War, but for ending it.

This was a new American line and represented a post-Dulles recognition of the existence and importance of Non-Alignment. Such a shift of policy made sense, because when the 1960 session of the UN General Assembly opened, more than half the members considered themselves as belonging to the Third World and being non-aligned. The West tended to see even fewer merits in the Non-Aligned Movement than did the Communist bloc, not least because the West regarded the movement as being primarily anti-colonial.

The history of Non-Alignment

The 1950s saw the birth and rapid growth of Non-Alignment as an approach to international politics before any formal movement came into being. Its growth coincided with the end of the European colonial empires. Nehru was the movement's father figure. Despite angry western denunciations of Non-Alignment, it did not mean non-involvement in international affairs; it was rather a refusal to take sides in the Cold War. In the mid-1980s a majority of all the countries outside the two ideological power blocs of East and West had come to regard themselves as belonging to the Non-Aligned Movement.

The movement began as an Asian initiative. It was joined in its early stages by Tito's Yugoslavia, whose historic break with Moscow had placed it in a dangerously exposed position, and Nasser's Egypt. Subsequently most new nations whether from Asia, Africa or the Caribbean joined the movement. Non-Alignment has found fewest adherents in Latin America, reflecting that area's delicately poised relationship with the United States.

On 1 June 1945, Sukarno enunciated a set of rules (*Pantjasila*) to guide the new Indonesian Republic, even though the Netherlands (with British help) made determined efforts over the next few years to regain control of its Asian empire.

Much of the impetus for Non-Alignment sprang from Asian revulsion against colonialism. India, Pakistan, Burma, Ceylon and Indonesia gained independence within a year or so of each other and these five countries accounted for nearly half the population of Asia, the world's most populous continent. They cherished their new freedom from colonialism and were not tempted to join either side in the Cold War. These Asian powers, moreover, did not see the Cold War in ideological terms. They saw it as a power struggle between two blocs each of which wished to dominate the very nations that had just achieved their independence. So they rejected Cold War alliances. This refusal to take part in Cold War confrontations represented an historic decision of immense importance and heralded the birth of the Third World.

In 1954 India and China agreed a treaty over the status of Tibet by which, in effect, India recognized China's control of Tibet which its forces had invaded and occupied in 1950. The two countries – Asia's giants – enunciated the Five Principles of Peaceful Co-existence, or the Panchsila: 'The principles and considerations which govern our mutual relations and the approach of the two countries to each other are as follows: (1) mutual respect for each other's territorial integrity and sovereignty; (2) mutual non-aggression; (3) mutual non-interference in each other's internal affairs; (4) equality and mutual benefit; and (5) peaceful co-existence.'

These principles were of particular importance to Asia during the following years. But not just to Asia. The concept of Peaceful Co-existence was one which the Non-Aligned Movement came to apply to its relations with the two sides in the Cold War.

But while Asian leaders were formulating the concept of Non-Alignment, the West was busy concluding the series of treaties which became the structural basis of its confrontation with the Communist bloc.

While the West was concerned to build up its system of anti-Communist defensive alliances, the driving force in the non-aligned countries was the new nationalism and a determined anti-colonialism. But the Bandung group of countries (see below) were by no means united in their approach and Ceylon, Pakistan and Thailand were clearly pro-western in their politics at that time. Nonetheless, this was the time when the concept of a Third Force came into vogue. The primary concern of the Third Force was peace – that is, peace between the two blocs because everyone saw clearly that a war in the nuclear age would engulf the whole world. Later, when the Cold War had settled into the more conventional, ritualistic responses of the 1960s, Non-Alignment (then virtually synonymous with the Third World) had become increasingly concerned with problems of development.

An important side effect of this triangular world was the extent to which both sides in the Cold War provided aid for the uncommitted nations in an attempt to woo them away from Non-Alignment. In a sense the Third World is the creation of the Cold War. The determination of newly independent Asian countries not to be drawn into the Cold War led them to formulate the principles of Non-Alignment. Later, as most of the new nations of Africa and Asia joined the movement, they were referred to increasingly as the Third World. The origins of the term Third World have been much debated. Yet its existence and very concept in fact depended upon a world already divided between East and West in the Cold War. The other vital characteristic of the Third World was that its peoples were poor and their countries underdeveloped. The poverty factor became the most important unifying theme for Third World countries from the early 1960s onwards.

The Bandung Conference

The Bandung Conference of April 1955 may be taken as the formal date which signalled the birth of Non-Alignment and perhaps also of the Third World, for the two are inextricably intertwined. Bandung's principal architects were Prime Minister Nehru of India, who represented the world's second most populous country and its largest democracy; President Tito of Yugoslavia, whose authority derived from his historic break with the USSR which enabled him to bring a genuinely Communist element into the movement; and President Nasser of Egypt, who had become the symbol of resurgent Arab nationalism. These men were to play a crucial role in the following years as they brought the world to accept Non-Alignment as a legitimate alternative to taking sides in the Cold War. Nehru more than anyone else can claim to be the creator of Non-Alignment and, as such, he was chiefly responsible for the emergence of the Third World as a new political force.

The Bandung Conference had five Asian sponsors: Burma (Myanmar), Ceylon (Sri Lanka), India, Indonesia and Pakistan. The Conference was concerned with five broad issues:

1. The reluctance of western powers to consult the new nations on issues concerning Asia;

2. The tensions between the USA and China which threatened the peace of the region;
3. The desire to find peaceful solutions especially between the rest of Asia and Communist China and also between China and the West;
4. Opposition to the continuation of colonialism in either Asia or elsewhere;
5. The more precise question of Indonesia's claim to West New Guinea (Irian Jaya). (This question was inevitable because Indonesia was the host country; in any case the issue could be seen as part of the question of decolonization.)

The conference witnessed the launching of Non-Alignment as a conscious alternative to membership of one or other side in the Cold War. The new nations wished to stand aside from the Cold War confrontations and concentrate instead upon their primary problem of development. Poverty was their first concern, not East–West ideological differences. The fact that they determined to maintain relations with both sides in the Cold War proved a consideration of great importance, influencing the amount of aid which some Third World countries were to receive over the next two decades. In part the new creed of Non-Alignment was a reaction to the useless and immensely costly Korean War.

While Nehru, Tito and Nasser can take the credit for giving the movement a remarkable impact, the deliberations of the Bandung Conference were further enhanced by the attendance of China's Zhou Enlai. His special concern was to propound the concept of Peaceful Co-existence. By his superb diplomacy he gained a respect for the new Communist China both as a major power and as a friend of the growing group of Afro-Asian countries. Nehru wanted the 29 countries which attended the conference to adopt the five principles of Panchsila and in the end these were incorporated in the *Bandung Declaration* of Ten Principles.

Bandung gave rise to the 'Bandung Spirit' of co-operation between the new nations of Africa and Asia. As such it may be seen as the formal beginning of the Third World policy of Non-Alignment.

Non-Aligned summit conferences

Although the Bandung Conference might be taken to have launched Non-Alignment, the idea of periodic Non-Aligned summits came later. The first such summit was held at Belgrade in 1961.

The decade began with high hopes; 1960 was the year when 17 new African countries became independent. John F. Kennedy won the American presidential election, giving rise to hopes of a more dynamic lead from the United States than had been provided during the last years of the Eisenhower–Dulles era. The Soviet Union had proposed the revolutionary idea of a Troika to run the UN: one representative for the West, one for the Communist bloc and one for the Non-Aligned or Third World. Even though the Troika idea came to nothing, the mere fact that the proposal had been put forward by one of the superpowers gave added legitimacy to the Third World. The concept had come of age.

The First Non-Aligned Summit, Belgrade, September 1961

This conference was timed to precede the 16th session of the UN General Assembly. The Summit was attended by 25 nations, out of a total UN membership at the beginning of the year of 100. (By the end of 1961, membership had reached 104.)

Presidents Nasser and Tito were the 'sponsors' of the Belgrade summit supported by presidents Achmed Sukarno (Indonesia), Kwame Nkrumah (Ghana), Modibo Keita (Mali) and Prime Minister Nehru (India). The summit was primarily concerned with colonialism and strengthening the new countries.

The Belgrade summit was preceded by a preparatory conference in Cairo in April 1961. At this conference a division occurred between Nasser and Tito on the one hand and Nehru on the other: the former wanted to define the principles of Non-Alignment, but Nehru wished the concept to be treated more liberally. He was against rigid interpretations and the subsequent history of Non-Alignment supports his approach. Nonetheless, Cairo laid down five criteria of Non-Alignment as follows:

1. A non-aligned country must follow an independent policy of co-existence of nations with varied political and social systems.
2. It must be consistent in its support for national independence.
3. It must not belong to a multilateral alliance concluded in the context of big power politics.
4. If it had a bilateral agreement with a big power or belonged to a regional defence pact these (agreements) should not have been concluded in the context of the Cold War.
5. If it had ceded bases to a big power, these should not have been in the context of the Cold War.

Such criteria highlighted the anti-Cold War stand of the non-aligned countries.

President Sukarno of Indonesia played a leading part at Belgrade. He defined Non-Alignment as follows: 'Non-alignment does not mean becoming a buffer state between two giant blocs. Non-alignment is active association in the cause of independence, abiding peace, social justice and freedom to be free... We are striving for the speedy establishment of a new equilibrium.'

The Belgrade Summit issued a Peace Appeal to both the Soviet Union and the USA. The previous year the shooting down of the American U-2 spy plane over the USSR had wrecked the Eisenhower-Khruschev summit and tensions remained high. The Peace Appeal of 5 September 1961 drew speedy responses from both super-powers, a further indication of the new climate of acceptance for the Non-Alignment Movement. In his reply to the Peace Appeal, for example, President Kennedy said: 'The US Government is aware that the non-aligned powers assembled at Belgrade represent an important segment of world opinion . . .'.

The summit declaration of 6 September 1961 called for a new international order to be based upon the liquidation of the remaining colonial empires.

The Second Non-Aligned Summit, Cairo, 28 November – 5 December 1964

This conference was attended by 47 countries, nearly twice the number present at Belgrade. The summit had been called on the initiative of Nasser

of Egypt, Mrs Bandaranaike of Ceylon backed by Nehru (who however had died earlier in the year) and Tito. A preliminary conference had been held earlier in the year.

The crisis in Congo (Léopoldville), now Zaïre, was still at its height and the beginning of the summit saw various manoeuvres to exclude Moise Tshombe of the breakaway Katanga (now Shaba) province from participating. The conference produced a 'Programme for Peace and International Co-operation' and established a Political and Economic Committee.

The main topics covered during the summit's deliberations were as follows: to prevent the spread of nuclear weapons; the liquidation of all foreign bases; non-interference in the internal affairs of other countries; an end to neo-colonialism and imperialism; the admission of China to the UN; support for the newly formed OAU; and concern over growing world economic disequilibrium.

The Third Non-Aligned Summit, Lusaka, 8–10 September 1970

The nature of the Non-Aligned summits had begun to change as they became routine, another of the mechanisms whereby Third World countries asserted their independence of great power politics. At the Lusaka summit resolutions were concerned primarily with problems of decolonization in Africa: the Portuguese territories; Rhodesia; apartheid in South Africa; Namibia; and the Israeli occupation of Sinai. Opening the summit President Kaunda of Zambia said: 'What we want is to make sure that our political freedom, economic and social progress are secure in our hands and are not subject to manipulation to benefit other nations against our interest.'

The Fourth Non-Aligned Summit, Algiers, 5–9 September 1973

This was the third summit to be held in Africa which reflected the new prominence of Africa in Third World councils. Attended by 75 nations, the summit produced a 'Declaration on the Struggle for National Liberation' and a majority of its resolutions – on apartheid, the Portuguese territories in Africa, Zimbabwe, Namibia, Spanish Sahara, Djibouti and the Comoros – concerned the end of colonialism in Africa. Other resolutions covered Israel and the Middle East, and economic affairs.

The Fifth Non-Aligned Summit, Colombo, 16–19 August 1976

At Colombo, the movement now consisted of 86 participating members, Belize having a special status. It took stock of the role of Non-Alignment and concluded that it represented mankind's search for peace. The questions included: imperialism, colonialism and neo-colonialism; decolonization; Southern Africa; combating racism and racial discrimination; the Middle East situation and the question of Palestine; an Indian Ocean Peace Zone Proposal; disarmament and security; interference in the internal affairs of other states; the United Nations; politics and economics; the press and news agencies. Observers at Colombo included 21 countries and organizations and a further seven attended as guests.

The Sixth Non-Aligned Summit, Havana, 3–9 September 1979

A number of countries (notably Yugoslavia, India, Sri Lanka, Tanzania) expressed their anxiety that the conference should be held in Cuba which was seen as too closely tied to the Communist bloc. They feared that the movement would thereby lose its anti-bloc stance. Cuba, however, advanced its 'radical thesis' which identified the socialist bloc as the 'natural ally' of the Non-Aligned against imperialism. The summit's declaration reaffirmed the principles of Non-Alignment. The principal subjects discussed were: South Africa; Western Sahara; the Middle East; Kampuchea (which was excluded from the conference because of its competing representatives); Indian Ocean and Mediterranean peace zones; Latin America.

The 95 members who attended included 54 heads of state or government, representatives of the Palestine Liberation Organization (PLO), the South West African People's Organization

(SWAPO) and the Zimbabwean Patriotic Front (Mugabe); 35 Foreign Ministers and various representatives of organizations, such as the UN Secretary-General. By now it had become the convention that the Head of State of the host country (in this case Fidel Castro of Cuba) became the chairman of the Non-Aligned Movement for the next 3 years or until the next summit took place.

The wide spectrum of interests represented by so many countries claiming to be non-aligned inevitably presented the movement with problems of reconciliation. Thus in 1966 Cuba had hosted a Tri-Continental Conference of 'radical' movements from Africa, Asia and Latin America. This expressed unity in the struggle against imperialism in all three continents. In fact the conference had little impact outside Communist circles.

The Seventh Non-Aligned Summit, New Delhi, March 1983

The seventh Non-Aligned summit was due to be held in Baghdad in 1982, but the date and venue were changed because of the Iran–Iraq war. By the 1980s the Non-Aligned Movement had become one of the firmly established instruments of Third World pressures and influence. In one sense its members, the great majority of Third World countries, were more assured than ever before in their dealings with the North. On the other hand, by 1983, they were facing especially difficult world economic conditions as well as a growing resistance in the North to many of their demands, particularly over economic matters.

The Final Declaration of the conference was equally divided between economic and political concerns. The Delhi Conference adopted a comprehensive declaration and the 'New Delhi Message' called on the major powers to pursue discussions on disarmament, and for the North to hold talks with the South on economic and technological co-operation.

By 1983, 99 countries and organizations were full members of the Non-Aligned Movement and 97 of these, including the PLO and SWAPO, attended the Delhi Summit. Some 60 heads of government were present.

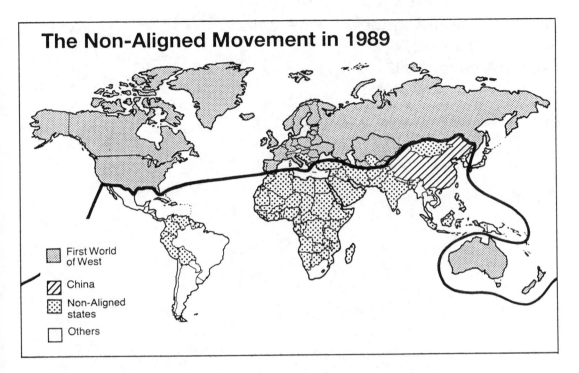

The Non-Aligned Movement in 1989

First World
of West

China

Non-Aligned
states

Others

The Eighth Non-Aligned Summit, Harare, 1–3 September 1986

Prime Minister Robert Mugabe of Zimbabwe became the new chairman of the Non-Aligned Movement. The summit concentrated upon the subject of South Africa (South African journalists covering the summit were told to leave) and members gave secret pledges of substantial aid to the frontline states for their impending confrontation with South Africa.

The summit condemned the US air raid on Libya but Gaddafi denounced the Non-Aligned Movement for its pretensions to neutrality between East and West and stormed out of the conference.

The Ninth Non-Aligned Summit, Belgrade, 4–7 September 1989

The summit was held in Belgrade shortly before Yugoslavia, which under Tito had been a founder member of the movement, collapsed in civil war and disintegrated. Venezuela joined the Non-Aligned Movement to become its 102nd member. The summit was attended by 65 heads of state or government and 69 guests or observers amongst whom, for the first time, were representatives of the six East European Warsaw Pact countries. Pressures were mounted for the Non-Aligned Movement to modernize itself and become more pragmatic. Reflecting the end of the Cold War, the final declaration referred to 'undisputed positive developments' between the superpowers which meant that 'tension (was) no longer at breaking point'. The summit reaffirmed that a new international economic order was a central goal. Other issues debated included the environment and debt.

(Ministerial conferences are held on a triennial basis between summits to plan for the forthcoming summit and at the tenth such conference held in Accra during 1991 at which 97 countries sent representatives, Argentina withdrew from the Non-Aligned Movement because the movement 'no longer had any reason to exist'. Mongolia was elected the 103rd member.)

The Tenth Non-Aligned Summit, Jakarta, 1–6 September 1992

The summit was attended by 59 heads of state and the UN Secretary-General Boutros Boutros-Ghali. New members included Brunei, Myanmar, the Philippines and Uzbekistan to bring total membership to 108. Armenia, China, Croatia and Thailand were given observer status.

The summit was concerned with its post-Cold War role. President Suharto of Indonesia (the conference chairman) called for a 'realistic re-ordering' of the Non-Aligned Movement's priorities to tackle the increasing polarization between North and South which loomed as 'the central unresolved issue of our time'. The conference condemned ethnic cleansing in former Yugoslavia. The final document reaffirmed the Non-Aligned Movement's intention to remain 'an independent political force despite the changes in the world' and noted the 'urgent need to accord high priority to the issues of development and equitable international economic relations.'

4 Third World Regional Groupings

Part 1 Africa

In 1945 only four African countries – Egypt, Ethiopia, Liberia and South Africa – were independent. But by 1980, when Rhodesia became Zimbabwe, the number of independent African countries had increased to 51 and all but one (South Africa) had joined the Organization of African Unity (OAU). This extraordinary historical phenomenon – the appearance of 47 new nations on a single continent over 35 years – was not, however, matched by an equal growth of economic or political power. The African bloc at the UN might be the largest in voting power; it remains the weakest in economic capacity or political influence.

Some of the huge new countries, such as Chad, Mali and Niger, may look impressive on a map. But when size is related to their tiny, fragmented populations and lack of economic development, it is easy to understand why the idea of continental unity had such a broad appeal – at least in theory. Pan-Africanism, or the search for continental unity, which played such an important role in the years immediately before and after independence, as much as anything represented the growing awareness of how weak the new nations were when they became independent. Colonialism had fragmented the continent, though just what might have emerged without the colonial carve-up of the nineteenth century it is impossible to say. But in most cases the size of a country bears little relation to the capacity of its economy to satisfy the needs of the population, often at a quite basic level. The annual gross domestic product (GDP) of many African countries is only equivalent to the municipal budget of a medium-sized British or French town. Nkrumah's famous dictum, 'Seek ye first the political kingdom', was no doubt correct as a tactic but as most African countries discovered soon after independence they were anything but economically free. The search for unity, then, became a crucial aspect of Africa in the 1950s and 1960s. It led to the emergence of a number of groups whose motives were a mixture: the common desire to resist further political and economic encroachments from outside; an assertion of a common identity as Africans; the need to co-operate to overcome problems.

Note: Of the four countries already independent in 1945:

Egypt

Britain formally ended its protectorate over Egypt in 1922 but the country remained within its 'sphere of influence' until Nasser's rise to power in the 1950s. The Anglo-Egyptian Treaty of 1936 (allowing Britain to station troops in the country) only came to an end in 1954 when Britain agreed (reluctantly) to remove its Suez base to Cyprus. The Suez Crisis (1956) represented a final attempt by Britain to employ old-style imperial gunboat diplomacy to control Egypt's policy – in this case unsuccessfully.

Ethiopia

The country's independence goes back to antiquity, dating at least from the Kingdom of Aksum (circa 500 BC). A powerful nation was created in the nineteenth century and, alone in Africa at the end of the century, Ethiopia was able to repel European colonialism when Menelik II defeated the invading Italian army at Adowa in 1896. Mussolini's Italy avenged this defeat when Italian troops invaded Ethiopia in 1935 although they only conquered the country in 1936 after protracted fighting. It was liberated in 1941 and Haile Selassie entered his capital on 5 May of that year. Apart from this brief period Ethiopia was not colonized like the rest of Africa.

Liberia

An independent Republic of Liberia was proclaimed in 1847; its creation was the work of American philanthropists who wished to assist freed slaves of the American South to find a home in Africa. Although it was never to be an American colony in the formal sense, for most of its existence Liberia was an economic colony of US interests and has been deeply influenced by the American connexion.

South Africa

Following the defeat of the Boers in the Anglo-Boer War of 1899-1902 South Africa became one of the self-governing Dominions of the British Empire in 1910 when the Act of Union came into effect. The country became fully independent under international law with the passing of the Statute of Westminster in 1931. According to the terms of the Act of Union, however, the British handed over power in South Africa to the representatives of the white minority. At that time and through to 1990 when President de Klerk initiated a process of real change, this minority showed its determination not to share power with the African majority, thus creating one of Africa's most intractable problems.

Dates of African independence since 1945

Country	Date
Libya	1951
Sudan	1956
Morocco	1956
Tunisia	1956
Ghana	1957
Guinea	1958
Cameroon	1960
Togo	1960
Mali	1960
Senegal	1960
Madagascar	1960
Congo (Léopoldville – now Zaïre)	1960
Somalia	1960

African Independence

Note: Egypt, Ethiopia, Liberia and South Africa were already independent in 1945

Dahomey (now Benin)	1960
Niger	1960
Upper Volta (now Burkina Faso)	1960
Côte d'Ivoire	1960
Chad	1960
Central African Republic	1960
Congo (Brazzaville)	1960
Gabon	1960
Nigeria	1960
Mauritania	1960
Sierra Leone	1961
Tanganyika (now Tanzania)	1961
Rwanda	1962
Burundi	1962
Algeria	1962
Uganda	1962
Zanzibar (now part of Tanzania)	1963
Kenya	1963
Malawi	1964
Zambia	1964
Gambia	1965
Botswana	1966
Lesotho	1966
Mauritius	1968
Swaziland	1968
Equatorial Guinea	1968
Guinea-Bissau	1974
Mozambique	1975
Cape Verde	1975
Comoros*	1975
São Tomé & Príncipe	1975
Angola	1975
Seychelles	1976
Djibouti	1977
Zimbabwe	1980
Namibia	1990
Eritrea	1993

Notes *The Comoros proclaimed itself independent on 6 July 1975; this was recognized in respect of three of the four islands (but not Mayotte) by France the following December.

Apart from the four countries already independent in 1945, an analysis of the 47 countries to become independent over these years shows as follows: 18 were French colonies; 16 British (Zanzibar merging with Tanganyika in 1964 to form the United Republic of Tanzania); five were Portuguese, three Belgian, one Italian and one Spanish. Cameroon and Togo were UN Mandates, Somalia comprised British Somaliland and the Italian Mandate of Somaliland, Sudan was an Anglo-Egyptian Condominion. The former Italian colony of Eritrea which became a Mandate of the UN after World War II was incorporated into Ethiopia in 1960 and for the next 30 years fought more or less ceaselessly against the government of Addis Ababa in its determination to secede until 1991 when the civil wars in Ethiopia finally came to an end. Eritrea became independent (following a referendum) in May 1993. Namibia which had been illegally occupied and controlled by South Africa became independent in 1990.

Once Zimbabwe became independent in April 1980, only three 'colonial' problems remained in Africa. First, in the North is the disputed territory of former Spanish Sahara (Rio de Oro). This territory was claimed and occupied by Morocco following Spain's withdrawal in 1975, but Morocco's claim has been disputed by the inhabitants whose independence movement POLISARIO has fought a liberation war against Morocco over the years since then. In September 1991 a UN-brokered ceasefire between Morocco and the POLISARIO Front came into effect pending a referendum. By mid-1993 conditions for such a referendum had still not been agreed and POLISARIO was threatening to renew the war.

Second, Namibia (formerly South West Africa) was occupied illegally by South Africa (according to the United Nations) which for years refused to admit UN jurisdiction over the former mandate which had been granted to South Africa in 1920. But in 1990, as a result of the new USA–USSR accommodation that was taking place as the Cold War came to an end, a settlement for Namibia was agreed and it became independent in March of that year.

Third, though South Africa itself is internationally recognized as independent, its policy of apartheid which denied equal political rights to the black four-fifths of the population (as well as the Coloured and Asian minorities) posed a major problem for the peace of the area. In Africa the ending of apartheid was equated with the ending of colonialism. Internal pressures in South Africa steadily mounted through the 1980s so that by the end of the decade South Africa was close to becoming ungovernable. Then the new President, F. W. de Klerk, gave his key speech of 2 February 1990 in which he announced the unbanning of the ANC and other banned political parties and organizations and so launched South Africa on a new path. By mid-1993, despite many setbacks and doubts as well as much violence, it did appear that the country which had abandoned apartheid, except in the crucial matter of 'one person one vote', was moving towards its target of democratic (i.e. all-race) elections set for April 1994.

Early moves to foster continental unity began in the 1950s when such colonies as the Gold Coast (Ghana) became independent. The danger that the continent would divide into a number of opposing groups was recognized by leaders such as Kwame Nkrumah, who saw these divisions being encouraged by the former colonial powers so as to prolong African weakness and allow them to continue exploiting the continent. It was Nkrumah who coined the phrase 'neo-colonialism' to cover such activities. The possible divisions at that time included: English- versus French-speaking Africa; the Arab North versus the Black South; the so-called moderates against the so-called radicals.

Meetings of two sets of newly independent nations, one half at Casablanca and the other at Monrovia, gave rise to two groups which were to be known as the 'radicals' (the Casablanca group) and 'moderates' (the Monrovia group) (see below). The years 1958 to 1963 witnessed a number of conferences and would-be unions which culminated in the formation of the Organization of African Unity in 1963. Some of the groups formed at this time have had little subsequent impact, but their later unimportance in no way detracts from their historical justification. They represented a search for ways to tackle acute continental problems: how to work together; how to present a united front to a big power world which otherwise would exploit their individual weaknesses; and how to create a greater sense of their shared 'African-ness' whatever political divisions might exist. Given the size of Africa and its diversity, the degree to which its many nations have managed to achieve common action and unity of purpose since 1960 is matter for congratulation rather than the reverse.

Pan-Africanism

The concept of Pan-Africanism goes back to the beginning of the century when the first Pan-African Conference sponsored by Trinidad barrister H. Sylvester Williams was held in London (1900), but its greatest flowering came in the late 1950s and early 1960s as the tide of independence began to sweep away the European colonial empires. The regional groups and organizations which sprang up at this time are now little more than historical footnotes. Nonetheless, they had their relevance at the time.

There was a Pan-African Congress in the immediate aftermath of World War I – at Paris in 1919 – which called upon the Allied and Associated Powers to establish a code of law for the international protection of the natives of Africa. At the Sixth Pan-African Congress held in 1945 in Manchester, Britain, such notable political leaders-to-be as Jomo Kenyatta from Kenya and Kwame Nkrumah from the Gold Coast took part.

The atmosphere had changed since 1919 and the scent of independence was in the air. The Congress called for an end to colonialism, stating 'We are determined to be free.'

The British colony of the Gold Coast achieved independence in March 1957 as Ghana, under the leadership of Kwame Nkrumah who became a leading figure in pressing for continental independence and unity. However, other African leaders often resented his powerful personality and suspected his motives. Nonetheless, he gave real impetus both to the continent-wide demand for an immediate end to colonialism and the desire for African unity.

A series of conferences was held at this time as follows:

1. The First Conference of Independent African States, Accra, Ghana, April 1958
2. The All-African Peoples Conference, Accra, December 1958
3. The All-African Peoples Conference, Tunis, January 1960
4. The Second Conference of Independent African States, Addis Ababa, June 1960 (By this time the divisions which were to be reflected in the Casablanca and Monrovia groups were already surfacing.)
5. The All-African Peoples Conference, Cairo, March 1961

As much as anything these meetings represented a search by the leaders of newly independent countries for a *modus vivendi* both with regard to each other and, hopefully, as a bloc in relation to the outside world. The fact that Africa was likely to achieve unity as much or as little as the Arab world, Europe or Asia was beside the point. The search was certainly worthwhile even if it only revealed the obstacles to real unity. In fact it did much more. The idea of unity was very much in the air, as shown by the following examples.

The Conakry Declaration

On 23 November 1958 Ghana and Guinea drafted a charter (which was later signed by Mali) to create an African Union of States. This led to the Conakry Declaration of 1 May 1959. Ghana and Guinea agreed to establish a union between their two countries. Later – 1 July 1961 – Mali also joined the 'union' although in real political terms the union never came to anything.

The Saniquellie Declaration

19 July 1959. At the village of Saniquellie, Liberia, President Tubman of Liberia, President Touré of Guinea and President Nkrumah of Ghana formulated the principles for achieving the Community of Independent African States.

The Casablanca group

In January 1961, representatives of Ghana, Guinea, Mali, Morocco, Libya, Egypt and the Algerian Provisional Government met in Casablanca where they adopted what came to be known as the *Casablanca Charter*. Their object was the creation of a joint military command and an African Common Market. The group was regarded as radical. It advocated a socialist path of development for Africa and a strong central authority. The movement received expressions of support from the Pan-African Movement for East, Central and Southern Africa (PAFMECSA) – also newly formed.

The Monrovia group

Opposition to the Casablanca group was not slow to appear. President Tubman of Liberia called a meeting in Monrovia (8–12 May 1961) which was attended by 19 other independent African nations. These were: Cameroon, the Central African Republic, Chad, Congo (Brazzaville), Dahomey (later Benin), Ethiopia, Gabon, Côte d'Ivoire, Libya, Madagascar, Mauritania, Niger, Nigeria, Senegal, Sierra Leone, Somalia, Togo, Tunisia, Upper Volta (later Burkina Faso). The same countries met again at Lagos in January 1962 but by then they had become known as the *Monrovia group*. The group adopted a draft charter for an Organization of Inter-African and Malagasy States. At Lagos (in January 1962) Tunisia did not attend, but Congo (Léopoldville, now Zaïre) did.

These manoeuvres and the groups which resulted from them threatened to split the continent. The formation of the Casablanca and Monrovia groups emphasized the dangerous nature of the ideological divisions which Africa faced before the Ethiopian Emperor Haile Selassie and others tried to resolve the differences which had surfaced between the two main groups. In perhaps his greatest contribution to independent Africa, Haile Selassie presided over meetings in Addis Ababa which led to the formation of the Organization of African Unity.

The Organization of African Unity (OAU)

In May 1963 the foreign ministers of 30 African countries met in Addis Ababa to prepare an agenda for a meeting of their heads of state. They discussed the creation of an Organization of African States which would be concerned with matters of collective defence, decolonization, and co-operation in economic, social, educational and scientific matters. Inevitably the meeting also dealt with apartheid in South Africa and racial discrimination.

Later that month (23 May) the heads of state or government of 30 countries met in Addis Ababa under the chairmanship of the Emperor Haile Selassie. They approved a Charter to create an Organization of African Unity (OAU). This Charter was signed by 30 heads of state on 26 May 1963. (Chad and Togo signed later to become founder members.)

The following countries were the founder members of the OAU: Algeria, Burundi, Cameroon, Central African Republic, Chad, Congo (Brazzaville), Congo (Léopoldville) (later Zaïre), Dahomey (later Benin), Ethiopia, Gabon, Ghana, Guinea, Ivory Coast (Côte d'Ivoire), Liberia, Libya, Madagascar, Mali, Mauritania, Morocco, Niger, Nigeria, Rwanda, Senegal, Sierra Leone, Somalia, Sudan, Tanzania, Togo, United Arab Republic (Egypt), Upper Volta (later Burkina Faso).

The Organization of African Unity represented a compromise between a strong federal type of structure that had been favoured by the Casablanca group and the looser association of states favoured by the Monrovia group.

The OAU Charter

The principal objects of the Organization as laid down by the Charter were:

A. To promote continental unity;
B. To co-ordinate efforts to improve the life of the African peoples;
C. To defend African sovereignty;
D. To eradicate colonialism;
E. To promote international co-operation.

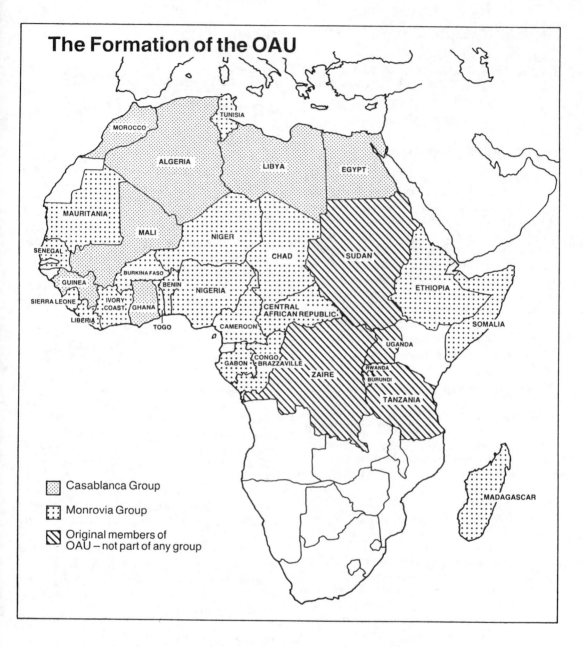

The Formation of the OAU

Casablanca Group

Monrovia Group

Original members of
OAU – not part of any group

Seven fundamental principles were laid down:
1.   Recognition of the sovereign equality of member countries;
2.   Non-interference in the internal affairs of countries;
3.   Respect for the sovereign equality and territorial integrity of each country and its inalienable right to independent existence;
4.   Peaceful settlement of disputes;
5.   Condemnation of assassination or subversion by one country in another;
6.   Dedication to the emancipation of those territories still colonies;
7.   Adherence to the principle of Non-Alignment.

Other important provisions included the following:
A.   Membership of the OAU was to be open to all independent African states and islands.

B. There was to be no recognition of the govern-
    ments of South Africa, South West Africa
    (later Namibia) or Rhodesia (now Zimbabwe)
    until the achievement of black majority rule in
    those territories.
C. The OAU agreed to give observer status to
    those liberation movements (such as the Afri-
    can National Congress (ANC) of South Africa)
    which it recognized.
D. Revenue was to be raised according to a
    member nation's UN assessment.
E. A fund was created to assist the liberation
    movements.
F. The OAU headquarters were established in
    Addis Ababa.

The structure of the Organization
1. The Annual Assembly of Heads of State and
    Government is the supreme policy making
    body.
2. The Council of Ministers consisting of foreign
    or other ministers is to meet twice a year (with
    provision for extraordinary meetings).
3. The General Secretariat is to carry out the
    functions assigned to it under the Charter. The
    Secretary-General is elected by the Annual
    Assembly of Heads of State or Government
    for a four-year term.
4. The Secretariat contains the following depart-
    ments: Political; Finance; Education, Science,
    Culture and Social Affairs; Economic
    Development and Co-operation; Adminis-
    tration and Conferences.
5. There is also an Arbitration Commission and
    other specialized commissions, including
    Defence and Labour.
6. A Liberation Committee co-ordinates the
    liberation movements.
7. The OAU includes a number of specialized
    agencies covering aviation, trade unions, Pan-
    African news, postal union, telecommunica-
    tions, scientific, technical and research, sports,
    railways.
8. Ad hoc committees may be set up as required
    (as in the case of emergencies).
    Broadly, the structure of the OAU is similar to
    that of the UN but without a Security Council
    or a veto.

The first Heads of State and Government
Summit was held in Cairo in 1964 when the most
important issues discussed concerned inter-African

borders; South Africa and apartheid; and decolonization. Of great importance to Africa were the
early resolutions calling upon OAU members to
observe their inherited colonial boundaries. The
alternative would have been continent-wide friction because the colonial boundaries had paid little
attention to ethnic realities. Other resolutions
called upon members not to establish diplomatic or
other relations with South Africa until apartheid
had been eliminated.

It is not easy to assess the achievements of the
OAU. Without doubt, it has helped shape the
direction of post-colonial African politics. 'Talking
out' a crisis between its members is possibly its
most important function. OAU insistence that its
members accept the inherited colonial boundaries
almost certainly lessened the possibilities of strife
between member nations. Sometimes the OAU
has achieved an impressive show of unity – over
economic objectives or questions of race (South
Africa). Its role as a forum which enables every
member country to put on record its views on
continental problems is also important. But it
suffers from similar defects to the UN and when
such an influential member as Morocco found
itself at odds with the organization over the
question of its claim to Western Sahara, it simply
withdrew from the OAU (November 1984). In
1988 the OAU celebrated its 25th anniversary.

By the beginning of the 1990s the OAU was
suffering from divisions that rendered it unable to
play any significant role in the trouble spots on the
continent. Its failure to do anything constructive
about the crisis in Somalia was a case in point.

Nonetheless, at its 27th summit meeting held at
Abuja, Nigeria, in June 1991, the OAU adopted a
51-nation treaty establishing the African Economic
Community (AEC) whose objectives were to
promote social, economic and cultural development and integrate African economies so as to
increase continental self-reliance. It envisaged a
six-stage development of the AEC before it
achieved a single economic community over a 34-
year period. The AEC would comprise six organs:
the Assembly of Heads of State and Governments,
a Pan-African Parliament, a Council of Ministers,
an Economic and Social Commission, a Court of
Justice, and a Specialized Technical Committee
with a General Secretariat.

When the 29th OAU summit was held in Cairo,
in June 1993, newly independent Eritrea was
admitted as the 52nd member. The Eritrean

President, Issaias Afewerki then 'stunned' the summit to which his country had just been admitted when he declared that the OAU had been 'an utter failure for 30 years'. As a result, he argued: 'Africa is not a place where its citizens can walk with raised heads but a continent scorned by all its partners, a continent that seems to produce endlessly the wrong manuals for economic development, democratization and political management.' The summit passed 10 resolutions of which the most important concerned: a) the establishment of a mechanism for resolving conflicts peacefully; b) a means for implementing the June 1991 (Abuja) treaty to establish an African Economic Community (AEC); and c) a means for easing the debt problem. Salim Ahmed Salim of Tanzania was re-elected OAU Secretary-General for a second 4-year term.

The Economic Commission for Africa (ECA)

The ECA was established by the Economic and Social Council of the United Nations on 29 April 1958. Its principal aim is to promote economic and social development in Africa. Membership of the ECA is open to all independent African countries which are also members of the UN, but on 24 July 1963, South Africa was barred by the Economic and Social Council until 'conditions for constructive co-operation have been restored by a change in its racial policy'.

The ECA headquarters are in Addis Ababa with sub-regional offices situated in Yaoundé, Gisenyi, Niamey, Tangier, Lusaka and Kinshasa. It is run by an Executive Secretary. His task – and that of the Secretariat – is to help organize African institutions and train their personnel, to advise governments in their development programmes, and to conduct investigations at the request of member countries.

The ECA pays special attention to agriculture and the problems of transition from subsistence to market agriculture. The agriculture division co-operates with the FAO.

The ECA is basically an advisory body with limited resources at its disposal. It sees its task as promoting co-operation between the sub-regions of Africa and promoting inter-African trade and it has become a source of statistics for Africa. Other areas in which it is involved include: manpower and training, social affairs (that is, the social aspects of economic development), transport, communications, natural resources.

The African Institute for Economic Development and Planning

In November 1963, in co-operation with UNESCO, FAO, WHO, and UNDP, the ECA established the African Institute for Economic Development and Planning at Dakar. The centre exists for the study of African development problems and for training specialists and government personnel involved in economic planning.

African Development Bank (ADB)

The African Development Bank (ADB) was brought into being in September 1964, when 20 African countries had ratified the agreement to set it up. The idea of such a bank had first been discussed at the All-Africa Peoples Conference of January 1960 in Tunisia. An agreement was worked out by finance ministers in Khartoum in 1963, the Bank's headquarters were established in 1965 at Abidjan and the ADB became operational on 1 July 1966.

A formula for subscriptions of members was based on a combination of population, gross national product, foreign trade and government revenue. A minimum subscription was set at $1 million, the maximum at $30 million.

Subscriptions were divided between paid up shares and *callable* (not paid up) shares. Through to the mid-1970s, subscriptions accounted for 70 per cent of the capital stock.

The Bank's stated aims were to contribute to the economic development and social advancement of its members both individually and collectively. It was to promote public and private capital investment and to provide technical assistance. The structure of the ADB was as follows:

A. The supreme organ of the Bank is the Board of Governors to which each member country nominates one Governor.

B. The Board of Directors consists of 18, of whom six are non-African, who are elected by the Board of Governors for 3 years. This is the operating organ of the Bank.

C. The President who is responsible for the day-to-day operations is elected for a 5-year term.

D. The Bank uses a unit of account equivalent at the beginning of the 1980s to $1.16.

E. There are two associated bodies:

1. *The African Development Fund*
   The ADF was established by the Bank in 1972 and grants interest-free loans for projects with repayment over 50 years.

2. *The Nigerian Trust Fund*
   The NTF was set up in 1976 (and is run by the ADB jointly with Nigeria) and grants loans for up to 25 years at 4 per cent interest rates. The NTF represents a Nigerian response to the oil crisis which Africa faced following the OPEC price rises of 1973.

F. There are a further four associated institutions of the ADB: *Société internationale financière pour les investissements et le développement en Afrique (SIFIDA)*; Africa Reinsurance Corporation; *Shelter-Afrique*; and the Association of African Development Finance Institutions (AADFI).

Originally the capital of the ADB was subscribed entirely by African countries in order to preserve the African nature of the Bank's operations. The ADB was the only regional development bank to do this. The drawback to this arrangement was the limitation which it placed upon available funds especially in view of the small size of most African economies and the very limited finances they could make available to the ADB. In 1978, therefore, at the 14th annual meeting of the Board of Governors held in Libreville (Gabon), it was agreed to open capital stock to non-regional subscribers. The decision was only ratified, however, in 1982, the delay resulting from genuine fears and hesitations of members that the nature of the operation would be changed and that it would lose its African bias. Nonetheless, by September 1984, 23 non-African countries had become members of the ADB. The African members continue to hold two-thirds of the share capital and all loans are limited to African members. The President must be an African. All independent African countries (except South Africa) belong to the ADB.

Arab Bank for Economic Development in Africa – Banque Arabe pour le Développement Économique en Afrique (BADEA)

BADEA was created in November 1973 at the Sixth Arab Summit at Algiers attended by members of the Arab League. It represents the Arab response to African support and solidarity at the time of the Yom Kippur War of October 1973 and is a vehicle whereby the rich OPEC Arab countries can channel development funds into black Africa.

The Bank began operations early in 1975. Its object is to assist African development by providing all or part of the finances needed for selected development projects. It also provides technical assistance. The Bank's subscribers are the members of the Arab League, less Djibouti, Somalia and Yemen. BADEA makes loans to the independent African countries (not members of the Arab League).

The three main organs of BADEA are: a Board of Governors (finance ministers of the Arab League); a Board of Directors; the Bank President. Loans are provided on concessional terms for development projects; they do not exceed $10 million or 40 per cent of the total costs of a project. BADEA loans have been provided in approximately equal proportions to West and East Africa.

Economic unions

A number of mainly economic unions were formed in the early 1960s among the Francophone countries. They were over-ambitious, they reflected the former colonial ties with France, and few had much impact. Nonetheless, they once again demonstrated an awareness of the possibilities for co-operation even if, in most cases, they also demonstrated fairly rapidly the constraints which limited such putative unions.

Union africaine et malgache – the Africa and Malagasy Union (UAM)

The UAM was formed on 12 September 1961. It grew out of a meeting in Brazzaville, capital of

Congo, in December 1960. Twelve Francophone nations had agreed to maintain close ties with each other and a special relationship with the ex-colonial power, France. The 12 were: Cameroon, Central African Republic, Chad, Congo (Brazzaville), Dahomey (later Benin), Gabon, Ivory Coast (Côte d'Ivoire), Madagascar, Mauritania, Niger, Senegal, Upper Volta (later Burkina Faso).

The aims of the UAM included the adoption of a common stand on international issues, the promotion of economic and cultural co-operation and the maintenance of a common defence organization. It soon became apparent, however, that the member countries were too diverse, too geographically widespread and too immersed in their individual development problems to allow the UAM ever to become significant.

In March 1964 the UAM changed its name to the Afro-Malagasy Union for Economic Co-operation (*Union africaine et malgache de co-opération économique* – UAMCE). From then on its principal preoccupation was with economic affairs. By 1966, however, the organization had become moribund.

African and Malagasy Common Organization – Organisation commune africaine et malgache (OCAM)

This successor to the UAMCE was formed in February 1965 at Nouakchott (Mauritania) and included 13 Francophone nations. These were: Cameroon, Central African Republic, Chad, Congo (Brazzaville), Dahomey (Benin), Gabon, Côte d'Ivoire, Madagascar, Mauritania, Niger, Senegal, Togo, Upper Volta (Burkina Faso). Later, in May 1965, Rwanda and Congo (Léopoldville) (Zaïre) joined the organization, although in June 1965 Mauritania withdrew. On 27 June at a meeting in Antananarivo (Madagascar), these 14 (without Mauritania) signed the OCAM Charter.

The original aims of OCAM were co-operation in economic, social, technical and cultural developments. Its principal organs are the Conference of Heads of State and Government; the Council of Ministers; and the Secretariat and Secretary-General. Its headquarters are in Bangui, Central African Republic. OCAM runs a number of joint services of which the multinational airline,

Air Afrique, was the most successful until it was detached from the organization in 1979.

OCAM has had a troubled history: Mauritius joined in 1970, Zaïre withdrew in 1972 and Congo in 1973, Cameroon, Chad and Madagascar withdrew in 1974 and Gabon in 1977. Some of these countries retained membership of OCAM's various agencies. The summit held in Côte d'Ivoire in 1982 decided to attempt to revitalize the organization by which time the initials stood for *Organisation commune africaine et mauricienne*.

UDE, UDEAC, UEAC

UDE, the Equatorial Customs Union, was created on 23 June 1959. It was replaced by UDEAC (Customs and Economic Union of Central Africa) which was established at Brazzaville in December 1964. Its members were: Cameroon, Central African Republic, Congo (Brazzaville), Gabon and Chad. The treaty formally replacing UDE came into force on 1 January 1966.

In 1968, however, the Central African Republic and Chad withdrew from UDEAC to join the Congo (Léopoldville) (Zaïre) in another union – UEAC (Union of Central African States). Then in December 1968 the Central African Republic rejoined UDEAC. The emphasis of these groups has been upon a customs union.

East African Community (EAC)

The East African Community comprising Kenya, Tanzania and Uganda was established on 6 June 1967. Its object was to strengthen economic, trade and industrial ties between the three countries. Its provisions included: a common excise tariff; no internal tariffs; and the establishment of an East African Development Bank (EADB). Its main organs were the Common Market Council; the Common Market Tribunal; the Secretariat; and the East African Authority (comprising the three heads of state) which was the ultimate authority of the EAC.

Other provisions in the treaty of the EAC included the establishment of five councils and an East African Legislative Assembly; a General Fund; the East African Railways Corporation; East African Harbours Corporation; East African Posts and Telecommunications Corporation; and the East African Airways Corporation.

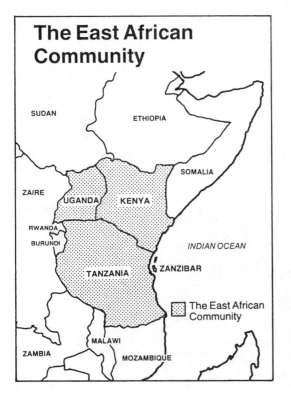

The East African Community

SUDAN

ETHIOPIA

SOMALIA

ZAIRE

UGANDA   KENYA

RWANDA

BURUNDI

INDIAN OCEAN

TANZANIA   ZANZIBAR

The East African Community

ZAMBIA

MALAWI

MOZAMBIQUE

The Community's headquarters were established at Arusha, the Railways at Nairobi, Harbours in Dar es Salaam, with Posts and Telecommunications in Kampala.

The three territories had a good deal in common. Kenya and Uganda became part of British Africa in the 1890s, while the League of Nations Mandate for Tanganyika was given to Britain at the end of World War I in 1919. The three territories came to independence within 2 years of one another (1961-63), were of comparable size and at a similar general stage of development. Moreover (a result of their colonial heritage) they shared in common the use of the English language, British law, similar institutions and systems of administration. In 1948 Britain had established the East Africa High Commission to co-ordinate activities in the three territories. In 1961 this was replaced by the East African Common Services Organization (EACSO). Thus the groundwork for operating a successful common market existed when the three countries became independent. Conditions were about as favourable as could be expected.

Yet between 1961 and 1967, Tanzania and Uganda complained that a majority of the economic benefits of EACSO went to Kenya which had a more advanced infrastructure than its two partners and a better developed industrial base. When the EAC was formed in 1967, therefore, attempts to adjust this imbalance were made by channelling a greater proportion of community revenues to Tanzania and Uganda.

But in the end the EAC foundered on political considerations. Following the coup of January 1971 which brought General Idi Amin Dada to power in Uganda, the East African Authority (the three heads of state) did not meet again because President Nyerere of Tanzania refused to meet Amin. Then in 1977 a quarrel between Kenya and Tanzania led the latter to close their joint border. Over the next 5 years, the EAC was wound up by mutual consent of the three countries, the principal task being a fair distribution of the Community's assets between the three countries (mainly the assets relating to the joint corporations, such as East African Airways).

Economic Community of West African States (ECOWAS)

The treaty establishing ECOWAS was signed in Lagos in May 1975 by 15 countries: Benin, The Gambia, Ghana, Guinea, Guinea-Bissau, Côte d'Ivoire, Liberia, Mali, Mauritania, Niger, Nigeria, Senegal, Sierra Leone, Togo, Upper Volta (Burkina Faso). Cape Verde became a member in 1977. The object of the treaty was to liberalize trade between members and work to create a full customs union over 15 years (by 1990). The main controlling bodies of ECOWAS are the Authority of Heads of State and Government; the Council of Ministers; the Executive Secretariat; the Tribunal of the Community; and four Technical and Specialized Commissions.

Earlier attempts to create some form of West African customs union included a meeting under the chairmanship of President Tubman of Liberia in 1964 between Liberia, Côte d'Ivoire, Guinea and Sierra Leone. The ECA also tried to foster such a union in 1967. Then in 1972 General Gowon of Nigeria and President Eyadema of Togo launched a new initiative which led to the formation of ECOWAS 3 years later.

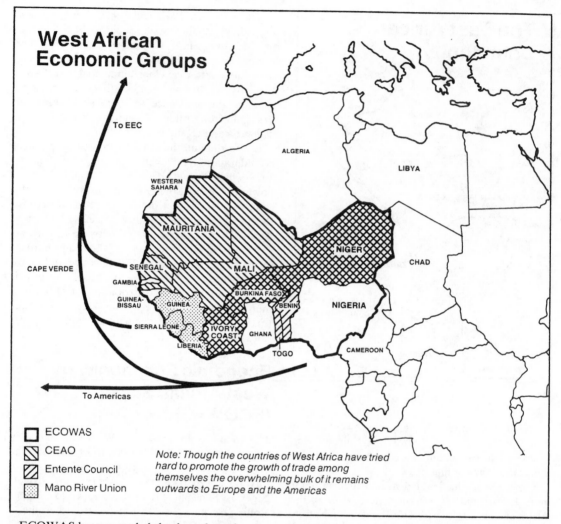

West African Economic Groups

To EEC

ALGERIA

LIBYA

WESTERN
SAHARA

MAURITANIA

NIGER

CHAD

CAPE VERDE

SENEGAL

MALI

GAMBIA

GUINEA-
BISSAU

GUINEA

BURKINA FASO

BENIN

NIGERIA

SIERRA LEONE

IVORY
COAST

GHANA

LIBERIA

TOGO

CAMEROON

To Americas

☐ ECOWAS

◩ CEAO

▨ Entente Council

▦ Mano River Union

Note: Though the countries of West Africa have tried
hard to promote the growth of trade among
themselves the overwhelming bulk of it remains
outwards to Europe and the Americas

ECOWAS has proceeded slowly and cautiously. The problems it faces and has to overcome are typical of the many barriers to closer co-operation which have often brought other African attempts at unity to an end. First, the 16 members cover an enormous area. Second, communications between them are usually poor and often almost non-existent, still reflecting colonial patterns which virtually excluded road or rail links between Anglophone and Francophone West African nations. Third, there is the Anglophone-Francophone divide (in language and administrative approach). Fourth, the direction of trade of most of the members of ECOWAS remains overhelmingly outward directed. When ECOWAS was formed only an estimated 6 per cent of members' trade was within Africa as a whole, another legacy of the way the economies were developed to suit colonial interests. Fifth, Nigeria with its huge population and oil wealth is regarded as a potential threat to the other far smaller economies and, therefore, must ensure that it is not seen to try to dominate the Organization. (The lesson of Kenya and the EAC should be remembered: in that case the disparity between Kenya and the other two members of the EAC was far less than that between Nigeria and all the other members of ECOWAS.) None of these problems is insuperable, though they do demand great care and much diplomacy. It is unrealistic to imagine that progress will be either fast or spectacular.

Listed below are other West African economic groups.

Communauté Économique de l'Afrique de l'Ouest – Economic Community of West Africa (CEAO)

This community was formed in 1974 to replace the earlier West African Customs Union (UDEAO). Its principal emphasis is upon trade although it also manages Community development funds and initiates regional economic programmes. The main controlling bodies are the Conference of Heads of State; the Council of Ministers; and the General Secretariat. The founder members were Côte d'Ivoire, Mali, Mauritania, Niger, Senegal and Upper Volta (Burkina Faso).

Conseil de l'Entente – Entente Council

Founded in May 1959 as a political and economic association of four West African nations – Dahomey (Benin), Côte d'Ivoire, Niger, Upper Volta (Burkina Faso) – the Conseil de l'Entente was joined in 1966 by Togo. The Council aims to promote economic development in the region through its Mutual Aid and Loan Guarantee Fund. Its Council consists of heads of state and ministers according to the business to be conducted. The emphasis is upon economic affairs.

Mano River Union

The Mano River Declaration was signed in 1973 to establish a customs and economic union between Liberia and Sierra Leone. Guinea joined the Union in 1980. A common external tariff was established in 1977.

Members of the above three groups – CEAO, the Entente Council and the Mano River Union – are also members of the far larger ECOWAS.

River basin authorities

There are two river basin authorities in West Africa: the Niger Basin Authority; and OMVS – Senegal.

Niger Basin Authority

This was originally known as the River Niger Commission (founded in 1964); it changed its name in 1980. Its members are Benin, Cameroon, Chad, Guinea, Côte d'Ivoire, Mali, Niger, Nigeria and Burkina Faso. Its principal organs are the Conference of Heads of State; the Council of Ministers; and the Executive Secretariat. It exists to ensure the most effective uses and development of the Niger River and its waters.

Organisation pour la Mise en Valeur du Fleuve Sénégal – Organization for the Development of the Senegal River (OMVS)

OMVS was founded in 1972 and replaced the earlier *Organisation des États Riverains du Sénégal*. It has three members: Mali, Mauritania and Senegal. Its organs are the Conference of Heads of State and Government; the Council of Ministers; and the High Commission. It is an economic agency concerned with the use of the waters of the Senegal River and the development of the River Basin area.

Southern African Development Co-ordination Conference (SADCC)

The SADCC (sometimes referred to as SADEK) was formed following a conference at Arusha in 1979. This was called to consider ways in which the nations near or bordering South Africa could reduce their economic dependence upon that country. SADCC had an original nine members: Angola, Botswana, Lesotho, Malawi, Mozambique, Swaziland, Tanzania, Zambia and Zimbabwe; in 1990 newly independent Namibia joined SADCC as its tenth member.

The main controlling bodies are the Annual Summit Conference (held in a different member country each year); the Council of Ministers; and the Secretariat (at Gaborone, Botswana). There are certain features about SADCC which are unique. Unlike a number of African regional organizations whose formation was the result of sometimes rather vague general aspirations, such as closer unity, SADCC was formed in response to a precise challenge: the pervasive economic and political influence of South Africa in the region. This is despite the fact that Malawi alone of the original nine countries had established diplomatic relations with South Africa. All nine were fundamentally opposed to South Africa's policies. Moreover, most of the nine – Angola, Botswana, Lesotho, Mozambique, Swaziland, Zambia and

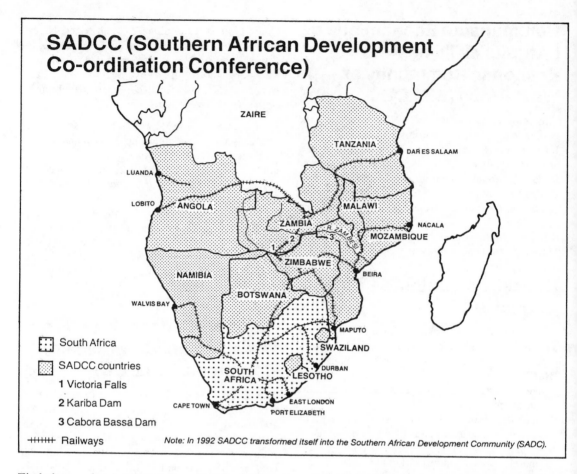

SADCC (Southern African Development Co-ordination Conference)

ZAIRE

TANZANIA

DAR ES SALAAM

LUANDA

LOBITO

ANGOLA

MALAWI

ZAMBIA

NACALA

MOZAMBIQUE

R. ZAMBESI

ZIMBABWE

NAMIBIA

BEIRA

BOTSWANA

WALVIS BAY

MAPUTO

□ South Africa

□ SADCC countries

1 Victoria Falls

2 Kariba Dam

3 Cabora Bassa Dam

+++++ Railways

SWAZILAND

SOUTH
AFRICA

DURBAN

LESOTHO

CAPE TOWN

EAST LONDON

PORT ELIZABETH

Note: In 1992 SADCC transformed itself into the Southern African Development Community (SADC).

Zimbabwe – have suffered from South Africa's destabilization tactics including periodic military incursions into their territories. Perhaps because it was a response to a particular situation, SADCC developed into one of the most successful of Africa's regional groupings both as to structure and in terms of its achievements.

One feature of SADCC structure is the allocation to member states of responsibilities for the study and co-ordination of particular policies. These allocations are as follows:

Angola	Energy
Botswana	Agriculture (foot and mouth disease and crop production)
Mozambique	Transport
Swaziland	Manpower development and training
Tanzania	Industrial development
Zambia	Development Fund
Zimbabwe	Regional food security

An indication of SADCC's impact was the relative success of its donor conference held in Maputo in November 1980 when representatives of industrialized countries as well as agencies attended, and pledges were made to the value of $650 million for SADCC's various development projects.

During 1990, with the rapid changes that were taking place in South Africa, SADCC had to rethink its role and work on the assumption that it would soon be able to collaborate with a newly democratic South Africa. For once South Africa has become acceptable to Africa as a whole it will automatically become the centre of economic growth for the Southern African region so that SADCC's original aims and *raison d'être* will be fundamentally altered. At its twelfth annual summit held in Windhoek (the capital of its new member, Namibia) in August 1992, SADCC recognized these new realities and transformed itself into the Southern African Development Community (SADC).

North–South Groupings

Many African states belong to groups which are not exclusive to Africa but also include countries of the North or countries from other regions of the Third World. Such groups – the ACP (The African, Caribbean and Pacific) states or the Commonwealth – are of vital importance to their Third World members because through them, hopefully, they exert pressures for change upon the major industrialized countries of the North. Four such groups are dealt with briefly here: the ACP–EC group; the Commonwealth; the Franc Zone; and the Franco-African Summit.

The African, Caribbean and Pacific states (ACP)

Under the terms of the Lomé Conventions (the First Lomé Convention came into force on 1 April 1976, and the Second Lomé Convention on 1 January 1981), the countries of the EC (Belgium, Denmark, France, the Federal Republic of Germany, Greece, Ireland, Italy, Luxembourg, Netherlands and the United Kingdom) agreed to allow the bulk of ACP agricultural goods into the EC duty free while other goods were to receive preferential treatment.

Under Lomé I, STABEX (Stabilization of Export Earnings) provides compensation for agricultural exports when there is a fluctuation in the market price. And under Lomé II, SYSMIN (similar to STABEX) operates to compensate for losses suffered by mineral exports to the EC under similar fluctuating market conditions.

In 1983 the Lomé Convention applied to 63 ACP countries of which 44 were African though excluding Algeria, Egypt, Libya, Morocco and Tunisia. Lomé III came into operation in March 1985, and Lomé IV at the beginning of 1990 by which time the number of ACP countries had risen to 69. Eritrea became the 70th ACP country in 1993. The Mediterranean countries of North Africa (Maghreb and Mashraq) entered into separate agreements with the EC in 1976 and 1977.

The main organs of the ACP are the Council of Ministers; the Committee of Ambassadors; the Consultative Assembly; the Secretariat; and the Centre for Industrial Development.

The EC–ACP agreements are the sequel to the earlier Yaoundé Conventions between the EC (before Britain became a member) and the mainly Francophone countries of Africa which were linked to the EC through France. The Lomé Conventions represent the limit to which the EC countries (enlarged to 12 with the admission of Portugal and Spain at the beginning of 1986) are prepared to go in making concessions to the ACP countries in terms of access for their products to the lucrative EC market. For further consideration of the importance of the Lomé Agreements for the Third World, see Chapter Seven of this book on a New International Economic Order (NIEO).

The Commonwealth

The Commonwealth is unique in that it is not a regional organization but includes members of all continents and from both sides of the North–South divide. A majority of its members, however, are from the Third World and over certain issues of vital concern to Africa – Rhodesia, South Africa, Namibia – it has played a particularly important role. The following African countries are members of the Commonwealth: Botswana, The Gambia, Ghana, Kenya, Lesotho, Malawi, Mauritius, Namibia, Nigeria, Seychelles, Sierra Leone, Swaziland, Tanzania, Uganda, Zambia, Zimbabwe. For a fuller treatment of the Commonwealth, see Chapter Four, Part 5.

The Franc Zone

Thirteen Francophone countries remain linked to the French franc at a fixed rate of exchange and their currencies are freely convertible into French francs. The 13 are Benin, Burkina Faso, Cameroon, Central African Republic, Chad, Comoros, Congo, Gabon, Côte d'Ivoire, Mali, Niger, Senegal and Togo. The advantage of linking small weak currencies to a major strong currency (in this case the French franc) is comparable to the former relationship of Commonwealth countries to Britain in the Sterling Area. However, the decision of January 1994 to devalue the CFA franc against the French franc by approximately 50 per cent represents a major blow to this stabilizing economic factor in Francophone Africa.

The Franco–African Summit

This has become an annual occasion and constitutes a link peculiar to France and Africa. The first such summit was held in Paris in 1973 under President Pompidou when 11 countries attended. But it was his successor, President Giscard d'Estaing, who encouraged the growth of the idea. A second such summit was held in Bangui in 1975 and attended by 14 countries and a third in Paris in 1976 with 19 countries taking part. Since then it has become an annual event. Thus in 1982 37 African countries (not all of them Francophone) attended the summit in Kinshasa. Its importance that year was emphasized by the fact that 37 represented the number of nations required by the OAU to form a quorum and in 1982 the OAU could not muster a quorum for the Tripoli Summit because of the split over the Western Sahara–Morocco question.

It is debatable just what this summit achieves. It is seen from Paris as a means of enhancing French influence in Africa. No doubt the African countries see it as a means of influencing French policies. France both relatively and absolutely of the major powers concentrates more of her aid and diplomacy upon the African continent than do any of the other powers. In this regard the summit has considerable significance.

Conclusion

Apart from the groups listed above, there are many other lesser known technical or economic regional organizations in Africa. Between them they cover aspects of co-operation in the fields of agriculture, aid, the arts, economics, finance, education, government, politics, law, the media, religion, science, social services, trade, industry and transport. Some are of a purely practical technical nature and for that reason attract little attention, although they do sound work. By their nature, groups which aim at political co-operation or union attract most attention and when they fail produce ready cynicism.

A feature of many Third World developments over the years which is important to understand is that so-called unions and regional co-operation groups often have purposes other than those stated. In a number of instances they represent the expression of a need: the determination to work together, to repudiate manipulation and interfer-

ence from outside. In this connection it has to be emphasized how weak – in economic, political or military terms – are almost all Third World countries. It is one thing to state an aim, such as greater unity or co-operation. It is something quite different to achieve the objective. One has only to examine the slow progress and seemingly futile arguments about trivia which have characterized the history of the EC to realize just how difficult is almost any form of international co-operation which has as its object closer integration of sovereign states. Africa (and the Third World generally) is no different from Europe or the other groups that have been formed in the rich, economically advanced North. Unions are often not expected to work in the precise sense of two or more countries merging their sovereignty. They are, rather, expressions of the desire to work together, a point lost upon critics of Third World activities from the North.

In historical terms we are still close to a time when the world was dominated by no more than a dozen powers from what we now term the North. At that time the present members of the Third World almost all belonged to one or other of the European empires. The Third World, then, is a new phenomenon. Far too many judgements of it are made in terms of the North which controls most of the world's effective media (a reason why the argument within UNESCO in the early 1980s about a new 'information order' was so important to Third World countries). Thus at the beginning of the 1960s when the Casablanca and Monrovia groups emerged as rivals in Africa, *moderate* was a western term meaning pro-West. *Radical* was also a western term meaning anti-West or, as Africans would qualify it, pursuing more independent policies. Even today almost all judgements of the Third World are western judgements formulated by those who have still to come to terms with a world that has rejected imperial control from the North.

Part 2 The Middle East

It is difficult to define the term Middle East to everyone's satisfaction and in recent years it has often been seen as synonymous with the Arab world. This is not the case, because the Arab world includes a number of North African countries. Nonetheless, the core of the Middle East consists of the Arabian peninsula and the other Arab countries to its north. Yet the region clearly overlaps into Africa (Egypt), Europe (Turkey and Cyprus) and the East (Iran and Afghanistan).

A number of Arab countries which must (in part) be considered here have already been treated in the previous section on Africa. These include the three countries of the Maghreb – Morocco, Algeria and Tunisia; Western Sahara (occupied and claimed by Morocco); and Mauritania, Libya, Sudan, Djibouti and Somalia, all of which are members of the Arab League; and the unique case of Egypt. Thus, for convenience, in the treatment of the Arab League or the Organization of Petroleum Exporting Countries (OPEC), countries which otherwise are part of Africa will be included.

Several Middle Eastern countries have a number of attributes which make them special cases. These are Turkey, Egypt and Israel.

Turkey is in an extraordinary position, straddling several worlds. In terms of development it belongs to the Third World. As a member of NATO throughout the years of the Cold War it did not qualify for membership of the Non-Aligned Movement. Although 99 per cent of the population are Muslims, Turkey is a determined secular state. And with a small part of the country in Europe and a special associate relationship with the EC, Turkey is very conscious of its European links. The country straddles the North–South divide with a foot poised uneasily in each camp.

Egypt, an Arab and Muslim nation (though with a people and history far more ancient than the Arabs who irrupted into Egypt only in the seventh century), was suspended from the Arab League, whose headquarters were moved from Cairo to Tunis in 1979, following its peace treaty with Israel. Egypt is the ancient bridge between Africa and Asia and has long been a vital geopolitical pivot country because of its geographical position and (since 1869) its possession of the strategic Suez Canal. Thus it plays an unique role in both Africa and the Middle East. During the 1950s and 1960s, when the major African nationalist struggles for independence were taking place, the radio *Voice of Cairo* was a prime instrument of anti-imperial propaganda. Following the Amman summit of the Arab League in November 1987, most Arab states resumed diplomatic relations with Egypt. By 1988 under Mubarak's skilful diplomacy, Egypt's relations with the rest of the Arab world were the best they had been in 10 years, an acknowledgement of the country's importance to the Arab Middle East as a whole. By the beginning of the 1990s, Egypt had moved back centre stage in Middle East affairs.

Israel is the third country of unique importance in the region. Created in 1948 and sustained by warfare with its neighbours and huge financial

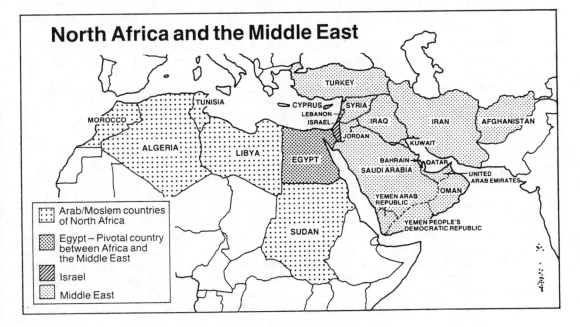

North Africa and the Middle East

TUNISIA
MOROCCO
ALGERIA
LIBYA
TURKEY
CYPRUS
LEBANON
SYRIA
ISRAEL
JORDAN
IRAQ
IRAN
AFGHANISTAN
KUWAIT
EGYPT
BAHRAIN
QATAR
SAUDI ARABIA
UNITED ARAB EMIRATES
OMAN
YEMEN ARAB REPUBLIC
SUDAN
YEMEN PEOPLE'S DEMOCRATIC REPUBLIC

Arab/Moslem countries of North Africa

Egypt – Pivotal country between Africa and the Middle East

Israel

Middle East

subventions from the USA, it has been a cause of permanent friction and hostility to its Arab neighbours. Israel cannot claim to be a developing country in the sense in which that term is normally used, nor yet a member of the Third World. Indeed, because of the make-up of its population, it is seen as being as much a projection of Europe and the West into the region (sustained against its Arab neighbours by western guilt and American money) as belonging to the Middle East. The reality of Israel, however, poses one of the most complex and dangerous political problems anywhere, as will be described later in this section.

Apart from the members of the Arab League (see above), which includes countries of North Africa, the core of the region consists of the Arabian peninsula, with the countries stretching as far north as Turkey and as far east as Iran and Afghanistan. Iran and Afghanistan are dealt with here as part of the Middle East, but this is as much for convenience as from any geographical definition.

In 1945 most of the region was poor, underdeveloped and generally in tutelage (even if technically independent) to the major colonial powers. With the rapid post-1945 development of oil, the USA came to play an increasingly influential role in the Middle East. This increased proportionately as the influence of the two colonial powers, France and especially Britain, diminished.

If we leave aside the Arab nations of North Africa, 16 countries are treated here as belonging to the Middle East. These are Afghanistan, Bahrain, Cyprus, Iran, Iraq, Israel, Jordan, Kuwait, Lebanon, Oman, Qatar, Saudi Arabia, Syria, Turkey, the United Arab Emirates and Yemen (with the Yemen Arab Republic (North Yemen) and the People's Democratic Republic of Yemen (South Yemen) uniting as one country, Yemen) in May 1990.

Independence

Leaving aside the North African countries but including Egypt, only nine Middle Eastern countries were fully independent in 1945. These were Afghanistan, Iran, Iraq, Lebanon, Saudi Arabia, Syria, Turkey, North Yemen and Egypt. Of these countries, Iraq had been a British mandate from World War I until 1932, while Lebanon and Syria were French mandates until the 1940s, becoming

fully independent in 1943 and 1946 respectively. North Yemen became independent in 1918 on the break-up of the Ottoman Empire, and the powers recognized the independence of Saudi Arabia in 1932 after it had been united by King Ibn Saud.

Following its defeat in 1918 Turkey had undergone a remarkable renaissance and modernization under President Kemal Ataturk during the 1920s and 1930s, while Iran, though nominally independent, had been occupied by British and Soviet forces during World War II and was to remain under British influence until the remarkable, if premature, rise and fall of the nationalist Dr Muhammad Mussadiq who challenged the power of the great oil companies 20 years before the time was ripe. At least the crisis he precipitated in 1951, by bringing the oil industry under government control, ended the British monopoly of Iranian oil production.

Throughout the nineteenth century Afghanistan had managed – if only just – to escape falling under the domination of either Czarist Russia or Imperial Britain (operating from India). But, ironically, at the end of the 1970s when the rest of the region, however precariously, had become independent, Afghanistan found itself with a huge Russian army in occupation in support of a government which certainly, without such backing, would have collapsed.

Seven Middle Eastern countries – Egypt, Iran, Iraq, Lebanon, Saudi Arabia, Syria, Turkey – were founder members of the United Nations in 1945, while two others, independent at that time, joined the organization later: Afghanistan in 1946 and North Yemen in 1947. Israel came into existence in 1948 and joined the UN in 1949.

Jordan (formerly Trans-Jordan), a British mandate, became independent in 1946; the British colony of Cyprus became independent in 1960; and Britain's Aden Colony and Protectorate became independent as the People's Democratic Republic of Yemen in 1967.

A number of small territories in the Gulf, often referred to as the Trucial States (because of the Truce which Britain had imposed on the area) had treaties of protection with Britain which were to be terminated during the decade of 1961-71. Kuwait became fully independent in 1961, following the termination of the 1899 agreement under which Britain had assumed responsibility for Kuwait's foreign policy in return for protection. Then in 1971 when Britain finally decided to end her military role in the Gulf, Bahrain, Oman, Qatar and the United Arab Emirates (UAE) became fully independent.

The countries of the region are divided in many ways, yet certain factors have acted to provide a kind of cohesion. Apart from the common membership of the Third World as developing nations, three sujects or themes unite them – at least in theory: Arab nationalism and the inheritance of Islam; opposition to Israel; and the possession of huge oil and gas resources.

Arab nationalism and the resurgence of Islam

In 1945 the whole region was backward. Those countries which were not then colonies, protectorates or mandates were, with few exceptions, very much within the spheres of influence of the major powers. Then the creation of Israel in 1948 changed fundamentally the climate in the Middle East. This new nation was seen by its Arab neighbours to be inimical to Arab nationalism. And, because the USA, Britain and France supported Israel, these big powers in turn were sometimes seen to be anti-Arab. The defeat of the Arabs (with the exception of Jordan) in the 1948 Arab-Israeli war was a further humiliation for Arab nationalism. But it also acted as a spur to revival.

In April 1951 the National Assembly of Iran passed a bill to nationalize the oil industry, then controlled by the Anglo-Iranian Oil Company and the following month Dr Muhammad Mussadiq became prime minister. He was the chief architect of oil nationalization and acted from nationalist principles. The quarrel between Iran and Britain led to a break in diplomatic relations (October 1952) and the further rejection of Anglo-American proposals to solve the dispute. But Mussadiq, meanwhile, quarrelled with some of his supporters and the military overthrew his government in August 1953 so that, by October 1954, it had been possible to work out an agreement to establish a consortium of eight (later 17) oil companies to run the Iranian industry in place of Anglo-Iranian. The British monopoly had been broken although oil production was to remain largely under the control of the international oil companies for many more years. The oil revolution was still 20 years in the future. Iran is not an Arab nation, but this nationalist 'revolt' against British economic domination was to have repercussions elsewhere in the Middle East.

Egypt now became the focus of Middle East nationalism. The coup of 1952 overthrew the monarchy. King Farouk went into exile and General Neguib (nominally) became the leader of Egypt, although he was soon replaced by the far more radical and charismatic Colonel Nasser. His nationalization of the Suez Canal in 1956, the subsequent war in which Israel invaded Sinai to provide Britain and France with a pretext to intervene, and the later withdrawal of the European powers under pressure from both the USA and the USSR enormously enhanced Nasser's prestige, though such an outcome could not have been foreseen. The USSR then provided the funds for building the Aswan High Dam in place of the World Bank, the USA and Britain, whose withdrawal from the project precipitated the Suez Crisis. The years following the Suez war saw the high point of Nasser's influence, the heyday of the *Voice of Cairo*, the union between Egypt and Syria (the United Arab Republic or UAR), and a new excitement throughout the Middle East. At last, it seemed that the old colonial powers were truly in retreat.

Two years after Suez a revolution in Iraq led to the overthrow of the pro-British monarchy and the establishment of a left wing socialist republic under Brigadier Abdul Karim Kassem. A further sign of Arab nationalism and shaking-off the shackles of semi-colonial control occurred in 1959 when Kassem withdrew Iraq from the Baghdad Pact.

Arab nationalism fed upon African nationalism and vice versa. While the above events were taking place, three North African Arab, or at least mainly Islamic, nations – Sudan, Morocco and Tunisia – became independent, all in 1956. And then, the culmination of a long and bitter struggle, Algeria became independent of France in 1962. Thereafter it acted as a member of the radical left in the politics of the Arab world. Arab nationalism swept away four monarchies: Egypt (1952), Iraq (1958), the Yemen Arab Republic (1962) and Libya (1969).

Arab nationalism, however, received a devastating setback in 1967 when, during the June Six Day War, Israel inflicted shattering defeats upon her neighbours and occupied the Sinai Peninsula, the West Bank, Arab Jerusalem and the Syrian Golan Heights.

The coup which overthrew King Idris of Libya in 1969 and brought the young Colonel Gaddafi to power was to have momentous impact because he, perhaps more than anyone else, began the process which Mussadiq had attempted, namely bringing the international oil companies under control and providing OPEC with teeth.

The 1973 Yom Kippur War did much to restore Arab pride, because it was the first Arab–Israeli conflict in which the honours were even. It led at once to the use of the oil weapon – the four-fold increase in the price of oil and the cutbacks in production, as well as the embargo (see below) against those western countries seen to be obvious supporters of Israel. The oil-rich nations of the Middle East now emerged as the spearhead of the Third World and, for the remainder of the 1970s, they played a vital role in advancing demands for a New International Economic Order (NIEO) and insisting upon North–South dialogue so that for the first time it appeared that weak Third World countries could begin to bargain with the rich North on somewhat more even terms. In the 1980s the shortlived oil power period came to an end, because of the world recession and an oil glut, and the OPEC nations had to revert to a tougher reality than the heady days of 1975. Nonetheless, they emerged from this experience with an enhanced sense of nationalism and identity, which did not disappear with the collapse of oil prices. The crisis gave to the Middle East a sense of self-confidence which it had never previously possessed.

The huge explosion of wealth and growth which resulted from the new-found oil power, also highlighted some potentially explosive problems. The first of these is the rapid rate of population growth in the region, varying between 2.3 and 3 per cent, so that the overall population figure is likely to double over the next 30 years. For a developing country, such rapid growth presents acute economic dangers. These are most obviously exemplified in Egypt whose population reached 53 million in 1990 and is expected to double in 24 years. These constant population increases swallow up most development gains.

There is also the huge and widening gap between the rich élites of the region and the majority who are poor. The conspicuous consumption of the ruling élites, made possible by the oil revolution, poses political and social questions which at the very least are highly dangerous and invite revolutionary assaults upon the existing régimes. Thus, glaring evidence of wealth at the top during the latter years of the Shah's rule in Iran was a major factor contributing to the revolution which brought about his downfall.

Third, and far more difficult to quantify, is the growth of Islamic fundamentalism whose most extreme expression has been in Iran since 1979 under the Ayatollah Khomeini. This fundamentalism is highlighted by the moves towards modernism and secularism in other parts of the Middle East. Arab socialism varies greatly between the brands to be found in Algeria, Libya or the Baathist régimes of Syria and Iraq.

Finally, the oil wealth of the 1970s caused a number of rapid, over-ambitious development plans to be launched. The glut and recession of the 1980s led to severe cutbacks and created a series of problems related to unfulfilled – and possibly unfulfillable – expectations. In the early 1990s the Middle East had to trim its general economic development according to the pressures emanating from the world recession.

Independence in the Middle East and North Africa

Nine countries of the region were independent in 1945 as follows:

Afghanistan	Lebanon	Yemen Arab
Egypt	Saudi Arabia	Republic
Iran	Syria	(North Yemen)
Iraq	Turkey	

Other countries became independent in the following years:

1946	Jordan
1948	Israel
1951	Libya
1956	Morocco
	Sudan
	Tunisia
1960	Cyprus
1961	Kuwait
1962	Algeria
1967	Yemen People's Democratic Republic (formerly Aden)
1971	Bahrain
	Oman
	Qatar
	United Arab Emirates (UAE)

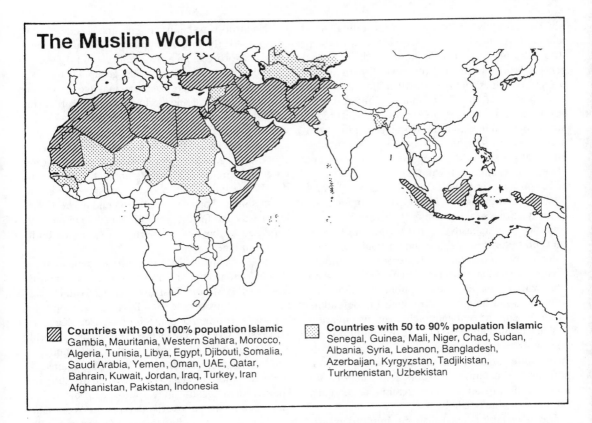

The Muslim World

Countries with 90 to 100% population Islamic
Gambia, Mauritania, Western Sahara, Morocco,
Algeria, Tunisia, Libya, Egypt, Djibouti, Somalia,
Saudi Arabia, Yemen, Oman, UAE, Qatar,
Bahrain, Kuwait, Jordan, Iraq, Turkey, Iran
Afghanistan, Pakistan, Indonesia

Countries with 50 to 90% population Islamic
Senegal, Guinea, Mali, Niger, Chad, Sudan,
Albania, Syria, Lebanon, Bangladesh,
Azerbaijan, Kyrgyzstan, Tadjikistan,
Turkmenistan, Uzbekistan

The role of Islam

Arab nationalism and the Islamic revival are intricately intertwined. Islam is far more absolutely part of the national and social structure in an Islamic society than is Christianity in the so-called Christian nations of the West. Saudi Arabia is the home of Islam and the heart of Islamic orthodoxy. Its strict adherence to Sharia law and its pressures upon surrounding Islamic countries to maintain strict religious standards are made easier because of its prestige. This prestige is derived both from Saudi Arabia's historic role as the birthplace of Islam, containing the two most holy places of the religion – Mecca and Medina – and from its huge oil wealth. Saudi aid to poorer neighbours is often conditional (indirectly) upon the attitude of the recipient towards Islam.

Growing opposition among the more conservative Islamic countries to imported western permissiveness has been a factor of considerable political importance. It has also been an aspect of nationalism in an area where religion and politics can be separated only with difficulty. Thus the

Note: The importance of Islam in the belt of countries immediately to the south of Europe and Russia gives to the core of the Islamic region – and especially Saudi Arabia – significant influence. Not only is Saudi Arabia the world's richest oil country but it is also the home and 'guardian' of one of the world's great religions, which at the present time is expanding fast. The break-up of the USSR meant that at the beginning of 1992 five successor states to the Soviet Union had substantial Islamic populations and were expected to look southwards to the Islamic world to which, in part, they belonged. The five were: Azerbaijan, Kyrgyzstan, Tadjikistan, Turkmenistan and Uzbekistan.

harsh revolution in Iran which the Ayatollah Khomeini launched in 1979 was only in part a fundamentalist religious revival. It was also a nationalist reaction – best expressed through religion – against the westernizing process that had gone too far and too fast under the Shah. Thus Islam has been used as an assertion of a new Iranian nationalism, enabling the country forcibly to throw off the last vestiges of western tutelage.

One of the most controversial Arab nationalist figures has been Muammar al-Gaddafi of Libya. His revolutionary ideology is a curious mixture which is certainly not popular outside Libya. As a rule his foreign adventures are viewed with deep suspicion, although his defiance of the USA is generally popular no matter what the rights or wrongs of the situation. In 1978, for example, Gaddafi claimed that the Islamic revolution should be extended to all parts of the world. He argues among other things that the Koran sanctions Arab nationalism, although his *Green Book* – his treatise on socialism and revolution – attacks the concept of an institutionalized revolution.

The mixture (in Islamic countries) of politics and religion is extremely difficult to disentangle or quantify. For example, some of the smaller Gulf countries look uneasily at what happens in Iran or Iraq and tailor their politics and approach to Islam accordingly. For different reasons President Nimeiri of Sudan introduced rigid Sharia law in 1983 with brutal excesses – public amputations, whippings and hangings. Although his defenders suggested that he had genuinely been reconverted to strict Islam, the more likely explanation for his behaviour was desperation as his régime was visibly faltering and running out of steam. It was, perhaps, in the nature of an appeal for support and funds from orthodox Saudi Arabia as Sudan's economy ground to a halt.

The power of Islam has been amply demonstrated in Afghanistan where, despite massive Soviet intervention (from December 1979 onwards), the Muslim *Mujahidin*, fighting a *jihad* against Communism, demonstrated that it was a war the USSR could not win. That realization, coupled with the new Soviet approach to foreign affairs which came with Gorbachev's *glasnost*, led the USSR to begin withrawing its troops from Afghanistan in May 1988; the last Soviet troops left the country in February 1989.

The growth of Islamic fundamentalism and the West

During 1988 there was a good deal of violence in the Islamic world although the Soviet decision to withdraw from Afghanistan eased some tensions while giving rise to others since various Afghan groups representing different Islamic sects began to fight each other. Although the ceasefire in the Iran–Iraq war heralded possible peace in the Gulf, disorders broke out in the Caucasus region of the USSR where Armenians in the autonomous region of Nagorno-Karabakh fought to secede from Muslim Azerbaijan. A number of Islamic countries – Morocco, Algeria, Tunisia and Egypt – moved to repress fundamentalist groups.

During 1989 there was a massive reaction throughout the Islamic world to the publication (in 1988) of Salman Rushdie's book *Satanic Verses* which was condemned as blasphemous by Muslims. In February 1989 the Ayatollah Khomeini called upon Muslims to kill Rushdie and the row led to an acrimonious and ongoing debate between the West and Islam about free speech versus censorship and blasphemy. By the end of the 1980s Islam was the fastest growing world religion and appeared to be making particular gains in both Africa and the USA.

On 2 August 1990 Saddam Hussein's Iraq invaded and occupied Kuwait to spark off a major crisis in the Middle East. The USA, Britain and France sent troops to Saudi Arabia to oppose Hussein's continued control of oil-rich Kuwait. The result was a split in the Arab–Islamic world with the more conservative Arab states condemning Iraq and supporting the coalition against it while the more radical states tended to support Hussein, less because they approved of his action than because he was overtly defying the West. The crisis escalated steadily (the West's concern with Kuwait was oil) and after a UN deadline for Iraqi withdrawal had passed the UN alliance led by the USA began an aerial bombardment of Iraq (16 January 1991). The main forces involved on the two sides were: the formidable (on paper) Iraqi army of 955,000 men; and facing it the coalition of approximately 400,000 US troops, 30,000 from Britain and 10,000 from France plus 100,000 troops from Saudi Arabia, Egypt and Syria as well as small contingents from other Arab states. What was remarkable about this war was the fact that a US-led alliance of Western and Arab states held together despite the fact that it was opposing an Arab state; and despite the fact that Iraq was launching missiles against Israel the latter was persuaded not to become involved in hostilities. Iraq's main allies were fundamentalist Iran (its recent enemy) and its small, weak neighbour Jordan which did not really have any choice. The PLO made the (longer-term) mistake of declaring its support for Hussein although the huge numbers of Palestinians in Kuwait had little alternative.

The aerial bombardment lasted from 16 January to 23 February; the ground war lasted 100 hours before Iraq capitulated, having withdrawn its forces from Kuwait. The aftermath of the war saw the opening of many wounds in the Islamic world. In Iraq itself the Kurds (Sunni Muslims) broke away in the North; while in the south a rebellion of Shi'ite Muslims was ruthlessly suppressed. Meanwhile, as the USSR collapsed, it became clear that some of its predominantly Muslim states in the south wished to establish closer relations with the Islamic world.

Throughout 1991 there was a growth of fundamentalist activity in Algeria where the *Front Islamique du Salut* (FIS) successfully challenged the government in local elections as the old FLN declined in authority. In the first round of legislative elections at the end of the year (26 December) the FIS won 188 out of 430 National Assembly seats and was leading in many other constituencies; it looked certain to win the second round of elections set for 15 January 1992. However, the Algerian army now stepped in to cancel the January round of elections and forced President Chadli Benjedid to resign. Subsequently the army created a High State Council and invited Mohammad Boudiaf to return from exile and head the government (he was later assassinated). Of vital North–South importance in the Algeria question was the attitude of the West. For several years by this time western aid donors had been exerting pressures upon African governments to abandon one-party rule and return to democracy as the price for continuing aid. Yet when the army overturned the democratic process in Algeria in order to thwart the fundamentalists the West was conspicuous by its silence.

During 1992–93 a new cause for Western–Islamic tension arose in former Yugoslavia where the plight of the Bosnian Muslims, losing in a civil war to both Croats and Serbs, led to accusations that the West wanted the Bosnian Muslims to be crushed.

Islam is a factor of such fundamental political importance throughout the region that even the strongest politician ignores it at his peril.

By 1992 the world Muslim population had reached 971,328,700.

Organization of the Islamic Conference (OIC)

The OIC was established in 1971 with headquarters in Jeddah, Saudi Arabia. Strictly speaking it is not a Middle East regional organization at all, because it includes all Muslim nations from The Gambia on the far western Atlantic seaboard of Africa to Indonesia in the Far East. However, the heartland of Islam remains in the Middle East, as do the majority of Muslim countries.

The Summit Conferences constitute the supreme decision-making body of OIC. Conferences of Foreign Ministers meet more frequently and the OIC is run by a Secretariat (and Secretary-General). There are six Specialized Committees. In addition there are a number of subsidiary organs and institutions within the OIC framework.

The Muslim Heads of State Summit which met at Rabat in 1969 decided to establish OIC. The next Heads of State Summit was held at Lahore, Pakistan, in 1974 and then at Mecca, Saudi Arabia, in 1981, and at Casablanca, Morocco, in 1984. The Summit is now held once every 3 years.

The aims of the Organization are set out in its Charter whose first and principal object is to promote Islamic solidarity among member states. The principal means of achieving this aim are through economic co-operation; cultural co-operation; humanitarian assistance; and political co-operation.

Membership of OIC

Afghanistan (membership suspended during the Soviet invasion/occupation	Lebanon Libya Malaysia
Algeria	Maldives
Bahrain	Mali
Bangladesh	Mauritania
Benin	Morocco
Brunei	Niger
Burkina Faso	Oman
Cameroon	Pakistan
Chad	Palestine Liberation
Comoros	Organization
Djibouti	Qatar
Egypt (suspended in 1979, restored in 1984)	Saudi Arabia Senegal
Gabon	Sierra Leone
Gambia	Somalia
Guinea	Sudan
Guinea-Bissau	Syria
Indonesia	Tunisia
Iran	Turkey
Iraq	Uganda
Jordan	United Arab Emirates
Kuwait	Yemen

The League of Arab States – the Arab League

The League of Arab States (commonly known as the Arab League) was founded in March 1945 and, perhaps ironically in view of subsequent history, its creation was encouraged by Britain. The League's principal objectives are to protect the independence and integrity of the member states, and to encourage economic and cultural co-operation. In November 1946, League members approved a Cultural Treaty.

The original parties to the Covenant of the League were: Egypt, Iraq, Lebanon, Saudi Arabia, Syria, Jordan and North Yemen (the Yemen Arab Republic), as well as representatives of the Palestine Arabs. The main concern of the League has always been the Palestine problem. Thus, at its inception, the League undertook the presentation of the Palestine case first in London and then at the UN (1946–48).

All members of the original League went to the aid of the Palestine Arabs – in some sense – during the war in 1948, although only Egypt, Syria and Jordan provided any effective military forces. Over the years the League can hardly claim any major political successes though it has experienced many reverses. In 1977, when Sadat visited Israel, a number of Arab governments refused to meet in Cairo and, in 1979, the League moved its headquarters from Cairo to Tunis and suspended Egypt's membership. But long before 1979 Egypt had come to be resented for dominating the League which it was seen to use to further its own political ambitions.

However, the League has achieved some modest successes in the social, cultural, health and educational fields. It has, for example, organized an Arab Cultural Treaty and a series of inter-Arab organizations (see below).

Members of the Arab League (with date of joining)

Algeria (1962)
Bahrain (1971)
Djibouti (1977)
Egypt (founder member)
Jordan (founder member)
Kuwait (1961)
Lebanon (founder member)
Libya (1953)
Mauritania (1973)
Morocco (1958)
Oman (1971)
Palestine (founder member – see below)
Qatar (1971)
Saudi Arabia (founder member)
Somalia (1974)
Sudan (1956)
Syria (founder member)
Tunisia (1958)
UAE (1971)
Yemen Arab Republic (founder member)*
Yemen People's Democratic Republic (1968)*

*The two Yemens united in May 1990.

Note: The term Arab is loosely used in relation to at least some members of the League whose claim to belong is based upon political sympathy and overwhelming adherence to Islam rather than a strict ethnic claim to being Arab. Thus Sudan is less an Arab nation than one whose northern peoples are Muslim and 'arabicized'; nor are the Somali peoples of Djibouti and Somalia Arabs. At least for some countries, membership of the League is, therefore, an expression of solidarity with like-minded nations whose powerful core group is Arab.

The Council is the supreme organ of the Arab League on which each member country has a representative and a vote. The Council includes a representative for Palestine. Attached to the Council are 16 committees of which the most important are the Political Committee, the Cultural Committee, and the Economic Committee. The General Secretariat consists of the administrative and financial offices of the League which implement the decisions of the Council. The Secretary-General is appointed by a two-thirds majority of the Council. There are seven assistant secretaries-general.

A number of groups have been established under Defence and Economic Co-operation including the Arab Unified Military Command; the Economic Council; the Joint Defence Council; and the Permanent Military Commission. The Arab Deterrent Force was set up in June 1976 by the League to supervise attempts to bring an end to the hostilities in Lebanon.

Specialized agencies directly under the Council include the Academy of Arab Music; the Administrative Tribunal of the Arab League; and the Special Bureau for Boycotting Israel.

All members of the League are also members of its specialized agencies. These are as follows:
Arab Academy of Maritime Transport
Arab Centre for the Study of Dry Regions and
    Arid Territories
Arab Civil Aviation Council

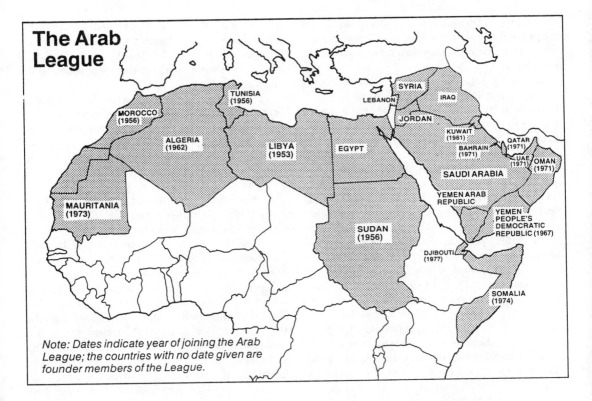

The Arab League

TUNISIA (1956)

MOROCCO (1956)

ALGERIA (1962)

LIBYA (1953)

EGYPT

LEBANON

SYRIA

IRAQ

JORDAN

KUWAIT (1961)

QATAR (1971)

BAHRAIN (1971)

UAE (1971)

OMAN (1971)

SAUDI ARABIA

YEMEN ARAB REPUBLIC

YEMEN PEOPLE'S DEMOCRATIC REPUBLIC (1967)

MAURITANIA (1973)

SUDAN (1956)

DJIBOUTI (1977)

SOMALIA (1974)

Note: Dates indicate year of joining the Arab League; the countries with no date given are founder members of the League.

Arab Industrial Development Organization

Arab League Educational, Cultural and Scientific Organization (ALECSO) (Within the framework of ALECSO are four bodies as follows:

    Institute for Arab Research and Studies

    Arab Literacy and Adult Education Organization

    Arab Manuscript Institute

    Permanent Bureau for Arabization)

Arab Labour Organization

Arab Organization of Administrative Sciences

Arab Organization for Agricultural Development

Arab Organization for Social Defence Against Crime

(Under this Organization come three bureaus as follows:

    Arab Bureau for Narcotics

    Arab Bureau for Prevention of Crime

    Arab Bureau of Criminal Police)

Arab Organization for Standards and Measures

Arab Postal Union

Arab Satellite Communications Organization (ASCO)

Arab States Broadcasting Union (ASBU)

Arab Telecommunications Union

The headquarters of these various bodies are found scattered in the different capital cities of League countries.

Under the Pact of the League of Arab States (22 March 1945) there is an *Annex Regarding Palestine* which effectively makes Palestine a full member state of the League. Today this means that the Palestine Liberation Organization, which represents the Palestine people, is given full membership status.

Israel in the Middle East

The existence since 1948 of Israel, the refusal of Arab nations to recognize its right to exist, and the Palestine Arab claims to a homeland, constitute the essential elements of the Arab–Israel problem.

The USA and the USSR both recognized Israel at once when it came into being. Subsequently, prior to the end of the Cold War, the USSR broadly supported the Arab cause though in recent years it was more interested to act as an arbiter with the USA. The USA, on the other hand, has unswervingly supported Israel. Indeed, the extent of its military and economic aid has been so great that Israel might be said to depend upon the USA for its survival.

The overwhelming nature of Israel's victory over the Arabs in the 1967 War was, psychologically, the moment for it to make concessions and reach a permanent settlement. Instead it retained the occupied territories, the defeated Arab powers as well as the Palestinians became increasingly bitter, and it became clear that nothing whatever had been solved.

The UN compromise Resolution 242 of 22 November 1967 (a compromise between supporters of Israel, principally the USA, and supporters of the Arabs) became the basis for subsequent negotiations. Its most important clauses are the following: withdrawal of Israeli armed forces from territories occupied in the recent conflict; termination of all claims on states of belligerency and respect for the acknowledgement of the sovereignty, territorial integrity and political independence of every State in the area and their right to live in peace within secure and recognized boundaries free from threats or acts of force; and for achieving a just settlement of the refugee problem.

In the following years, however, Israel announced its intention of keeping Arab Jerusalem; it annexed the Golan Heights; and it destroyed Arab villages and expelled their inhabitants. The result was simply to harden Arab attitudes. Then in 1970 the Palestinian guerrillas, who argued for a Palestinian state in which both Jews and Arabs could live instead of a Zionist state, launched a fierce war against the government of Jordan because at that time King Hussein was apparently ready to recognize Israel.

Negotiations continued endlessly through to 1973 but no settlement appeared any closer. Then came the 1973 Yom Kippur War. The initial surprise, together with impressive Egyptian and Syrian military successes, represented an important turning point. The war substantially redressed the balance of power in the area and led to the use of the oil weapon for the first time so that, though the fundamental position with regard to Israel had not changed, that of the Arabs had. They emerged from the war with greatly enhanced self-confidence and by deploying the oil weapon and increasing oil prices gave themselves huge new economic power, enabling the Gulf countries led by Saudi Arabia to force the West to talk of a New

International Economic Order and hold North–South discussions. Another result of the change of fortunes was that the EC for the first time called for the legitimate rights of the Palestinians to be taken into account.

By 1974 the PLO position could be divided between those – a majority – prepared to accept a Palestine state comprising the West Bank and the Gaza Strip, and those led by Yasir Arafat (a minority, the rejectionists) who in effect demanded the end of Israel and the creation of a Palestine state in its place.

In November 1975 three UN resolutions were passed. The first two called for the Palestinian right of self-determination and the PLO to take part in all future debates on the Middle East; while the third resolution condemned Zionism as a form of racism and racial discrimination.

Most Arab governments wanted the PLO to accept a Palestinian state consisting of the West Bank and Gaza and to reject the idea of a secular Palestine in place of Israel. Israel refused to deal with the PLO under any circumstances. With variations this situation continued until the Sadat initiative of 1977 when he visited Israel and addressed the Knesset (Parliament) in Jerusalem. This in turn led to the Camp David Summit and the 1979 Peace Treaty between Israel and Egypt.

Total Arab opposition to the Egypt–Israel accord followed, leading to the isolation of Egypt in the Arab world, its suspension from the Arab League, and the withdrawal of Arab aid mainly because the treaty did nothing for the Palestinians.

The period 1981-83 saw an escalation of the Middle East problem, where confrontation became more pronounced than possible solutions, though these continued to be offered. The period included the assassination of President Sadat; the Fahd Plan which included recognition by the Arabs of Israel's right to exist in return for Israeli withdrawal from the 1967 lines and a Palestinian state; Israel's annexation of the Golan Heights; the Israeli withdrawal (by April 1982) from Sinai; revolts against Israel in the West Bank; the Israeli invasion of Lebanon; the siege of Beirut; the Sabra/Chatila massacre; the bloody battle in Tripoli in which Syrian and dissident PLO factions attempted to dislodge Arafat from the leadership of the PLO and his consequent move of PLO headquarters to Tunis at the end of 1983.

In the end Israel gained nothing – or very little – from its invasion of Lebanon, while its withdrawal in 1985 was a bloody and costly affair. By 1986 neither Israel nor the USA was prepared to deal with the PLO and the stalemate continued. Israel maintained a 'security zone' in the south of Lebanon, following her 1985 withdrawal, and in 1988 made a number of forays north into Lebanon again.

But 1988 was to be a year of great importance for the PLO. On 8 December 1987, following the killing of four Arabs by an Israeli army truck, the consequent violence signalled the beginning of the *Intifada* or Arab uprising in the West Bank which was to give both the PLO and Arafat a new credibility. On 15 November 1988, the Palestine National Council made a Declaration of Statehood in Algiers. On this occasion the PLO also declared that it accepted UN Resolution 242 (effectively recognizing Israel's right to exist). As a result some 50 countries proceeded to recognize the PLO. By the end of the year the USA (after a 13-year ban) held formal talks at ambassador level with the PLO.

During the first year of the *Intifada* 300 Palestinians were killed and thousands injured and it was the *Intifada* that changed PLO policy to one in which the Arabs inside Israeli-controlled territory became the spearhead of the movement rather than those outside Israel which had been the case up to that time. Also during the year, King Hussein of Jordan accepted the secession of the West Bank from his kingdom (it had been annexed by his grandfather in 1950 and occupied by Israel in 1967); by doing so he abandoned his role as representative of the Palestinians.

1989 was to be a year of manoeuvres with various versions of a peace plan being advanced by Israel, Egypt and the USA in which each envisaged some form of autonomy for the Palestinians in the West Bank and Gaza Strip. During 1990 when the Gulf Crisis (Iraq's invasion of Kuwait) dominated Middle East affairs after August, Israel continued to insist that it would not talk with the PLO; but observers detected a shift in US attitudes (all-important to Israel) towards an international conference on Palestine. There were calls from the left of the Palestine Movement for an escalation of the *Intifada* uprising in the West Bank.

A substantive breakthrough was achieved in 1991 when formal talks between Israel and its Arab neighbours opened in Madrid on 30 October. What had now come to be accepted as a possible outcome was self-government for 1.7 million Palestinians in the West Bank and Gaza Strip. But the intransigence of Israel's prime minister, Yitzhak Shamir, led to recriminations at the closing session of the first Madrid round on 1 November and then Israel officially opened new Israeli settlements on the annexed Golan Heights and continued its military activities in southern Lebanon. But during the year Israel found itself subjected to increasing pressures for a settlement from the EC.

Although the US-sponsored Arab–Israeli talks continued through 1992 they were almost wrecked at the end of the year when Israel expelled 415 Muslim fundamentalists who had to live in tents in the freezing mountains of southern Lebanon. A change of government in Israel brought Yitzhak Rabin to power in place of Yitzhak Shamir and the peace talks continued into 1993.

The real breakthrough came dramatically at the end of August 1993 when it was revealed that parallel to the talks in Washington DC another series of highly secret negotiations had also been conducted in Norway. Israel and the PLO in direct talks had agreed: that Jericho in the West Bank and the Gaza Strip should be given self-rule. It was only a fraction of what the PLO wanted but it was a beginning and represented changed perceptions of new realities on both sides. The PLO – or its mainstream Fatah movement under the enduring Yasir Arafat – has transformed itself from a revolutionary organization committed to the armed struggle into an organization espousing diplomacy and negotiations; while Israel has realized that the end of the Cold War and the changing attitudes which have followed mean that this is its best chance to achieve a settlement before its main backer, the USA, loses patience while others, most notably the EC, are ready to exert greater pressures upon Tel Aviv than ever before. Whether or not the agreement would be ratified and implemented remained to be seen, but it was an historic breakthrough nonetheless.

There has long been a parallel between the Middle East question and Israel's refusal to talk with the PLO and the apartheid question and South Africa's refusal to talk with the ANC. But just as President de Klerk broke the deadlock in South Africa by unbanning the ANC and releasing Nelson Mandela in 1990, so in September 1993 it appeared that the Middle East deadlock had at last been broken because the Israeli government and the PLO had negotiated at the same table.

The Palestine refugees

The Palestine Liberation Organization (PLO) and the Palestine Liberation Army (PLA) were established in 1964. The Palestine National Council (PNC) is the supreme body of the PLO. In 1968 Al

Israel and Its Neighbours

Note: The refugee numbers given were as registered with UNRWA as at 30 June 1984. The total number of refugees comes to 2,034,314 while the estimated mid-year 1983 population of Israel was given as 4,106,100.

Palestine Refugees 1984

Jordan 781,564 (of which 198,896 in camps)
West Bank 350,779 (of which 89,295 in camps)
Gaza Strip 410,745 (of which 226,937 in camps)
Lebanon 256,207 (of which 131,909 in camps)
Syria 235,019 (of which 69,664 in camps)

By the end of March 1992, UNWRA had provided essential health, education, relief and social services to over 2.6 million registered Palestine refugees. Of this number over 900,000 resided in 61 refugee camps in Jordan, Lebanon, the Syrian Arab Republic and the occupied territory of the West Bank and Gaza Strip. As a result of the Gulf War of 1991 over 300,000 Palestine refugees were displaced from Kuwait and the Gulf region and moved into the UNWRA area of operations.

Note: By 1993 there were an estimated 1.7 million Palestinians in the West Bank and Gaza Strip.

Fatah (the Palestine National Liberation Movement) joined the PNC and in 1969 the other guerrilla groups did the same.

The PLO is represented in all the Arab countries and also in the USA, the USSR (prior to the break-up of the Soviet Union), China, Cuba, Yugoslavia (prior to its disintegration), Switzerland and Britain. At the 1974 Rabat Arab Summit the PLO was recognized as the sole legitimate representative of the Palestinian people. That year it was also granted observer status at the UN. Its main organs are the Palestine National Council (PNC); the Central Council; the Executive Committee; the Palestine Liberation Army (PLA); and the Palestine National Fund. There are other bodies, such as the Central Council of the Palestine Resistance Movement, which represent all the guerrilla groups. The Palestine National Charter is the constitution of the PLO.

The United Nations Relief and Works Agency for Palestine Refugees in the Near East (UNRWA) has provided relief for Palestine refugees since 1950. Its funds come almost entirely as voluntary contributions from governments. The refugees it serves – in effect the Palestine people – are represented by the PLO. In the mid-1980s, when the PLO fortunes were at a low ebb and there was no indication of an early settlement in the Middle East, UNRWA (which had initially begun operations in 1950, providing emergency relief to 750,000 Palestinians who had become refugees as a result of the 1948 Arab–Israeli conflict) was then looking after more than 2 million Palestine refugees. (See map – Israel and its neighbours – for details of refugees in the three areas: the Gaza Strip; the West Bank; the Golan Heights.)

Middle East regional organizations

There are many regional organizations covering the Middle East. One problem concerns the overlap between the African and Arab worlds, so that some countries belong to institutions in both groups: Africa because they are a geographic part of the continent; the Middle East because they are Arab and Muslim. Thus a number of countries which belong to the Arab League are also members of the OAU.

The United Nations is responsible for a number of regional activities in the Middle East, but most of these are dealt with in Chapter Two of this book on the United Nations. Only two are examined here: the Economic Commission for Western Asia (ECWA) which is comparable to the ECA in Africa (Egypt alone belongs to both Commissions); and UNRWA (see above).

In addition the UN has four longstanding observer or peacekeeping missions in the Middle East as follows:

1. UNTSO – the United Nations Truce Supervision Organization – set up in 1948 to observe the truce in Palestine. Its headquarters are in Jerusalem.
2. UNDOF – the United Nations Disengagement Observer Force – established in 1974 to oversee Syrian–Israeli disengagement. Its headquarters are in Damascus.
3. UNIFIL – the United Nations Interim Force in Lebanon – established in 1978 with headquarters in Naqoura, Lebanon.
4. UNFICYP – the United Nations Peace-Keeping Force in Cyprus – set up in 1964 and maintained following the Turkish invasion and partition of Cyprus in 1974 with headquarters in Nicosia.

Following the end of the Iran–Iraq War in 1988 the Security Council set up UNIMOG (United Nations Iran-Iraq Military Observer Group) to supervise the withdrawal of forces. Its mandate was terminated in February 1991.

On 9 April 1991, following the end of the Gulf War, the Security Council set up UNIKOM (the United Nations Iraq–Kuwait Observer Mission) to monitor the 200-kilometre demilitarized zone between the two countries. The United Nations also established UNSCOM (the United Nations Special Commission) to carry out immediate on-site inspections of Iraq's biological, chemical and missile capabilities and to supervise their removal or destruction.

Economic Commission for Western Asia (ECWA)

The ECWA was established in 1974 with the following membership:

Bahrain, Egypt, Iraq, Jordan, Kuwait, Lebanon, Oman, PLO, Qatar, Saudi Arabia, Syria, UAE,

Yemen Arab Republic* and Yemen People's Democratic Republic*.

Turkey, Israel, Iran and Afghanistan are not members of the ECWA, which as a consequence is entirely Arab in its composition. The ECWA's principal activities concern studies of economic and technological problems, the collection and dissemination of information and the provision of advisory services. It has a very limited budget. The ECWA works in close collaboration with other UN bodies operating in the region.

Its organs include the Commission whose annual sessions are attended by representatives of all member states; and the Secretariat (headquarters in Baghdad) which includes a number of divisions ranging from Development Planning to Information. The ECWA is smaller in both scope and impact than the ECA.

The other regional organizations are almost all entirely Arab in membership. Only the most important ones are dealt with here. Certain organizations appear elsewhere in this book. Two of these are BADEA and OPEC.

BADEA (the Arab Bank for Economic Development in Africa), with its headquarters in Khartoum, has already been described in the regional section on Africa, because it was established in November 1973 following the Yom Kippur War and was intended specifically to assist African development, in part perhaps as compensation for the effects of higher oil prices on the African continent.

OPEC (Organization of Petroleum Exporting Countries) is dealt with below in Chapter Six on OPEC and Oil Power, as also is the OPEC Fund for International Development.

Arab Fund for Economic and Social Development (AFESD)

AFESD, an Arab agency, was established in 1968 by the Economic Council of the Arab League, though it did not begin operations until 1973. All member countries of the Arab League (including the PLO) belong to it, although Egypt was suspended in 1979 for the period of its isolation by the rest of the Arab world. It is run by a Board of Governors, a Board of Directors and Director-General, and Chairman of the Board of Governors.

*The two Yemens united to form a single nation in 1990.

Its headquarters are in Kuwait City and its authorized capital (calculated in Kuwait Dinars) is KD800 million. Members may take up shares of which there are 80,000 worth KD10,000 each.

AFESD is concerned to make loans and grants for economic and social development projects in Arab countries. It also co-operates with other Arab organizations, such as the Organization of Arab Petroleum Exporting Countries (OAPEC).

The Arab Monetary Fund

The Arab Monetary Fund was established (like AFESD) by the Economic Council of Arab States in 1976 and began operations the following year. All the members of the Arab League belong (Egypt was suspended in 1979).

Its organs are the Board of Governors; the Board of Executive Directors; and the President. Its finances are computed in the Arab Accounting Dinar (AAD), which is worth three IMF Special Drawing Rights (SDRs).

Its object is to assist a move towards Arab economic integration. It helps members with balance of payments problems and (in terms of its articles of agreement) is not unlike a regional IMF.

Co-operation Council for the Arab States of the Gulf

More generally known as the Gulf Co-operation Council (GCC), the organization was created in 1981 and has as its members the six Gulf states – Bahrain, Kuwait, Oman, Qatar, Saudi Arabia and the UAE. The aim of the GCC is to encourage unity among the Gulf States and its object is to co-ordinate, integrate and co-operate in economic, social and cultural affairs.

The organs of the GCC are the Supreme Council consisting of the heads of the six member states; a Ministerial Council; a Secretariat-General with Secretary-General and two assistant secretaries-general – one for political and one for economic affairs.

The work of the GCC can be covered by various headings, such as economic co-operation, industry, agriculture, transport and energy. After its creation the GCC decided also to deal with defence questions and in 1984 its members agreed to set up a joint defence force.

At their summit of November 1986, held in Abu Dhabi, the GCC heads of state called for an immediate ceasefire in the Iran-Iraq war and an end to attacks upon shipping in the Gulf. The GCC joint defence force, the Peninsula Shield, decided to purchase maritime patrol craft.

The GCC has established an Investment Corporation for the Gulf, the capital of $2100 million being subscribed in equal amounts of $350 million per member.

The GCC played an active co-ordinating role among its members during the Gulf Crisis of 1990–91.

Council of Arab Economic Unity

The Council of Arab Economic Unity held its first meeting in 1964. Twelve Arab states belong: Egypt, Iraq, Jordan, Kuwait, Libya, Mauritania, the PLO, Somalia, Sudan, Syria, UAE and Yemen. Its organs are the Council; the General Secretariat and Secretary-General.

Under the aegis of the Council, an Arab Common Market was established in 1964, consisting of Iraq, Jordan, Libya, Mauritania, Syria, Yemen PDR and Egypt (suspended 1979). The object was a full customs union though this has yet to be achieved.

The Council of Arab Economic Unity has initiated a number of multilateral agreements among its members to cover Social Insurance, Reciprocity of Social Services, Labour Mobility, Transit Trade, Taxes, Capital Investment and Mobility and the Settlement of Investment Disputes. The Council has assisted in the creation of a number of joint ventures.

Islamic Development Bank

The Bank opened in 1975. The decision to establish the bank was taken in December 1973 at Jeddah during the Conference of Islamic Finance Ministers. The Bank has 44 members (all the members of OIC, see above, except Iran).

Its organs are a Board of Governors and a Board of Executive Directors. The Bank has authorized capital of 2000 million Islamic Dinars (one Islamic Dinar – 1 IMF SDR) divided into 200,000 shares each valued at 10,000 Islamic dinars.

The Bank maintains the Islamic principle of no usury and so only charges a service fee on loans

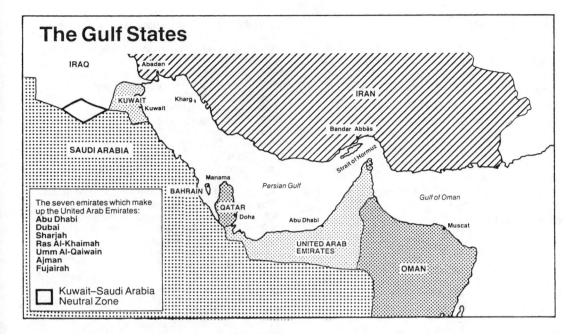

The Gulf States

IRAQ

Abadan

KUWAIT

Kuwait

Kharg

IRAN

Bandar Abbás

SAUDI ARABIA

Manama

BAHRAIN

Persian Gulf

Strait of Hormuz

Gulf of Oman

The seven emirates which make up the United Arab Emirates:
Abu Dhabi
Dubai
Sharjah
Ras Al-Khaimah
Umm Al-Qaiwain
Ajman
Fujairah

QATAR

Doha

Abu Dhabi

Muscat

UNITED ARAB EMIRATES

OMAN

Kuwait–Saudi Arabia Neutral Zone

and no interest. It concentrates upon projects concerned with infrastructure which should have a long term impact upon development.

Organization of Arab Petroleum Exporting Countries (OAPEC)

OAPEC was formed in 1968 to safeguard the interests of the oil-producing Arab states and to encourage co-operation among them. The members are Algeria, Bahrain, Egypt, Iraq, Kuwait, Libya, Qatar, Saudi Arabia, Syria, Tunisia and the UAE.

Unlike OPEC, OAPEC is confined to Arab countries and so includes minor Arab oil producers – Egypt, Syria and Tunisia – who do not qualify as members of OPEC. The main organs are the Council of Ministers; the Executive Bureau; the Secretariat (Secretary-General and Assistant Secretary-General); and the Judicial Tribunal to settle differences of interpretation of the OAPEC Charter. OAPEC is involved in a number of joint ventures, such as the Arab Engineering Company.

Arab Maghreb Union (UMA)

In February 1989 five North African countries – Algeria, Morocco, Tunisia, Libya and Mauritania

– announced the formation of the Arab Maghreb Union (UMA) and on 19 October of that year a 50-member Maghreb Assembly met in Rabat. The first President of the Assembly was Ahmed Osman of Morocco. A second summit was held in Tunis in January 1990 to deal with defence co-operation. Then, at Algiers in July 1990 (the third summit), UMA leaders agreed to unify customs tariffs on imports by 1991 and to establish a full customs union by 1995. However, during 1992 UMA ran into problems following the crisis in Algeria relating to the Islamic Fundamentalists, and the heads of state meeting scheduled for Benghazi in June of that year was cancelled.

Other organizations

There is a great range of other organizations in the region. They are concerned with subjects ranging from agriculture to defence, religion or transport and welfare.

The region has some particular relations with the North. Thus the EC has a special policy of association with all the countries of the Mediterranean: it has co-operation agreements with Algeria, Morocco, Tunisia, Egypt, Jordan, Lebanon and Syria, as also with Israel and Yemen. Cyprus and Turkey have associate agreements with the EC.

Conclusions

Although the Middle East and Africa overlap, it is easier to treat Africa as a regional entity than it is to do the same for the Middle East. Two Middle Eastern countries in particular, Israel and Turkey, are in anomalous positions when related to the Third World. Except for Cyprus and Israel every country has an Islamic majority and most countries are also clearly Arab in ethnic composition (except for Turkey, Cyprus, Lebanon, Iran and Afghanistan).

Although the state of the oil market had been depressed for a decade by 1993, it was OPEC and oil power in the period immediately after the Yom Kippur War of 1973 which provided the thrust that brought the countries of the Middle East into the forefront of the North–South dialogue and provided the region with the power and influence which have done so much to fuel Arab nationalist resurgence. That process will continue.

Important dates in the Middle East 1945–93

1945 Formation of the Arab League.
1947 UN proposes the partition of Palestine between Arabs and Jews; the proposal rejected by the Arabs.
1948 UN sanctions the creation of Israel; the first Arab–Israeli War.
1951 Mussadiq attempts to nationalize the Anglo-Iranian Oil Company: crisis between Iran and Britain continues to 1954.
Egypt abrogates 1936 Treaty with Britain: British troops occupy the Canal Zone.
1952 Ahmed Ben Bella forms the Algeria Revolutionary Committee in Cairo.
Revolt in Morocco against France.
Neguib and Nasser seize power in Egypt; King Farouk abdicates.
1954 Nasser takes full control in Egypt; the Anglo-Egyptian Agreement on the Suez Canal.
Beginning of the Algerian war of independence – to 1962.
1955 The Baghdad Pact: Iran, Iraq, Pakistan, Turkey and Britain.
The Cyprus Emergency, which goes on to 1959.
1956 Nasser nationalizes the Suez Canal; Israel invades Sinai; Britain and France invade Egypt; the UN Peacekeeping Force takes over and Britain and France withdraw; the Canal is blocked.
Archbishop Makarios of Cyprus deported by the British to the Seychelles.
1957 Suez Canal reopened and run by the Egyptian Suez Canal Authority.
1958 Egypt and Syria form the United Arab Republic (UAR).

Revolution in Iraq: King Faisal killed, a republic proclaimed under Brigadier (later General) Kassem; US marines sent to Lebanon and British troops to Jordan.
1959 Iraq withdraws from the Baghdad Pact.
1960 Cyprus becomes independent with Archbishop Makarios as President.
The formation of OPEC.
1962 Algeria independent.
1964 Civil war in Cyprus between Greeks and Turks; UN Peace Mission established in Cyprus.
1967 The Six Day War (5–10 June) between Israel and its Arab neighbours: Israel occupies Sinai, Arab Jerusalem, the West Bank of Jordan, the Golan Heights; a UN ceasefire arranged; the Suez Canal blocked; UN Resolution 242.
1969 Yasir Arafat becomes leader of the PLO.
1970 Civil war in Jordan: the Palestine guerrillas against the government forces.
The death of Nasser ends an era.
1972 Civil war in Lebanon.
1973 The Yom Kippur War between Egypt and Syria and Israel; Arabs impose oil embargo on western nations supporting Israel; OPEC quadruples oil prices.
1974 Turkey invades Cyprus; partition of the island.
1975 Renewed civil war in Lebanon.
Suez Canal reopened.
1977 President Sadat of Egypt visits Israel and addresses the Knesset in Jerusalem.
1978 The Camp David Summit: President Carter, Prime Minister Menachim Begin and President Sadat. Israel agrees to withdraw from Sinai.
1979 Revolution in Iran; the Shah abdicates; an Islamic Republic is proclaimed under the Ayatollah Khomeini.
Egypt and Israel sign peace treaty in Washington.
The Arab League expels Egypt and moves its headquarters from Cairo to Tunis.
Raid on Grand Mosque at Mecca by Islamic extremists.
1980 Saudi Arabia publicly executes 63 for raid on Grand Mosque.
Conference of Islamic nations meeting in Pakistan condemns Soviet invasion of Afghanistan.
US rescue mission to Iran (for Embassy hostages) fails.
Israel allows Jews to settle in occupied Hebron.
Outbreak of Gulf War between Iraq and Iran.
1981 Iran frees the US hostages after 444 days' captivity.
Israeli air attack upon Iraq nuclear plant at Baghdad.
Assassination of President Sadat.
Israel annexes the Golan Heights.
1982 Israel finally withdraws from Sinai which is fully occupied by Egypt.
Israel invades southern Lebanon to drive PLO to a line 25 miles (40 km) beyond the border; it develops into an exercise – after the siege of Beirut – to expel the PLO from Lebanon; eventually the PLO headquarters are moved to Tunis.
1984 The USA, Britain, Italy and then France withdraw their peacekeeping troops from Lebanon.
1985 Israel withdraws from Lebanon.
Nimeiri overthrown in Sudan.

1986 Increase in terrorism and hostage taking.
   USA bombs Libya claiming it allowed terrorist bases.
1987 Iran-Iraq War enters its seventh year.
1988 The USSR starts to withdraw its troops from Afghanistan in May.
   End of Iran-Iraq War.
   King Hussein of Jordan abandons claims to the West Bank.
   Yasir Arafat proclaims Palestinian State.
1989 USA downs two Libyan fighters.
   Israel closes Palestinian schools in West Bank and Gaza Strip.
   Ayatollah Khomeini announces death sentence on Salman Rushdie for his novel *The Satanic Verses*.
   Egypt accepted back into Arab fold.
   Death of Ayatollah Khomeini.
1990 Iraq invades and annexes Kuwait.
   UN trade embargo against Iraq.
   UN sanctions the use of force to drive Iraqi occupying troops out of Kuwait.
1991 Saddam Hussein ignores UN deadline (15 January) for withdrawing from Kuwait; Alliance commences aerial bombardment of Iraq.
   Mogadishu falls to Somali rebels.
   President Bush (27 February) declares Gulf War over; the Iraqis have been ousted from Kuwait.
   Algeria state of emergency.
   The Egyptian, Boutros Boutros-Ghali, is named as new UN Secretary-General.
   The USA and Scotland indict two Libyans for the bombing of Pan Am flight 103 over Scotland in 1988.
1992 The Algerian Army annuls elections (to prevent Islamic Fundamentalists from coming to power) and forces President Chadli Benjedid to step down.
   The USA sends troops to Somalia to assist in the distribution of food.
1993 Historic agreement between Israel and the PLO for autonomy of Jericho and the Gaza Strip.

Part 3   Eastern Asia

The emergence of the Third World began with the rise of independent Asia. The power shift since 1945 has been enormous. This shift has been from Europe to Asia, a return swing of the pendulum from West to East. When late-medieval Europe looked east for its silks and spices, power lay in the East but the maritime age which followed gave rise to the worldwide European empires. The age lasted for approximately 400 years and then European domination came to an astonishingly abrupt end in the 1940s, although the West needed another two decades for a true appreciation of its real power decline.

The collapse of western control in Asia was swift, spectacular and traumatic. The break-up of the British Indian Empire, the Communist victory in China, the disintegration of Dutch power in the East Indies, the American intervention and then withdrawal from Vietnam, and the elimination of British bases in the Far East are the main signposts of this Asian revival. The emergence from the ashes of defeat of an incredibly wealthy, industrious Japan to become the world's second economy after that of the USA is further testimony to Asia's revival. Japan has joined the ranks of the North. It is a capitalist country, one of the Group of Seven (the major western economic powers).

Numbers alone speak for Asia. China and India together contain a third of the world's population, while more than half the total population of the world lives in Asia. India and China are the two focal points of Asia and their influence since 1945 has been profound. Indian independence in 1947 and the Communist victory throughout mainland China in 1949 meant that two huge nations, each with vast populations, had finally succeeded in throwing off western control or tutelage. In the case of India this meant the direct end of imperial control. In the case of China, it meant the emergence of a strong central government after more than a century of weakness, internal strife and constant western manipulation that came close to a colonial carve-up. Asia's new-found influence comes as much as anything from a perception of what these two powers will become over the next 50 years. Both have the potential in land, people and resources to enter the superpower league.

At Bandung in 1955 (see Chapter Three of this book on the Third World and Non-Alignment), India and China, though poles apart ideologically, served notice that Asia intended to pursue its own policies in its own fashion. And though the message was also meant for the Soviet Union, it was aimed primarily at the West as western imperialism was forced on the defensive on all fronts. The West found this hard to take. The USA could not come to terms with such an approach until the collapse of its Vietnam policy in 1975.

The simultaneous decline of Europe, the emergence of the superpowers and the growth of fierce Asian nationalism together ensured the end of empires and the appearance of what we came to call the Third World. Asia's revival was led by China under Mao Zedong, fiercely opposing any western role in Asia, and India under Nehru, insisting upon Non-Alignment.

The population factor

The preponderance of world population in Asia is a factor of immense significance for the future. When such countries as China and India make industrial and technological breakthroughs on a par with those in the West, the balance will be tilted still more towards Asia and away from the West in a second economic revolution, arguably more important than the political revolution after World War II. One simple calculation demonstrates the point. When China's technology is comparable to that of the USA, its population need produce only at one quarter of the capacity of the US population to achieve an equal output. This may still lie some distance in the future but the lesson of Japan should not be forgotten. What Japan has done, China could do over the next 30 or 40 years as the enormous industrial growth in southeast China in the years since 1985 already suggests.

The converse of this picture, however, are the huge pressures that such vast numbers exert upon resources. Chinese production has to increase by the equivalent of an extra 12 million people a year simply to ensure the same standard of living for everyone. That is to add the total population of Ghana to China every year.

Asian independence

The struggle for independence in Asia began as soon as World War II came to an end. In Indochina and Malaya, Communist guerrillas who had fought the Japanese became the spearhead of independence movements. In Indonesia the Nationalists proclaimed their independence from the Dutch. The first break came in 1946 when the USA gave independence to the Philippines. Britain dismantled its Indian Empire and its periphery – Ceylon and Burma – in 1947 and 1948. In China the years 1945–49 witnessed a fierce civil war that ended with the expulsion of the rump of the Nationalist armies to Formosa (Taiwan) and the triumph of the Chinese Communists under Mao Zedong on the mainland. In Malaya the British were to fight an ultimately successful jungle campaign against the Communist guerrillas before handing over power to a conservative régime in 1957. But everywhere Asians were resuming control: the only question was the manner in which they were to do so.

Dates of independence

1946	Philippines (USA)
1947	India (Britain)
	Pakistan (Britain)
1948	Burma – later Myanmar (Britain)
	Ceylon – later Sri Lanka (Britain)
1949	Indonesia (Netherlands)
1953	Laos (France)
	Cambodia – later Kampuchea (France)
1954	North Vietnam (France)
	South Vietnam (France)
1957	Malaya (Britain)
1963	Malaya, Sabah, Sarawak and Singapore join together in the Malaysian Federation (Britain)
1965	Singapore (leaves Malaysia)
	Maldives (Britain)
1975	Papua New Guinea (Australia)
1976	Formation of the united Socialist Republic of Vietnam
1983	Brunei (Britain)
1991	Federated States of Micronesia (USA)
1991	Marshall Is. (USA)

India

India can boast the oldest continuous civilization in the world and perhaps the country's greatest attribute is its capacity to absorb outsiders: invaders, new religions, ideologies – many have found a place in India to contribute to its sponge-like growth. This is in marked contrast to China whose approach to the world has been one of exclusiveness personified in its monument, the Great Wall.

Kashmir and Pakistan

Since partition in 1947, India's relations with Pakistan have never been easy. Partition saw an estimated 500,000 deaths as Hindus crossed from Pakistan into India and Muslims from India into Pakistan.

The first open cause of quarrel was Kashmir. The state of Jammu and Kashmir had a Hindu ruler but a predominantly Muslim population. Shortly after independence in October 1947, Pathan tribesmen from Pakistan invaded Kashmir whose ruler appealed to India for assistance. Indian troops then occupied the greater part of Kashmir. India refused to hold a plebiscite and since 1954 has treated the parts of Kashmir it holds as belonging to India, while Pakistan retains those parts overrun by its tribesmen in 1947. This was one cause of the first Indo-Pakistan War in 1948.

India has had three wars with Pakistan. The

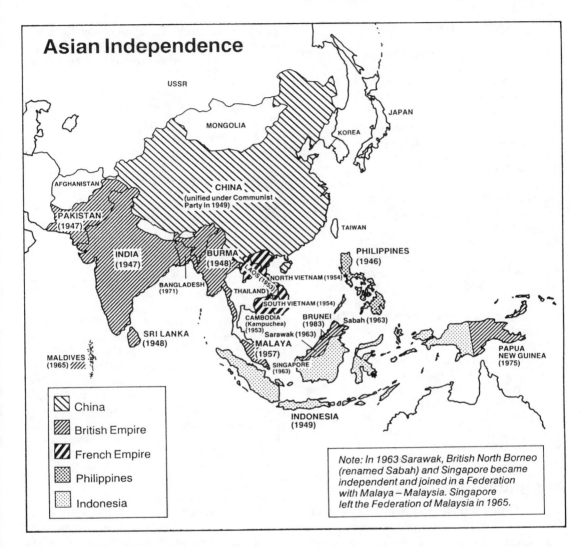

Asian Independence

USSR

MONGOLIA

JAPAN

KOREA

AFGHANISTAN

CHINA
(unified under Communist
Party in 1949)

PAKISTAN
(1947)

TAIWAN

INDIA
(1947)

BURMA
(1948)

PHILIPPINES
(1946)

LAOS (1953)

NORTH VIETNAM (1954)

BANGLADESH
(1971)

THAILAND

SOUTH VIETNAM (1954)

CAMBODIA
(Kampuchea)
(1953)

BRUNEI
(1983)

Sabah (1963)

SRI LANKA
(1948)

Sarawak (1963)

MALAYA
(1957)

PAPUA
NEW GUINEA
(1975)

MALDIVES
(1965)

SINGAPORE
(1963)

INDONESIA
(1949)

Legend:
- China
- British Empire
- French Empire
- Philippines
- Indonesia

Note: In 1963 Sarawak, British North Borneo (renamed Sabah) and Singapore became independent and joined in a Federation with Malaya – Malaysia. Singapore left the Federation of Malaysia in 1965.

Note – Annexations: In what might be described as tidy-up operations in the post-imperial phase, China, India and Indonesia annexed or 'absorbed' territories on their peripheries as follows:

1961 India annexed the three tiny Portuguese enclaves of Goa, Daman and Diu without opposition from the Portugese.

1962 Indonesia took over Dutch New Guinea (West Irian).

1965 China 'absorbed' Tibet, though it had invaded that remote territory in 1950–51.

1975 Sikkim, a former Indian protectorate, became an Indian state.

1976 Indonesia annexed Portuguese Timor.

second came in 1965 over the Rann of Kutch with border incidents in April and a three-week war in September. But far more important for the sub-continent were the events which led to the breakaway of East Pakistan to form the state of Bangladesh. In 1971 a revolt against dominance from West Pakistan took place in East Pakistan, resulting among other things in around 7 million East Pakistani refugees crossing into West Bengal, India. To safeguard its own position and ensure Russian neutrality, India concluded a treaty with the USSR in August 1971. Only then was it prepared to train and later support Bangladeshi guerrillas opposed to Pakistan government forces. As a result of providing such support India again found itself at war with Pakistan. In the west there was stalemate, but in the east India achieved a rapid victory, the 12-day war leading to the emergence of an independent Bangladesh.

India and China

India's relations with China have been through several different phases. In the early stages of the Cold War, while India was insisting upon the right of Third World countries to be non-aligned, China's Communist party was consolidating its power and defying a hostile world. Yet despite China's invasion of Tibet in 1950, Nehru and Zhou Enlai agreed *panchsila* together (see Chapter Three of this book on the Third World and Non-Alignment). And at Bandung in 1955, these two leaders dominated the proceedings to suggest that a non-aligned Asia could accept a non-aggressive Communist China. But border fighting between the two powers occurred in 1959 and then in 1962 came China's invasion of northeastern India. China's refusal to accept the boundaries laid down by Britain proved a humiliation for India and Nehru. This was more than a border incident or small-scale war to adjust boundaries. China, at that time almost totally isolated, was determined to demonstrate to the rest of Asia that it rather than India was the dominant Asian power.

In September 1993 India and China signed a pact agreeing to reduce their armed forces along their 2433-mile border; each side said it would abide by the existing Line of Actual Control while continuing their search for a mutually acceptable boundary settlement.

International affairs

India's decision to remain in the Commonwealth when it became a republic in 1949 was a turning point for the association; in effect it ensured the emergence of what became known as the New Commonwealth. Nehru's personal determination to push Non-Alignment and his insistence upon championing the right of the new Asian nations to stand aside from Cold War entanglements was probably the most important factor in the formation of the Third World as an identifiable group.

More controversial was India's entry into the nuclear club with the explosion of its first nuclear device in 1974. This event upset many who regarded India as the chief proponent of Non-Alignment. Instead it was behaving as a would-be great power rather than as the leader of the Non-Aligned Movement searching for a peace formula between the two sides in the Cold War. Indeed,

other fears surfaced at that time and India was suspected of wishing to dominate the affairs of the subcontinent in relation to both Pakistan and Bangladesh. Then when it annexed Sikkim in 1975, Nepal also became fearful of India's intentions. By the mid-1970s India's image as the champion of Third World Non-Alignment had become tarnished.

Communal strife

Communal strife has been an unfortunate feature of the subcontinent since 1947. Given its enormous size, its huge population, as well as its mix of cultures and religions, this is perhaps hardly surprising. Nonetheless, a priority of the Indian government has always been to maintain strong central control to counteract the constant pulls away from the centre.

The worst communal violence took place at the time of independence between Hindus and Muslims when about half a million people were killed in the two-way movement of Hindus and Muslims across the Punjab. During the 1970s and 1980s, the Tamil separatist movement in the south threatened relations with Sri Lanka. The Naxalites in Bengal or the remote Naga tribesmen of Assam also challenged the idea that central government must be supreme.

A major communal crisis erupted in 1984 when Sikh separatist demands came to a climax with appalling riots followed by the storming of the Golden Temple in Amritsar by Indian army troops in June of that year. This action provoked the assassination of the prime minister, Indira Gandhi, by two of her Sikh bodyguards four months later (October). That crisis simmered on for the rest of the decade.

The two bloody bus massacres of July 1987 in which 72 Hindus were killed in 24 hours brought the death toll for the year to more than 500. The Khalistan Commando Force, most radical of the Sikh terrorist groups, claimed responsibility. In May 1988 Sikh militants were again in possession of the Golden Temple which was surrounded by troops in yet another confrontation.

India finally became physically involved in Sri Lanka in 1987 when 20,000 troops were despatched as a peace-keeping force to the troubled Jaffna Peninsula during July. By May 1988 official Indian troop strength in Sri Lanka was put

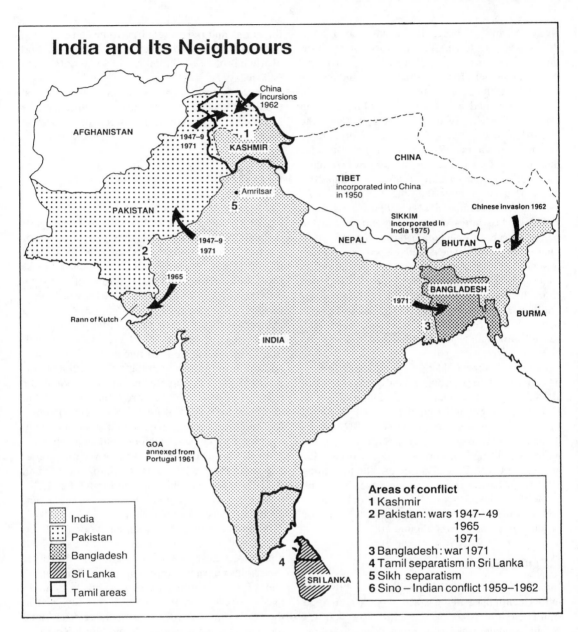

India and Its Neighbours

Areas of conflict
1 Kashmir
2 Pakistan: wars 1947–49
                1965
                1971
3 Bangladesh : war 1971
4 Tamil separatism in Sri Lanka
5 Sikh separatism
6 Sino – Indian conflict 1959–1962

India
Pakistan
Bangladesh
Sri Lanka
Tamil areas

at 52,000 men although Sri Lankan officials suggested it was between 60,000 and 70,000. Following an accord to end the Tamil rebellion India began a partial withdrawal of its troops in June 1988; the total withdrawal of its troops was completed in 1990.

Communal violence escalated at the end of the 1980s and into the 1990s: it included extensive terrorist activities in Jammu and Kashmir, the Punjab (Sikhs) and Assam. Then Hindu–Muslim tensions exploded in 1992 following the destruction of the Babri Mosque in Ayodha (6 December 1991) by Hindu militants.

Politics

Despite immense problems and the attraction that the imposition of authoritarian or dictatorial rule always seems to hold, India has remained a democracy, the largest in the world. Its institutions, based partly on British and partly on American models, have become wholly Indian.

Following the assassination of Gandhi in 1948, Nehru dominated Indian politics until his death in 1964. During the 1950s he also dominated the Non-Aligned Movement of the Third World. After an interregnum in 1964–66 when Lal Bahadur Shastri served as prime minister, Nehru's daughter, Indira Gandhi, was to dominate Indian politics, perhaps even more than had her father, from 1966 to her death in 1984. She ruled from 1966 to 1977, but lost her seat in parliament during the period of rule by the Janata party, a coalition of opposition parties which had united in order to oust her and Congress. The Janata party fell apart while in office. Indira Gandhi returned to power triumphantly in 1980 to remain prime minister until her assassination in 1984. Her rule was both personal and centralizing. Her son Rajiv succeeded her in 1984 to continue (for a time) the Nehru dynasty.

But in 1989 the hold of Congress was broken when Rajiv Gandhi's Congress party only obtained 192 seats and Vishwanath Pratap Singh of Janata Dal became prime minister of a minority National Front. Then during the elections of 1991, Rajiv Gandhi was assassinated near Madras by Tamil extremists. Congress, however, again formed the government with P. V. Rao as president. During 1992 India had to come to terms with the dissolution of the USSR – usually a dependable ally – and consider what would now happen to the obsolete principle of non-alignment.

Economics

India's GDP at US$221,925 million in 1991 put it in fourteenth place in the world table. When that is translated into per capita wealth, however, the country remains one of the poorest on earth. Yet the resources are there. India has the land, the people, a highly trained and efficient civil service, a good infrastructure. With extended irrigation it could feed at least double the present population. India also possesses large mineral resources, especially coal and iron ore, as well as some oil.

Despite prophecies of doom related to the ever-increasing population during the 1960s, India demonstrated that with the help of the 'green revolution' and better irrigation it could produce

the grains and pulses required to be self-sufficient in food. But self-sufficiency is a relative term and nearly half the population are lucky to obtain one meal a day.

On the industrial front a series of 5-year plans, the first launched in 1950, have raised India to the status of a major industrial power – of the second rank.

China

The victory of the Communists over the Nationalists at the end of the 1945–49 civil war gave mainland China a powerful central government for the first time in more than a century and changed the direction of Asian politics. This Chinese revolution helped all Asia throw off western dominance, including those countries which were ideologically opposed to Communism. China had managed – if only just – to avoid formal colonization during the high point of European imperialism. Now a China united under the Communists appeared, in alliance with the USSR – though this was an illusion – to create an enormous monolithic Communist bloc stretching from the River Elbe in Germany to the Sea of Japan. A united Communist China represented triumphant Asian nationalism opposed to western imperialism and economic control. However, in its relations with Korea, Vietnam, Burma (Myanmar), India, Tibet and Pakistan, the new China insisted upon a series of border adjustments and, in the case of Tibet, eventual incorporation in China.

Almost at once the Korean War (1950-53) threatened China and when UN (western and mainly American) forces reached the Yalu River, the border between North Korea and China, at the end of 1950, China's response was to send in massive forces and to remain deeply involved in the war until the truce eventually re-established the boundary between North and South Korea on the 38th parallel. Chinese intervention in Korea was as much to protect Manchuria and reassert Chinese power over an area which was traditionally within its sphere of influence, as it was dictated by considerations of Cold War strategy.

China's invasion of Tibet in 1950 was the assertion of an old suzerainty. In 1959 China further tightened its hold on that country and Tibet's leader, the Dalai Lama, fled to India. China then had a confrontation with India. In 1960

China repudiated the India-Tibet boundaries which Britain had imposed in 1914 and this produced border clashes with India. In the meantime, beginning in 1953, China became a major source of military aid to the Communists in South Vietnam.

As a result of the Communist victory in 1949, the Nationalists under Chiang Kai-shek had retreated to Formosa (Taiwan). There he established a government which persisted in claiming to represent all China. Taiwan had been taken from China by the Japanese in 1895 and restored to the Nationalist Chinese government in 1945. China now claimed Taiwan, but the USA committed itself to defend it on behalf of the Nationalists against a Communist invasion. Further, the USA was prepared to defend the two Nationalist-held offshore islands of Quemoy and Matsu. This American support for the Nationalists led both the USSR and India publicly to support China in its claims to these islands.

Nehru was sympathetic to the new China throughout the 1950s, but when China tightened its grip upon Tibet in 1959 and repudiated the existing borders, clashes with India became inevitable. In 1962 these developed into a full-scale war when a Chinese army invaded the northeast of India. Though border claims were the ostensible reason for hostilities, the war of 1962 had more profound geopolitical causes. China at the time was internationally isolated; it wished to emphasize its pre-eminence as the leading Asian power, a position which, in the long run, only India could challenge. During the crisis Nehru felt obliged to turn to both the USA and the USSR for support against China.

China's post-revolutionary relations with the USSR were anything but easy. Nationalism was at the root of their mutual suspicions, with the USSR deeply disturbed by China's vast population which it saw as a threat to Siberia. Their ideological differences were profound. In 1960 the USSR ended its economic assistance to China and in 1963 the ideological quarrel came into the open. China denounced the USSR for cutting off its aid and the western world suddenly saw the apparently monolithic Communist bloc split in two, its giants pulling in separate directions. One result of this division was that China had to pay increasing attention to fortifying its northern border as well as its southern periphery. Including Mongolia which became a Soviet satellite in 1946, the Soviet–Chinese border stretched for 4500 miles (7242 km).

With the explosion of its first atomic device in 1964, China joined the nuclear club. It followed this with a hydrogen bomb in 1967, thus emphasizing its entry into the big power league.

Despite its economic backwardness, China with its huge population was regarded as a threat by the USSR and, indeed, by the West. In 1950 its population stood at an estimated 545 million; by the mid-1960s it had reached the 700 million mark. The fear of Chinese numbers was not eased by Mao's cynical remark in relation to possible nuclear warfare: that if 300 million Chinese were killed, there would still be another 300 million to replace them.

The internal revolution was all important and, as Mao taught, it was a continuous process. Although Mao experienced setbacks, he was to dominate China for a quarter of a century. The Chinese revolution was marked by extraordinary features: campaigns, such as that to allow a hundred flowers to bloom, the 'great leap forward' which turned into something of a disaster, or the Cultural Revolution of 1966–69 designed to prevent the emergence of a new ruling class. The use of the Red Guards to discipline the old officialdom or revolutionary backsliders and the veneration accorded publicly to the *Little Red Book* of Mao's sayings were other aspects of the on-going revolution. The elevation of Mao was in keeping with an older Chinese tradition which accepted and revered the authoritarian leader, the emperor. These revolutionary tactics, which left western observers bemused, had a profound influence in the Third World where the Chinese model came to be looked upon as an alternative approach to development.

Despite its isolation China displayed growing confidence in the 1960s. It became a substantial aid donor in the Third World, most notably in Africa where its spectacular project to build the TAN-ZAM railway from Dar es Salaam on the Indian Ocean coast of Tanzania to Kapiri Mposhi in central Zambia became the largest single aid project anywhere. China had had virtually no contact with Africa before this time and the obvious area for assistance lay in the neighbouring countries. However, this was a deliberate Chinese political gambit, a demonstration to the Third World that it was in sympathy with its aspirations and would help where it could, and a defiant gesture to the West that still would not recognize it, as well as to the USSR – a serving of notice that China was a factor to be reckoned with.

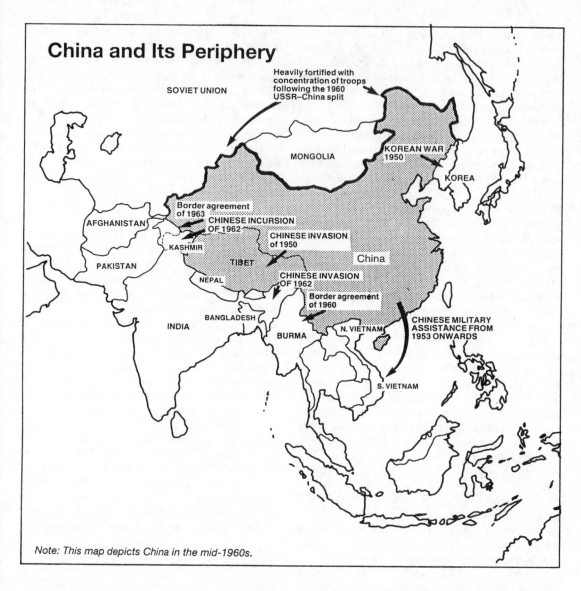

China and Its Periphery

SOVIET UNION

Heavily fortified with concentration of troops following the 1960 USSR–China split

MONGOLIA

KOREAN WAR 1950

KOREA

AFGHANISTAN

Border agreement of 1963

CHINESE INCURSION OF 1962

CHINESE INVASION of 1950

KASHMIR

CHINESE INVASION of 1962

China

PAKISTAN

TIBET

NEPAL

Border agreement of 1960

BANGLADESH

INDIA

BURMA

N. VIETNAM

CHINESE MILITARY ASSISTANCE FROM 1953 ONWARDS

S. VIETNAM

Note: This map depicts China in the mid-1960s.

The Chinese revolution which followed the Communist triumph of 1949 was one of the most far-reaching events of the century. Its impact upon Asia was profound.

Vietnam

The war in Vietnam included in their harshest form all the elements which have shaped the Third World: the rearguard determination of a colonial power to hold on; a growing ideological struggle that involved the big powers of East and West; and poverty pitched against military might. Above all the Vietnamese were determined not to be controlled by the West. On the one hand Vietnamese nationalism was not understood by a West which reduced everything to Cold War considerations; on the other hand Vietnamese nationalism was actually sharpened by the Cold War conflict. If the only way to achieve nationalist independence was through adopting thoroughgoing Communism, then that was what the Vietnamese people would do.

Indo-China had been French since 1858. It was invaded and occupied by the Japanese in 1940. At the end of the war, as Japanese power collapsed,

British forces moved into Indo-China. On 2 September 1945 in Hanoi, a Vietnam Communist, Ho Chi Minh, made a Vietnamese 'Declaration of Independence', but that lasted only for 3 weeks before the British took over on behalf of the returning French. By November 1946, the French were bombarding the port of Haiphong and Ho Chi Minh was calling upon the people of Vietnam to defend their new republic. By 1950 the struggle had become bound up in the spreading Cold War and, between 1950 and 1954, the USA bore 80 per cent of the costs of the war. The French, who had been fighting a war to regain control of a colony in nationalist revolt, were transformed into defenders of an outpost of the Free World against spreading Communism. By 1953 France had decided to pull out of neighbouring Laos and Cambodia, which became independent. Yet by then its forces in Vietnam totalled 250,000 men.

John Foster Dulles, the American Secretary of State, believed in the 'domino theory'; that is, allow one country to fall to Communism and its neighbours would follow one by one. He regarded Vietnam as essential to western security in southeast Asia. Then came the siege of Dien Bien Phu, a French military fortress in northwest Vietnam, and the spectacular French collapse and surrender. Significantly, during the siege which lasted from 13 March to 7 May, Foster Dulles was to say of Vietnam: 'It is rich in many raw materials, such as tin, oil, rubber and iron ore . . . The area has great strategic value.' Here were clearly set out the reasons why France was making such an effort to hold on and why the USA was prepared to provide support. The French surrender at Dien Bien Phu was followed by a French withdrawal and the Geneva Conference which recognized two Vietnams.

The USA now provided support for its nominee in South Vietnam, Ngo Dinh Diem, who, after a rigged referendum, ousted Bao Dai to become president, prime minister and minister of defence. From 1954 onwards the USA steadily increased its support to the régime in the south, while the nature of the conflict changed. For the West, which now meant the USA, it became a struggle to prevent the spread of Communism; for North Vietnam, which argued that the terms of the Geneva Conference had been broken, the struggle was to achieve a united Vietnam.

By 1960 the Vietcong Communist guerrillas were in control of much of South Vietnam. In 1962 President Kennedy made his fateful decision to dispatch military advisers to South Vietnam. The conflict escalated. The USA had become involved in a major war on the mainland of Asia which was to last for years and become an international and domestic disaster. From 1965 onwards, under President Lyndon B. Johnson, the USA committed increasing numbers of combat troops to the struggle and began to bomb targets in North Vietnam. By 1968, at the height of the struggle, there were about 500,000 American troops in Vietnam. At the end of that year a much quoted statistic – that the Americans had dropped upon North Vietnam a heavier tonnage of bombs than the total dropped on Germany and Japan throughout World War II – had become true. Yet no end was in sight and the lesson which emerged became increasingly clear: that not even the greatest power on earth could win in a situation where a determined people were set upon fighting to achieve their objective no matter how high the cost.

It fell to that most controversial of American presidents, Richard Nixon, to end American involvement in Vietnam. After lengthy and tortuous negotiations a ceasefire was signed in Paris on 27 January 1973. This was followed by a rapid phase-down of American aid to the government in South Vietnam. The assistance came to an end in 1975 when the last American personnel were withdrawn and the South was abandoned to the North. In 1976 following nationwide elections a united Socialist Republic of Vietnam was proclaimed.

In the end the rights and wrongs of the struggle in Vietnam, even its ideological aspects, were forgotten as the world watched the greatest of the superpowers deploying massive resources against a determined peasantry – and losing. This spectacle had profound effects in the USA for years afterwards and was seen in Asia as the triumph of determined nationalism over western imperialism. No other struggle in the Third World has had such a psychological impact. This impact was in no way diminished because the socialist Vietnam which emerged from the conflict was regarded with caution, if not downright hostility, by most of its neighbours.

The Cold War in Asia

No other region of the world has been so obviously affected by the Cold War as was Asia in the 1950s.

Latin America remained relatively insulated, Africa was still under colonial control, while the Middle East, despite the Suez Crisis of 1956, continued to be part of the western camp. But in Asia the emergence of Communist China in 1949, the Korean War of 1950, the on-going struggle in Vietnam and the determination of Nehru's India to maintain Non-Alignment in face of Cold War pressures to take sides ensured that Asia became the battleground for the struggle whose most obvious western exponent was the American Secretary of State, John Foster Dulles.

Most of the newly independent countries of Asia tried to stay clear of Cold War entanglements, but had their work cut out to do so. China under the Communists was committed to one side and yet as Zhou Enlai made plain at Bandung, as well as earlier on his visit to India, his country wished to pursue a policy of peaceful co-existence. The Korean War, however, highlighted the ruthless, dangerous nature of the global ideological conflict, although India did manage to achieve a breakthrough for the idea of a Third Force when, despite Dulles, it was included in the 1953 peace negotiations.

The Cold War achieved two paradoxical results in Asia. On the one hand, it almost certainly ensured that many countries became independent sooner than might otherwise have been the case, because the USA in particular pressed the colonial powers to grant independence, while both super-powers sought allies among the new nations. On the other hand, the Cold War helped prolong a colonial presence in other parts of Asia which otherwise might have been withdrawn sooner, namely the French in Indo-China and the British in their East of Suez role which lasted to 1968 in Singapore and another 2 years in the Gulf.

In both Malaya and Vietnam, the Communists, who had led the nationalist opposition to the Japanese, later led the guerrilla movements which opposed the returning imperial powers – Britain and France. It is possible, though by no means certain, that without the Cold War the British and French would have held on somewhat longer to at least parts of their Asian empires.

The Korean War which left 580,000 South Korean and UN troops dead on the one side and between 1 and 1.5 million North Koreans and Chinese dead on the other (apart from civilian casualties) set the stage for Cold War confronta-tion in Asia for a generation. Just as a Korean truce was being laboriously worked out, the first

phase of the Vietnam struggle was also coming to a climax (the fall of Dien Bien Phu occurred the following year). But if those were the two most dangerous Cold War struggles there were others.

Widespread Communist or Communist-inspired insurgency occurred in a number of Asian coun-tries after 1945. In Malaya this led to a full-scale jungle war between British troops and the Com-munists before that country became independent in 1957. The successor government, however, still had to deal with some guerrilla activity in the mid-1970s. Burma (Myanmar), Indonesia and the Philippines also experienced various forms of Communist revolt. Burma (Myanmar) which became independent in 1948 suffered from appa-rently endless civil strife until in 1962 General Ne Win overthrew the government of U Nu and established a military dictatorship. In 1974 the country became a one-party socialist republic. Insurgency continued, however, with the Com-munists as the largest, though by no means only, opposition group.

A number of countries – Thailand, Malaya (later Malaysia), Singapore, Pakistan – were to remain firmly pro-western, though India, Indonesia, Sri Lanka and Burma (Myanmar) maintained a non-aligned status. Thailand in any case faced constant threats to its stability with coups in 1947, 1951, 1957, 1971, 1973 and 1976. Later other communal problems unconnected with the Cold War were to trouble the region. In Burma (Myanmar) there were the separatist Karens, Shans and Kachins; in Sri Lanka the Tamils; in India the Nagas and then the Sikhs. The overthrow of the corrupt régime of Ferdinand Marcos in the Philippines in 1986 with tacit (if late) American approval arguably heralded a new pattern. Marcos' successor, Mrs Aquino, faced a Communist insurgency movement when she came to power.

The government of Indonesia, huge and sprawl-ing with 13,000 islands and Hindu–Muslim com-munities, faces many problems at the best of times. What is astonishing about its performance since independence has been the extent to which it has coped successfully. There was the long-drawn-out quarrel with the Netherlands over West Irian, which eventually became part of Indonesia, and with Portugal over Timor. There was also the deliberate confrontation with British Borneo from 1957 onwards. The government had to fight would-be independence movements in Sulawesi and the Moluccas while in 1965, at the time of the attempted coup against Sukarno, between 100,000 and 750,000 people are variously estimated to have been killed.

During this period the politics of the region were characterized by constant manoeuvring and unexpected realignments: China and Pakistan; India turning to the USSR; Burma (Myanmar) attempting desperately to remain non-involved. Such moves were complicated by the roles which the great powers adopted.

The Great Powers in Asia

The USA, the USSR, Britain and France were always on the sidelines and sometimes deeply involved in Asian manoeuvres during these years, though first France and then Britain withdrew from more active Asian interventions leaving these to the USA and the USSR.

The USA

Overwhelming American power ensured the surrender of Japan in 1945, although the other Allies had played a part in the victory. Yet only 4 years later the man the USA had backed with huge military and financial support in China, Chiang Kai-shek, retreated to Taiwan. More than 20 years were to pass before the Nixon administration made it possible for Communist China to enter the United Nations. In the meantime the USA (with the South Koreans) bore the brunt of the fighting in South Korea and then became deeply involved over 20 years in the Vietnam War. American Asian policies were not rewarded with much success over this period. India and a majority of other Asian countries insisted upon Non-Alignment. Only in South Korea did US action lead to the subsequent establishment of a 'client' state. And in Japan, American policy could claim a victory.

The Japanese factor

The startling post-war recovery of Japan was a phenomenon of the 1950s and 1960s. That it took place without any obvious setbacks was mainly a result of Cold War calculations, because the USA was prepared to encourage its rapid recovery as a counterweight to both China and the USSR. In consequence Japan rapidly emerged as a highly successful bastion of capitalism in an otherwise dangerous Communist or non-aligned Asia – dangerous from the viewpoint of the West.

By the 1970s the Japanese economy ranked second in the non-Communist world and third after the two superpowers. Japan, moreover, was firmly committed to the western camp, one of the 'Group of Seven' who acted as host to the leaders of these major western economies for their 1986 summit.

The USSR

This same period also saw growing Soviet involvement in Asia. Probably the USSR was as surprised as the West at the rapid and overwhelming victory of Mao and the Chinese Communists in 1949. As a result the Soviet Union had to come to terms with the Chinese giant in the Communist camp, a potential equal partner who made plain from the beginning that it would not be treated by Moscow as a satellite. The 1950 Sino-Soviet Treaty might have persuaded the West that a monolithic Communist bloc had come into existence but the reality was more complex.

China had long regarded the USSR as an imperialist power. For example, the USSR had established a protectorate over Tannu Tuva (now the autonomous republic of Tuva) in 1914 and annexed it in 1944. It turned Mongolia into a satellite in 1946. Russian armies entered Manchuria in 1945; they stayed in Sinkiang until 1949 and in Port Arthur until 1955.

For their part the Russians regarded China's huge numbers with suspicion akin to fear. They saw these as a threat to the vast expanses of near-empty Siberia. Thus it was always an uneasy alliance, which collapsed at the beginning of the 1960s. And when China and India faced each other with increasing antagonism at the turn of the decade it made geopolitical sense for India to turn to the USSR, which it came to regard as the most important power in relation to its Asian policies.

France

French imperial interests in Asia were centred upon Indo-China, a small though rich imperial fief when compared with the huge sprawling Dutch East Indies. In the post-1945 politics of Asia, the Netherlands were eliminated as a factor almost at once and Indonesia became fully independent in 1949. France, however, held on grimly in Indo-

China until its defeat at Dien Bien Phu. Thereafter, only Britain of the old imperial powers
remained for some years longer to play an Asian
role.

Britain

Britain's decision to decolonize its Indian Empire
immediately after World War II set the pace for
the end of empires. The success of this exercise
and the subsequent good relations which Britain
enjoyed with India and Pakistan made it easier for
Britain to continue an imperial role in other parts
of Asia for some years. The Commonwealth
initiative which established the Colombo Plan in
1950 also helped (see Chapter Five of this book on
Aid and its Agencies).

Britain remained in Malaya to fight a successful
war against Communist insurgents until that country became independent in 1957. It kept its Borneo
colonies until Sabah and Sarawak were united with
Malaya and Singapore in the Malaysian Federation
(1963). Britain also provided military forces to
assist them against Indonesian 'confrontation'.
And when Singapore seceded from the Malaysian
Federation in 1965, Britain kept its substantial
military base there – the key to its Far East role –
until 1968. Finally, Britain's protectorate over
Brunei was only ended in 1983 when that country
became fully independent.

It suited Communist China to leave Hong Kong
as a capitalist enclave on its coast until, after a
number of 'hiccups', Britain and China agreed a
settlement in 1984: the Colony and Territory will
revert to China in 1997. Thus Britain did manage
to withdraw from Asia with a certain grace, though
its equivalent of Dien Bien Phu had been the
ignominious surrender of Singapore to the Japanese in 1942.

By the mid-1980s only a few colonial anomalies
remained in Asia: Hong Kong and Macau. The
French also remained in the island territory of New
Caledonia, where white French settlers and the
Kanaks confronted each other, with 7000 French
troops stationed in the island to keep the peace
while France worked out a solution to the last of its
Far Eastern colonial problems.

The end of the Cold War

The end of the Cold War followed by the disintegration of the USSR at the beginning of the 1990s

and the consequent emergence of a number of
newly independent states in Asia – Azerbaijan,
Armenia, Georgia, Kazakhstan, Kyrgyzstan,
Tajikistan, Turkmenistan and Uzbekistan – pro-
foundly altered the geography as well as the
politics of Asia. China's determination to continue
as a centralized, Communist state was emphasized
– to its disadvantage world-wide – when on 4 June
1989 the government ordered the military to crack
down on the student-led pro-democracy movement. The subsequent massacre of about 1000
students in Tiananmen Square was condemned
world-wide.

Asian economic advance

Through these traumatic political events, the new
nations of Asia made considerable and in some
cases dramatic advances. Despite the setbacks of
the Great Leap Forward or the Cultural Revolution, China's economic development since 1949
has been spectacular and, overall, its people have
achieved a better standard of living than ever
before in their history. Similarly India has made
enormous advances. Yet in each case their huge
populations and the sheer size of development
problems mean that, on a per capita basis, their
people remain among the poorest in the world.

Taiwan, South Korea and Singapore, the first
two helped by massive injections of American
assistance and all three displaying commendable
entrepreneurial skill, have achieved considerable
prosperity and in the case of South Korea had
achieved the world's twelfth largest GDP by 1991.
The countries of South-east Asia working together
in ASEAN (see below) have also made substantial
economic advances. But whatever the variations,
Asia's people are still among the world's poorest.
It will be years before even the major nations are
able to achieve the economic breakthroughs which
will put them in the category of Japan. Then, and
only then, should they so choose, will they be able
to end their Third World status at least in
economic terms, whatever political road they may
wish to pursue.

Asian and Pacific regional organizations

Unlike Africa, the Middle East or to a lesser extent Latin America, which between them have spawned a large number of regional organizations, there are relatively few in Asia and the Pacific. This reflects a different kind of political reality. Such huge countries as China or India are more likely to create spheres of influence around their peripheries than feel the need to join regional groups for purposes of economic or political co-operation. Moreover, the size of these countries inhibits smaller neighbours from entering associations with them if they believe that such associations will be dominated by the larger power. Thus there is no Asian equivalent of the Organization of American States (OAS) in the Americas or the OAU in Africa. The OAS, in any case, is generally seen not to be very effective, because of the dominant role inevitably assumed by the USA. While the OAU cannot be dominated by any one member, it does reflect the urgent search for unity in Africa against what are sometimes seen as overwhelming outside pressures. The proliferation of organizations in the Middle East represents the great surge of Arab and Islamic confidence derived from OPEC power in the 1970s, although the Arab League which dates from the end of World War II is the one organization most obviously based upon ethnic and religious considerations. Broadly it is the smaller powers which most need to belong to regional groups, from which they hope to draw support.

Economic and Social Commission for Asia and the Pacific (ESCAP)

Like the Economic Commissions for Africa and for Latin America and the Caribbean, ESCAP is the UN regional development organization for Asia. Founded in 1947 it was first known as ECAFE (Economic Commission for Asia and the Far East) but changed its name to its present title in 1974. Membership includes non-regional powers, such as Britain and France, as well as Australia, New Zealand, Japan, the USA and Russia (formerly the USSR). It also has associate members.

ESCAP's headquarters are in Bangkok, Thailand. Its organs consist of a Commission and a Secretariat, while a number of committees meet annually or on a 2-yearly basis. ESCAP has a Pacific office in Vanuatu. ESCAP activities cover the fields of agriculture, development planning, industry, technology, human settlements, international trade, natural resources, population, shipping and ports, social development, statistics, transport and communications.

ESCAP is the only organization covering all Asia and the Pacific. It assists development programmes through technical assistance or advice to governments and with research and training. The biennial budget in the 1980s stood at only $35 million, although this was supplemented by funds from members to cover the costs of technical assistance programmes.

As with other regions, the UN has many programmes in Asia and the Pacific. These fall under the UNDP, UNHCR, FAO, the World Bank Group and IMF, UNESCO, WHO, and so on.

Asian Development Bank (ADB)

The ADB was formed in 1966. It has a membership of 34 countries from the Asian and Pacific regions and a further 17 non-regional members. The ADB raises funds from both private and public sources to finance development projects in the region. Its principal activities are to provide assistance to governments to help them co-ordinate economic policies. It provides technical assistance.

Its organs consist of a Board of Governors, a Board of Directors and the Administration. The Administration includes a number of departments which cover the Bank's development activities as well as being responsible for funding.

The ADB differentiates between its ordinary capital resources, which are used to provide loans at market rates to the more economically advanced countries of the region, and its Special Funds. The Asian Development Fund which was set up in 1974 provides loans at concessional rates to the Bank's least developed members. The majority of loans go to specific projects, such as those that build up a country's infrastructure. They are not provided for general purposes, budgetary support or balance of payments assistance.

Association of South East Asian Nations (ASEAN)

ASEAN is one of the relatively few groupings of nations in the region. Formed at Bangkok in 1967, ASEAN's principal objectives are to achieve regional peace and greater stability in the region (ASEAN was created at the height of the Vietnam war); and to assist the economic development of its members.

In 1991 ASEAN agreed to form an ASEAN Free Trade Area with the object of phasing out tariffs between members over a period of 15 years.

The original members of the Association (five in number) were Indonesia, Malaysia, Philippines, Singapore and Thailand. Brunei joined in 1984 shortly after achieving independence and Papua New Guinea has observer status.

ASEAN's organs are the Summit Meeting (the High Authority); the Ministerial Conferences (foreign ministers who meet annually by rotation in member countries); the Standing Committee; the Secretariat (the main secretariat is in Jakarta but each member has its own national ASEAN secretariat); and various Committees which oversee the association's main activities. At its first summit in 1976 ASEAN agreed a Treaty of Amity and Co-operation and a Declaration of Concord.

Other regional groupings

The Colombo Plan is the most important development agency in the region (see Chapter Five of this book on Aid and Its Agencies). Now known as the Colombo Plan for Co-operative Economic and Social Development in Asia and the Pacific, it was formed in 1950 and over the years has proved one of the more successful channels for aid.

A number of Asian and Pacific countries, including India, are members of the Commonwealth and others (the Pacific members of the ACP) benefit from an associate status with the EC.

Two Islamic organizations play a role in Asia. These are the Islamic Development Bank and the Organization of Islamic Conference (OIC). Both are dealt with above under the Middle East.

South Pacific Commission (SPC)

The SPC was formed in 1947 by the colonial powers of the region – Australia, France, Netherlands, New Zealand, UK and USA. It is concerned with regional issues and provides economic assistance for approximately 5 million people in 22 territories, mainly small islands. Its organs are the South Pacific Conference; the Committee of Representatives of Governments and Administrations; and the Secretariat.

South Pacific Forum

The Forum consists of heads of government of independent and self-governing territories in the South Pacific. It first met in 1971. There are 15 members: Australia, New Zealand, Cook Is., Fiji, Kiribati, Nauru, Niue, Papua New Guinea, Solomon Is., Tonga, Tuvalu, Vanuatu and Western Samoa. The Federated States of Micronesia and the Marshall Is. joined the Forum as full members in 1991 on the achievement of independence.

The Forum discusses the problems of the area. In 1983 it called upon France to give greater autonomy to New Caledonia and speed up the advance to independence. The Forum has repeatedly opposed French nuclear tests in the Pacific.

South Pacific Bureau for Economic Co-operation (SPEC)

SPEC was established in 1973 to assist co-operation and consultation between members of the South Pacific Forum in matters of trade and economic development, transport, tourism, and so on. SPEC is run by a Committee and Secretariat.

Part 4   Latin America and the Caribbean

Unlike the rest of the Third World, most Central and South American countries achieved independence in the first half of the nineteenth century following the collapse of Spanish and Portuguese power in the region. Only the Caribbean islands remained colonies until after World War II. Except for the islands and the Guianas the region had been colonized exclusively by the two Latin powers so that it has a certain cohesion, including the almost universal adherence to the Roman Catholic religion and the use of Spanish or Portuguese, unifying factors not to be found in Africa or Asia. Latin American élites are more Eurocentred than is the case elsewhere in the Third World. Finally, because most of the countries have enjoyed about 150 years of independence, attitudes towards the North differ from those of other Third World groupings. This comes out clearly in relation to the Non-Aligned Movement.

History of the region

After 1492, when Christopher Columbus made his first landfalls on territories of the New World, the Bahamas, Cuba and Hispaniola, years were to pass before the explorers realized that a huge landmass (North and South America) lay between them and their objective of the East Indies. Yet within an astonishingly short time Spain, then Europe's greatest power, and Portugal had carved out for themselves huge empires in this New World.

Spain and Portugal agreed a division of this New World between them at the Treaty of Tordesillas in 1494. Spain was to have any lands to the west of longitude 40 degrees west and Portugal was to have what lay to the east of the line, in effect Brazil. During the 1520s the Spanish conquistador Hernando Cortés destroyed the Aztec Empire and conquered Mexico. In the 1530s Francisco Pizarro did the same for the Inca civilization centred upon Peru. Great silver mines gave Spain enormous wealth and by 1600 the Spanish Empire, as yet unchallenged, stretched from the Rio Grande to the Straits of Magellan. The colonization of Brazil went more slowly. The Portuguese were primarily concerned with their Asian empire although, in the last quarter of the sixteenth century, Brazil was developed as the world's leading sugar producer. For the next three centuries, Portugal provided Brazil with slaves from her African colony of Angola.

In the seventeenth century, the Dutch, English and French challenged Spanish power throughout the Caribbean, which in this book, for cultural and political reasons, includes four mainland enclaves: Belize in Central America, and Guyana, Surinam and French Guiana in South America. The Dutch fell out of the imperial race at the end of the seventeenth century. Anglo-French rivalry came to a climax in the eighteenth century at a time when the Caribbean islands developed as sugar producers and slaves were immensely valuable. Thus in the restitutions and bargaining at the conclusion of the Seven Years War in 1763, Britain seriously considered keeping Martinique, which it had taken from France, rather than retaining Quebec which General James Wolfe had just conquered. This pattern persisted to the end of the eighteenth century: Brazil was Portuguese, most of the rest of South and Central America, apart from British, Dutch and French Guiana, made up the Spanish Empire while the Caribbean presented a colonial mixture of Spanish, British, French and Dutch possessions.

The only link between this huge area and other parts of what became the Third World was the Atlantic slave trade. For 300 years Brazil and the Caribbean islands (as well as the southern states of North America) were to be the recipients of African slaves from the Gulf of Guinea to Angola. In 1791 the slaves in Haiti rose in revolt against the French. This uprising, sparked off by the French Revolution, signalled the beginning of the independence struggles which were to dominate the region for the next 50 years. Under the black leader, Toussaint l'Ouverture, Haiti became the first Latin American country to achieve independence (1804).

Independence movements are infectious and before long Latin America was in turmoil. The first half of the nineteenth century saw virtually the whole mainland from Mexico to Chile achieve independence. Napoleon's invasion of the Iberian peninsula in 1808 brought an end to Portuguese and Spanish control of their South American colonies. One great struggle, centred upon Venezuela, was led by the Venezuelans Simón Bolivar and Antonio José de Sucre; a second struggle further south was led by the Argentinian José de San Martín and the Chilean Bernardo O'Higgins. In Brazil the Portuguese regent, Dom Pedro, proclaimed an independent empire and, there at least, a relatively peaceful transition from colony to free nation took place. In most of Latin America, however, bitter civil wars and endless faction fights followed the ousting of the Spanish.

The Mexican story illustrates the turbulence which characterized the times. A 10-year struggle – 1810 to 1820 – led to independence from Spain, but over the next 50 years Mexico had 30 presidents and many bitter internal power struggles. Nationalist development, moreover, was complicated by the struggle with the United States. Although the Mexicans wiped out an American garrison at the Alamo in 1836, they were defeated a decade later in the Mexican War (1846-48) with the USA. Mexico was then forced to cede California, Utah and New Mexico, about 40 per cent of its territory, to the United States. During the American Civil War, France attempted to gain influence in Mexico by putting forward (and supporting with French troops) its own candidate, Maximilian I of Austria, as emperor of the territory, but he was defeated and executed in 1867. A long period of oppression produced the revolution of 1910.

The nineteenth century was a period of much bloodshed and strife both within the successor states to the Spanish Empire and between them, usually over border disputes. Slavery was abolished in all the Spanish-speaking republics by the 1850s although in Brazil it was to last until the 1880s. During this period American, British and other European financial and trading interests moved into what had been a closely guarded Spanish preserve: these interests were to dominate much of the subsequent economic development.

Although economic growth was often spectacular, it was also very uneven: mining and plantation agriculture rarely produced much benefit for the peasant masses. Typical of such progress was the nitrates boom in Chile which lasted from 1880 to 1919.

The Caribbean remained largely immune to these momentous events. The island colonies continued as part of the European empires. On the mainland of South America the three enclave territories of British, Dutch and French Guiana were extensions of Caribbean culture and politics rather than belonging to Latin America, as was British Honduras (Belize) in Central America. In the South Atlantic the British held the Falkland Islands which they had taken from Argentina in 1832.

In 1945 most of the countries of Central and South America were already independent. Yet in terms of their stages of development they each qualified for membership of the Third World. Though some sectors of Latin America were far more advanced economically than the countries of Africa or Asia, development had always been grossly uneven. Wealthy ruling élites of great power and relatively influential middle classes

contrasted with the peasant masses and urban unemployed, whose poverty sometimes was amost indescribable.

The revolts against Spain at the beginning of the nineteenth century were led by Spanish settler classes or mestizos so that the colonial class divide was perpetuated after independence and the successor states retained many colonial features.
• Latin America's external affairs have always been dominated by relations with the United States. The Monroe Doctrine of 1823 was designed to warn off European intervention and most especially attempts by Spain and Portugal to regain control of their empires. It also signalled the beginning of a policy which has lasted down to the present – the American determination to treat the region as its exclusive sphere of influence.

Latin America since 1945

The Great Depression of the 1930s made a harsh impact upon the economies of Latin America although, during World War II, a degree of industrialization took place because the war in Europe cut off traditional supplies of consumer goods. After 1945 the reformist zeal of Mexico, the home of revolution, had slowed down and the country became more closely tied to the economy of the USA.

One result of bad economic conditions was to make the urban middle classes, generally the most important group politically, look to strong dictator-like figures. In Brazil from 1930 to 1954 the man was Getúlio Vargas; in Argentina after 1946 Juan Perón. His overthrow by the army in 1955 illustrates one of the most abiding aspects of South American politics: namely, the tremendously strong army tradition. For much of their independent history, many Latin American countries have been ruled by military juntas or strong men – the dictator or 'caudillo', that figure peculiar to Latin America. Since 1970, however, there has been an appreciable turn towards democracy.

Since the 1950s poor or uneven economic performance has been further complicated by the huge population explosion. The increase in numbers has constantly outstripped economic growth. And though World War II did lead to substantial industrialization, not many of the benefits found

Latin America: Independence

MEXICO
(1821)

CUBA
(1898)

DOMINICAN REPUBLIC
(1844)

GUATEMALA
(1838)

HONDURAS
(1838)

HAITI
(1804)

EL SALVADOR
(1821)

NICARAGUA
(1838)

COSTA RICA
(1838)

PANAMA
(1903)

VENEZUELA
(1830)

COLOMBIA*
(1830)

ECUADOR
(1830)

PERU
(1821)

BRAZIL
(1822)

BOLIVIA
(1825)

PARAGUAY
(1811)

CHILE
(1818)

URUGUAY
(1828)

ARGENTINA
(1816)

*Bolívar had created a 'Gran Colombia' which
included Ecuador and Venezuela but this broke up
in 1830.

THE FALKLAND IS.
(BRITISH)

their way downwards to the urban poor or peasant masses. Latin America presents many glaring examples of extreme wealth at one end of the scale and mass poverty at the other, with wretched peons exploited and oppressed in the countryside, and huge slums surrounding the skyscraper inner cities of Rio de Janeiro and São Paulo.

With such a background, Latin America presents fertile possibilities of revolution and insurgency. A revolution in Guatemala in 1944 led to major changes and under President Jacobo Arbenz Guzmán (1951) a series of agrarian reforms were implemented. A counter-revolution with American backing was mounted from Honduras in 1954.

In Bolivia a successful left wing revolution was launched against the army in 1952, though it had lost its impetus by 1960. Castro's rise to power in Cuba has attracted the most international attention but his was only one of many – in his case successful – attempts to overthrow reactionary and corrupt oligarchies or dictatorships. Often when left-of-centre parties achieve power, they are accused of doing too little too late. Alternatively when the left comes to power it tries to go too fast and invites – and as a rule gets – violent right wing reaction against it. Thus in 1970 the Popular Unity Party brought Salvador Allende Gossens to power in Chile but by 1973 his Marxist policies produced a right wing reaction and an army takeover led by General Augusto Pinochet Ugarte, backed by the American Central Intelligence Agency (CIA).

The glaring differences between rich and poor in Latin America have been the subject of much political comment. For example, in El Salvador 2 per cent of the people own 57 per cent of the cultivable land. That kind of situation is an open invitation to left wing revolutionary forces to attempt a redress.

Conscious of economic vulnerability to outside forces – the USA in particular, but also other transnational interests – the countries of Latin America have made a number of attempts to create free trade areas or common markets, though to date without much obvious success. The Latin American Free Trade area was established in 1960 but had collapsed by 1980. Also in 1960 El Salvador, Guatemala, Honduras and Nicaragua formed the Central American Common Market. In 1969 Bolivia, Chile, Colombia, Ecuador and Peru formed the Andean Group. In 1975, 25 countries of the region banded together in the loose *Sistema Económico Latinoamericano* (SELA). In their various ways, these groups represent regional attempts to boost self-reliance.

Latin America and the United Nations

When the United Nations was formed in 1945, 20 Latin American countries (Argentina, Bolivia, Brazil, Chile, Colombia, Costa Rica, Cuba, Dominican Republic, Ecuador, El Salvador, Guatemala, Haiti, Honduras, Mexico, Nicaragua, Panama, Paraguay, Peru, Uruguay and Venezuela) were among the 51 founder members. For years they formed the biggest UN bloc.

The Latin American bloc was to remain the largest until 1960. In the 1950s these countries, in alliance with the new nations of Asia, pressed for economic redress and demanded aid. It can be argued that the concept of the Third World, at least as far as aid is concerned, was the creation of Latin America and the new nations of Asia. During the early stages of the Cold War, apart from such target countries as Turkey or South Korea, the USA regarded the countries of Latin America as the most obvious recipients of its aid.

Two problems complicated the economic scene. The first was the huge growth of population which was encouraged by the overwhelming preponderance of the Roman Catholic Church. The second was the rapid increase in urbanization. Today more than 60 per cent of the people of Latin America are urban and enormous slums have grown up around many cities, such as Mexico City and São Paulo.

Between 1945 and 1992, though there have been some spectacular sectoral advances, most Latin American economies have remained deeply troubled. At the beginning of the 1980s, for example, a group of Latin American countries accounted for half of the world's debts.

International orientations

As a result of their history, the countries of the region see themselves as being more closely connected with the North than is the case with Asia, Africa or the Middle East. Argentinian or Brazilian middle classes are more obviously Europeanized (and regard themselves as such) than their counterparts in Bombay or Singapore. This is a political factor of importance.

In 1961 when the first Non-Aligned Summit was held in Belgrade, only Cuba attended as a full member of the movement although Bolivia, Brazil and Ecuador were present as observers. In 1964 at the Cairo Non-Aligned Summit, Cuba was still the only non-aligned country from Latin America, though the presence of an increased number of observers – Argentina, Bolivia, Brazil, Chile, Jamaica, Mexico, Trinidad and Tobago, Uruguay and Venezuela – indicated a growing regional interest in the movement. So far only one Non-Aligned Summit (Havana in 1979) has been held in the hemisphere and that was controversial because some non-aligned countries were unhappy that Cuba should be the host in view of its close ties with Moscow.

But by 1983 when the Non-Aligned Summit was held in New Delhi and 99 full members attended, the number from Latin America and the Caribbean had risen to 16, namely Argentina, Bahamas, Barbados, Belize, Bolivia, Colombia, Cuba, Ecuador, Grenada, Guyana, Jamaica, Nicaragua, Panama, Peru, Surinam and Trinidad and Tobago. Including Cuba, Belize and Guyana, half of these are Caribbean and mainly mini-states. At the same time eight countries attended as observers: Antigua and Barbuda, Brazil, Costa Rica, Dominica, El Salvador, Mexico, Uruguay and Venezuela.

This 'holding back' from full commitment to the Non-Aligned Movement is indicative of several regional concerns, none of which is easy to quantify. For example, there is a certain sense of apartness from the broad stream of Third World opinion; a desire not to offend the USA; the fact that some countries, such as Chile or Paraguay, have not been candidates for the movement under their dictators. The issue of Non-Alignment highlights a certain ambivalence in the position of the major countries of the region. In development terms, Argentina and Brazil are halfway between the majority of the Third World and the advanced North. This middle position is often reflected in their approaches to international politics.

The Church, violence and Big Power intervention

Ever since independence, the region has had a history of violence between the forces of right and left or wealth and poverty. There have been many dictatorships, revolutions, military takeovers and coups.

The present era is characterized by some of the less pleasant aspects of this violence. In Brazil big business interests, whether mining or ranching, have adopted policies which have decimated the American Indians, driving them ruthlessly from their habitats and on some occasions pursuing virtually genocidal tactics.

During the 1970s in Argentina, guerrilla groups such as the Montoneros or People's Revolutionary Army (ERP) opposed the right-wing military régime, which produced death squads in reaction to them. When President Raúl Alfonsín came to power in 1983, it was claimed that at least 10,000 people had either been murdered by these squads or simply made to disappear.

By 1988 Nicaragua had been in a state of war for years following the ousting in 1979 of the long-standing, brutal dictatorship of President Somoza. The subsequent left wing Sandinista government was opposed by a right wing counter-revolution of Contras who were heavily and openly backed by the US government on the grounds that it did not wish to see a left wing government of the Cuban kind in Central America. By April 1986 President Reagan had run into trouble with Congress which had twice (using different tactics) managed to prevent him supplying the Contras with aid to the tune of $100 million. President Reagan made plain his determination to try again and obtained congressional approval for his $100 million aid in August 1986. By mid-1987 the Iran–Contra arms scandal, under investigation by a House of Representatives committee, was inflicting great damage upon the credibility of the Reagan administration.

In the meantime the Contadora group of moderate states – Mexico, Venezuela, Colombia and Panama – tried to mediate between the Sandinista and the US governments in the hope of preventing a situation of the Vietnam type developing in Central America. In April 1986 the Contadora group announced that the USA had agreed to stop backing the Contras if the Sandinista government signed a Central American peace accord which the group had proposed. This came to nothing, but a ceasefire was agreed in 1988. Then, after lengthy negotiations, elections were held on 25 February 1990, when the Sandinista government was voted out of office to be replaced by a 14-party coalition, the National Opposition Union, and a woman, Violeta Barrios de Chamorro, became president. During the early 1990s it appeared that Nicaragua might at last enjoy a period of democracy without constant civil war although the peace was a fragile one. By mid-1993, however, Chamorro was relying upon the Sandinistas for her political survival – they remained the biggest political party – and as the American Elliott Abrams, who had been a major supporter of the Contras under President Bush, said in September 1993: 'The Sandinistas more or less won, like in Vietnam. What was not decided in the war or in the elections must be decided now.' He said this at a time when thousands of men on both sides of the divide were taking up arms again and a renewal of civil war seemed inevitable.

In Costa Rica the newly elected president, Oscar Arias Sánchez, said in April 1986, prior to his 8 May inauguration, that he would stop the US-backed Contras using Costa Rica as a base for their operations against the government of Nicaragua. The majority of the Contras – between 10,000 and 12,000 – operated from Honduras and, according to most impartial estimates, were so undisciplined and badly trained that they were unlikely to achieve anything without American aid.

In El Salvador, a brutal civil war continued throughout the 1980s with the Christian Democrat (centre) government fighting left wing guerrillas. However, after 12 years of war a peace accord was finally signed between the government and the rebels – the Farabundo Martí National Liberation Front (FMLN) – on 16 January 1992. By then the civil war had cost 80,000 lives, displaced 1 million of the population and caused about $1 billion worth of damage to the country's infrastructure.

In Guatemala a right wing government is opposed by left wing guerrillas. A constant problem in attempting to assess such situations is the easy trap of equating everything with 'left wing' or 'right wing'. More accurately one should talk of vested autocratic or oligarchical interests on the one hand, and the urban poor or rural peasants on the other. These confrontations go back to the days following independence. During the 1970s and 1980s they took on inevitable Cold War overtones and the equation of peasant guerrilla movements with Soviet or Cuban-backed Communism.

In Chile the brutal dictatorship of Pinochet was constantly challenged through the 1980s; at the end of the decade he allowed a return to democracy. In elections of March 1990 Patricio Aylwin Azocar became the president at the head of a coalition government. Pinochet retained control of the army, a position that was written into the constitution.

In Argentina a popular reversal replaced the generals who were responsible for the Falklands War with a democratic régime under Alfonsín. Only in Paraguay did dictatorship seem absolutely secure. There President Stroessner (born 1912) had ruled unchallenged since 1954. But on 3 February 1989 General Andrés Rodríguez led a military coup to overthrow Stroessner's régime and return the country to democracy. Stroessner went into exile.

These many ingredients of violence pose exceptionally dangerous problems into the foreseeable future. Throughout the Cold War years there was the possibility, recognized both inside and outside

the USA, that a US government might embark upon a policy that would draw the country into another open-ended Vietnam situation and in the spring of 1986, for example, Nicaragua appeared the most likely candidate for this unwelcome role. The end of the Cold War in 1989 removed the likelihood of an American intervention for ideological reasons of the kind that had dominated its ·Latin American policies over the previous three decades but not the possibility of intervention for other 'policing' reasons and, in fact, a US intervention did take place at the very end of the 1980s in Panama.

Panama 1989

General Manuel Noriega came to power in Panama in 1981 and had for some time been on the CIA payroll. By 1984, however, he began to play off the CIA and the drug traffickers (who routed supplies to North America through Panama) against one another. On 5 February 1988, Noriega was indicted on drug trafficking charges in the USA and on 26 February the Panamanian National Assembly appointed Manuel Solis Palma as President in place of Eric Delvalle, who had been ousted after trying to dismiss Noriega who controlled the powerful Panama Defence Force. On 15 March 1988, after violent confrontations between police and anti-Noriega demonstrators, President Reagan called on Noriega to step down; following an abortive uprising, Panama declared a state of emergency.

The presidential elections of 7 May 1989 were nullified by the government (effectively controlled by Noriega) which declared its candidate, Carlos Duque, the winner although the opposition and independent observers insisted that Guillermo Endara was the winner. Then the new US President, George Bush, also called on Noriega to step down. On 3 November 1989, the US Justice Department ruled that the US military had the right to arrest wanted criminals in foreign countries. On 15 December the Panama Assembly named Noriega head of government and 'maximum leader' and declared a state of war with the USA. Anti-American violence escalated and on 20 December 1989 the USA invaded Panama with 14,000 troops (in addition to the 12,700 already stationed in the Panama Canal Zone). A government headed by Endara was sworn in by a judge at the US military base. Fighting did great damage to

Panama City and lasted for several days. Noriega took refuge in the Vatican Nunciature which was besieged by US troops over Christmas, but two weeks after the invasion Noriega surrendered and was flown to Miami to stand trial for his alleged drug-trafficking offences. Whatever Noriega's crimes, the story is one of blatant big power policing with scant regard for international law.

Poverty and inequality

The fundamental problem concerns poverty and inequality, the classic ingredients of revolution. Latin American critics of US intervention argue that the answer to revolutionary situations must be to tackle the root problem of poverty. If the USA were to use some of its awesome wealth to assist these troubled economies to break out of their circles of poverty, much of the current militarism and left–right violence might then fall away.

Central American conflicts focus attention upon three immensely powerful ideas: North American capitalism; the Roman Catholic faith; and Marxism (though the extent to which the end of the Cold War will now discredit this third idea remains to be seen). Because of overwhelming American economic and political power in the region, the desire for revolutionary change has sometimes been tempered by restraint for fear of the alternative of American intervention. Since 1945 the USA has intervened (not necessarily successfully) in Guatemala (1954), Cuba (1961 and 1962, at the time of the missile crisis and US–USSR confrontation), the Dominican Republic (1965–66), Nicaragua in support of the Contras (1985–87) and in Panama (1989).

The fact that over 90 per cent of the people of these countries are Roman Catholics gives the Church enormous influence. But the Church has often been seen to support the status quo rather than changes which would benefit the masses. In recent years this has presented it with a major challenge as its role has been queried, at least tacitly, by its traditional supporters.

The cycle follows a predictable pattern: a ruthless government, representative only of entrenched minority interests, is challenged by rebellion which may develop into a war or, more likely, will take the form of a guerrilla movement harassing the government. The Church denounces violence and so is seen to support the government and the status quo. One result of this historic situation has

been the emergence of liberation theology, which has taken its intellectual approach from Marxism while retaining emotional ties with the Roman Catholic faith.

After a century and a half of class warfare in which, too often, the Church has been identified with the ruling classes, a religious 'revolt' has occurred. Its two principal components are worker priests and liberation theology. Together they have exercised immense appeal on a predominantly Roman Catholic continent. In 1984 the Vatican made investigations and then the Sacred Congregation for the Doctrine of the Faith repudiated errors which it claimed were emerging from liberation theology in Latin America. But in 1986, reacting to the growing crisis in Central America, the Vatican produced a more positive approach which in part at least recognized the legitimacy of the class struggle.

These problems of violence will not be solved by military intervention or repression. What is required is an attack upon their root cause and in almost every case that is poverty.

The debt problem

Most countries of the Third World are in debt to the North, but Latin America leads the rest in this respect, although through the 1980s Africa – if on a smaller scale – became commensurately more indebted, given the size of its economies. By 1982 Latin American debts had become so large that there was a distinct possibility of a South American default. This would have sparked off a major banking crisis. At that time the US banking system had become overexposed to Latin American debts.

At the end of 1983, seven Latin American countries between them – Argentina, Brazil, Chile, Colombia, Mexico, Peru and Venezuela – owed $300 billion in external debts. Interest payments for these seven came to 40 per cent of export earnings; with capital repayments after rescheduling operations that figure rose to 60 per cent of all foreign earnings.

In one sense it may be argued that the size of a country's debts indicates the extent of its collateral and capacity to repay. This is the reason why Brazil, Mexico and Argentina (the three largest debtor nations) have managed to run up such enormous debts. Yet beyond a certain point such a comforting argument becomes meaningless, because the debts turn into a crippling burden

Latin American debts by country 1991

Country	$ billion
Argentina	63
Bolivia	4
Brazil	116
Chile	17
Colombia	17
Costa Rica	4
Dominican Republic	4
Ecuador	12
Mexico	101
Nicaragua	10
Panama	6
Peru	20
Uruguay	4
Venezuela	34
	$412 billion

Note: Figures have been rounded downwards to the nearest billion.

The World's Principal Debtor Nations

Countries paying in excess of 20% foreign exchange earnings to service debts.

Latin America

Argentina (48.4%)	Honduras (30.6%)
Bolivia (34.0%)	Jamaica (29.4%)
Brazil (30.0%)	Nicaragua
Chile (33.9%)	(109.3%)
Colombia (35.2%)	Peru (27.7%)
Ecuador (32.2%)	Uruguay (38.2%)

Africa

Algeria (73.7%)	Malawi (25.0%)
Burundi (31.5%)	Morocco (27.8%)
Congo (25.3%)	Niger (50.4%)
Côte d'Ivoire	Nigeria (25.2%)
(43.4%)	Tanzania (24.6%)
Ghana (26.9%)	Tunisia (22.7%)
Kenya (32.7%)	Uganda (70.0%)
Madagascar	Zambia (50.3%)
(32.0%)	Zimbabwe (27.2%)

Asia

India (30.7%)	PapuaNew
Indonesia (32.7%)	Guinea (29.6%)
Jordan (20.9%)	Philippines (23.2%)
Pakistan (21.1%)	Turkey (30.5%)

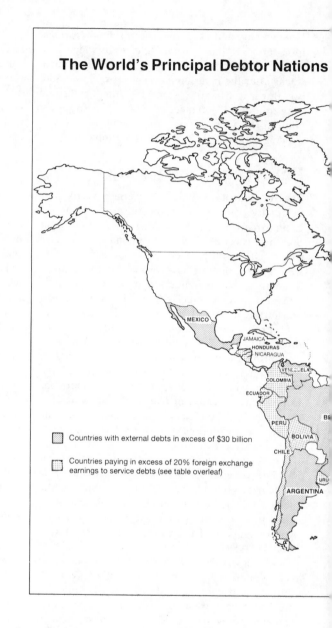

The World's Principal Debtor Nations

☐ Countries with external debts in excess of $30 billion

▦ Countries paying in excess of 20% foreign exchange earnings to service debts (see table overleaf)

whose servicing affects every other aspect of economic development and retards growth. Thus a 1 per cent increase in American interest rates costs Latin American countries an additional $1 billion in servicing charges. For the balance of the 1980s the most indebted countries of Latin America paid – on average – one third of their foreign exchange earnings in servicing debts.

When debtor nations borrow money and use it only to pay interest on their previous borrowings – as is the case for certain Latin American (and other) borrowers – then the debts have become unmanageable. In 1984, for example, Latin American debtors paid out $20 billion more in servicing than came into the region in the form of new development loans. This is a nonsensical position for so-called developing nations.

In 1986, the fourth year of its austerity programme, Mexico projected a growth rate of 4 per cent; meanwhile between 1981 and 1983 it had cut back imports from its principal creditor, the USA, by $33.2 billion. There is a sort of equation when

governments, such as the new Alfonsín govern-ment in Argentina (which came into office in 1983), risk collapse if in order to repay their debts they are obliged to offer their people more austerity than they can be expected politically to bear; then the time has come for the creditors to reschedule, since not to do so is to put the entire debt at risk. Thus, late in 1984, the International Monetary Fund (IMF) rescheduled Argentina's debts. It allowed Argentina to defer the repayment of $13 billion which was due by the end of 1985 and provided a standby credit of $1.4 billion. As a result of this exercise, Argentina was at once able to raise fresh loans to the value of $4.2 billion. Similarly in 1984 the economic positions of both Brazil and Mexico improved after they had agreed IMF reform packages. But a more or less endless process of rescheduling goes on. As a percentage of export earnings, debt servicing for Latin America increased from 13 per cent in 1970, to 33.3 per cent in 1980, 39.6 per cent in 1981 and 53.2 per cent in 1982 when the debt crisis almost got out of hand.

The overall picture had not greatly changed by 1991 when five Latin American countries had debts in excess of $20 billion: Argentina, Brazil, Mexico, Peru and Venezuela.

The question of debt was to dominate the economies of Latin America through the 1980s. 1983 was a crucial year for debt problems when 15 arrangements were made with the IMF, while 47 per cent of regional exports went to service debts. Debt service ratios in 1983 were Argentina (58.5 per cent), Mexico (56.7 per cent), Brazil (52.8 per cent) and Bolivia (50.0 per cent). Colombia, Ecuador, Peru, Uruguay and Venezuela were between 20 and 50 per cent with Panama at a low of 6.8 per cent. By the end of 1984 the regional debt figure had risen to $360 billion.

On 24 June 1984, a group of 11 nations met at Cartagena, Colombia, to discuss debt problems. The meeting consisted of foreign and finance ministers of the following countries: Argentina, Bolivia, Brazil, Colombia, Chile, Ecuador, Mexico, Peru, Dominican Republic, Uruguay and Venezuela. Their object was to resolve the debt problem. Between them the 11 accounted for 94 per cent of the region's debts at the end of 1984. At the first meeting Argentina floated the idea of unilateral action to cut back on debt repayments but this was blocked. Another meeting of the group took place later in the year (September) at Mar del Plata in Argentina which led to calls for direct talks with the principal western creditor nations and for more lending by the IMF and the World Bank. The group reviewed its relationship with the banking North with caution but the problem remained. The Latin American region suffers from high inflation and a low total share of world trade.

During 1987 Brazil, whose debts had reached $110 billion, tried contradictory policies: it suspended interest payments; then, later in the year, adopted an austerity programme indistinguishable from an IMF package. Then it floated the idea of turning debts to banks into risk equity (or bonds) to be taken up by private companies since there seemed little prospect that banks would be able to get their money back and turning debts into bonds became one feature of the attack upon the debt problem.

Although there was a slight easing of the debt situation for the two largest debtors – Brazil and Mexico – at the beginning of the 1990s, this represented only relative relief. Thus in 1989 Mexico secured a rescheduling of $54 billion worth of debts for the period 1989-92. Brazil's fortunes also improved marginally at this time. In January 1992 Brazil obtained an IMF standby loan of $2.1 billion; in February the Paris Club agreed a rescheduling operation and this – for $44 billion of bank debts – had been approved by the Club at the end of the year.

Total Latin American (but not Caribbean) debts in 1991 stood at $429,792 billion.

The Caribbean

The Caribbean, the world's most concentrated area of mini-states, has an entirely colonial history. In the seventeenth and eighteenth centuries, the European colonial powers – Britain, France and the Netherlands – struggled for mastery in the area largely at the expense of the declining Spanish Empire. In most cases, except for Cuba and the Dominican Republic, they ousted the Spanish although some islands changed hands half a dozen times or more. In cultural and political terms the Caribbean includes the four mainland enclaves: British Honduras (now Belize) in Central America, and Guyana (formerly British), Surinam (formerly Dutch) and French Guiana on the South American mainland. In the final division of spoils, the United States also became involved.

By world standards, most Caribbean nations are minute in size, population and resources. All are characterized by poverty. A history of colonialism, slavery and sugar is common throughout the region, while today these mini-economies are still chiefly dependent upon sugar, bananas, certain spices and tourism. In terms of economic development one or two stand out from the rest. Trinidad, the most notable exception, is blessed with more varied resources, including oil and its asphalt lake.

In 1945 only Cuba, the Dominican Republic and Haiti were independent. Cuba had become independent in 1898 following a war between the USA and the colonial power, Spain, and though Cuba achieved nominal independence, the USA reserved the right to intervene. This 'right' was only relinquished under President Franklin D. Roosevelt in 1934. The Americans established a huge military base at Guantánamo which has been retained to the present time.

The first Dominican Republic was proclaimed in 1809 but at the Treaty of Paris in 1814 the territory was returned to Spain by the victorious allies. A

The West Indies: Independence

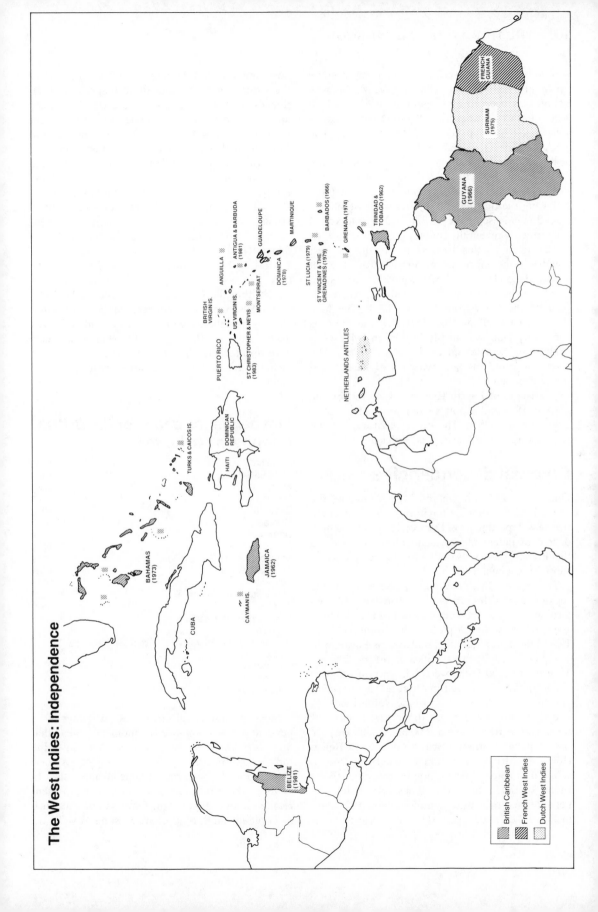

FRENCH GUIANA

SURINAM (1975)

GUYANA (1966)

TRINIDAD & TOBAGO (1962)

GRENADA (1974)

BARBADOS (1966)

ST VINCENT & THE GRENADINES (1979)

ST LUCIA (1979)

MARTINIQUE

DOMINICA (1978)

GUADELOUPE

ANTIGUA & BARBUDA (1981)

ANGUILLA

MONTSERRAT

ST CHRISTOPHER & NEVIS (1983)

US VIRGIN IS.

BRITISH VIRGIN IS.

PUERTO RICO

NETHERLANDS ANTILLES

DOMINICAN REPUBLIC

HAITI

TURKS & CAICOS IS.

BAHAMAS (1973)

JAMAICA (1962)

CAYMAN IS.

CUBA

BELIZE (1981)

British Caribbean
French West Indies
Dutch West Indies

second republic was proclaimed and recognized by Spain in 1821 but, the following year, the new nation was overrun by neighbouring Haiti which held it until 1844 when Juan Pablo Duarte successfully made it independent of its neighbour. The USA occupied the country in 1916 at a time of political anarchy and its forces remained until 1924. From 1930 to 1961 it was ruled by the dictator Rafael Leónidas Trujillo Molina. In 1963, following the ousting of Trujillo's socialist successor, Juan Bosch, the USA again intervened militarily to prevent the country going Communist.

The third of this trio, Haiti, is the poorest country in the entire region. French from 1697, it won independence in 1804 following the slave revolt led by Toussaint l'Ouverture. It was occupied by the USA from 1915 to 1934. The long régime first of 'Papa Doc' Duvalier and then his son 'Baby Doc' was finally broken in 1986 when 'Baby Doc' was forced to flee the country. The economic problems and extremes of wealth and poverty remain.

The island of Puerto Rico was acquired by the USA in 1898 and is now a Commonwealth associated with the USA. The other territories of the region were all colonial dependencies in 1945.

Colonial dependencies

Guadeloupe, Martinique and French Guiana, the three French colonial territories, have become overseas departments of France. They enjoy a high degree of independence, send representatives to the French Assembly and are the recipients of substantial annual French aid.

The main Dutch colonial possession in the region was Dutch Guiana. The British established a colony there in 1650 but ceded it to the Dutch in 1667. It was declared part of the Netherlands in 1954, but gained full independence as Surinam in 1975. The Netherlands Antilles lie off the coast of Venezuela towards the west. The largest island is Curaçao. They have full internal self-government and are part of the Kingdom of the Netherlands.

Britain, which had by far the largest number of territories scattered over a 2000 mile (3200 km) arc from Guyana (formerly British Guiana) to Belize (formerly British Honduras), tried to find a solution to colonial devolution by creating a West Indian Federation in the 1950s. After lengthy negotiations this was established in 1958 and included the three biggest island territories: Barba-

dos, Jamaica, and Trinidad and Tobago. Part of the strategy was to make these bigger and wealthier islands bear the cost for the tiny Windward and Leeward Islands. The Federation was inaugurated in 1958 and became fully independent in 1962 but by then it was already disintegrating. First Jamaica and then Trinidad opted out, demanding full independence on their own. As a result the rump Federation only lasted until 1966 when Barbados also demanded its independence. British Guiana, which had refused to contemplate membership of the Federation, also became independent as Guyana in 1966.

Most of the remaining islands, which at best are only just economically viable, became independent within the Commonwealth during the 1970s and 1980s. British Honduras, claimed ever since 1821 by neighbouring Guatemala, finally achieved inependence as Belize in 1981 when Guatemala gave up its claims in return for guarantees which included access through the territory to the Caribbean.

Independence dates for the British Caribbean territories

Jamaica	1962
Trinidad & Tobago	1962
Barbados	1966
Guyana	1966
Bahamas	1973
Grenada	1974
Dominica	1978
St Lucia	1979
St Vincent & the Grenadines	1979
Antigua & Barbuda	1981
Belize	1981
St Christopher & Nevis	1983

British colonies in 1993
Anguilla
Bermuda (in the Atlantic, not part of the Caribbean)
British Virgin Is.
Cayman Is.
Montserrat
Turks & Caicos Is.

Most of these small territories – whether independent or not – remain so economically weak that they are likely to be aid-dependent into the foreseeable future. They are subject to easy penetration by external financial interests. In many of them the normal rate of unemployment remains above 20 per cent. Only one or two, such as Trinidad and Barbados, are reasonably well off.

The crisis in Grenada (1983)

Grenada covers a mere 133 square miles (344 km^2) and in 1991 had an estimated population of 90,000. It achieved independence within the Commonwealth in 1974. The corrupt government of Sir Eric Gairey was ousted in 1979 by Maurice Bishop and the New Jewel Movement. The new government suspended the constitution and promised elections although these were not held. Bishop was a popular figure and, though a Marxist, allowed Grenada to continue a mixed economy (in reality he had little choice). This depends upon bananas, cocoa, spices (mace and nutmeg) and tourism.

In 1983 a new airport was being constructed at Point Salines with EC and OPEC money and Cuban engineers and labour. The USA regarded the use of Cubans as ominous and saw the new airport as a possible Cuban–Soviet military base. Then an internal power struggle within the New Jewel Movement came to a head and General Hudson Austin carried out a coup and had Bishop and others murdered. In October 1983, following the Austin coup, the USA intervened. The island was invaded by 1900 American and 300 Caribbean troops, the latter from the Organization of Eastern Caribbean States (OECS). (It remains a matter of argument whether a request for intervention was made by the Governor-General Sir Paul Scoon before the intervention took place or after the *fait accompli*.) By December, when the Cubans had been expelled, most of the American troops were withdrawn but 300 US military police and 500 OECS security forces remained on the island. Elections were held in 1984 returning to power the New National Party under the old politician Herbert Blaize.

The crisis in Grenada and the US intervention spotlight some of the problems faced by mini-states: to what extent can they be taken over by thugs within or manipulated from outside? And to whom do they turn in such circumstances? Whatever the rights or wrongs of the Grenada crisis, the American intervention, which was widely welcomed by the OECS and Grenada, was nonetheless in a long tradition of preventing left wing regimes from consolidating their power.

Cuba

Fulgencia Batista Zalvidar, who became dictator of Cuba in 1935, was a corrupt, brutal man whose overthrow by Fidel Castro and his revolutionaries in 1959 was widely welcomed. The Castro régime has managed both social change and moderate economic growth at the same time. But American hostility to the new régime, stemming initially from opposition to Castro's nationalization measures, made it easier (as well as imperative) for the new government to turn to the Soviet Union. When the USA cut off purchases of Cuba's huge sugar crop, the country's basic source of income, the Soviet Union offered an alternative market. This offer, which Castro accepted, emphasized both the switch of political allegiance and Cuba's dependence on its sugar exports.

Under the new government, land was collectivized, business nationalized, and education given a Marxist orientation. A great measure of social equality was achieved at the price of political freedom. But despite its many advances, Cuba remained essentially a one-crop culture, dependent upon the USSR as a secure market for its sugar and for huge aid subventions.

The quarrel with the USA led in 1961 to the abortive Bay of Pigs invasion by CIA-trained refugees who attempted to launch a counter-revolution. Far more dangerous was the missile crisis of 1962. The USSR had begun to build up a missile base in Cuba and the US fleet blockaded the island. The Soviet leader Nikita Khruschev drew back from a direct confrontation with the USA and ordered his fleet to withdraw in mid-Atlantic as it headed for Cuba.

During the remainder of the decade, Cuban policy was to spread revolution to mainland Latin America. Havana encouraged or became involved in revolutionary movements in Guatemala, Venezuela, Colombia, Peru and Bolivia. This phase of policy came to a climax in 1967 with the death of Che Guevara, Cuba's second best known revolutionary, who was executed in Bolivia after his capture while operating with anti-government guerrillas. He became a major cult figure of the Third World.

During the 1970s the emphasis was on change. Cuba achieved some remarkable social advances in education and health. Castro became one of the most enduring Third World leaders, a constant thorn in the side of the USA, whose overt hostility to him was undoubtedly a source of at least part of his appeal. In the mid-1970s Cuba became heavily involved in African politics.

In 1975 Cuba began to provide massive military

support to Aghostino Neto's Popular Movement for the Liberation of Angola (MPLA) after the Portuguese withdrawal when Neto was opposed by rival guerrilla movements, principally the National Union for the Total Independence of Angola (UNITA). These Cuban forces were later to play a vital role helping defend the new government against South African incursions. Cuba also supplied Angola with several thousand technicians, often at quite low levels, because the country had been almost entirely denuded of quite elementary skills when the bulk of the 500,000 Portuguese settlers left at independence. Cuban assistance included medical teams and engineers. The civil war in Angola continued into the 1980s and right through that decade with UNITA receiving support from both South Africa and the USA (through the CIA) and the MPLA government obtaining support from the USSR and Cuba.

By 1987 the number of Cuban troops in Angola had risen to about 50,000; they played a significant role in turning the battle of Cuito Cuanavale in south-eastern Angola (1987-88) against the South African army which had laid siege to the town. Cuito Cuanavale was of vital strategic importance to the government. Then, during 1988 (as part of the USA–USSR détente) an agreement, largely brokered by the USA but with Soviet acquiescence, was forged whereby the following settlement was accepted: that Cuba would withdraw its troops from Angola over a period of 30 months; that all South African forces should be withdrawn from Angola; that South Africa and the USA should cease supporting UNITA; that the African National Congress (ANC) should withdraw its bases from Angola; and that United Nations Resolution 435 bringing Namibia to independence should be implemented. The agreement was carried out over the period 1989–91 and the last of Cuba's forces returned home in May 1991, ending what had been the most effective of Cuba's interventions in other countries.

In 1977 Cuba supplied assistance on a comparable scale to the left wing government of General Mengistu in Ethiopia during that country's war with Somalia. Cuba's military involvement has been a major factor in the politics of southern Africa and the Horn of Africa. In addition, Cuba has provided aid on a much smaller scale (military training or technical assistance) in a number of other African countries, such as Mozambique and Zimbabwe. The efforts made by the USA to persuade Cuba to withdraw its forces from Angola demonstrated both Castro's ability to irritate the world's leading superpower and his capacity, out of proportion to his country's actual strength, to make an impact upon political and military situations far from home.

Why Cuba should make this effort is not easy to pinpoint. Many of its people are of African descent although the link has become fairly remote over the centuries. Castro has always insisted that Cuban aid was in defence of socialist revolutions and in that claim no doubt is a desire to 'cock a snook' at the USA with whom Cuba has had such poor relations. It would, however, be wrong to assume that Cuban interventions in Africa have been solely at the instigation of the (former) USSR.

The strength of Cuban influence has been due to the personality of Castro himself and to the strategic position of Cuba in relation to Latin America where it has been the only Marxist–Communist state. Its influence has been made easier, if not possible, by massive Soviet aid and because of the spread of social services and education to all the population, something that was not contemplated under the preceding régime.

Despite these achievements Cuba remains basically a one-crop economy. Sugar accounts for over 75 per cent of exports and these became over-dependent upon the Soviet market (as Cuba discovered to its cost at the beginning of the 1990s). In 1983, however, sugar and sugar products accounted for 74 per cent of exports and the Soviet Union then took 72 per cent of Cuba's total exports, while a further 10.9 per cent went to the East European countries.

During the 1980s Cuba supplied advisers to the government of Nicaragua. But, after the American intervention in Grenada, it became more muted in its approach to the politics of Central America and in 1990 ended its involvement in Nicaragua.

Although Mikhail Gorbachev visited Cuba in April 1989 he did not exert any pressures to make it pursue a policy of *perestroika* or *glasnost* and in December of that year Castro stated his determination to resist the kind of reforms then sweeping Eastern Europe. Yet, despite his insistence upon Communism and refusal to contemplate reforms, Castro's relations with the rest of Latin America improved through 1990. But, changes in the USSR were to have a major impact upon Cuba, which in 1989 received $3 to $6 billion of aid from Moscow.

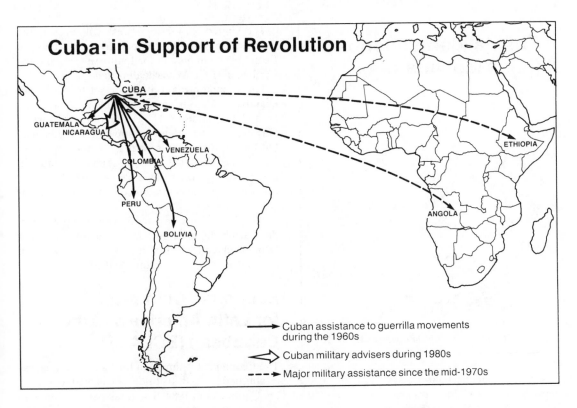

Cuba: in Support of Revolution

CUBA

GUATEMALA
NICARAGUA

VENEZUELA

COLOMBIA

PERU

BOLIVIA

ETHIOPIA

ANGOLA

→ Cuban assistance to guerrilla movements
during the 1960s

⇨ Cuban military advisers during 1980s

---▶ Major military assistance since the mid-1970s

In December 1990 the USSR agreed to continue economic aid and oil exports to Cuba but at reduced rates. During 1991 Cuba entered upon a period of economic stringency and rationing as a direct result of the drastic fall-off in trade with the USSR and Eastern Europe. Then the USSR withdrew 11,000 troops from Cuba and President Gorbachev announced that in future relations would be based solely on political and economic links. In 1992 Cuba's economic position further deteriorated since the break-up of the USSR and Eastern European bloc meant that it no longer had any secure markets. Both exports and imports fell drastically with exports earning approximately $4 billion as opposed to $8 billion in 1989 while imports of oil fell from 13 million metric tonnes (mt) to 6 million metric tonnes as a result of the ending of the Soviet subsidy. The country was subjected to increased rationing and power cuts. Perhaps uniquely of former Soviet allies, Cuba suffered drastic economic cutbacks as a result of the collapse of Communism in the Soviet empire; moreover, in direct proportion as Soviet support disappeared so the USA increased its embargo pressures upon Cuba. By 1993, therefore, Cuba

was making cautious moves to open up part of the economy to limited private investment.

The Falkland Islands

These islands in the South Atlantic off the coast of Argentina were held by Spain from 1770 to 1820 and by the newly independent Argentina from 1820. The British expelled the Argentinian settlers from the islands in 1832 and declared them a colony in 1833. They have been the subject of a dispute between Britain and Argentina for years.

Slow negotiations about the islands took place from 1966 onwards between the two countries but almost no progress was achieved. Then on 2 April 1982, Argentina invaded and occupied the Falkland Islands; its government clearly did not believe that Britain would retaliate with military force. In this it was mistaken. A British military task force reminiscent of World War II steamed across the Atlantic, landed its troops and defeated the Argentinian forces on the Falklands, forcing them to surrender on 14 June 1982. Casualties were 750 Argentinians dead, 255 British and three Falkland Islanders.

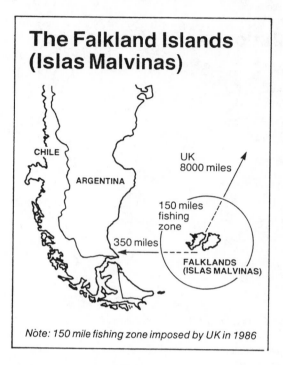

The Falkland Islands (Islas Malvinas)

CHILE

ARGENTINA

UK
8000 miles

150 miles
fishing
zone

350 miles

FALKLANDS
(ISLAS MALVINAS)

Note: 150 mile fishing zone imposed by UK in 1986

The fact that the failure of the war led to the downfall of the Galtieri régime did not alter the general Argentinian enthusiasm for reclaiming what to them are the Islas Malvinas.

Since the end of this little 'colonial' war a British garrison of 4000 men has been maintained on the Falklands at enormous expense. Through the 1980s Argentina refused to declare an end to formal hostilities with Britain and the British government refused to discuss the issue of sovereignty. The two countries finally restored diplomatic relations in 1990 although the issue of the Falklands was unresolved.

Latin American and Caribbean regional organizations

Most Latin American or Caribbean regional organizations are concerned with economic co-operation although some are political. The Organization of American States (OAS) is the major exception, although the Contadora Group of countries which seeks to find a peaceful solution in Central America is also political in intent.

The United Nations operates at all levels in the region as does the World Bank group, but only the Economic Commission for Latin America and the Caribbean (ECLAC) is dealt with here.

The Commonwealth is important to the Caribbean because no fewer than 12 of its 50 members are to be found here. The largest of these in size is Guyana and the largest in population is Jamaica, but by world standards both are small. The other 10 can be classified as mini-states. In addition there are six British dependencies which qualify for Commonwealth assistance and eventual membership.

The European Community is also important in the Caribbean since 13 nations qualify under the Lóme Conventions as members of the ACP group of countries with special links to the EC.

Economic Commission for Latin America and the Caribbean (ECLAC)

The Economic Commission for Latin America was established in 1948. Its title was changed to include the Caribbean in 1984. The total membership is 40 countries. In addition to the countries of Latin America and the Caribbean, Canada, France, Netherlands, Portugal, Spain, UK and USA are also members. These powers are important as aid donors in the region and, apart from Canada, are the former and, in certain cases, continuing colonial powers.

ECLAC is run by a Commission and Secretariat. The Commission normally meets every 2 years in different capitals. The Secretariat has its headquarters in Santiago, Chile. ECLAC's principal role is to assist in the analysis of regional and national economic development problems. It co-operates closely with other UN agencies.

Andean group

Established in 1969 by the Cartagena Agreement, the group aims to assist economic and social integration of its members. The member nations are Bolivia, Colombia, Ecuador, Peru and Venezuela. Chile was a member but withdrew in 1977. The principal organs of the group are the Commission, the Andean Council, the Junta, a Parliament, the Court of Justice, a Reserve Fund, and the Development Corporation.

So far the group has been more of an aspiration than an achievement. The size and spread of the countries belonging to it, and the fact that at different times disputes between members have led to temporary withdrawals or threats to withdraw, have hampered progress. In May 1983 the heads of government of the five member states reaffirmed their commitment to regional integration but it was not until December 1991 that the group, meeting in Cartegena, decided to form a free trade zone from January 1992 with universal external tariffs from 1993.

Caribbean Community and Common Market (CARICOM)

A Caribbean Free Trade Association (CARIFTA), founded in 1965, was replaced by CARICOM in 1973. CARICOM is confined to 12 Commonwealth Caribbean territories and Montserrat (a British dependency). The Dominican Republic, Haiti and Surinam are observers.

The Heads of Government Conference is the final authority of the Community. Under this come the Common Market Council and the Secretariat. There are also a number of institutions concerned with health, education, labour, foreign affairs, finance, agriculture, industry, transport, energy, mines and natural resources, science and technology.

The principal object of CARICOM is economic integration by the creation of a common market. However, the extent of intra-regional trade is both relatively and absolutely very small, ranging between 8 and 14 per cent of the total of member states.

Members of CARICOM failed to meet their deadline of October 1991 to establish a common tariff to be applied to imports from third countries due to conflicts between members. In November 1992, however, they agreed to cut external tariffs from 1993.

Central American Common Market (CACM)

CACM was established in 1960. It has five members: Costa Rica, El Salvador, Guatemala, Honduras and Nicaragua. Its organs are Ministerial Meetings which formulate policy, and a Permanent Secretariat in Guatemala City.

The principal object of CACM is to liberalize trade between members and establish a customs union. Ideological differences between members and the general political turmoil of the region have prevented any obvious advance. In 1984 ministers of member countries agreed a progamme to reactivate CACM which by then had lost most of its momentum. Attempts to revitalize CACM at the beginning of the 1990s met with small success although the group did obtain preferential access to the Venezuelan market.

Inter-American Development Bank (IDB)

Originally known as the IADB, the IDB was the first of the regional development banks to be established. It was set up in 1959 with the object of promoting the development of the developing members of the region. It then included the USA and Canada. Later, during 1976 and 1977, countries from other regions, principally Europe but also Japan, joined so as to widen its financial resource base. Its organs are the Board of Governors, the Board of Executive Directors, and the Administration, under which come eight departments.

The IDB makes loans to governments, public and private bodies for specific development projects. Loans are repayable over periods ranging from 10 to 25 years in the currencies that were loaned. Up to the end of 1984 the Bank had lent $27,772 million. There is a special programme designed to finance small projects. The Bank also provides a certain amount of technical co-operation.

Under the IDB (established in 1964) is the Institute for Latin American Integration.

In 1992 the IDB had a total membership of 44 including non-American members.

Latin American Integration Association (LAIA)

In 1960 a Latin American Free Trade Association (LAFTA) was established although by 1980 it had collapsed. LAIA was formed on the ruins of LAFTA in 1980. It is a deliberately loose, pragmatic association in contrast to its predecessor. Its members are Argentina, Bolivia, Brazil, Chile, Colombia, Ecuador, Mexico, Paraguay, Peru,

Uruguay and Venezuela. Its organs are the Council of Ministers, a Committee of Representatives, an Evaluation and Convergence Conference, and the Secretariat.

Its objects are to establish economic preferences and regional tariff preferences; trade and preferences between members have to take account of the different stages of development of members.

The Treaty of Montevideo which created the LAIA envisages outward agreement between member states and non-members. This piecemeal, pragmatic approach is a recognition of the great differences in size and stage of development of the members and the impracticability of trying by means of such an association to achieve too much too quickly.

Organization of American States (OAS)

The OAS was founded in 1948 to foster peace, security and understanding among the countries of the region. Its members include the 35 countries of Latin America and the Caribbean, as well as the USA. (Canada which for years was the only major country of the region which did not join the OAS, finally did so at the beginning of the 1990s.) A number of other countries and Vatican City have permanent observer status. The organs of the OAS are a General Assembly, Meetings of Consultation of Ministers of Foreign Affairs, a Permanent Council and the General Secretariat. The headquarters are in Washington DC.

The OAS is a North–South organization and suffers from the fact of US membership in the sense that the other members have always been wary of American domination and so have been reluctant to use the Organization. Nonetheless, the OAS has an antecedent history going back to 1826 when Simón Bolivar called the First Congress of American States which met in Panama City. And in 1947, the Rio Treaty established the Inter-American Treaty of Reciprocal Assistance, a joint security pact for the western hemisphere against attack from outside.

A number of specialized institutions of the OAS deal with education, social affairs, law, energy, and the Pan-American Highway.

The Treaty of Asunción

In March 1991 the presidents of what are known as the Southern Cone countries – Argentina, Brazil, Uruguay and Paraguay – signed the Treaty of Asunción. This is designed to create a common market for the region (Mercosur) by the beginning of 1995. Full integration was scheduled to begin in 1994.

There are many other lesser known regional organizations covering between them a huge number of subjects.

Part 5
The Commonwealth

The Commonwealth is especially important to any consideration of the Third World, because it is one of the few associations of nations which has grown organically rather than having been artificially created to answer a need. It bridges a number of gaps between North and South and provides a pattern for co-operation between rich and poor, powerful and mini-state, while its members embrace most of the world's races, religions, political systems and ideologies, and are to be found on all the world's continents, although at the beginning of the 1990s the emphasis was upon the encouragement of multiparty democracy.

The Commonwealth grew out of the British Empire in two phases. Between 1900 and 1939, the old Dominions – Canada, Australia, New Zealand (and, in this context, South Africa) – determined to achieve equality of status with Britain as independent countries. When Britain declared war on Germany in 1914 it acted on behalf of its entire Empire. In 1919, however, the Dominions signed the Versailles Peace Treaty separately. Then the Balfour Report of 1926 and the Statute of Westminster of 1931 clarified further the international status of the Dominions as independent countries. In consequence, when Britain went to war with Germany for a second time in 1939, the Dominions made their own declarations.

Thus by 1945 the British Empire and Commonwealth contained both colonies and Dominions. That year, however, saw the beginning of the end of empires and the question was soon to arise whether the Commonwealth could change to accommodate the new nations of Asia and Africa. The answer lay with India.

British India (greater India with Burma and Ceylon) became independent over the years 1947-48. The attitude towards the Commonwealth of India and particularly of Nehru proved crucial to the development of the association. India decided to become a republic at a time when each of the Dominions still recognized the British monarch as their own. No mechanism existed to accommodate a republic within the Commonwealth. Ceylon which became independent in 1948 joined the Commonwealth as had Pakistan the previous year, but Burma decided not to do so. The fact that Britain exerted no pressure upon Burma to join was taken as proof of the genuinely voluntary nature of the association. At this time, moreover, Ireland decided to leave the Commonwealth to become a republic.

In April 1949, after India had become a republic, the Commonwealth devised a new formula to enable a republic to become a member of the association, namely, that the British monarch was to become the 'symbol of the free association of its independent member nations and as such Head of the Commonwealth'.

This Indian decision changed the nature of the Commonwealth, which ceased to be a 'club' of the white settler Dominions. Instead it admitted republics from that year onwards. It is, moreover, unlikely that most of the African and other colonies which became independent subsequently would have been so ready to join the Commonwealth – if they had done so at all – had the Republic of India decided against joining. The Indian decision gave the association a world appeal which cut across racial, religious, political and economic barriers.

Explaining his country's decision to join the Commonwealth in 1949, by which time he was already emerging as the leader of what became the Non-Aligned Movement, Nehru said: 'We join the Commonwealth obviously because we think it is beneficial to us and to certain causes in the world that we wish to advance. The other countries of the Commonwealth wish us to remain, because they think it is beneficial to them.'

When the second wave of independence got under way in the 1950s, first Ghana and then Malaya, which both became independent in 1957, joined the Commonwealth. From 1960 onwards the association grew rapidly as the empire was dismantled until by 1985 the Commonwealth numbered 49 independent countries. In 1987,

however, Fiji was suspended following two coups that led to a government which was dominated by ethnic Fijians. In 1989 Pakistan, which had left the Commonwealth in 1972 after Bangladesh had become a member of the association, rejoined. And in 1990 newly independent Namibia joined. The great majority of British colonies on achieving independence elected to become members of the Commonwealth (see Chapter 1 of this book, 'End of Empires').

The Commonwealth in 1993

Country	Population
Antigua & Barbuda	64,000
Australia	17,562,000
Bahamas	264,000
Bangladesh	110,602,000
Barbados	259,000
Belize	196,000
Botswana	1,359,000
Britain	57,561,000
Brunei	268,000
Canada	27,737,000
Cyprus (Greek republic only)	580,000
Dominica	71,500
Fiji (suspended in 1987)	748,000
Gambia, The	921,000
Ghana	15,237,000
Grenada	90,900
Guyana	748,000
India	889,700,000
Jamaica	2,445,000
Kenya	26,985,000
Kiribati	74,700
Lesotho	1,854,000
Malawi	9,484,000
Malaysia	18,630,000
Maldives	230,000
Malta	360,000
Mauritius	1,081,000
Namibia	1,512,000
Nauru	8,000
New Zealand	3,481,000
Nigeria	89,666,000
Pakistan (rejoined in 1989)	130,129,000
Papua New Guinea	3,834,000
St Christopher-Nevis	43,100
St Lucia	135,000
St Vincent & the Grenadines	109,000
Seychelles	71,000
Sierra Leone	4,373,000
Singapore	2,792,000
Solomon Is.	339,000
Sri Lanka	17,464,000
Swaziland	826,000
Tanzania	25,809,000
Tonga	97,300
Trinidad & Tobago	1,261,000
Tuvalu	8,500

The Commonwealth

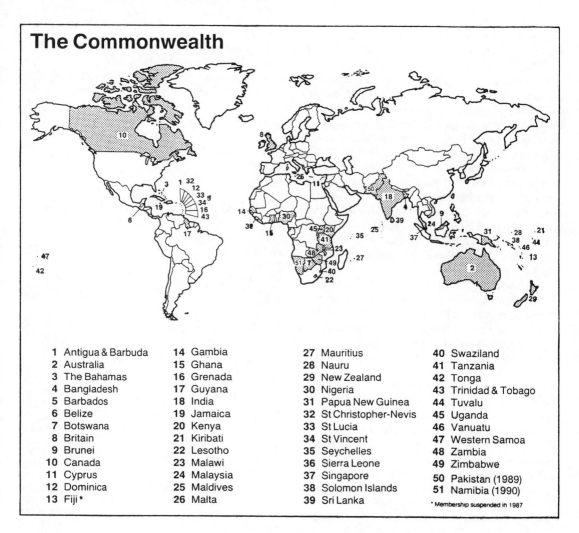

1	Antigua & Barbuda	14 Gambia	27 Mauritius	40 Swaziland

1 Antigua & Barbuda	14 Gambia	27 Mauritius	40 Swaziland
2 Australia	15 Ghana	28 Nauru	41 Tanzania
3 The Bahamas	16 Grenada	29 New Zealand	42 Tonga
4 Bangladesh	17 Guyana	30 Nigeria	43 Trinidad & Tobago
5 Barbados	18 India	31 Papua New Guinea	44 Tuvalu
6 Belize	19 Jamaica	32 St Christopher-Nevis	45 Uganda
7 Botswana	20 Kenya	33 St Lucia	46 Vanuatu
8 Britain	21 Kiribati	34 St Vincent	47 Western Samoa
9 Brunei	22 Lesotho	35 Seychelles	48 Zambia
10 Canada	23 Malawi	36 Sierra Leone	49 Zimbabwe
11 Cyprus	24 Malaysia	37 Singapore	50 Pakistan (1989)
12 Dominica	25 Maldives	38 Solomon Islands	51 Namibia (1990)
13 Fiji*	26 Malta	39 Sri Lanka	* Membership suspended in 1987

Country	Population
Uganda	17,194,000
Vanuatu	154,000
Western Samoa	160,000
Zambia	8,303,000
Zimbabwe	9,871,000
Total	1,503,453,000*

*The total population of the Commonwealth represents slightly more than a quarter of the world total.

What the association offers its 50 widely different members, a majority of whom belong to the Third World, may perhaps be better gauged if the Commonwealth is broken down into the following categories:

1. Four countries belong to the rich advanced economies of the North – Britain, Canada, Australia and New Zealand.

2. Fifteen nations belong to Africa – Botswana, the Gambia, Ghana, Kenya, Lesotho, Malawi, Mauritius, Namibia, Nigeria, Sierra Leone, Swaziland, Tanzania, Uganda, Zambia and Zimbabwe.

3. Eight nations belong to Asia and Oceania – Bangladesh, Brunei, India, Malaysia, Pakistan, Papua New Guinea, Singapore and Sri Lanka.

4. Two members are European mini-states on the borderline between North and South – Cyprus and Malta.

5. Twenty-one nations are mini-states and mainly islands, situated in the Caribbean, the Atlantic, Indian and Pacific Oceans.

The nature of the Commonwealth

The Commonwealth has a minimum of working structures and operates on a basis of consensus, maintaining wherever possible an informal approach to decision-making. Because its members were all former colonies or dependencies of Britain, which remains its most powerful member, the suspicion has persisted that the Commonwealth is little more than an easy 'let-down' from empire for Britain. This is denied by members, though most of the rows within the Commonwealth have fallen into a pattern with Britain supporting a position which the majority have attacked.

In terms of the association's membership and the problems members face and attempt jointly to tackle, the Commonwealth may be seen as a microcosm of those aspects of international relations which divide North and South. There is the great disparity between its rich and poor members so that four – Britain, Canada, Australia and New Zealand – belong to the North and are members of the OECD (Organization for Economic Co-operation and Development) and DAC (Development Assistance Committee) groups of countries. The rest are members of the Third World, nearly all belong to the non-aligned group of nations, and are recipients of aid for their development. Race issues, which have played so important a part in the long process of decolonization, have been central to Commonwealth deliberations, including UDI in Rhodesia, apartheid in South Africa, and the question of Namibia. Most Commonwealth countries are affected by the population explosion in the Third World. This is especially significant as a factor in India, the Asian giant of the association, and Bangladesh, Nigeria and Pakistan, each with populations at the 100 million mark.

The Commonwealth is in an unique position to assist mini-states to find ways to overcome their particular restrictions. Of the 50 Commonwealth members, 24 have populations of under 1 million. Of these five have less than half a million, and 15 less than a quarter of a million. Finally, as with any other group of nations, Commonwealth relations are concerned with power and, because Britain is by far the most powerful member, it is unsurprising that a great deal of effort on the part of the remainder has been directed at influencing its policies. This is normal. It is perhaps particularly

the case in view of Britain's former imperial role. From the point of view of Third World members, a major argument in favour of the Commonwealth association is the fact that it gives them an unique opportunity to influence one of the most powerful countries of the North in areas of particular concern to them.

The value of the Commonwealth must be seen in terms of how it tackles North–South problems and the extent to which it assists in their solutions. There are many Commonwealth organizations, but the key to its achievements is the biennial Commonwealth Heads of Government Meeting at which its leaders confer informally and take decisions which subsequently are put into practice by the Secretariat.

Commonwealth Heads of Government Meetings (CHOGMs)

CHOGMs now take place once every 2 years and may be held in any Commonwealth country. The Commonwealth Secretariat in London prepares the CHOGM agendas, and an examination of the principal topics discussed at those meetings over the years shows the extent to which the association is concerned with two kinds of question: political problems arising out of the end of empire, most notably those with racial overtones, such as Rhodesia and South Africa; and problems of economic development. Meetings have always been kept as informal as possible but, inevitably, as the Commonwealth has expanded a certain structural approach which once did not exist has crept into CHOGMs.

The meetings listed here (not all are included) show a progression in Commonwealth ideas or are notable for the solutions they devised for particular problems.

1944 One of the last old-style meetings attended only by Britain, Australia, Canada, New Zealand and South Africa. Prior to 1939 such meetings were known as Imperial Conferences; now it was called a meeting of the British Empire and Commonwealth of Nations.
1949 A new formula was agreed allowing India to remain in the Commonwealth while the British monarch was recognized as the Head of the Association.
1960 The issue of South Africa's continued membership of the Commonwealth was raised since it persisted in its policy of apartheid.

1961   The meeting insisted upon the principle of racial equality. South Africa which had just voted to become a republic (by referendum among its whites) did not apply to remain in the Commonwealth and so departed.

1965   The meeting agreed to the establishment (in London) of a Commonwealth Secretariat. The meeting was overshadowed by the issue of Rhodesia which five months later (11 November) made its Unilateral Declaration of Independence (UDI).

1966   *January* The first meeting held outside London (Lagos) was devoted to the subject of Rhodesia following UDI the previous November. It was concerned to find ways to end UDI, to implement UN sanctions and safeguard Zambia from any resultant damage (from sanctions).

1966   *September* Back in London this CHOGM was again dominated by Rhodesia and Britain declared NIBMAR (no independence before majority rule).

1969   Still dominated by Rhodesia although an easier atmosphere prevailed as other members, especially those from Africa, felt more assured that Britain did not intend a 'sell out' over Rhodesia.

1971   *Singapore* With the exception of the Lagos meeting which had been specially convened to discuss Rhodesia only, this meeting began the practice of rotating CHOGMs among the Commonwealth countries rather than always holding them in London. The meeting issued the *Declaration of Commonwealth Principles* and established the Commonwealth Fund for Technical Co-operation (CFTC).

1973   *Ottawa* This followed Britain's accession to the EC and provided the first occasion for a CHOGM to assess the impact of its decision upon the rest of the Commonwealth.

1975   *Kingston* A group of Commonwealth experts was appointed to assist progress towards a New International Economic Order (NIEO); aid was offered to Mozambique to assist it to apply sanctions against Rhodesia.

1977   *London* Zimbabwe (where the armed struggle was reaching a climax) featured prominently again in the discussions. *The Gleneagles Agreement* reaffirmed the total opposition to apartheid. An Industrial Development Unit within the CFTC was agreed.

1979   *Lusaka* was dominated by the subject of Rhodesia and a formula was worked out which led to the Lancaster House Conference, the end of UDI and independence for Zimbabwe in 1980.

1981   *Melbourne* For the first time since 1966 it was possible to hold a CHOGM without Rhodesia dominating the proceedings and Melbourne was especially concerned with economic questions.

1983   New Delhi produced two declarations: *The Goa Declaration on International Security* and *The New Delhi Statement on Economic Action*. The subject of South Africa became increasingly prominent.

1985   *Nassau* Dominated by the growing crisis in South Africa the CHOGM produced *The Commonwealth Accord on Southern Africa*.

1986   *London* Mini-summit concerned only with the report of the Eminent Persons Group (EPG) on South Africa (see below).

1987   *Vancouver* was again concerned with South Africa and the other members made clear to Britain that they would adopt joint policies even if Britain refused to join with them in doing so. The issue of Fiji where the object of a successful military coup was to exclude the Indian community from political power was also the subject of deep concern. The new régime in Fiji having proclaimed a republic in the country was – at least for the time being – excluded from the Commonwealth.

1989   *Kuala Lumpur* was principally concerned with South Africa – the CHOGM produced a statement on southern Africa *The Way Ahead* and *The Langkawi Declaration* on the environment. Pakistan, having rejoined the Commonwealth, took part in this summit. The Nigerian, Chief Emeka Anyaoku, was elected third Commonwealth Secretary-General.

1991   *Harare* Agreed a three-stage lifting of sanctions against South Africa as that country moved away from apartheid. *The Harare Declaration* was concerned with Commonwealth principles. The CHOGM welcomed as its fiftieth member Namibia (which had become independent in 1990) but shelved the application of Cameroon to join the association.

Over the years the CHOGMs have produced a number of declarations which, as the product of consensus from a growing number of members, have their limitations. Yet they also, clearly, establish the thrust of the Commonwealth approach to the world's major problems. These Declarations are as follows:

1. *The Declaration of Commonwealth Principles (Singapore 1971)* Emphasizing the wide membership of the association and its voluntary nature, the Declaration sets out six principles as follows:

    A. We believe that international peace and order are essential to the security and prosperity of mankind.

    B. We believe in the liberty of the individual.

    C. We recognize racial prejudice as a dangerous sickness.

    D. We oppose all forms of colonial domination and racial oppression.

    E. We believe that the wide disparities in wealth now existing between different sections of mankind are too great to be tolerated.

    F. We believe that international co-operation is essential.

2. *The Gleneagles Agreement on Sporting Contacts with South Africa (1977)*

This agreement accepted that it was the urgent duty of member governments to take every practical step to prevent sporting contacts with South Africa.

3. *The Lusaka Declaration on Racism and Racial Prejudice (1979)*
(Since the setting was Lusaka and the principal topic of discussion Rhodesia, while the problem of South Africa loomed large, it is understandable and fitting that this CHOGM produced such a declaration.) It sets out a series of principles opposed to racism in all its forms.

4. *The Melbourne Declaration (1981)*
(Perhaps in reaction to the subject of Rhodesia and race, the Melbourne Declaration is concerned with the widening economic gap between North and South.) It calls for greater dialogue to solve the problems of poverty.

5. *The Goa Declaration on International Security (1983)*
Reflecting India's pre-eminent position in the history of Non-Alignment, the Goa Declaration is a call for dialogue between the superpowers so as to relax world tensions.

6. *The New Delhi Statement on Economic Action (1983)*
A second statement of principles to emerge from the New Delhi CHOGM was concerned with the continuing economic crisis especially as it affected the Third World. It called for a comprehensive review of the international monetary, financial and relevant trade issues.

7. *The Nassau Declaration on World Order (1985)*
On the occasion of the 40th anniversary of the founding of the United Nations, it is a Commonwealth assertion of support for the world body.

8. *The Okanagan Statement and Programme of Action on Southern Africa (1987)*
This sets out immediate Commonwealth objectives and proposals designed to put pressure on South Africa and provide assistance to the border countries of SADCC.

Note: By 1985 the practice appeared to have become normal for each CHOGM to issue its own Declaration.

Commonwealth structure

Apart from the biennial CHOGMs, which provide the main decision-making instrument of the association, there are various regular Ministerial Meetings as well as the on-going work of the Commonwealth Secretariat with its headquarters in London.

Apart from the 50 member states in 1993, the dependent territories of Britain, Australia and New Zealand also benefit from Commonwealth activities. They are free to apply for membership on achieving independence and it is generally assumed they will do so. There are also special cases – countries which may join the Commonwealth at a future date – of which South Africa is the obvious remaining example.

Namibia (as the former German South West Africa) became a mandate of the League of Nations at the end of World War I and as such was mandated to George V who delegated the responsibility to the then Union of South Africa so that, technically, the British monarch retained a responsibility for Namibia. At the 1975 Kingston CHOGM, Namibia was invited to join the Commonwealth on achieving independence and did so in March 1990.

Pakistan was a member of the Commonwealth from its independence in 1947. In 1972, following the war in which East Pakistan broke away from West Pakistan to form Bangladesh (which joined the Commonwealth), Pakistan left the Commonwealth. The hope was expressed at the time that Pakistan would rejoin the Commonwealth at a later date and it did so in 1989.

South Africa left the Commonwealth in 1961. When majority rule is achieved in that country, the new South Africa would certainly be welcomed back into the Commonwealth should it wish to rejoin it, especially as the Commonwealth has played a leading role in trying to bring an end to apartheid. Moreover, most of the African nations active in promoting change in South Africa are also in the Commonwealth. By 1993 this likelihood appeared to be appreciably closer.

Commonwealth ministers of finance meet once a year (reflecting the importance of economic questions and the aid mechanisms of the association) and ministers of education, health and law meet once every 3 years. Other ministers meet as necessary.

A new Commonwealth role to promote democracy among its members developed in the early

1990s, following the 1991 Harare summit; a number of governments requested Commonwealth help in monitoring their electoral process as they changed from one-party to multi-party or from military to civilian rule. Countries seeking such monitoring have included Seychelles, Guyana, Ghana, Lesotho and Kenya.

The Commonwealth Secretariat

This was established by a decision of the 1965 CHOGM and was provided with headquarters in London (Marlborough House) by the British government. The Secretariat's basic task is to organize consultations between the members of the Commonwealth and run the various programmes of co-operation. The Secretariat comes under the control of the CHOGMs and other ministerial meetings. The Secretary-General and two deputy secretaries-general are elected by the CHOGM, while the Secretary-General is responsible for the rest of the Secretariat appointments. There are approximately 350 staff drawn from the countries of the Commonwealth. It is a policy for Commonwealth countries to release senior staff to serve for a few years with the Secretariat so as to learn about the Commonwealth at first hand. The first Secretary-General was Arnold Smith of Canada (1965–75); the second was Shridath Ramphal of Guyana (1975–89); and he was succeeded by Emeka Anyaoku of Nigeria (1989–). The Secretariat has three divisions: the International Affairs Division; the Legal Division; and the Information Division.

The Commonwealth Fund for Technical Co-operation (CFTC)

The CFTC provides experts, finances training and offers consultancy services in a variety of fields. It is financed by voluntary subscriptions from all member governments. There are three groups under the CFTC: the General Technical Assistance Division; the Technical Assistance Group (TAG); and the Industrial Development Unit.

In 1983 the Human Resource Development Group was formed to act as an umbrella to six existing Commonwealth programmes, namely the Education Programme; the Fellowships and Training Programme; the Management Development Programme; the Medical Programme; the Women

THE COMMONWEALTH SECRETARIAT

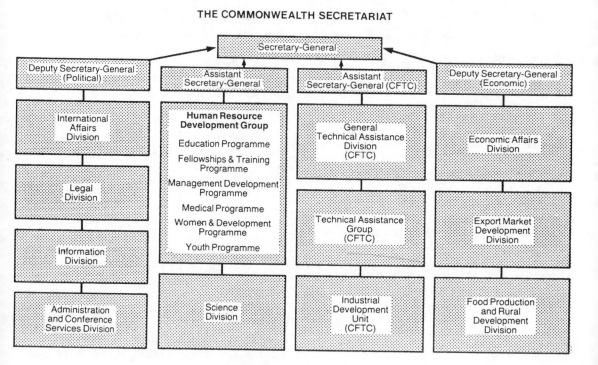

and Development Programme; and the Commonwealth Youth Programme.

Other divisions of the Secretariat are the Science Division, the Economic Affairs Division, the Export Market Development Division, and the Food Production and Rural Development Division.

Commonwealth crises

Over the years three questions have provoked Commonwealth crises and potentially disastrous splits in the membership. They are of great significance because each arose directly out of the end of empire and, in two of the three cases, the problem was about race. The three crises concern Suez in 1956, South Africa and Rhodesia. In each case Britain was to be found on one side (sometimes supported by the old Dominions), with the members of the new Commonwealth on the other side, creating a North–South confrontation. These crises are important not least because they show how the Commonwealth, which straddles the North–South divide, has been used with increasing skill by its 'south' members to bring pressures to bear upon Britain to persuade it to modify and then change its policies.

Suez 1956

The Suez crisis is dealt with elsewhere in this book and may be regarded as the last major attempt by the old colonial powers (Britain and France) to discipline a weak Third World nation by gunboat diplomacy. When the Suez War of 1956 took place the Commonwealth consisted of eight members: Britain, Australia, Canada, New Zealand, South Africa, India, Pakistan and Ceylon (Sri Lanka). Britain presented its Suez intervention as (among other things) a means of safeguarding the lifeline route of the Canal to the Far East. Australia, New Zealand and South Africa supported Britain. But the new Commonwealth countries – India, Pakistan and Ceylon – saw themselves as part of the Third World and considered the British action as a return to imperial behaviour. They, therefore, supported Nasser and the danger arose that the Commonwealth would split along North–South lines (though the terms North and South were not then in use) or even more dangerously along racial lines with Britain and the old 'white' Dominions set against the new Asian members. This danger,

however, was averted by Canada whose prime minister, Louis St Laurent, and his external affairs minister, Lester Pearson, refused to endorse British action. By its stand Canada saved the Commonwealth from a clear-cut split. The Canadian position at this time was of great significance to the future of the Commonwealth, to the idea that the association represented a genuinely new departure and was not a disguised version of empire expected to fall into line behind Britain.

South Africa

Once the Commonwealth began to grow in size with the addition of its first Asian and later African members, it was inevitable that South Africa's policy of apartheid would, sooner or later, come under attack. The Nationalists under Daniel Malan came to power in 1948 and began at once to formalize racial separation by law, while the word *apartheid* came into international usage to describe that policy. At the beginning of 1960 the membership of the Commonwealth had increased by two countries, Ghana and Malaya, which created a five-five balance between Britain and the old Dominions on the one hand and the new Third World members on the other. 1960 was the year of Sharpeville which focused world attention upon the inequities of the apartheid system. The subject of South Africa's race policies was raised at that year's Commonwealth Conference though it was diplomatically shelved. But everyone knew this to be no more than a temporary respite for South Africa's prime minister Hendrik Verwoerd. In October 1960 Nigeria became independent and joined the Commonwealth.

Prior to the Commonwealth Conference of 1961 two events occurred which had a precise bearing upon what was to come. White South Africans voted in a referendum to turn the Union of South Africa into a republic. Since it was already the Commonwealth convention (arising out of India's decision to become a republic in 1949) that a member which changed its status had to seek readmision to the Commonwealth, South Africa would require Commonwealth approval to remain in the association. Second, Julius Nyerere, then the premier of Tanganyika which was due to become independent in December 1961, wrote an important article which appeared in the London *Observer*. His basic argument was that should South Africa remain a member of the

Commonwealth while retaining its apartheid policy, Tanganyika would find it difficult to join the association on independence.

When the Commonwealth heads of government met in London it was not an African, but Tunku Abdul Rahman, the prime minister of Malaya, who led the attack upon apartheid. As at the time of Suez, the Commonwealth divided. Britain, Australia and New Zealand supported South Africa's continuing membership, but they were opposed by India, Pakistan, Ceylon, Ghana, Malaya and Nigeria. For the second time on a fundamental issue, Canada sided with the Third World members of the Commonwealth and so again prevented a straight North–South divide. In the event South Africa did not seek readmission to the Commonwealth as a republic. It thus saved face and was not actually expelled.

Throughout the period of UDI in Rhodesia (1965-80), that subject took precedence in Commonwealth deliberations, but the problem of South Africa was always lurking in the background, a menacing issue that would have to be faced again. Major events are listed below:

1966 The beginning of the armed struggle in Namibia by the South West African People's Organization (SWAPO) against the forces of South Africa. The UN terminates South African Trusteeship of South West Africa (Namibia).

1970 The Lusaka Non-Aligned Summit adopts the *Lusaka Declaration* denouncing South Africa's subversion of neighbouring countries.

1971 At the Singapore Commonwealth Conference, the new British prime minister, Edward Heath, and his foreign secretary, Sir Alec Douglas-Home, have a confrontation with the African members over the announced British intention of resuming the sale of arms to South Africa (terminated under the previous administration of Harold Wilson).

1974 The UN Institute for Namibia is established in Lusaka.

1975 At the Kingston CHOGM Namibia is invited to join the Commonwealth on achieving its independence.

1977 The Gleneagles Agreement against sporting contacts with South Africa. The Commonwealth Sanctions Committee becomes the Committee on Southern Africa.

1979 SADCC is formed: of its nine members, seven – Botswana, Lesotho, Malawi, Swaziland, Tanzania, Zambia and Zimbabwe – are members of the Commonwealth. The 1979 Lusaka CHOGM devises the formula to end UDI and issues the Lusaka Declaration against Racism and Racial Discrimination.

1980 Zimbabwe becomes independent and, inevitably, the problem of South Africa moves to the top of CHOGM agendas.

1982 The Commonwealth Games Federation agrees a Code of Conduct to strengthen the Gleneagles Agreement.

1983 The CHOGM in New Delhi agrees Commonwealth–UN co-operation to combat apartheid propaganda.

1985 With the escalation of violence in South Africa and growing unrest in the townships it was predictable that the South African issue would dominate the Nassau CHOGM. There the Commonwealth Accord on South Africa was agreed: this, clearly, was much less forthright than it might have been, solely because of the opposition of Britain to any meaningful steps to apply pressures to South Africa.

1986 The Eminent Persons Group (EPG), set up by the Nassau CHOGM, visits South Africa, but its recommendations are rebuffed by Pretoria. In August a Commonwealth mini-summit in London considered sanctions against South Africa but Britain refused to agree with the other members to even minimum action.

1987 South Africa again dominates the Vancouver CHOGM with Britain's prime minister, Margaret Thatcher, isolated on the issue of sanctions.

1989 At the Kuala Lumpur summit the British prime minister, Margaret Thatcher, issues a separate statement on South Africa, against the spirit of the summit consensus to which (earlier) she had agreed.

1990 A group of Commonwealth leaders meet Nelson Mandela, the leader of the African National Congress (ANC), in Lusaka on 27 February 2 weeks after his release from 27 years in prison.

1991 At the Harare CHOGM a three-stage lifting of sanctions is proposed as South Africa dismantles apartheid and makes progress towards a new constitution.

Rhodesia

Rhodesia was to be central to Commonwealth discussions (and rows) for 15 years (1965-80). When the ill-fated Central African Federation (CAF) of Northern Rhodesia, Southern Rhodesia and Nyasaland was in the process of being dismantled, Kenneth Kaunda of Northern Rhodesia begged the British minister (Rab Butler) not to allow all the military equipment of the Federation to be handed over to Southern Rhodesia, but his plea was ignored. The possibility of UDI became increasingly likely from the beginning of 1964. The subsequent sequence of events was as follows:

1965 UDI proclaimed by Ian Smith: the beginning of 15 years of OAU, Commonwealth and UN pressures upon Britain to prevent a 'sell out' to the Smith régime. An emergency session of the OAU in November 1965 called upon members to break diplomatic relations with Britain if it had not taken stronger action by mid-December. In the event nine of 36 OAU members broke relations with Britain including two Commonwealth countries – Ghana and Tanzania.

1966 Lagos (January): a special Commonwealth meeting to examine Rhodesia; Harold Wilson declared that sanctions would work in weeks rather than months. During the succeeding years the majority of the Commonwealth members constantly exerted pressures upon Britain to prevent the possibility of a 'sell out' to Smith and his Rhodesian Front. This was particularly the case at the 1966, 1969 and 1971 CHOGMs.

1966 Talks between Wilson and Smith fail.

1968 May: UN Mandatory Sanctions against Rhodesia. Proposals on the table to end UDI, but in January 1969 at the CHOGM in London the rest of the Commonwealth say these are unacceptable.

1970 Guerrilla action in Rhodesia increases. Edward Heath comes to power in the British general election (June) and 'talks about talks' get under way.

1971 Sir Alec Douglas-Home and Smith agree settlement terms (subject to a Commission of Inquiry). Nyerere comments: 'If they have agreed, then they have agreed on a sell out.'

1972 The Pearce Commission reports a resounding 'No' to the Home–Smith terms.

1973 The guerrilla war escalates.

1975 Independence in Mozambique turns Rhodesia's flank and the war escalates still further.

1979 Margaret Thatcher becomes prime minister of Britain; in Australia 6 weeks before the Lusaka CHOGM she indicates readiness to accept a solution involving Ian Smith and Bishop Abel Muzorewa in Rhodesia. (A great deal of remarkable Commonwealth diplomacy orchestrated by Malcolm Fraser of Australia, Julius Nyerere of Tanzania, Kenneth Kaunda of Zambia and Michael Manley of Jamaica ensured that at Lusaka Britain agreed to a new strategy which led to the Lancaster House Conference and then independence for Zimbabwe in April 1980. This will rank as one of the best examples of carefully planned and executed diplomacy by a group of nations in order to alter the political approach and policy of a major power in the direction the majority wanted it to go. The Lusaka solution for Rhodesia was a Commonwealth idea: and in this case it was also a triumph that such an organization could successfully influence the policy of Britain.)

The stories relating to both South Africa and Rhodesia contain the same elements: Britain fighting a rearguard action on behalf of white racist minorities (whether negatively or positively), while the majority of the Commonwealth (including the old Dominions which, increasingly on these issues, lined up with the new Commonwealth) exerted pressures upon Britain through the mechanism of the Commonwealth.

At the CHOGM at Melbourne in 1981, there was a collective sigh of relief that after so many years Rhodesia was out of the way and the Commonwealth could look at other problems, such as development. There have been other crises. The violent overthrow of the government in the tiny island of Grenada in 1983, the subsequent US invasion with a Caribbean Peace-keeping Force drawn from Barbados and Jamaica highlighted one of the most complex areas of Commonwealth concern, namely, what to do to help the many, very small nations in the world when they have dangerous problems. Half the membership of the Commonwealth consists of such small nations.

A Third World comment upon the Commonwealth came years ago from Mrs Pandit, sister of Jawaharlal Nehru, of India: 'Only the greatest good can come from such an association of unlike people.'

Part 6   The EC and the African, Caribbean and Pacific Group (ACP)

The creation of the European Economic Community (EEC – referred to hereafter as simply the EC) in 1957 and the subsequent growth of its economic power posed a new problem for the Third World. Two members of the original six, France and Italy, had a number of existing or recent colonial connections with Africa. When Britain joined the EC in 1973, it brought with it Commonwealth or colonial ties in Africa, the Caribbean and the Pacific. In essence the EC–ACP relationship is neo-colonial. The 70 ACP states have small, weak economies, often dependent for 50 per cent or more of their foreign earnings upon the export of one or two mineral or agricultural commodities. Through the EC–ACP arrangement, these countries have sought access on favourable terms to the lucrative EC market. Inevitably, despite the rhetoric about interdependence which, for example, was a part of the 1984 Lomé III Convention, the ACP countries are in effect suppliants to the EC for better conditions of trade, easier access to the European market and more aid. The relationship does represent a form of North–South dialogue, but all the advantages lie with the EC.

Highlights in the development of EC–ACP relations are as follows:

EC and African, Caribbean and Pacific Group (ACP)

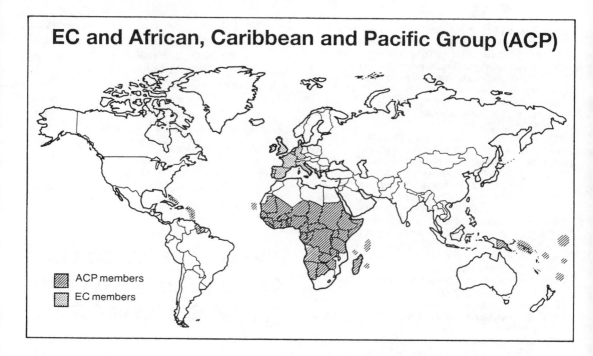

ACP members
EC members

1957   *The Treaty of Rome* between the original six – France, West Germany, Italy, Belgium, Netherlands and Luxembourg – made provision among other things for association between the Community and the overseas territories of its members in the fields of aid and trade. The first European Development Fund (EDF) was established with 581 million Units of Account. Originally virtually all EDF assistance went to the Francophone territories which were then still dependent.

1963   After most of France's colonies in Africa become independent, a new form of agreement between them and the EC was required. The Francophone countries formed the Associated States of Africa and Madagascar and then sought continued access to the European Common Market on favourable terms. The *First Yaoundé Convention* provided for bilateral negotiations between the two groups. It was to run for 5 years and dealt with preferential access to the EC (mainly for ACP primary products) and the provision of aid. It also established joint institutions at ministerial and parliamentary levels. EDF funds were increased.

1969   *The Second Yaoundé Convention* continued the policy of the first convention but by 1969 Commonwealth African countries were beginning to explore the possibility of a special relationship with the EC.

1973   Britain, Ireland and Denmark join the EC. Lengthy negotiations now got underway to enable Commonwealth countries also to become associates of the EC and 43 ACP countries from Africa, the Caribbean and the Pacific determined to negotiate as a bloc. The result was Lomé I.

1975   *Lomé I* was negotiated between the EC of the Nine and (now) 46 ACP countries. This agreement included the STABEX (Stabilization of Export Earnings) mechanism to maintain revenues from primary commodities when world prices became depressed. Lomé I established a Council of Ministers, a Committee of Ambassadors and a Consultative Assembly. EDF funds for the 5-year period were set at 3457.8 million Units of Account.

1979   *Lomé II* continued the broad policies set out under Lomé I. The number of ACP countries had risen to 57. SYSMIN, a mechanism similar to STABEX, was launched to assist the ACP mining sector. The EDF fund was increased to 5700 million European Currency Units (ECUs).

1984   *Lomé III* was negotiated between the EC of the Ten (Greece had joined in 1981) and (by then) 65 ACP countries. The accent was more on the private sector. The EDF fund was set at 7400 million ECUs.

1990–92   *Lomé III* expired in March 1990 to be replaced by *Lomé IV*. The principal worry of the ACP countries, as the Cold War came to an end, was the extent to which the new western concern with Eastern Europe and the states of the former Soviet Union would affect assistance to them under Lomé IV. The Convention is now between the EC of the Twelve (with the addition to the Ten of Portugal and Spain) and 70 ACP countries (additional members joining since Lomé III being Angola, Dominican Republic, Eritrea, Haiti and Namibia).

Members of the EC and ACP at the time of Lomé IV (1993)

EC
Belgium
Denmark
France
Germany
Greece
Ireland
Italy
Luxembourg
Netherlands
Portugal
Spain
United Kingdom

ACP
Angola
Antigua & Barbuda
Bahamas
Barbados
Belize
Benin
Botswana

Madagascar
Malawi
Mali
Mauritania
Mauritius
Mozambique
Namibia

Burkina Faso
Burundi
Cameroon
Cape Verde
Central African Republic
Chad
Comoros
Congo
Côte d'Ivoire
Djibouti
Dominica
Dominican Republic
Equatorial Guinea
Eritrea
Ethiopia
Fiji
Gabon
Gambia
Ghana
Grenada
Guinea
Guinea-Bissau
Guyana
Haiti
Jamaica
Kenya
Kiribati
Lesotho

Liberia
Niger
Nigeria
Papua New Guinea
Rwanda
St Christopher-Nevis
St Lucia
St Vincent & the Grenadines
São Tomé & Príncipe
Senegal
Seychelles
Sierra Leone
Solomon Is.
Somalia
Sudan
Surinam
Swaziland
Tanzania
Togo
Tonga
Trinidad & Tobago
Tuvalu
Uganda
Western Samoa
Vanuatu
Zaïre
Zambia
Zimbabwe

5 Aid and Its Agencies

The growth of the aid idea

Although there are earlier precedents for aid (prior to World War II) the growth of the aid idea broadly parallels the end of empires and, indeed, was related precisely to that development. There are two strands to the process. On the one hand the newly independent countries discovered just how weak and underdeveloped were their economies. If they were to develop in line with the expectations of their people, following the excitement of political independence, then they urgently needed two things: capital and technical assistance. To obtain either they were obliged to turn to the rich countries of the North. They did, it is true, have a choice: the capitalist countries of the western world, including their old colonial masters, and also the USA, the rest of Europe and, later, Japan; and the Communist nations. Both groups, they discovered, were ready enough to supply aid – on their own terms.

Most of the aid-giving advantages, however, lay with the West rather than with the Communist bloc. First, the West had far greater wealth. Relatively and absolutely the Communist countries were far more sparing in their aid, the great bulk of which was provided only for socialist régimes or where there was a powerful Cold War reason – as in the case of Egypt when the West withdrew its offer to build the Aswan High Dam in 1956 and the USSR promptly stepped in. Second, the newly independent countries had close ties with the ex-imperial powers – ties of language, custom, methods of procedure – which they had inherited from the colonial period. All these made it easier to seek, obtain and use aid from such sources, certainly in the years immediately after independence. These various factors made up one side of the new aid equation.

On the other hand the ex-imperial powers of the North whose colonies one by one were becoming independent, urgently sought a means to perpetuate or at least maintain as much influence as possible in the new countries which they had controlled until recently. Aid provided the most obvious instrument for this purpose. Aid from the old colonial powers allowed them three advantages: to maintain good relations in the post-independence age; to maintain substantial economic influence which, hopefully, would supplement their existing investments and trade relations with those countries; to provide the appearance of enlightenment especially against the background of the Cold War as this escalated during the 1950s.

There were historic precedents for the flow of resources from rich to poor, from developed to developing. These could be seen on a purely capitalist basis during the nineteenth century when wealth from Europe and especially Britain was invested in the USA, Canada and Australia, and, at a somewhat more altruistic level, with the beginning of Colonial Development and Welfare. The first British Colonial Development Act was passed in 1929; then in 1940 the British Parliament passed the Colonial Development and Welfare Act under which development funds on a small scale were made available to the colonies. Between 1940 and 1960, some £230 million sterling was provided in the form of grants to the colonies under the Colonial Development and Welfare Acts. But the real impetus for the aid idea came with the Marshall Plan for European recovery.

The Marshall Plan

The American Marshall Plan was named after the US Secretary of State from 1947 to 1949, George C. Marshall. It was launched to bring about the financial and economic recovery of war-torn Europe. The US Foreign Aid Act was passed in April 1948. Sixteen countries of western Europe, led by Britain and France, set up the Organization of European Economic Co-operation (OEEC, now the OECD) in Paris, although the USSR

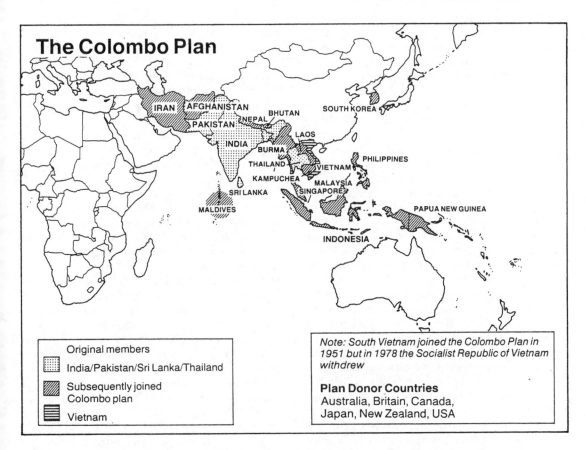

The Colombo Plan

Original members

India/Pakistan/Sri Lanka/Thailand

Subsequently joined
Colombo plan

Vietnam

Note: South Vietnam joined the Colombo Plan in 1951 but in 1978 the Socialist Republic of Vietnam withdrew

Plan Donor Countries
Australia, Britain, Canada, Japan, New Zealand, USA

rejected the idea of receiving American economic assistance. In the next few years massive amounts of American capital assistance helped western Europe back on its feet.

Marshall Aid, however, was different in kind from what we now describe as aid. It was a once-for-all operation, the injection of relatively massive assistance into economies which were already advanced or developed. The technology existed in Europe although the economies had been badly disrupted and run down by the effects of war. What was needed was a large, swift injection of capital resources to enable those economies to reorganize. This was provided by Marshall Aid. But if Marshall Aid was essentially concerned with the recovery of Europe, it also familiarized the countries of the North with the idea of aid – which at its best is the transfer of resources from advanced economies to less advanced economies in order to assist the latter to make crucial economic breakthroughs.

The Colombo Plan

The Colombo Plan may be taken as the real beginning of modern aid in the sense of transfer of resources, both technical and financial, from developed to developing economies. The Plan has certain unique features and over the years has been one of the most successful means of supplying aid. Originally the Plan aimed to foster co-operative economic development in south and south-east Asia. The concept was worked out during 1950 and the Plan went into operation in 1951. The Plan was a logical consequence of the impact of war and the end of European empires in Asia, where the newly independent countries found themselves in urgent need of economic assistance with their development. All the new nations of Asia were economically underdeveloped.

The Colombo Plan was a Commonwealth initiative. Ministers of seven Commonwealth countries met in the capital of Ceylon (now Sri Lanka) in January 1950. These were Australia, Britain,

Canada, Ceylon, India, New Zealand and Pakistan. The Plan was intended to benefit countries of South and South-east Asia, but it was later extended to include a much wider area stretching from Iran to South Korea and from Fiji in the Pacific to the Maldives in the Indian Ocean. Four of the founding countries – Australia, Britain, Canada and New Zealand – were non-Asian and donors. The other three – India, Pakistan and Ceylon – were the successor states of British India and only achieved independence in 1947 and 1948. The USA (1951) and Japan (1954) joined the Plan as donor nations.

In 1977 the name of the Plan was changed to the Colombo Plan for Co-operative Economic and Social Development in Asia and the Pacific. Assistance under the Plan is approved by ministers at meetings of the Consultative Committee, but each aid programme is negotiated bilaterally on a government-to-government basis within the framework of the Plan. The Colombo Plan has been acknowledged as the pioneer of bilateral aid. There is no central planning or common fund. Instead, a developing member determines its needs and approaches one of the donor members. Then, together they work out how to implement the programme. The Plan acts to bring the two sides, donor and recipient, together. The main sources of Plan aid are Australia, Britain, Canada, Japan, New Zealand and the USA, although the developing members also provide some technical assistance for each other.

The achievements of the Colombo Plan over the years have been considerable. From 1950 to 1981 donors provided a total of $65.1 billion in aid. In addition they supplied technical assistance (training, experts, volunteers and equipment) worth $4284.9 million, while technical co-operation exchanged between the developing members of the Plan amounted to $30,188,800 of which India supplied $22,534,300. The significance of the Colombo Plan, most particularly in its early years, was that it came much closer to a partnership approach to development problems than did later aid relationships.

Bilateral aid

Aid has grown in direct relationship to the process of decolonization. As the new nations appeared on the world stage, they sought aid for their development and the principal donor nations, recognizing the neo-colonialist advantages to be derived from giving aid, signalled their readiness to do so. As Professor Bauer[*] argues: 'The concept of the Third World or the South and the policy of official aid are inseparable. They are two sides of the same coin. The Third World is the creation of foreign aid: without foreign aid there is no Third World.' One does not have to accept all Professor Bauer's arguments to admit the uncomfortable accuracy of this particular claim.

Aid grew rapidly in the 1950s, its growth encouraged by decolonization and the rivalries of the Cold War. Its value as an instrument for winning allies in the world struggle of the Cold War was seen at its starkest in 1956, when the West withdrew its offer to build the Aswan High Dam and the Soviet Union willingly filled the gap.

The end of the decade and the early years of the 1960s were the high point of aid optimism (on both sides of the equation), but thereafter the flow of aid levelled off. Then in 1973 came the Yom Kippur War, the oil crisis and a number of pressures, including the apparently uncontrollable welter of problems retarding development in Africa, as well as the new strategies for the poorest associated with the name of Robert McNamara, President of the World Bank (1968–81), which led to a further substantial growth in aid (assisted now by huge injections of development funds from the Organization of Petroleum Exporting Countries). Yet the second half of the 1970s and the early 1980s were a time of disillusionment with the aid idea, especially in the leading donor countries. Even so, by the mid-1980s aid had become a permanent aspect of North–South relations.

Bilateral aid flows

Bilateral or country-to-country aid allows the donor to control the way in which the aid is given and take political credit for its results. Two-thirds or more of western (Development Assistance Committee or DAC) aid is bilateral, while a much higher proportion (almost all) Council for Mutual Economic Assistance (CMEA or Communist) aid was bilateral.

In the first half of the 1950s, as aid became an important factor in international affairs, the annual bilateral aid flow came to $1.8 billion.

[*]*Equality, the Third World and Economic Delusion*, Weidenfeld and Nicolson, 1981.

During this period and up to 1960, the great majority of African and Caribbean territories remained colonies and so were dependent for aid upon the metropolitan powers. It was the Latin American and Asian countries which pushed for aid at this time. During this period the USA provided approximately 50 per cent of world aid. The Cold War was at its height and a high proportion of all American aid was channelled into countries, such as Turkey and South Korea, on the southern periphery of what was then seen to be the monolithic Communist bloc. After the USA, the two major colonial powers, France and Britain, ranked next as aid donors. Later, West Germany and Japan (rehabilitated and recovering rapidly in economic terms) joined the former three as substantial aid donors.

Although the Colombo Plan may be taken as the beginning of the aid age, it was at the end of the 1950s that a series of international and national mechanisms to further the aid process were created in the UN or the countries of the North. Thus in 1958 and 1960 the western aid consortia for India and Pakistan were created; in 1959 the EC set up the European Development Fund (EDF) and in the Americas the Inter-American Development Bank (IDB) was created. In 1960 the World Bank established its 'soft' arm for finance on easy terms – the International Development Association (IDA) – and the OECD countries established the Development Assistance Committee (DAC). The United Nations proclaimed the 1960s the First Development Decade. Between 1960 and 1962, Canada, Kuwait, Japan, Britain, Denmark, Sweden, Norway, France and West Germany each set up aid departments or ministries. Aid had become an international fashion.

The Development Assistance Committee (DAC)

In world terms, the western nations which form the Development Assistance Committee, or DAC, are by far the largest source of aid. The DAC, which is part of the Organization for Economic Co-operation and Development (OECD), was established in 1960 and comprised 17 countries. The DAC plays an important role in co-ordinating the aid of member nations. Most DAC members have accepted a commitment to provide 0.7 per cent of their GNPs in aid. Yet few have got anywhere near that figure.

By the mid-1980s bilateral aid flows from both DAC and the Communist countries appeared to have settled into a pattern that reflected the apparently unchanging nature of the Cold War. It is worth examining the flows of that time and the prevailing attitudes of the major donors because there were shortly to be a number of dramatic changes in perceptions about aid with the actual flow, though increasing slowly, in fact contracting in real financial terms.

Changes in attitudes were already apparent by the late 1980s and were to be enormously accelerated as a result of the end of the Cold War and the consequent collapse of the Soviet Union. The disappearance of the USSR and the countries of Eastern Europe as an alternative source of aid (they had become, instead, suppliants for aid on a massive scale to enable their economies to realign themselves with the West) meant a western reappraisal of its aid policies and raised acute fears in the South that much of the aid it had long taken for granted might now begin to dry up. In any case, even before the end of the Cold War, the main donors had begun to attach far tougher conditions to their aid, discovering a convenient new morality which allowed them to link it to privatization, a return (by one-party states) to democracy and a new concern with human rights, none of which had overtly concerned them during the heyday of the Cold War.

It is worth examining the DAC pattern of aid giving in the mid-1980s for this shows how aid had been shaped by two parallel sets of considerations: the Cold War; and the post-imperial concerns of the former colonial powers, especially Britain and France. (Thereafter, we jump to the early 1990s when most of the factors operating in 1984 – apart from on-going neo-colonialism – had ceased to be valid.)

DAC aid 1983–84 in $ millions and as a percentage of GNP

Country	Total aid 1983–84 ($ million)	As % of GNP
Australia	760	0.47
Austria	170	0.26
Belgium	460	0.58
Canada	1530	0.48
Denmark	420	0.79
Finland	170	0.34
France	3800	0.75*
West Germany	2980	0.47

The Development Assistance Committee (DAC) 1985

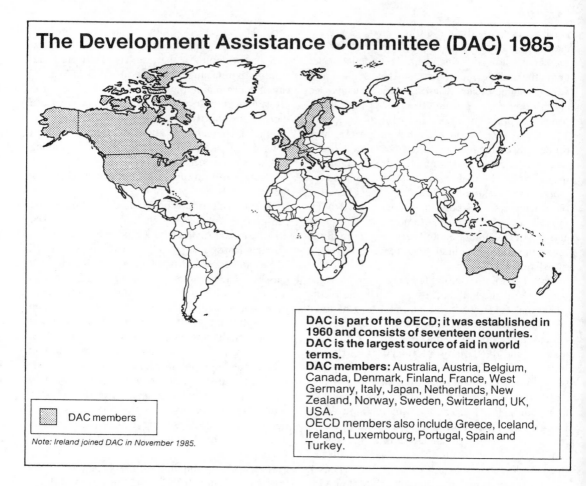

DAC members

Note: Ireland joined DAC in November 1985.

DAC is part of the OECD; it was established in 1960 and consists of seventeen countries. DAC is the largest source of aid in world terms.
DAC members: Australia, Austria, Belgium, Canada, Denmark, Finland, France, West Germany, Italy, Japan, Netherlands, New Zealand, Norway, Sweden, Switzerland, UK, USA.
OECD members also include Greece, Iceland, Ireland, Luxembourg, Portugal, Spain and Turkey.

Country	Total aid 1983–84 ($ million)	As % of GNP
Italy	980	0.28
Japan	4040	0.34
Netherlands	1230	0.96
New Zealand	60	0.26
Norway	560	1.06
Sweden	750	0.82
Switzerland	300	0.31
UK	1510	0.34
USA	8400	0.24

*If the aid France provides for its overseas territories and departments is deducted from the above figure then its aid to independent countries was running at the level of $2.53 billion a year representing 0.50% of GNP.
Source: DAC Report 1985

At this time the five leading members of DAC in terms of total aid disbursed were the USA, France, West Germany, Japan and Britain. In 1983-84 total DAC aid came to US$28.12 billion.

DAC policies – individual countries

The approaches to aid considered here under individual countries operated through the central period of the Cold War – 1960 to 1985. In the latter year Mikhail Gorbachev came to power in the USSR and initiated his policies of *glasnost* and *perestroika* whose consequences he could hardly have expected: not only did they bring an end to the Cold War but they also brought about the disintegration of the Soviet empire with almost incalculable results for the Third World. These may be summarised as follows: a) The main donors of the West no longer felt compelled to provide aid as part of the matching process that had been so important an element during the Cold War period; b) Much western effort was now withdrawn from the South as they concentrated upon East Europe and the former Soviet Union; c) The CMEA as a source of aid disappeared as Russia and the East European countries sought western assistance with their economic restructuring problems; d) In addition, the main western donors – now freed from Cold War restraints – were able to apply their 'new morality' (see above) insisting upon far greater political responses in return for less aid in absolute terms.

The USA's share of total development aid 1950–85

1950–55	1960–61	1970–71	1975–76	1983–84
50.2%	46.3%	30.8%	21.7%	22.2%

The Cold War provided the impetus for early American aid, but at the beginning of the 1960s, under the Kennedy administration, aid reached a peak. This was the brief idealistic period of the 'New Frontier' and the Alliance for Progress, a co-operative programme to promote development in Latin America. In 1960, when DAC was formed, the USA provided just under half the world's aid. Later in the 1960s, aid became unfashionable as the Vietnam War moved to the forefront of American politics. By the 1980s, despite a generally lukewarm approach to aid (sometimes downright antagonistic), the USA was still providing an annual average of $8.4 billion (1983-84). This was only 0.24 per cent of GNP, but it reflected the huge size of the American economy in relation to all others. Perhaps more than other countries – or at least more obviously and openly – the USA used its aid to reward friends and withheld it to punish enemies.

The USA, inevitably, acts as the western aid pacemaker. When it decides to cut back or fails adequately to support the International Development Association (IDA), its actions are usually taken by other donors as an excuse for doing the same thing. In 1984 the direction of US aid clearly reflected the country's political priorities. The top recipients were Israel, Egypt and Central America, with a marked decline in assistance to most other areas.

France

Of the big five France is the largest western bilateral donor on the basis of a percentage of its GNP. Of the old colonial powers France was always a larger donor than Britain and, if aid to its overseas territories and departments is included, it ranked third in volume for 1983-84 after the USA and Japan. On that calculation France provided $3.8 billion of aid (0.75 per cent GNP) of which $1.27 billion went to its overseas territories and departments and $2.53 billion to independent countries.

A high proportion of all French aid is always concentrated upon Francophone countries, mainly in Africa. When France makes an exception to this pattern (as it did in the early 1980s towards Nigeria), this was as part of a policy to assist France to break into a new market (in Nigeria's case one that was traditionally British). More than 80 per cent of French aid is bilateral and 60 per cent of this is in the form of technical co-operation, with great emphasis upon linguistic and cultural ties.

Britain

Britain lay fifth in the DAC league at this time (a position it maintained subsequently) and most of its bilateral assistance goes to Commonwealth countries, with two areas of concentration: Africa and South Asia. The main recipients of British aid in Africa (at this time) were Botswana, Ghana, Kenya, Malawi, Sudan, Tanzania, Uganda, Zambia and Zimbabwe. In Asia they were Bangladesh, India, Nepal, Pakistan and Sri Lanka. In the Middle East, Egypt and Turkey were substantial recipients of British aid. With few exceptions, most recipients of British aid on any scale are former imperial possessions or, as in the case of Egypt, once within its 'sphere of influence'. Britain provides a higher proportion of multilateral aid (on a percentage basis) than does France. As a proportion of GNP British aid declined through the 1970s and by 1984 (according to DAC) its aid was only slightly higher in real terms than in 1970.

West Germany

West German aid was unaffected by post-imperial considerations (as in the cases of Britain and France) and to that extent Germany has had a freer hand. Its approach to aid has been orthodox and Germany has concentrated upon obvious target countries, such as India or Tanzania. Broadly, it followed American lines in its aid giving, at least with regard to Cold War considerations.

Japan

As a major donor Japan was a latecomer to aid. About 60 per cent of Japanese assistance has been bilateral. Japan was increasingly criticized for the small amount of aid it provided long after its economy had moved into second place in the western world behind that of the USA. In the mid-1970s, therefore, it made the political decision to expand the volume of its aid with the result that it doubled betwen 1977 and 1980 and then doubled again between 1981 and 1985. This brought Japan into second place as a donor after the USA. The majority of Japanese aid is concentrated upon south-east Asia, in part following the pattern of its war reparations.

Scandinavia

As a group, the three Scandinavian countries – Norway, Sweden and Denmark (Finland at this stage was still a very minor donor) – have consistently been at the top end of the DAC scale as its most generous donors, each having passed the DAC aid target of 0.7 per cent GNP. Both Norway and Sweden have concentrated their efforts upon a relatively small number of selected countries and in the mid-1980s these were, for Norway: Bangladesh, India, Kenya, Pakistan and Tanzania; and for Sweden: Bangladesh, India, Ethiopia, Kenya, Mozambique, Sri Lanka, Tanzania, Vietnam and Zambia with about 80 per cent of Swedish aid going to programmes rather than projects.

Netherlands and Belgium

The Netherlands has been one of the most generous of DAC donors (with the Scandinavian countries) on a percentage of GNP basis, passing 1.08 per cent in both 1981 and 1982. Dutch policy has been to concentrate on low-income countries with special attention (at this time) to four – Bangladesh, India, Indonesia (its former colonial empire) and Tanzania. A majority of Belgium's bilateral assistance was channelled into its former dependencies in Africa – Zaïre, Burundi and Rwanda.

Canada

Canada set itself the target of reaching 0.7 per cent GNP in aid by 1990 (though worsening economic conditions and changing attitudes meant it only achieved 0.44 per cent GNP by that year). About 58 per cent of its bilateral aid goes to low-income countries. Canada has enjoyed a fairly liberal reputation over aid matters. For example, it has been able to supply technical assistance personnel with equal facility to both Anglophone and Francophone countries in Africa – a reflection of its own colonial background.

Australia

Australia concentrates its aid overwhelmingly upon countries in its region, south-east Asia and the Pacific. Nearly half of all Australian aid has been channelled into Papua New Guinea, its former colonial territory, with which it has maintained a special post-independence relationship.

The shares of world ODA (official development assistance) of the six main DAC donors in 1983-84, on a percentage basis, were the USA (22.2 per cent), West Germany (8.4 per cent), France (10.6 per cent), Britain (4.2 per cent), Japan (10.9 per cent) and Canada (4.3 per cent).

Aid directions of the top five donors to their top five recipients (percentages – 1982–83)

USA

Israel	12.2%
Egypt	11.3
Turkey	3.6
El Salvador	2.3
Bangladesh	2.3

France

Réunion	9.9%
Martinique	7.4
New Caledonia	4.5
Polynesia	4.5
Guadeloupe	4.1

Note: The top five recipients of French aid are either French overseas departments or overseas territories.

Britain

India	7.9%
Sudan	3.2
Sri Lanka	2.8
Kenya	2.8
Tanzania	2.3

Japan

Indonesia	9.7%
China	9.4
Thailand	6.1
Philippines	4.4
Bangladesh	4.2

West Germany

India	5.3%
Indonesia	3.8
Egypt	3.2
Israel	2.7
Turkey	2.6

An analysis of the direction of aid by these five donors at this time reveals a good deal about western political reasons for providing aid. Six countries are among the top five recipients with regard to two major donors. Thus Egypt, Turkey and Israel are in the top five of the list for both the USA and West Germany; Bangladesh for the USA and Japan; India for Britain and West Germany; Indonesia for Japan and West Germany.

France's top five recipients are all overseas territories or departments, but its second five recipients (in terms of volume of aid) are Morocco, Côte d'Ivoire, Senegal, Cameroon (each in Francophone Africa) and French Guiana, an overseas department.

Of the top 18 recipients of American aid in 1982–83, the first three – Israel, Egypt, Turkey – were in the Middle East; El Salvador, Costa Rica, Jamaica, Peru, Honduras, the Dominican Republic were seen as strategically important to US policy in Central and South America; Bangladesh, India, Pakistan, Indonesia and the Philippines were countries of huge populations in Asia; while Sudan, Kenya and Liberia in Africa were seen as vital strategic countries, though in the case of Liberia there is a long-standing historic, semi-colonial relationship. Finally, aid to the Trust Territory of the Pacific Islands represented a US Trusteeship responsibility.

Of the top 22 recipients of French aid, six were overseas departments or territories; 13 were in Francophone Africa; and only Indonesia, Brazil and Egypt were outside the Francophone world.

Of the top 18 recipients of British aid, ten were in the Commonwealth and four – Sudan, Pakistan, Egypt and Nepal – enjoyed special links with Britain from imperial days. The other four reci-

pients were Mexico, Turkey, Indonesia and Brazil.

Japan concentrates overwhelmingly upon Asian countries. Its top recipients were each invaded by Japan during World War II. West Germany, with no recent colonial ties, had a more diffuse pattern to its aid-giving.

There were three main sources of aid in the mid-1980s: the DAC group of countries, OPEC and the Council for Mutual Economic Assistance (CMEA) which was the Communist bloc's equivalent to DAC. (For OPEC aid see Chapter Six.)

The Council for Mutual Economic Assistance (CMEA)

The USSR and the East European countries were all members of the Communist economic grouping, the Council for Mutual Economic Assistance (CMEA). Their aid, however, was on a small scale both by comparison with DAC and in its total amount. Only in a few carefully chosen countries which Moscow regarded as socialist in their policies or clearly socialist leaning did Soviet aid make any real impact. A DAC estimate for the years 1979–81, for example, shows as follows:

USSR
($ millions)

	1979	1980	1981
Total gross disbursements	1811	2085	2096
Net disbursements	1403	1664	1661
As percentage of GNP	0.13	0.15	0.15

Eastern Europe
($ millions)

	1979	1980	1981
Total gross disbursements	513	604	579
Net disbursements	358	489	468
As percentage GNP	0.09	0.12	0.12

Countries of concentration for Soviet aid were Afghanistan, Kampuchea, Cuba, North Korea, Laos and Vietnam. In Africa the main recipients of Soviet aid have been Egypt, Algeria, Nigeria, Ethiopia, Congo, Somalia (prior to 1977) and Guinea. Most East German aid (often military

World aid sources to the mid-1980s by group on a percentage basis

Group	1950-55	1960-61	1970-71	1975-76	1983-84
DAC	99.7	86.9	78.1	63.3	76.8
CMEA	–	9.9	11.3	6.7	8.5
OPEC	–	–	4.6	27.8	13.6
other	0.3	3.2	6.0	2.2	1.1
	100.0	100.0	100.0	100.0	100.0

Source: DAC Report 1985

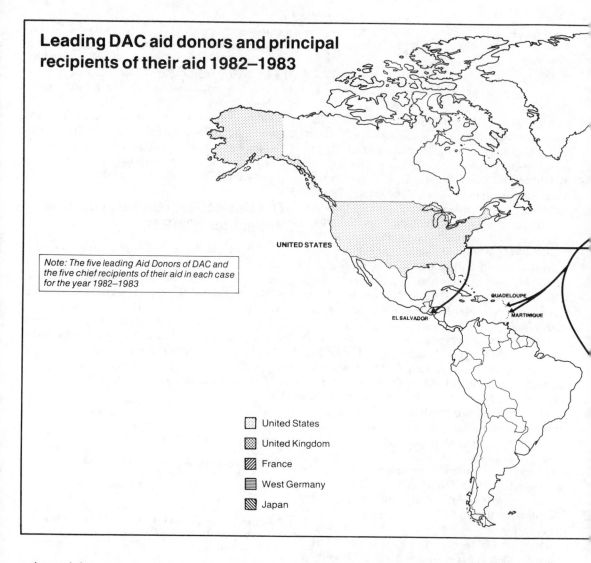

Leading DAC aid donors and principal recipients of their aid 1982–1983

Note: The five leading Aid Donors of DAC and the five chief recipients of their aid in each case for the year 1982–1983

- ▢ United States
- ▨ United Kingdom
- ▨ France
- ▤ West Germany
- ▨ Japan

assistance) has gone to a few African countries: Angola, Mozambique, Zambia.

During 1983–85, CMEA aid from the Soviet Union and East Europe ran at approximately $3 billion a year of which the USSR accounted for 80 per cent. Nearly all CMEA aid was provided on a bilateral basis. In 1984 approximately 85,000 students and trainees from Third World countries were on courses in the CMEA countries and about two-thirds of these were in the USSR. Only socialist countries got much in the way of a grant element in CMEA aid.

The main recipients of CMEA aid in 1983-84 were Vietnam ($1180 million), Cuba ($680 million), Mongolia ($620 million), Afghanistan ($203 million), Ethiopia ($155 million) and India ($84 million). In addition, during 1984, $78 million went to sub-Saharan Africa and $65 million to Kampuchea. The only important recipient of CMEA aid which was not a socialist country with close Moscow alignments was India which has received substantial Soviet assistance since 1955.

China

China is a developing country itself, yet in the 1960s it emerged as a major aid donor concentrating especially upon sub-Saharan Africa. Unlike the two superpowers, China did accept the target figure of 0.7 per cent of GNP for aid.

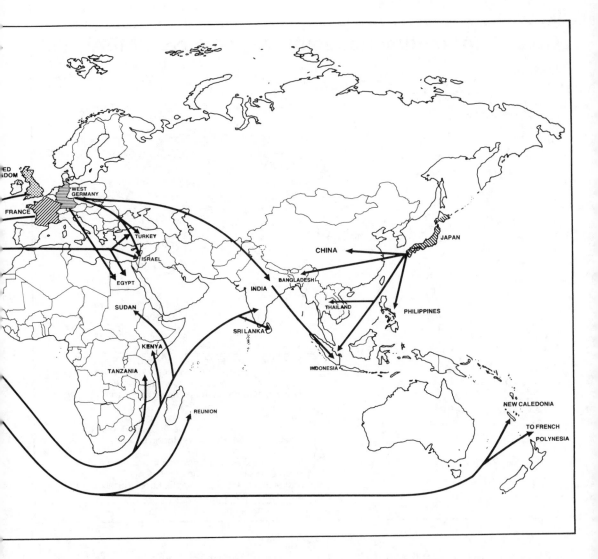

In 1964 while on a visit to West Africa in the course of an important tour of the continent, Zhou Enlai visited Mali and laid down eight principles which should govern Chinese aid:

1. Chinese aid mutually benefits both donor and recipient; it is not a kind of unilateral alms.
2. China respects the sovereignty of recipient countries, and never asks for privileges or attaches any conditions.
3. Aid is provided free or with low interest rates.
4. The purpose of Chinese aid is to help recipients embark on the road to self-reliance.
5. China tries to help recipients build projects which require less investment while yielding quicker results, thus helping to accumulate capital.
6. China will provide its own equipment at international market prices. If it is not up to agreed specifications, it will be replaced.
7. China will ensure that technical personnel of the recipient country master appropriate techniques.
8. Chinese experts will have the same standard of living as the experts of recipient countries.

Most Chinese aid was on a modest scale though with the massive exception of the TANZAM railway. This was built from Dar es Salaam in Tanzania on the Indian Ocean to Kapiri Mposhi in

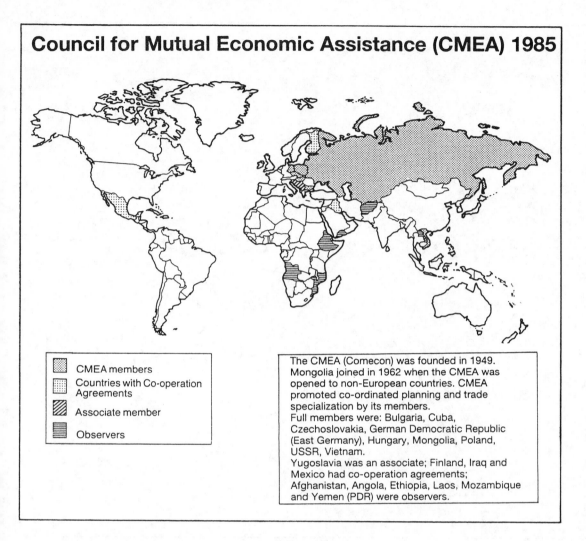

Council for Mutual Economic Assistance (CMEA) 1985

CMEA members

Countries with Co-operation Agreements

Associate member

Observers

The CMEA (Comecon) was founded in 1949. Mongolia joined in 1962 when the CMEA was opened to non-European countries. CMEA promoted co-ordinated planning and trade specialization by its members.
Full members were: Bulgaria, Cuba, Czechoslovakia, German Democratic Republic (East Germany), Hungary, Mongolia, Poland, USSR, Vietnam.
Yugoslavia was an associate; Finland, Iraq and Mexico had co-operation agreements; Afghanistan, Angola, Ethiopia, Laos, Mozambique and Yemen (PDR) were observers.

central Zambia between 1968 and 1975 at an eventual cost of $400 million, although subsequent extra construction and training costs came to a further $53 million. After 1978 Chinese aid was restructured and more geared to assisting the development of commercial projects. Its technologies are often more adapted to the requirements of poor developing countries than are the technologies of western donors.

Cuba

Though itself a developing country, heavily dependent upon the USSR for massive aid, Cuba was to become a donor of significance in three or four countries. From 1975 onwards it became a major source of both military and then technical assistance to the new government of Aghostino Neto and the MPLA in Angola. Then on a comparable scale from 1977 onwards, it also became a donor, again of military and technical assistance, to the radical government of General Mengistu in Ethiopia. The extent of its military assistance to Angola and Ethiopia made Cuba an important factor in the highly charged politics of the African continent through the period 1975 to 1990. For example, the USA exerted great pressure to make Cuba withdraw its troops from Angola (see above, Chapter Four Regional Groupings, Part 4 Latin America and the Caribbean).

These percentage aid flows from the three main groups in 1983-84 represented in financial terms –

Shares (%) of world aid: USA France   Britain   CMEA OPEC

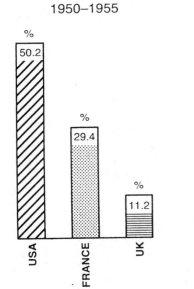

1950–1955

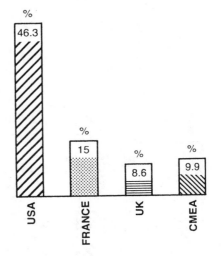

1960–1961

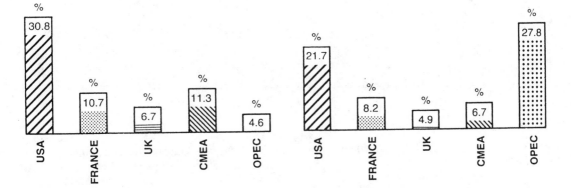

1970–1971

1975–1976

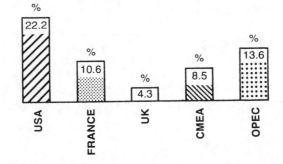

1983–1984

Total world aid as shared by DAC   CMEA   OPEC

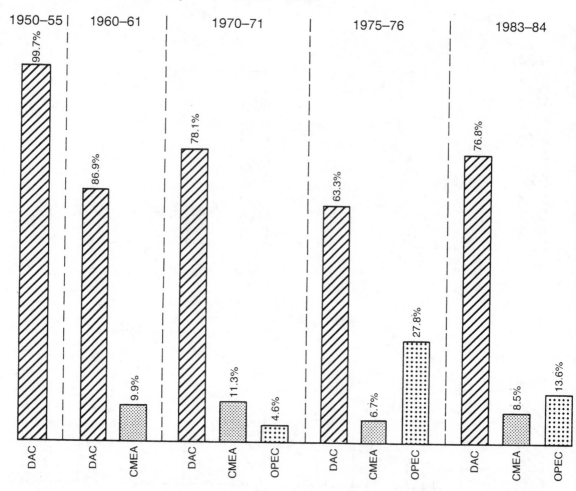

out of a total world aid flow of $37,049,000,000 – the following:

DAC	$28,433 million
CMEA	$3135 million
OPEC	$5027 million

Source: All figures upon which the above diagrams have been based have been extracted from the 1985 Report of DAC – *Twenty-five years of development co-operation* – a review (OECD).

The changed aid climate of the 1990s

Although by the mid-1980s aid had – apparently – become a permanent, set feature of North–South relations, few any longer believed it would achieve more than helping the poorest keep their heads above water. At the beginning of the 1990s the industrial (OECD) countries were providing 0.35 per cent of their combined GNP as ODA and in 1990 the total aid flow was $54 billion of which $52 billion came from the OECD.

But significant changes in attitudes on the part of donors also had to be taken into account. During the late 1980s the West, increasingly confident that it could discount the USSR as a serious donor rival, began to attach ever more stringent conditions to its aid. At the same time western leaders linked aid to new economic and political aims; for example, the one major contribution to North–South dialogue made by Britain's prime minister, Margaret Thatcher, was to popularize the idea that privatization measures should be linked to aid packages, especially in those countries which had large state sectors of one kind or another. In addition, western donors began to insist upon democracy and 'good governance' (though precisely what good governance means is subject to endless debate) as part of the overall aid package. Thus, a number of countries such as Kenya and Malawi in Africa were told that continuing aid would depend upon improvements to their democratic or human rights records.

The crucial change, however, came with the end of the Cold War. Once it became obvious that the end of the Cold War also meant an end to the world-wide confrontation of the superpowers – and, indeed, to the disappearance of the USSR as an effective superpower – the Third World began to realize what had already been emerging during the recession-dominated 1980s: that it was largely expendable. Further, the suspicion grew that sudden western concern with democracy and human rights or insistence upon 'good governance' had less to do with the establishment of such concepts than with providing an excuse for donors to cut back on their aid. The true nature of the aid business and the growing unwillingness of the North to help the South were highlighted in the 1992 *Human Development Report* of the UNDP which pointed out that while the West was unwilling to write off Africa's debts it was prepared to reduce the debts of Poland by 50 per cent despite the fact that Poland's per capita income was five times that of the average for Africa. At the May 1992 conference of the IMF and World Bank in Washington DC the Group of Seven (G-7) countries agreed to offer Moscow financial aid to the tune of $24 billion. Understandably, this produced a sense of grievance in the South, for if the rich western donors could offer aid on such a scale so quickly to their erstwhile Cold War enemy, why could they not do a little better in relation to the Third World?

The break-up of the USSR created a number of prospective new Third World countries such as Uzbekistan and these, as well as Russia itself, were all seeking aid from the West. Moreover, the end of the Cold War had not only eliminated the Third World's alternative court of appeal (for aid), but had also eliminated the aid from that source as well which meant that the total amount of aid on offer was drastically reduced in real terms since a proportion of OECD aid would be diverted from

the South to the former Soviet empire countries.

ODA from the 18 DAC countries in 1991 came to $55.5 billion and represented 0.33 per cent of their combined GNP, down slightly from the 0.34 per cent figure for 1985 when ODA from DAC came to $29.4 billion. Below are given the DAC figures for 1991 (these should be compared with the DAC figures for 1983–84 given above).

Country	Amount $ millions	%GNP
Ireland	72	0.19
New Zealand	100	0.25
United Kingdom	3348	0.32
Australia	1050	0.38
Italy	3352	0.30
Netherlands	2517	0.88
Belgium	831	0.42
Austria	548	0.34
France	7484	0.62
Canada	2604	0.45
United States	11,362	0.20
Germany (WG figures)	6890	0.41
Denmark	1300	0.96
Finland	930	0.76
Norway	1178	1.14
Sweden	2116	0.92
Japan	10,952	0.32
Switzerland	863	0.36

Note: Figures derived from 1993 World Development Report

An analysis of these figures (as compared with those for the mid-1980s), reveals the following:

Of the five major donors – the USA, Japan, France, Germany and Britain – the level of US aid has dropped significantly from 0.24 per cent of GNP to 0.20; Japan has dropped slightly (0.34 to 0.32) but because of the huge growth of the Japanese economy in the intervening years now almost matches the USA in cash terms; France has dropped from 0.75 per cent to 0.62; Germany from 0.47 to 0.41; and Britain from 0.34 to 0.32. And, a major development, Italy has replaced Britain as the fifth largest donor. Thus, the order of the top donors with their aid in dollars is as follows:

USA	$11,362m
Japan	$10,952m
France	$7484m
Germany	$6890m
Italy	$3352m
UK	$3348m
Canada	$2604m

Otherwise the pattern remains much as in the mid-1980s with only the Netherlands and the three

Scandinavian countries – Norway, Sweden and Denmark (but now joined by Finland) – achieving the 0.7 per cent of GNP target.

Britain in 1993

Britain, in particular, has been an advocate of the new moral values which it has argued should now be attached to its aid giving; recipients of British aid are world-wide although it concentrates most of its bilateral aid upon Commonwealth countries. Britain's approach to aid in the early 1990s may be taken as a reasonable guide to western donor attitudes in general.

The Overseas Development Administration (ODA) states its main priorities to be the following: to promote economic reform; to promote good government; to reduce poverty; to promote human development (better education and health, children by choice); to tackle environmental problems; to promote the private sector; to improve responses to emergencies; to improve aid management overseas. The overt political nature of at least three of these priorities represents a new aspect of aid in the 1990s: the readiness of donors to impose their political ideas upon recipients in return for aid.

In relation to Eastern Europe and the former Soviet Union, Britain presented a financial assistance plan that envisaged a cash flow of £104 million sterling for 1991/92, £188 million sterling for 1992/93, £231 million sterling for 1993/94 and £227 million sterling for 1994/95, stating baldly that the programme was to support the establishment of plural democracies and market economies in Eastern Europe and the former Soviet Union and insisting that it is both separate from and additional to the programme of aid to developing countries.

The top 20 recipients of British bilateral aid at the beginning of the decade (1990) were as follows:

Country	Pounds sterling millions
India	87.8
Bangladesh	55.8
Pakistan	47.6
Kenya	44.4
Malawi	37.2
Mozambique	25.4
Zambia	24.5
Uganda	24.0
Tanzania	23.2
Indonesia	22.7
Sudan	21.4
Malaysia	21.1
Zimbabwe	20.7
Ethiopia	20.0
Ghana	19.9
China	18.7
Sri Lanka	17.1
Guyana	15.3
Nepal	15.2
Jamaica	14.8

Fourteen of these countries are members of the Commonwealth including the top five recipients (India, Bangladesh and Pakistan being the successor states to the old British Indian Empire) and altogether Commonwealth countries receive 70 per cent of Britain's bilateral aid. Disbursements of multilateral aid in 1990 came to £683 million sterling divided between the European Community (£333 million), the World Bank Group (£184 million) and UN Agencies and others (£166 million).

Most revealing about the programme is the argument advanced that the bulk of British aid finances British goods and services. Thus, since 1978, Aid and Trade Provision (ATP) finance worth £937 million sterling has helped win British exports worth £3.8 billion, while Britain is estimated to gain commercially from its contributions to the multilateral agencies, at the rate of orders for British goods and services valued at approximately £1.40 for every £1 contributed.

Multilateral donors

Multilateral aid is provided by the World Bank Group, the United Nations Specialized Agencies and the regional development banks. The EC and OPEC also provide aid through group mechanisms, but these are more like collectives of like-minded donors and a different principle is involved.

The World Bank Group

The World Bank (IBRD) and the International Monetary Fund (IMF) were founded in 1944 at the Bretton Woods meetings in the USA when it was hoped (principally by the American' and British architects of the system – H.D. White and Lord Maynard Keynes) to establish a new world financial system.

Membership of the World Bank is open to all members of the IMF and at mid-1993 membership stood at 176 for the World Bank and 153 for its 'soft' arm, the IDA.

The Bank is divided into two institutions each of which provides development assistance. These are the International Bank for Reconstruction and Development (IBRD) and the International Development Association (IDA). The IBRD lends at variable interest rates which are 0.5 per cent above the average cost of borrowing. Repayment of World Bank loans is usually over 20 years or less and includes a grace period. Bank loans are either made to governments or have to be guaranteed by governments. A third World Bank institution, the International Finance Corporation (IFC), was established in 1956. Its object is to provide support for the private sector in developing countries. The IFC can make equity investments and provide loans without government guarantees.

The IDA is the 'soft' arm of the Bank. It provides soft loans on easy terms to the poorest countries and only to governments. Its loans are for 50 years and without interest, although there are certain service charges.

Almost all Bank loans are for specific projects (as opposed to programme support although a change of emphasis following much criticism of its project support became apparent in the 1990s) and Bank money cannot be restricted to purchases in any one country, an advantage for recipients. Bank loans are based on economic considerations, carry market interest rates and have to be repaid over 20 years, so there is very little concessional element about them.

On the other hand the IDA (established in 1960) provides wholly concessional assistance. It is dependent for its funds upon replenishments negotiated every 3 years from its principal donors. Its loans go only to the poorest countries and in 1991 the criterion for these was a per capita GNP of $635 or less.

In April 1993 the president and chairman of the World Bank said: 'Poverty reduction must be the benchmark against which performance (by the Bank) as a development institution is measured.' During 1992/93 agreement was reached on the tenth replenishment of the IDA's resources (IDA-10) for 1994-96 equivalent to SDR13 billion ($18 billion) which would maintain the value of the ninth replenishment in real terms.

A new World Bank development of the 1980s was the creation of the Special Programme of Assistance (SPA) for Africa. Eligibility for assistance through the SPA is determined on the basis of poverty (countries cannot be eligible for IBRD loans), indebtedness (countries have to have projected debt service ratios of 30 per cent or more), and efforts to adjust (countries have to be implementing a policy-reform programme) endorsed by the World Bank and the IMF.

Control of the World Bank

The World Bank is owned by its members, with each country subscribing shares according to its GNP. What this means in practice is that the western economies led by the USA (which has 17.46 per cent voting power) effectively control the Bank's policies. When it was established in 1944 the World Bank was not seen as a development agency. Today, however, it is the world's largest source of development finance. The USSR was never a member of the World Bank for both ideological reasons and (presumably) because it saw it would always be outvoted. However, in 1992-93, following the break-up of the USSR, the Bank welcomed 11 additional republics of the former Soviet Union to its ranks as well as the three Baltic states. As a result it extended its operations massively into Eastern Europe and Central Asia and total lending to these ex-

IBRD and IDA lending over the period 1989–93 (commitments) in millions of dollars

	1989	1990	1991	1992	1993
IBRD	16,433	15,180	16,392	15,156	16,945
IDA	4,934	5,522	6,293	6,550	6,751
TOTAL	21,367	20,702	22,685	21,706	23,696

IBRD and IDA lending to the poorest countries over the period 1984–93 in millions of dollars

1984–88	1989	1990	1991	1992	1993
		(annual average)			
9,965.5	12,436.2	9,482.6	10,860.0	10,756.8	9,956.6

Note: The poorest countries are defined as those with a per capita income of $635 or less in 1991.

Communist states in fiscal year 1993 amounted to $3844 million and included initial loans to Albania, Armenia, Estonia, Kyrgyzstan, Latvia, Lithuania, Moldova, Russia and Ukraine.

Because of overwhelming dominance of western voting power the crucial question for the Third World concerns the kind of developments the World Bank encourages and is willing to finance.

Voting powers in the IBRD and IDA

	IBRD	IDA
	%	%
USA	17.46	16.26
Japan	6.74	10.29
Germany	5.21	6.97
France	5.00	4.07
UK	5.00	5.36

Governors of these five countries are appointed; other governors are elected and represent groups of countries. The major western economies are always able to control a majority of votes.

World Bank policies

As the largest source of development aid, the World Bank is clearly of the greatest significance to the Third World. The Bank developed a new strategy for the 1990s: investment in human resources whose main objective is the reduction of poverty through intensified support for effective primary-level services. As the 1993 World Bank Report states: 'The rapidly increasing involvement of the Bank in lending for social and human development provides a good indication of the growing awareness of social programmes as good investments.'

But criticisms of the World Bank have grown: broadly that it is too remote from the problems on the ground. For years the World Bank has worked on two broad assumptions: that it should raise and lend more money each year and that from its investments some prosperity will trickle down to the poorest. Most of its investments have been in projects – usually of major size and chosen in collaboration with Third World governments – that have often resulted in both environmental damage and adverse social consequences. Third World countries, however, will accept World Bank loans, even for projects that are obviously unsuitable, since this means regular injections of new money that can be used to service existing debts. It is a vicious circle.

The Annual Report of the World Bank and the annual meeting of the IBRD and IMF have become events of significance for the Third World. In the Report the Bank says what needs to be done; at the meeting much lobbying takes place.

The Bank's review of the state of development in the Third World is too often delivered as though from on high. Thus, in relation to Africa (generally regarded as the poorest, least developed region), the Bank tends to act as if it is owned by the rich countries of the North and is doing African countries a favour when it provides loans. But if the Bank acts like a 'nanny' instructing the developing world, the IMF is the 'policeman'. At Seoul in 1985 the idea was advanced that the World Bank as well as the IMF should provide a *seal of approval* for developing countries (so as to make it easier for them to find development finance on world markets). Subsequently, the concept of an IMF seal of approval has come to haunt much of the relationship between North and South.

One of the World Bank's most acclaimed documents was its 1981 *Accelerated Development in Sub-Saharan Africa* (An Agenda for Action). This was badly received in Africa. Its analysis of the continent's problems was accepted, but the Bank descended upon the continent like a *deus ex machina*, analysed its ills and then prescribed solutions with far too little reference to what Africans wanted or were trying to achieve. Such attitudes are too often the story of the aid relationship. Furthermore, most of the solutions offered are too akin to market-force policies favoured by the West.

In its 1992 *World Development Report* the World Bank called for a $75 billion a year programme by the year 2000 to raise the living standards of the world's poor by improving their environment, admitted that some of its own programmes had harmed the environment and cautiously moved towards greater support for 'green' policies. But great damage was done to the Bank's image in 1992 when details of an internal Bank memorandum were leaked. The World Bank's chief economist had proposed increased pollution for Africa. In an internal Bank memorandum Lawrence Summers asked: 'I've always thought under-populated countries in Africa are vastly under-polluted. Shouldn't the World Bank be encouraging more migration of the dirty industries (to such countries)? I think the economic logic behind dumping toxic waste in the lowest-wage countries is impeccable.' As long as such ideas surface from its senior staff it will be unsurprising that Third World countries view the Bank with suspicion.

The International Monetary Fund (IMF)

Also born out of the Bretton Woods talks of 1944, the IMF is historically closely allied to the World Bank. When it was set up, the IMF was not seen as a development agency, but as a permanent means of establishing a world multilateral system of payments. It is a form of co-operative deposit bank. Members with balance of payments problems can draw over 4 years up to four times their deposit quotas in exchange for their own currencies. Then, if a member wants help over and above its full drawing rights, it is obliged to submit to stringent IMF conditions. These *conditionalities* as they have come to be called go beyond normal banking requirements. It is IMF conditionality which has become a major bone of political contention between the Fund and many would-be borrowers from the Third World.

The IMF is not a source of aid but a source of short-term funds to tide countries over immediate problems when their economies are in crisis. But the problem for the Third World is that the IMF has come to be seen, with its *seal of approval* which western bankers require if they are to lend, as a kind of policeman for western capitalism, prescribing policies which developing countries should follow. Too often, these policies appear to be what the western capitalist governments would prescribe, not necessarily what Third World countries want.

According to the *Human Development Report* of 1992 the IMF no longer performs the function for which it was created, which was to maintain monetary stability with the burden of adjustments shared between surplus and deficit countries; moreover, it has ceased to perform this original function because it is unable to control or exert authority over the rich industrial nations. By the beginning of the 1980s (and ever since) it has been clear that the rich nations (in effect the Group of Seven) who between them can control the voting of the IMF had come to see it as their instrument and not as their mentor, and though the IMF should have become the guardian of the poor, in fact it became the policeman for the rich. Thus a high proportion of Third World countries now operate IMF-inspired structural adjustment programmes (SAPs) through which the IMF instructs governments how to run their economies in return for a measure of debt relief in the form of rescheduling.

The United Nations agencies

The UN agencies have become a major source of multilateral aid, mainly in the form of technical assistance. In the early 1950s such agencies as the FAO and WHO were seen as advisers on problems rather than as disbursers of aid. Then during the 1960s (the decade when aid took off and was, for a time, fashionable) four new agencies were created: the IDA of the World Bank in 1960 which has been described above; the World Food Programme (WFP) in 1962; the United Nations Development Programme (UNDP) in 1965; and the United Nations Fund for Population Activities (UNFPA) in 1966.

UN agencies have a particular importance in the field of multilateral aid, because recipients have a voice in their decisions. Thus in the UNDP and UNICEF, decisions depend upon consensus rather than a vote. An important function for these agencies, as far as the Third World is concerned, is to compensate for the inequalities which result from the system of bilateral aid. For example, principal bilateral donors such as Britain and France tend to concentrate their aid upon the Commonwealth (Britain) or Francophone Africa (France) so that some countries not covered by such groupings find difficulty in attracting aid. It is in such cases that UN multilateral assistance may turn out to be crucial. Moreover, the UN agencies tend to concentrate their efforts on the poorer developing countries and the bulk of UN assistance goes to countries with per capita GNP below the $635 mark. About 50 per cent of UN funds are channelled through the UNDP; the balance goes through agencies, such as FAO or WHO, and the money is administered by their trust funds.

The United Nations Development Programme (UNDP)

UNDP technical asistance funds can be used to employ personnel from almost any source and are not confined to the countries supplying the funds.

The UNDP relies upon annual voluntary contributions from most countries of the world, although the bulk of its funds (90 per cent) come from the DAC countries of the West. Its funds for 1991 came to $1.5 billion and in 1993 the UNDP was supporting 6000 projects world-wide.

The World Food Programme (WFP)

The WFP handles food resources valued at about $1.6 billion a year, a quarter of all food aid disbursed. WFP aid is tied to specific projects and, unlike bilateral food donors, WFP does not allow its food to be sold on the recipient country market so that funds raised can then be used for general purposes. At the end of 1991 the WFP was assisting 266 development projects at a total cost of $3 billion and during the life of these on-going projects an estimated 80 million people will receive WFP food aid.

For the other UN agencies see Chapter Two on the United Nations and Chapter Seven for coverage of IFAD (International Food for Agricultural Development).

Regional banks

There are three regional banks: the Inter-American Development Bank (IDB), the Asian Development Bank and the African Development Bank. For a breakdown of their activities and impact, see Chapter Four on Regional Groupings.

Other multilateral agencies

Other multilateral aid agencies relate to the EC and OPEC. These, however, may be described as donor collectives. In each case they are agencies representative of like-minded donor groups disbursing a proportion of their aid on a multilateral basis. The EC operates the European Development Fund (EDF) and the European Investment Bank (EIB) as well as providing substantial food aid. A donor, such as Britain, will include its contributions to the EDF as part of its total aid for any given year. For details of the OPEC Fund see Chapter Six on OPEC and Oil Power. Finally the Commonwealth (see Chapter Four, Part 5) operates a limited multilateral aid programme through the CFTC.

Non-government Organizations (NGOs)

There is another considerable flow of resources and people from rich to poor countries, apart from government or private enterprise. These are the non-government organizations (NGOs) which are wholly or partly concerned with development problems in the Third World. Contributions to aid and development projects through NGOs from the DAC countries are substantial; part of their funds come from government support grants to individual organizations. As a matter of policy some countries, such as Norway, disburse substantial amounts of aid through voluntary organizations. The USA, for example, channels quantities of food aid through the private organization CARE (Cooperative for American Relief Everywhere).

The range of these NGOs is enormous: some are hard-headed and cost-effective in their approach; others are amateur in the extreme. Broadly they may be divided into five categories:

1. Churches and missions whose primary concern is proselytization, though in recent times they have become involved in aspects of development, especially in education and health.

2. Large national organizations, such as the US Ford Foundation. These have assured funds and often mount major studies of problems concerning development though they do not operate only in the Third World.

3. National agencies, such as OXFAM in Britain or NOVIB in Holland, which were created specifically to assist with problems of the Third World.

4. International organizations which originally were not designed for Third World operations at all, but have become increasingly involved in Third World development problems. These include the International Red Cross, the Planned Parenthood Federation, World University Service and the World Council of Churches.

5. A number of countries have created volunteer-sending agencies, such as Britain's Voluntary Service Overseas (VSO). Some of these are entirely government run; others which began as voluntary organizations have come to rely for the bulk of their funds upon their govern-

ments even though they continue to act as independent voluntary organizations.

Such organizations often operate in the field at levels at which governments would not be prepared to undertake anything. Thus in the early 1970s at an extremely sensitive level (as far as western governments were concerned) the World Council of Churches (WCC) provided aid to African guerrilla movements in southern Africa (Mozambique and Rhodesia), although specifying that the funds should only be used for medical or other non-violent purposes.

In the troubled 1990s the NGOs (or some of them) tended to take on a new role, insisting upon delivering humanitarian aid where governments were loath to become involved and so setting the pace for later official interventions (Bosnia and Somalia are examples of this). Sometimes, ironically, the activities of NGOs in such circumstances are welcome to governments since they provide them with an excuse not to take action themselves.

Aid distribution

For the fiscal year 1991, the total ODA (official development assistance) from OECD and OPEC members was as follows: OECD a total of $55,519 million; OPEC (1990) $6,341 million.

In all aid considerations it is the donors who call the tune: generally this is equally true whether it is bilateral or multilateral aid. Countries which are heavily dependent upon aid are not in a position to take part in *equal* bargains. In any case, aid is about an *unequal* relationship. This, perhaps, is most obvious when examining the role of major donors, such as the USA in its bilateral capacity, or the World Bank as a multilateral donor. In the latter case, throughout the Bank's history, policies have clearly been dictated by the major western members of the Bank in tune with western economic interests in the Third World. The greatest weakness of the Third World in relation to the North lies in its economic dependence. This is as true in matters of trade as in the aid relationship.

Important dates in the development of aid

1944   Establishment of the World Bank and IMF.
1945   FAO established (headquarters in Rome).
1947   Marshall Plan put forward.
1948   OEEC (later OECD) established.
1949   President Truman proposes 'Point Four' programme of assistance.
1950   The Colombo Plan is launched.
1956   Suez Crisis: the West (including World Bank) withdraws offer of aid to Egypt for Aswan High Dam and USSR takes over; high point of Cold War aid rivalries.
1959   The Inter-American Development Bank (IDB) is set up.
1960   The International Development Association (IDA), the soft arm of the World Bank, is established. DAC is established.
1961   The UN General Assembly designates the 1960s as the United Nations Development Decade.
1962   The World Food Programme (WFP) established in Rome.
1963   The First Yaoundé Convention between the EC and the Associated African and Malagasy states.
1964   The African Development Bank is established. The first United Nations Conference on Trade and Development (UNCTAD I) is held in Geneva.
1965   The United Nations Development Programme (UNDP) is established.
1966   The Asian Development Bank is established.

1968   UNCTAD II in New Delhi proposes a Generalized System of Preferences to favour exports of developing countries.
1969   The Pearson Report *Partners in Development* calls for 0.7 per cent GNP as ODA.
1970   UN General Assembly proclaims Second Development Decade.
1971   UN General Assembly designates 25 countries as Least Developed Countries (LDCs).
1973   The Fourth Non-Aligned Summit in Algiers advances the idea of a New International Economic Order (NIEO). The Yom Kippur War and the oil crisis leads to a quadrupling of oil prices by the end of 1974.
1974   Sixth Special Session of the UN General Assembly adopts Declaration and Programme of Action on the Establishment of a New International Economic Order.
1975   The high point of Arab (OPEC) aid: Arab Bank for Economic Development in Africa (BADEA), the Islamic Development Bank and the Saudi Fund for development each becomes operational. Lomé I between EC and ACP countries.
1976   OPEC Special Fund is established in Vienna. The formation of the Club du Sahel to assist development of the Sahel region.
1977   Japan announces intention to double its aid by 1980 from $1.4 billion to $2.8 billion.

1978   The World Bank produces its first World Development Report.
1979   Lomé II signed by EC and ACP states.
1980   UN General Assembly proclaims 1980s the Third UN Development Decade.
The Brandt Report: *North–South: A Programme for Survival*.
1981   The CANCUN Summit: 22 representatives of North and South meet to discuss 'Co-operation and Development' but against a background of the UK government white paper of 1980 and President Reagan's pre-summit speech, both of which emphasize free market forces.
1982   Debt crisis sparked off by Mexico and then Brazil declaring inability to meet debts.
1983   The African development crisis continues: World Bank report *Sub-Saharan Africa: Progress Report on Development Prospects and Programmes*.
Second Brandt Report.
1984   Lomé III between EC (10) and ACP (65) countries.
1985   World Bank establishes a Special Facility for Sub-Saharan Africa.
At Seoul meeting of World Bank and IMF the concept of a *seal of approval* is floated.
1990-92   The end of the Cold War brings about major reappraisals of aid.
1991   Lomé IV between EC (12) and ACP (69) countries.
1992   The Rio Earth Summit or UNCED (UN Conference on the Environment and Development).

6 OPEC and Oil Power

Although the Organization of Petroleum Exporting Countries (OPEC) was formed in 1960, it attracted little public attention and was virtually ignored by the international oil companies for the first decade of its existence. Only in the 1970s did it come into prominence.

Following the closure of the Suez Canal in 1956, oil prices rose in 1957 although 2 years later there was a general reduction. It was still very much the era of cheap oil. The fall in the price of Gulf crudes in 1959 adversely affected those Middle Eastern countries whose budgets depended upon oil revenues. As a result in September 1960, following another oil price reduction, ministers from five major oil-producing countries – Iran, Iraq, Kuwait, Saudi Arabia and Venezuela – met in Baghdad where they decided to establish a permanent body to act in the interest of oil producers: in effect a cartel.

The original five were joined by others as follows: Qatar (1961), Libya and Indonesia (1962), Abu Dhabi – later the United Arab Emirates (1967), Algeria (1969), Nigeria (1971), Ecuador (1973) and Gabon (1975, although it had been an associate from 1973).

The Conference, the supreme authority of OPEC, formulates general policies and is made up of representatives of member countries who appoint governors and elect the Chairman. The Conference works on the unanimity principle and meets two (or more) times a year.

The Board of Governors directs the management of OPEC, implements the resolutions of the Conference and draws up the budget. One governor is appointed from each member country. The Economic Commission is concerned to promote stability in international oil prices. The Secretariat, the administrative organ of OPEC with a Secretary-General, is divided into a number of departments, namely the Research Division, the Economic and Finance Department, the

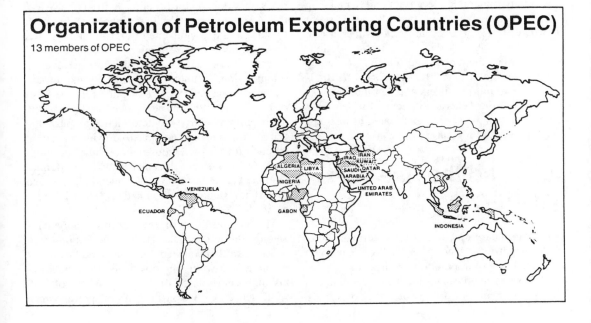

Organization of Petroleum Exporting Countries (OPEC)

13 members of OPEC

ALGERIA LIBYA
NIGERIA
VENEZUELA
ECUADOR
GABON
IRAN
IRAQ KUWAIT
SAUDI ARABIA QATAR
UNITED ARAB EMIRATES
INDONESIA

Information Services Department, the Statistics Unit, the Personnel and Administrative Department, the Public Relations Department, and the Legal Affairs Unit.

Oil wealth in the Gulf was becoming an increasingly important political factor during the 1960s. Thus as early as 1961 Kuwait established the Kuwait Fund for Arab Economic Development which to begin with was only a modest disburser of aid providing no more than KD60 million ($200 million) from 1962 to 1971. Then in 1967 at the time of the Six Day War against Israel the rich Arab oil states – Saudi Arabia, Kuwait, Libya – made massive grants to the three non-oil front line states – Egypt, Jordan and Syria – which had borne the brunt of Israel's military actions.

By 1970, however, Libya began to mount pressure upon the independents for a change in price structure. It forced Occidental to cut production by a third and then used production cuts as a lever to achieve further changes. This was the beginning of OPEC power. At Caracas in December of that year the OPEC Conference decided to press for price increases and raised the tax on oil company incomes to 55 per cent.

A factor of great importance, which now operated in OPEC's favour, was that from 1970 onwards production in the USA began to fall. Thus by 1973 US demand from the Middle East had reached 1.7 million barrels per day. This meant that the world's greatest consumer became increasingly vulnerable, because it had to make up a growing shortfall from the Middle East or elsewhere. It was to need as great an increase in supplies each year as did Europe. Negotiations between the companies and OPEC continued between 1970 and 1973. In February 1971, it is true, the six Gulf producers and 23 oil companies did work out the Teheran Agreement which fixed prices – but this soon became outdated by insistent OPEC pressures for greater price changes.

1973 and the rise of OPEC

The extraordinary way in which a handful of Third World countries which possessed oil came to dominate much of international politics during the mid-1970s was an unusual – and inevitably temporary – phenomenon of power, or rather of a brief

power imbalance which upset the more usual ways in which international affairs are conducted. The rise of OPEC had repercussions throughout the world. For a time it gave great hope to the Third World that a new world order more to its liking could be brought into being. This was not to be, though the changes wrought at that time did leave some permanent results and gave to Third World countries a greater sense of their potential ability to alter things – provided they acted together.

On 6 October 1973, the Yom Kippur War was launched against Israel, by Egypt and Syria. This was the first Arab–Israeli encounter in which the Arabs held their own so that the military honours were by no means one-sided. And during the war, on 16 October, the Arab oil producers met in Kuwait to raise posted oil prices by 70 per cent, so that Arabian 'marker' crude increased in price from $3.01 a barrel to $5.12 a barrel. Later Libya was to raise its prices still higher to $8.92 a barrel. On 17 October, just a day after the first price rise had been agreed, a more drastic decision was taken in Kuwait. Under the terms of the Organization of Arab Petroleum Exporting Countries (OAPEC), it was decided to use the oil weapon in support of Egypt and Syria in their war with Israel, then still raging. Iraq opted out of this decision. The other Arab producers decided upon cumulative 5 per cent production cuts from the September level of output until Israel had withdrawn from the territories occupied in 1967. But though these decisions looked drastic enough from the West, the Arab producers hesitated about taking such tough measures and their implementation was accompanied by many misgivings. Nonetheless, by December the agreed cutbacks had achieved a dramatic impact upon the world's oil market and Iranian oil was selling at $17.40 a barrel. The Shah of Iran, with ambitions of his own unrelated to the Yom Kippur War, was determined to push the price of oil as high as possible to provide maximum revenue for his own industrial and other development plans. He was the chief 'hawk' who dominated the December 1973 OPEC meeting, by which time the posted price of oil had settled at $11.65 a barrel.

The complexities of the various manoeuvres among the oil producers, the hesitations and divisions in their ranks did not alter the fact that a remarkable revolution took place over an astonishingly short period of time. The events of 1973 witnessed an explosion of Arab oil power which was to lead to North–South Dialogue, demands for a New International Economic Order and, at least briefly, Third World euphoria that at last the world economic balance had been tilted in the South's favour. What immediately made these expectations possible was the fact that the Arab oil producers were able to build up huge cash surpluses in a very short time. The possession of these surpluses was the weapon which provided the OPEC countries with their temporary bargaining strength. In the West the big question was just how they would deploy their surpluses.

By December 1974 both OPEC government revenues and the price paid for oil by consumers had multiplied by a factor of five. For example, OECD estimates for 1973 to 1977 suggest that OPEC recycling (the jargon word of the time meaning spending the surpluses to purchase western goods and industrial expertise) was equivalent to creating about 900,000 jobs in the industrialized countries over this period. Clearly *this* was the basis of OPEC power. If the situation could continue indefinitely in which this small group of countries were thus able to affect the western industrial scene, their influence would remain considerable.

Saudi Arabia was the most cautious of the Arab oil producers. It was also by far the largest producer and the *swing* country whose increase or decrease of production could substantially alter the entire pattern. Saudi Arabia believed, realistically, that the continued well-being and prosperity of OPEC was dependent upon an equally continuing health among the western economies. But precisely because it was the richest oil country, Saudi Arabia had to allow itself to be carried along by the others – at least in part – for it was especially susceptible to the argument that the needs of the smaller producers for large returns were greater than its own.

From December 1974 until January 1979 the price of oil went up twice: the first time in September 1975 (the Vienna OPEC meeting) by 10 per cent, and then again in December 1976 when the majority – but not Saudi Arabia or the UAE – raised the price by another 10 per cent. Thus OPEC was split but not disastrously even though the division between the price hawks and price doves foreshadowed deeper splits which would become far more evident in the troubled 1980s.

By 1979 the price hawks in OPEC were once again pushing oil prices higher (following a partial glut in 1978). Their prospects of even higher prices seemed the greater following the revolution in Iran, the fall of the Shah and the uncertainty as to what policy the new government would follow, though in the beginning it seemed clear that there would be a deliberate cutback in Iranian production.

In June 1979 OPEC imposed a ceiling of $23.50 a barrel, but events were getting out of hand. At an extraordinary meeting at Geneva in October prices were raised another 9 per cent. The rise did not appear to stop even there for by the end of the year best African 'sweet crudes' were selling at $37 a barrel. The end of the decade saw the OPEC oil prices peak, although financiers at the time were predicting a $50 barrel of oil. At Algiers in June 1980 OPEC set the market price for crude at $32 a barrel and fixed that the value differentials above this ceiling should not be allowed to rise more than another $5 – achieving a peak of $37 a barrel which had already been reached.

All this time the consumers had looked on apparently helpless as the world's most valuable traded fuel rocketed in price. For once the major trading countries of the West seemed unable to control the price to their satisfaction. Over these years the West's inability to control the price – and the enormous success (in the short run) of the OPEC cartel in pushing it up – gave rise to many Third World hopes, often wildly optimistic and soon to be disappointed, that at last the Third World had found a means of redressing the North–South imbalance. This short period of less than a decade – 1973 to 1980 – can be described as the era of OPEC power. The vital question for the Third World was – and remains – what did it gain in any permanent sense from the exercise of OPEC power?

The year 1980 may be taken as the high point of OPEC power for the decade which followed altered the situation drastically at least for the short term as follows:

a) Recession and the emergence of new producers reduced demand for oil and brought the prices down from the high level they had reached at the beginning of the decade.

b) Despite the 8-year war between Iraq and Iran this did not have the expected effect of pushing up oil prices.

c) Squabbles within OPEC prevented it from producing a single, coherent policy to cope with

Distribution of oil reserves 1992

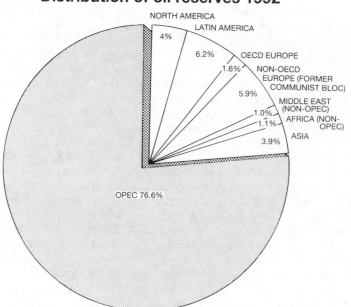

Note

Production figures have to be related to total demand. In 1992 the pattern was as follows:

OPEC

produced 26m b/d

consumed 4.5m b/d

and so had a surplus of 21.5m b/d for export.

The USA

produced 8.85m b/d

consumed 16.24m b/d

and so had a deficit of 7.39m b/d which had to be imported.

Europe (OECD and non-OECD)

produced 14m b/d

consumed 21.5m b/d

and so had a deficit of 7.5m b/d which had to be imported.

Japan

consumed 5.545m b/d

which had to be imported.

Rest of world

produced 16m b/d

consumed 17.5m b/d

and so had a deficit of 1.5m b/d which had to be imported.

(NB. Discrepancies between total surplus and total deficit are accounted for either by the consumption of reserves or by untraced trading.)

WORLD OIL OUTPUT IN 1992

Production is shown in four main groups: OPEC; Europe, both OECD and non-OECD (former Communist) states; the USA; and the rest of the world. In 1992 total world oil output came to 65 m b/d. In the diagram the figures have been rounded to the nearest million barrels.

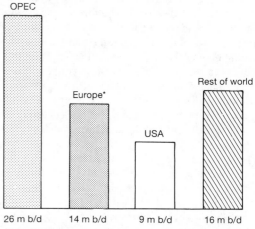

*Both OECD and non-OECD (former Communist bloc)

the new conditions. Thus, at the OPEC meeting of 16–17 September 1992, Ecuador withdrew in protest at the high annual fee ($2m) and its low quota of only 320,000 barrels a day (b/d).

d) The potentially calamitous results of the 1991

Gulf War, which led to the firing of oil wells in Kuwait, nonetheless did not alter by much the generally sluggish world demand for oil.

e) By 1993 it had become clear that until the western economies moved out of recession, OPEC would continue to remain in the doldrums.

Yet, despite the above developments, an examination of world oil resources and production in 1992 (see diagrams opposite) reveals that the OPEC position for the future remains remarkably strong.

OPEC resources and production*

OPEC power and, most especially, Middle Eastern oil power is based upon the extent of its share of total world oil resources and its ability to meet consumer demands. And this situation will operate in the future despite the period of recession and the decline in OPEC influence which took place over the period 1984-1993. OPEC resources, therefore, have to be related first to OPEC's own energy needs; second to the demand of the world's main consumers; and third to alternative sources of supply.

At the end of 1992, OPEC possessed 76.6 per cent of the world's proved resources (the figure includes non-OPEC Middle East countries). Of this amount 65.7 per cent was in the hands of the Middle East OPEC members, while five non-Middle East OPEC countries between them controlled 11.9 per cent of world proved resources as follows:

Algeria	0.9%	Libya	2.3%
Gabon	0.1%	Nigeria	1.8%
Indonesia	0.6%	Venezuela	6.2%

OPEC's share of proved oil reserves (by country) end 1992

Country	Thousand million barrels	% of world total
Algeria	9.2	0.9
Gabon	0.7	0.1
Indonesia	5.8	0.6
Iran	92.9	9.2
Iraq	100.0	9.9
Kuwait	94.0	9.3
Neutral Zone[a]	5.0	0.5
Libya	22.8	2.3
Nigeria	17.9	1.8
Qatar	3.7	0.4
Saudi Arabia	257.8	25.6
UAE[b]	98.1	9.8
Venezuela	62.6	6.2
	Total	76.6

[a] Oil from the Neutral Zone is shared equally by Kuwait and Saudi Arabia.

[b] The two Emirates of Abu Dhabi (9.2%) and Dubai (0.6%) together make up the percentage share of 9.8% of the UAE.

The significance of this table is that OPEC's huge surplus to its requirements is sufficient to supply all the additional needs of the USA (7.3m b/d), Western Europe (7.5m b/d), and Japan (5.5m b/d) as well as giving it an additional 2m b/d. However, OPEC consumption may rise sharply once the recession ends. Moreover, so great are the reserves of such countries as Saudi Arabia and Kuwait that if world demand were suddenly to double they – and only they – would have the capacity to meet the extra demand.

The condition of the world oil market in 1993 may be very different from the position in 1975 or 1985 yet the basic surplus and deficit situation as demonstrated here will remain relatively the same – unless some major new discoveries are made.

The future potential influence of OPEC has also to be related to the level of production and consumption of the major consumers. The USA with reserves of 32.1 thousand million barrels (3.2 per cent of world total reserves) is by far the greatest consumer. In terms of its 1992 production, the USA only has 9.8 more years of its own oil to use if it continues to produce at the same level and finds no further reserves. Of the major users the USA is the most vulnerable. Russia with reserves of 48.4 thousand million barrels (4.8 per cent of total world reserves) has a further 16.7 years of oil if it produces constantly at the 1992 output level.

On the other hand, since the disruptions of 1990-92 in the Gulf, Iran could nonetheless produce for 73.6 years and Saudi Arabia for 82 years if they maintained output at their 1992 levels.

*All figures for reserves, production and consumption have been extracted from *BP Statistical Review of World Energy* (June 1993).

OPEC output (barrels per day 1992)

Country	b/d
Algeria	1,325,000
Gabon	295,000
Indonesia	1,540,000
Iran	3,455,000
Iraq	480,000*
Kuwait	905,000
Neutral Zone	325,000
Libya	1,520,000
Nigeria	1,850,000
Qatar	485,000
Saudi Arabia	8,735,000
UAE	2,490,000
Venezuela	2,500,000
Total	25,905,000

*The reduction is due to the UN embargo after the Gulf War.

This picture of OPEC resources (as in 1992) highlights the huge preponderance of reserves which lie in the Arab countries of the Middle East. Even though the 1980s proved an especially difficult period of glut and saw a collapse of OPEC solidarity in the face of other producers, such as Britain and Mexico, capturing at least a proportion of their dwindling markets, this was a temporary setback; already by the 1990s most of the new discoveries were in the Middle East rather than elsewhere and their possession of the vast majority of total world resources gives OPEC formidable long-term assets.

During the mid-1970s, when OPEC countries first realized the extent of their power and made conscious efforts to exercise it, they did so in very different world market conditions so that the OPEC price rise, cutback in production and boycott decisions of 1973-74 had an immediate and devastating effect. The fact that by the mid-1980s world recession had produced an oil glut meant that OPEC was in temporary disarray. This disarray, along with depressed demand, continued into the 1990s which were ushered in by the Gulf War of 1991 which in turn led to the disruption of the Kuwait fields and the forced cutback of Iraqi production. Yet none of this diminishes the long-term oil strength which the group as a whole commands.

Of total world oil reserves of 1006.5 thousand million barrels at the end of 1992, five Middle East countries between them possessed well over half at 547.8 thousand million barrels. These five were:

Iran	92.9
Iraq	100.0
Kuwait	94.0
Neutral Zone	5.0
Saudi Arabia	257.8
UAE	98.1
Total	647.8

These figures add up to great power; they also make the five – and the Gulf – exceptionally vulnerable to military pressures and such vulnerability could well become greater in a future of dwindling oil reserves world-wide.

OPEC power and after

Between 1973 and 1979 the world's media watched the deliberations of OPEC as though everything else depended upon them, which in a sense was the case. The OPEC-induced price rises, the oil production cutbacks and the boycott brought a new dimension into relations between the advanced economies and those of the Third World. For a time there was panic in the West as oil prices rose, including the spectacle in European countries of huge lines of motor vehicles filling their tanks with petrol as though in a wartime emergency. And in international politics, the demand for a New International Economic Order suddenly came to the forefront, as did the new concept of a North–South dialogue, with a confident OPEC led by its militant 'hawks' insisting upon change and a less than usually assured North apparently, at least, ready to listen and take part in a two-way discussion. These changes were seen by the rest of the Third World to be the achievements of OPEC power. It is little wonder that for a time the features of Saudi Arabia's oil minister, Sheikh Yamani, became among the most familiar on the world's television screens.

Third World excitement at this new-found OPEC power was reinforced by the fact that every member of OPEC was also a Third World country facing huge development problems of its own. As a result they were assumed to be entirely in sympathy with wider Third World aspirations. In consequence OPEC's successes were regarded as an assertion of *all* the Third World's rights in confrontation with the North.

Thus the Third World had a vested interest in OPEC even when the huge price increases inflicted major economic hardship upon non-oil producing countries of the South. The need for solidarity was paramount and Third World countries lined up behind OPEC as it faced the major industrialized countries of the North. (The Communist bloc was largely insulated from the impact of OPEC price rises, because it was self-sufficient in oil and also produced a substantial surplus to its total needs.)

In March 1975 OPEC leaders met at a summit in Algiers where they presented themselves as the vanguard of the Third World demanding a New International Economic Order. Later that year, in June 1975, OPEC met in Gabon. There the Organization proposed that oil prices should be quoted in SDRs (Special Drawing Rights) of the IMF rather than in US dollars and that prices should be indexed to world inflation rates. These proposals were not at all palatable to the West. The result of such demands, combined with continuing OPEC pressures, led to the convening of the 1976 Paris Conference on International Economic Co-operation and Development (CIEC). At this meeting 19 representatives of the Third World met eight representatives of the western capitalist world and the idea of a North–South dialogue was born.

A vital aspect of the OPEC-dominated 1970s (which was also the UN's Second Development Decade) was the large scale and continuous transfer of financial resources from the advanced industrial economies to the oil-exporters so that such countries as Iran, Saudi Arabia and Nigeria could embark upon development plans of a scope undreamt of only a few years earlier. The size of the OPEC surpluses and the question of how they would use them is what gave OPEC its power. Thus payments from the rich oil-importing countries to members of OPEC rose from $35 billion a year in 1973-74 to $140 billion a year by 1978. This represented a net annual transfer of about $40 billion a year, or one and a half times the total capital flow (both public and private) to the Third World in 1973.

Western fears that in its triumphant heyday, OPEC might use its sudden new wealth to do irreversible damage to the West – such as reducing oil output until it was just sufficient to supply what OPEC members needed for immediate development purposes – did not materialize. The OPEC states behaved *responsibly* in western terms and used their surpluses to increase imports from the West (in the end greatly to the West's advantage), while also placing much of the balance of their wealth as investments in the West: either through the purchase of business interests and by building up share portfolios, or by making the money available on the international money markets.

Thus, after the first triumphant display of its power, OPEC behaved more as a junior but acceptable partner in the western-dominated economic system than as the spearhead of the Third World, though for a time it did raise a hope that this would be its role. Despite this failure OPEC's importance to the Third World – both positively and negatively – was very great. It did demonstrate, however briefly, that Third World solidarity, backed in this case by oil power, could force the West to consider the Third World case in a manner that had simply not been evident before. OPEC solidarity was a mirage, however, and by 1980, as world economic conditions changed for the worse, Third World support for OPEC also began to collapse. The idea of a New International Economic Order appeared to have been shelved. What North–South dialogue took place at all had become acrimonious and unconstructive. There were also deepening divisions in the Arab world and OPEC ranks, and two of the best endowed OPEC nations – Iran and Iraq – had embarked upon a brutal war with one another. The greatest success to be recorded by then was the ability of the West to stall and do nothing until conditions had changed in its favour.

The troubled 1980s

The contrast between the all-powerful OPEC of 1979, whose decisions were awaited by the rest of the world with bated breath, and the OPEC of 1986 trying to persuade Britain and the USSR to cut back their production so that OPEC could maintain its prices (with these then sliding well below $15 a barrel) illustrates perfectly how quickly international political fortunes can alter. In 10 years (1975-1985) OPEC's position had changed: instead of being the spearhead of a newly resurgent Third World at last forcing the old imperial capitalist West to make concessions, it became the suppliant pleading with Mrs Thatcher's Britain to cut back its (non-OPEC) production so as to help keep the cartel together.

For example, by 1982 Nigeria, which had become a modest aid donor when it was producing 2.3 million barrels a day, found that it had to make savage cutbacks in its development plans as it was forced to reduce oil production to 1.3 million barrels a day (and sometimes below 1 million barrels a day). Other members of OPEC were obliged to do the same and even Saudi Arabia – the *swing* country of the Organization – had reduced output from a mammoth 10 million barrels a day and more to less than 5 million barrels a day. By the mid-1980s OPEC was struggling simply to maintain itself in being as a coherent organization.

Moreover, the war between Iraq and Iran did so much damage to those two countries that when it ended in 1988 they faced enormous bills for reconstruction. Further, the end of that war was to be followed by another crisis in 1990–91 when Iraq invaded Kuwait and subsequently fired the Kuwait oilfields. As a consequence of these developments in the 1980s and early 1990s, the possibility of continuing huge cash surpluses in the future (assuming the end of the world-wide recession) will probably now be confined to Saudi Arabia, a renewed Kuwait, the UAE and possibly Libya.

OPEC members' percentage share of world oil resources related to population

Country	% world oil resources 1992	Population (mid-1992)
Algeria	0.9	26,401,000
Gabon	0.1	1,253,000
Indonesia	0.6	184,796,000
Iran	9.2	59,570,000
Iraq	9.9	18,838,000
Kuwait	9.3	1,190,000
Libya	2.3	4,447,000
Nigeria	1.8	89,666,000
Qatar	0.4	520,000
Saudi Arabia	25.6	15,267,000
UAE	9.8	1,969,000
Venezuela	6.2	20,184,000

An examination of these population figures related to oil resources shows that the non-Middle East members of OPEC, with the exception of Libya, have sufficiently large populations and, therefore, development needs of their own to ensure that they will be price 'hawks' into the foreseeable future, needing all the revenue they can obtain for the improvement of their own economies. Iran and Iraq, in their post-war recovery phases, should also be included in this group and Iran in any case has a sufficiently large population to absorb all it earns. Effectively, then, this means that only Saudi

Arabia, the UAE, Kuwait and Libya will be able to create large financial surpluses in the future over and above their own development needs.

Arab and OPEC aid

One of the most positive aspects of oil power was the rapid growth of Arab and OPEC aid and the creation of a number of new aid agencies based in the Middle East. Between them these added significantly to the flow of aid into the Third World, although in part they came to be seen by the non-oil producing countries as no more than compensation for the huge extra amounts they were obliged to pay for their oil.

Of the 12 members of OPEC, 10 became substantial international donors. These were Algeria, Iran, Iraq, Kuwait, Libya, Nigeria, Qatar, Saudi Arabia, the UAE and Venezuela. If we take into account the huge differences in population between OPEC members, then it is not reasonable to expect either Indonesia or Nigeria (with populations then of 165.4 million and 103.1 million respectively) to be major donors. Each had enough development problems of its own to overcome and so needed all the money it could raise. Nonetheless, Nigeria did provide aid at least to its neighbours in Africa. (Ecuador and Gabon did not become aid donors.)

Nigerian aid

At the end of 1974 Nigeria made available substantial sums to both the IMF and the World Bank: $120 million to the IMF to be used to finance oil credits; and $240 million to the World Bank at 8 per cent interest. In the Commonwealth to which it belongs, Nigeria was the only developing member to increase its contributions to the Commonwealth Fund for Technical Co-operation (CFTC). On a bilateral basis it provided £2 million to the Sahel countries in the wake of the 1973 drought, $500,000 to Guinea-Bissau at its independence and further aid to Mali, Botswana and Zambia. In West Africa, Nigeria also provided substantial grants to Togo, Benin and Niger to help balance their budgets. The amounts involved were not great, but then Nigeria at this time had more than enough of its own development problems including post-civil war reconstruction and, given the size of its population, it would have been quite reasonable for it to provide no aid at all.

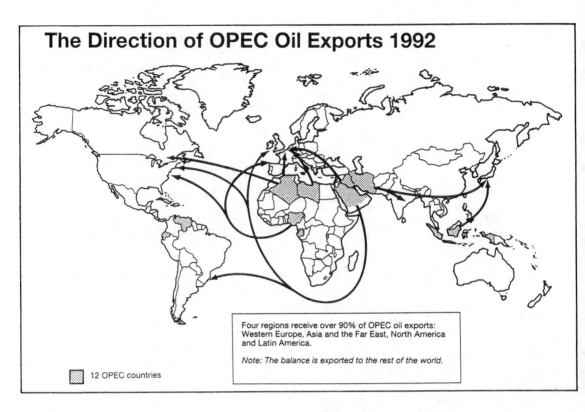

The Direction of OPEC Oil Exports 1992

Four regions receive over 90% of OPEC oil exports: Western Europe, Asia and the Far East, North America and Latin America.

Note: The balance is exported to the rest of the world.

▨ 12 OPEC countries

Nigerian aid (US$ millions) 1976–90*

1976	1980	1984	1985	1986
$80	$35	$51	$45	$52

1987	1988	1989	1990
$30	$14	$70	$13

*Figures extracted from the 1993 World Development Report.

The extent of OPEC aid

As a group the OPEC states proved far more generous with their aid on a percentage of GNP basis than any other group. Arab aid was already beginning to make an impact before the oil price rises of 1973. Between 1970 and 1972 allocations were as follows:

1970	1971	1972
$443.5 million	$630.9 million	$688.9 million

In 1973 a sharp rise occurred and the official disbursement figures (on a 2-year basis) over the peak period were as follows:

1973	1975 (peak)	1978
$1750 million	$8710 million	$5780 million

These figures are even more impressive when seen as a percentage of the GNP of the 10 principal OPEC donors:

1973	1975	1979
1.43%	2.71%	1.48%

At no time have any OECD donors reached even the lowest of these figures (1.43 per cent) for their aid disbursements. Indeed in 1979, aid from the 10 OPEC donors on a percentage of GNP basis surpassed that of the 17 OECD donors by more than four times and that of the eastern bloc countries by 36 times (according to OECD statistics). And in 1981, when the signs of recession were multiplying, OPEC aid was still running at $8 billion, equivalent to 20 per cent of all ODA and equal to that of the USA, the world's richest nation.

Whatever criticisms are levelled at OPEC aid – and there are a number – it was nonetheless provided at a level whose generosity was unmatched by any other donor. Moreover, it should be remembered that oil is usually the sole and certainly the main source of wealth of the OPEC nations. It is a capital resource which once used cannot be replaced, a fact that makes the aid even more generous. This is certainly the case when matched against aid from the North. The OPEC countries, too, are themselves developing and on that count could have justified providing no aid at all.

OPEC aid (US$ millions) 1976 – 90

1976	1980	1984	1985	1986
5877	9636	4559	3615	4704

1987	1988	1989	1990
3333	2369	1514	6341

Conditions of OPEC aid

OPEC aid is not tied to goods and services (for the obvious reason that the OPEC countries themselves do not have the goods or services that could be used in this way). Nor does it come with technical assistance, again reflecting the stage of development of the donors. Essentially, then, it comes in the form of capital – grants or loans. During the 1970s, 58 per cent or more of OPEC aid came in grant form, a much higher grant level than aid from any other source.

A small amount of OPEC aid was equivalent to commodity assistance – that is, oil supplied at concessional rates by means of extended credits. Iraq, Iran and Saudi Arabia did this to a limited extent, as did Venezuela in Latin America. The grant element in OPEC loans was as high as 80 per cent, while 50 per cent of its aid was in direct grant form and not tied to donor procurements as its OECD equivalent would almost certainly be. Most OPEC aid (about 70 per cent of the total) has been non-project aid.

Multilateral aid

Only a small proportion of OPEC aid is channelled through multilateral agencies, such as the World Bank. This is understandable against the background of OPEC's emergence as a major source of assistance, just as it was also leading the demand for a New International Economic Order. OPEC countries did not see why a large proportion of

their surplus funds should go into multilateral organizations which they could not control. Instead they established their own multilateral agency, the OPEC Fund. But in one instance, IFAD (the International Fund for Agricultural Development), which was created in 1976, OPEC countries paid a leading part in bringing this new UN body into existence (see Chapter Seven on a New International Economic Order). Nonetheless, between 1978 and 1981, approximately 5 per cent of OPEC aid, worth $420 million a year, was channelled through multilateral agencies.

The direction of OPEC aid flows

Unsurprisingly most OPEC aid has gone to other Arab or Islamic countries. About 75 per cent has been provided for Arab nations and of that up to 43 per cent (over the years) has been channelled to the Palestine refugees in Syria, Jordan and Egypt. Otherwise the main non-Arab recipients have been Pakistan, India and Turkey. By the end of 1981 OPEC countries had provided aid for more than 300 projects which they had co-financed (for example with the World Bank) worth a total of $23 billion, of which the OPEC share was $8 billion.

Despite the far more difficult conditions of the 1980s, OPEC maintained a high level of aid (see table above) although there were huge fluctuations in the amounts on offer with 1987, 1988 and 1989 being especially poor years, though the amount increased dramatically again in 1990.

The OPEC Fund for International Development

The OPEC Fund (known until 1980 as the OPEC Special Fund) was established in 1976, with headquarters in Vienna. It is in part a co-ordinating agency, making OPEC contributions to IFAD as well as co-ordinating other OPEC aid. (We have been speaking of OPEC aid as though it has all been channelled through OPEC. This is not the case; OPEC members have, of course, made their own bilateral aid-giving arrangements for the majority of their aid.)

The objects of the OPEC Fund are:

1. The co-ordination of OPEC aid policy.
2. The disbursement of concessional funds to

multilateral organizations, such as IFAD, the UNCTAD Common Fund etc.

3. Acting as a donor agency for both programme and project assistance.

4. The criterion for Fund lending was initially a 70 per cent grant element in loans which were made available interest free over 25 years with a 5-year grace period.

5. In 1981, however, new terms were introduced: these included interest charges ranging from 1 to 8 per cent according to the per capita income of recipients, while the grant element was drastically reduced to 4 per cent – a sign of the changes in the international economic climate.

6. Loan recipients up to 1981 were divided geographically as follows: Africa – 49 per cent; Asia – 39 per cent; Latin America – 12 per cent.

Other Arab aid funds

Arab OPEC donors between them have created a number of aid and financial institutions. The three best known national funds are KFAED (the Kuwait Fund for Arab Economic Development), the Saudi Fund for Development, and the Abu Dhabi Fund for Arab Economic Development. Inter-Arab organizations include: AFESD (Arab Fund for Economic and Social Development) (see Chapter Four, Part 2); AAAID (Arab Fund for Agricultural Development in Africa); the Islamic Development Bank (see Chapter Four, Part 2); and BADEA (Arab Bank for Economic Development in Africa) (see Chapter Four, Part 1). Conditions attaching to loans from these various funds may vary substantially.

Since 1974 the charters of the Kuwait Fund, the Abu Dhabi Fund, the Saudi Fund and the Iraqi Fund have each been amended with a specific provision for aid in principle to be made available to *all* developing countries.

Conclusions

OPEC aid, which in the main means Arab aid, reached its peak in 1977, the year when Kuwait disbursed over 10 per cent of GNP in concessional aid, though the figure had dropped to 5.14 per cent by 1979. In the same two years Saudi Arabia disbursed 4.3 per cent of GNP and 3.13 per cent of GNP respectively. On the other hand the USA disbursed a mere 0.19 per cent of GNP in aid in 1979 and a substantial proportion of that went to Israel and southern Europe rather than to countries which could truly be regarded as belonging to the Third World.

The great value of OPEC aid lies in the fact that it is not (and cannot be) tied to procurements from the donor countries, nor is it conditional upon the donors supplying technical assistance personnel. This, of course, reflects the state of development of the OPEC donors, but it does mean the provision of aid which has far fewer strings attached to it than most aid from other sources. Yet though OPEC aid was immensely more generous on a GNP percentage basis than aid from any other source, it has not had an impact commensurate with the excitement that OPEC generated during the 1970s when it was leading the demands for a North–South dialogue.

7 A New International Economic Order

The idea of a New International Economic Order (NIEO), which played a significant part in the politics of North–South during the mid- and later 1970s, was important not because it succeeded – it did not – but because it helped emphasize the principal problems which surround all North–South issues. These are not questions of compassion, equity or justice, though each has its place, but questions of power. The countries of the North which wield approximately 90 per cent of the world's power in terms of the decisions they both take and can enforce are in this position precisely because they control the world economy. To ask them to surrender this power, therefore, is unrealistic.

The concept of a New International Economic Order

Though its roots may be traced back much further, the idea of a NIEO was born in the changed atmosphere of 1973-75 when OPEC briefly threatened to turn the accepted world hierarchy on its head. Even so, the concept of a NIEO was flawed from the beginning, because self-interest does not work towards a one-world community – the idea inherent in the concept. In the initial demands for a NIEO, there was implicit the more realistic threat that the OPEC countries would use the oil weapon to force the advanced economies to make substantial economic concessions to the Third World. These were seen to be in terms of trade and the structure of the international bodies which control the world economy, so that Third World members would have a greater say in the decision-making process. As a result, so the theory went, some of the advantages enjoyed by the advanced economies would be surrendered, or at any rate reduced, in favour of the Third World.

Such demands for change – unless backed by oil or other weapons which the advanced economies cannot ignore – really amounted to a demand for the rich North to show greater generosity in its dealings with the poor South.

In the broadest sense the concept of NIEO is essentially socialist. It assumes that the better-off will – in statesmanlike fashion – surrender advantage for the sake of a wider world harmony and international – as opposed to national – interests. There is, however, little evidence to suggest that those now in positions of power – in this context the rich North – are prepared to make any such willing surrender of their advantages, while there is a great deal of evidence to the contrary. A NIEO, if it means anything, means the termination of the existing order of the world economy and its replacement by a new one that has quite different priorities. The concept suffered from the further disadvantage that it was too all-embracing. Demands for NIEO were on behalf of the oil-rich countries of OPEC; the poor nations of Africa; huge, newly industrializing ones, such as Brazil, Argentina and Mexico; small, newly industrializing countries, such as Singapore or Taiwan; as well as the giant India. It was unreasonable to suppose that all their varying needs could be accommodated in the new dispensation.

Any demand for redress of an unfair balance by a disadvantaged group is essentially revolutionary. In consequence it is only likely to succeed if accompanied by pressure – 'out of the barrel of a gun' to quote Mao's phrase – and in this case by the sustained pressure of OPEC. In the event the pressure was not, and could not be, maintained long enough to bring about any major changes and, not surprisingly, little came of the demands for a NIEO.

The roots of the NIEO idea can be traced back to the writings of Raoul Prebish, the Argentinian economist whose name was well known in UN circles during the organization's early days. In *Towards a New Trade Policy for Development*, he attacked the old concept of comparative advantage so much favoured by the capitalist West both then and later, to argue instead that this kept developing countries permanently underdeveloped because it meant that they remained producers of raw materials or one or two commodities. He advocated interventionist policies which would alter the balance in favour of the developing world. A NIEO would do the same thing.

The United Nations and NIEO

The UN declared its First Development Decade to run from 1961 to 1970; towards its end there was the clear need for a new strategy. Lester B. Pearson, the former Liberal prime minister of Canada, chaired (just a decade before the Brandt Report) what became known as the Pearson Report: *Partners in Development*, the Report of the Commission on International Development which appeared in 1969. Like the Brandt Report it analysed the state of rich-poor relations and development in the Third World. Its most memorable recommendation was that the donor countries should strive to achieve an aid target of 0.7 per cent of their GNP.

In 1970 the UN General Assembly adopted an international development strategy for its Second Development Decade (1971-80). This was adopted unanimously though just what that was to mean in terms of performance was another matter.

In May 1974 the United Nations held its Sixth Special Session in Algiers. This was the first ever convened solely to look at economic affairs and it was here that the idea of a NIEO was adopted by the world body. The Special Session adopted a *Declaration and Programme of Action on the Establishment of a New International Economic Order*. This NIEO demanded: 'the establishment of a new international economic order based on equity, sovereignty, interdependence, common interest and co-operation among states, irrespective of their economic and social systems' which would 'correct inequalities and redress existing injustices, make it possible to eliminate the widening gap between the developed and the developing countries and ensure steadily accelerating economic and social development in peace and justice for present and future generations'. The sentiments were splendid.

The *Programme for Action* is concerned essentially with changes in the structure of global production, consumption and trade. Its aims are:

1. To give a greater share of industrial produc-

tion to developing countries.
2. To make developing countries technologically self-sufficient.
3. To see they obtain the maximum benefits from the operation of transnational corporations in their territories.
4. To see that developing countries take full control over their resources.
5. Generally, to restructure the framework of international control over trade.

These proposals were later spelt out in the *Charter of Economic Rights and Duties of States* which was voted upon at the UN General Assembly in November 1974. Some 120 nations voted for the Charter, six voted against and 10 abstained. The 16 who voted against or abstained were 'free' western economies. Nonetheless, the Charter was adopted that December. It stipulated that every nation has the right to exercise *full permanent sovereignty* over its wealth and natural resources. This, clearly, was seen as a crucial part of the Charter in the light of transnational activities generally in the Third World, and the recent OPEC experience of the oil companies in particular. The Charter sets forth the rights of nations to associate in organizations of primary producers in order to develop their national economies (a clear endorsement of the operations of the OPEC cartel).

In September 1975, the UN held another Special Session on development and international co-operation during which the General Assembly enumerated measures to be taken as the basis for negotiations on the issues of raw materials; energy; trade; development; and money and finance. On this occasion the Assembly called for a restructuring of the UN's own economic and social sectors so that they could deal with problems of economic co-operation and development.

In 1979 the UN called for a third special session to be held in 1980. Little new transpired although the UN proclaimed its Third Development Decade to run from 1981 to 1990. The strategy for the Third UN Development Decade 1981-90 included the following targets for developing countries:

1. 7 per cent growth for GDP.
2. 7.5 per cent per annum expansion of exports and an 8 per cent per annum expansion of imports of goods and services.
3. Increases in domestic savings with a target figure of 24 per cent by 1990.

4. A rapid increase in ODA to reach and then pass 0.7 per cent GNP, a target few OECD countries have ever attained.
5. 4 per cent expansion of agricultural production.
6. 9 per cent expansion of manufacturing output.

The targets set out here were hopeful (few were attained), but by 1980 the world climate was visibly changing. OPEC was about to pass its peak of influence, recession was beginning to bite in the western economies and the political attitudes of key western governments – the USA, Britain and West Germany – had noticeably hardened against either aid or, even more, such concepts as NIEO.

Assumptions behind calls for a NIEO

The demands for a NIEO which became so insistent in the mid-1970s were based upon two (unstated) assumptions. The first was that the rich North was heavily dependent upon resources controlled by the poor South (OPEC's exercise of oil power was behind this assumption) and that these resources, therefore, could and, if necessary, would be withheld in order to force the North to agree to a NIEO. The second assumption was that OPEC (which had made the entire dialogue possible in the first place) would maintain its solidarity with the rest of the Third World and continue to use its economic strength as a weapon to force concessions from the North on behalf of all the Third World.

Apart from these tactical considerations, however, demands for a NIEO also imply that those with advantage will be prepared to surrender it. Broadly, in historical terms, this never happens. Equally, such demands assume a continuing solidarity among members of the South, not simply in the sense of maintaining a united front in relation to the North, but also in the sense that all members of the South have identical or near identical aims. Given the huge spread and variety of Third World countries – in terms of their political persuasions, their stages of development and their population sizes – this was always a most dubious assumption upon which to work.

In fact the evidence points in quite another direction. Most Third World countries wish to escape from that (development) status as fast as possible. This is more likely to mean that those

with a major resource, such as oil, will be tempted to break ranks with the other Third World countries as soon as they see the chance of moving up in the scale of development: first, to join the ranks of the newly industrializing countries and then to become junior developed nations.

In broad terms the calls for a NIEO represented a demand for changes in the way that international trade is conducted. They also covered a wide range of subjects concerned with how rich-poor relations should be conducted. In effect, the *Charter of Economic Rights and Duties of States* gives the advantages to the developing countries by proposals, for example, covering market intervention in favour of their products and by placing an obligation upon the advanced economies to redress the balance. In particular, calls for a greater Third World say in the decision-making processes of the World Bank or IMF should make up for their lack of money in those organizations and were to be totally resisted by the North.

A time of dialogue

The mid-1970s were a time of dialogue, though not one that the North had sought. For example, in 1975, there was a meeting in Dakar (West Africa) of developing countries on raw materials which proposed the establishment of a series of 'OPECs' to put pressure on the advanced economies. Calls for North–South dialogue were sufficiently insistent and, with OPEC power at its height, a reluctant West did agree to a series of talks of which the most important but ultimately sterile were those held in Paris late in 1975. At these the skilful diplomacy of the US Secretary of State, Henry Kissinger, for the West diffused demands for NIEO, suggested endless committees and ensured that little action was taken at a time when the demands were at their height. Kissinger's was a brilliant negative performance.

Then for the rest of the 1970s various other pressures were exerted upon the West for a continuing dialogue, although from 1976 the West had recovered from its initial shock and panic at the application of oil power by OPEC and, moreover, had discovered the economic advantages of 'recycling' Middle East oil wealth. To begin with the Third World was enthusiastic about dialogue and the North apprehensive, but, as always, the rich could afford to wait while the poor needed quick action to alleviate their problems.

The time for action on NIEO was in the years 1974-76 and if anything concrete was to come of the demands it would be due to OPEC's strength and its solidarity with the Third World as a whole. In the event the North rode out the storm. Almost nothing concrete was achieved though at least OPEC forced the principal DAC countries to discuss the grievances of the South. One new body was created as a direct result of OPEC power.

The International Fund for Agricultural Development (IFAD)

IFAD grew out of the 1974 World Food Conference and owed its creation largely to pressures exerted by OPEC. It came into formal existence in 1976. IFAD had 136 member states (on its foundation): its method of voting and the cash contributions required of its members did represent a victory for the NIEO idea. Thus the western industrialized countries were asked to provide 56.7 per cent of the finances, but only have 33 per cent of the voting power. The OPEC members supplied 41.5 per cent of the finances and also had 33 per cent of the voting power, while 104 developing countries without oil were obliged to contribute only 1.8 per cent of IFAD's finances, though they too had 33 per cent of the voting power. The principle of voting equity enshrined in IFAD for once ignored the general principle which obtains in most international organizations concerned with the disbursement of funds: that voting strength should depend upon the size of national financial contributions.

Western attitudes to NIEO

When at the height of the oil crisis North and South met in Paris and the Conference on International Economic Co-operation and Development (CIEC) was established, it did look as though some progress might be achieved. At the CIEC meeting in 1976 eight representatives of the developed North met 19 representatives of the South: this was the beginning of the short-lived North–South dialogue. On that occasion at least the South maintained its solidarity. For example, it refused to discuss only energy as the North demanded, but insisted that energy should be linked to all raw materials and that the price of a 'basket' of principal western exports be related to the price of oil. Nothing was decided. The West's main strategy was to adopt delaying tactics in the hope and expectation that Third World solidarity would be eroded, which proved to be the case.

The western approach was to undermine OPEC–Third World solidarity; so the West talked but did nothing until recycling became the primary concern of the OPEC members. Their desire to develop their own economies became paramount at the expense of considerations of Third World solidarity. If such countries as Iran, Nigeria and Saudi Arabia were to carry out the ambitious development plans which they had launched at this time, they needed the recycling process to go ahead at once so that they could obtain the sophisticated machinery, technology and technical assistance the West had to supply. In the process of obtaining these development requirements, they inevitably undermined their solidarity with the rest of the Third World, because only by withholding their surplus finances long enough from the West could they have expected to force significant changes.

Some western countries, such as Norway, gave a qualified welcome to the idea of NIEO – a watered-down version – but only if everyone else went along with the concept. The USA, however, was positively hostile to any form of NIEO and Japan and the countries of Europe only a little less so. In fact, while participating in North–South dialogue, the West set out to kill NIEO. The Third World needed solidarity if it was to achieve anything, and the West was determined to divide. By the end of the decade the concept of NIEO had become a dead letter.

In a sense, calls for a NIEO were about the aid relationship. An important, indeed vital, aspect of this is the assumption on the part of donors that recipients *want* to be more like them. It is a question of mimicry and the donors call the tune. Since the basic North–South or Rich–Poor relationship is one of exploitation anyway, aid represents a gesture towards the 'have-nots' by the 'haves' to keep them moderately content. It is largesse rather than a serious effort to redress existing imbalances. Indeed, donors do not want to do that since real redress would reduce their position of dominance.

The patterns of the 1970s

There was a clear pattern to the events of the decade which tells us much about the real attitudes of North and South. First OPEC demonstrated its strength and willingness to use oil as a weapon in the period immediately after the Yom Kippur War. The organization became the vanguard of the South in a confrontation with the rich North. This confrontation, the first of its kind, induced initial western panic and so led to a willingness – reluctant, perhaps, but there if only as a stalling device – to talk. And so the idea of dialogue was born. The West stalled most effectively, while waiting to see what would happen in the South. At the same time it was determined to give nothing of substance away. The major OPEC nations, meanwhile, had embarked upon huge development plans and these required goods and services which only the West could supply. To obtain them, therefore, they recycled their oil wealth and the North sighed with relief as its huge outgoings for oil were now returning. Once this process had got underway, NIEO effectively was dead and the OPEC countries had ceased to act as the vanguard for the Third World as a whole.

This pattern raised some significant questions. First, fundamental yet unstated throughout the meetings of the time, is the simple question: does the Third World really want a NIEO at all? Or rather, do its individual members merely resent their poverty and exploitation by the North and wish to rise above these as soon as possible by any means which are to hand, in order to join the ranks of the rich? The whole concept of aid and development implies acceptance of international upward mobility, which is the antithesis of Third World solidarity upon which any NIEO would have to depend. Moreover, upward mobility also implies acceptance of a single world economic order. Third World countries at present are the poor members of this order. The underlying assumption is that if they can rise into a higher rank they will quickly and happily enough forget their Third World status.

Africa 2000

In 1979 an African symposium of economists and others met in Monrovia, Liberia, to discuss the state of the continent's development. Their deliberations took place at the latter end of the period of dialogue and by that time it must have been clear that any hopes of a NIEO had already passed.

The symposium's report, *What Kind of Africa by the Year 2000?* became known subsequently by the more simple title *Africa 2000*. The symposium called for measures, including an African Common Market, that would lessen the continent's dependence upon the North. In theory, at least, this represented a more realistic approach to the development problems of Africa than did wider calls for an all-embracing NIEO. A NIEO could only be put into effect with the co-operation of the North. The African plan called upon Africans alone to co-operate on a continent-wide basis and because the members of the Organization of African Unity (OAU) were all developing countries at much the same stage of economic advance, this made practical sense. One telling phrase in the report called upon African countries to 'break with excessive mimicry in every field'. The group argued: 'The objective for the year 2000 is to rid the continent of the general approach that currently prevails and which accepts without question the concept and practice of "transfer of technology" – an expression which the symposium suggests should be stricken from the international vocabulary.'

This was to face up to hard political, as well as economic, realities. Little is given free and because both a NIEO and the transfer of technology depend upon the vastly more powerful North divesting itself in effect of part of its advantage, neither makes much real development sense. In fact, by the early 1980s, African development was generally in deep trouble and urgent appeals for yet more aid became stronger just as the world recession began to bite. This, however, does not detract from the logic behind *Africa 2000*.

By 1980 Third World demands for a NIEO might still be made as part of the ritualistic ongoing North–South debate. But they no longer had much force behind them nor did they any longer represent any real hope that concessions were likely to be made by the North. What the Third World had to digest instead was the Brandt Report.

The Brandt Report

After the failure of the Paris dialogue talks of 1976 it was clear that the North had to make some kind of gesture if there was not to be a continuing and potentially dangerous confrontation, because OPEC was still very much in its militant heyday. Classic delaying tactics were therefore employed by the North whose immediate answer to demands for dialogue was the Brandt Report.

Early in 1977 the President of the World Bank, Robert McNamara, in a speech delivered at Boston (obviously pre-arranged) suggested that the former West German Chancellor, Willy Brandt, should chair an independent inquiry. On 28 September 1977, Willy Brandt announced that he was ready to launch and chair an 'Independent Commission on International Development Issues'. This announcement followed a long round of consultations and discussions. The object of the Commission was to 'present recommendations which could improve the climate for further deliberations on North–South relations'. At this point cynics will no doubt note the phrase *for further deliberations*: action was clearly to be pushed ever further into the future. Various distinguished political figures and economists from the spectrum of both North and South, including Britain's Edward Heath, Sweden's Olof Palme and Tanzania's Amir Jamal – from the establishments on both sides of the dialogue – sat on the Commission to give it balance. The terms of reference included: 'to suggest ways of promoting adequate solutions to the problems involved in development and in attacking absolute poverty'.

It is worth looking at the Report in some detail because it is likely to remain the principal reference document on North–South deliberations until another retired, eminent politician is asked to do a repeat exercise, perhaps in the late 1990s. The Report is good on general analysis of the problems and the key word subsequently picked up by the media is 'interdependence', a nice comfortable word, acceptable to both sides, implying that 'we are all in this together'. It is a word designed to play down the problems and divisions and move its hearers (or readers) away from the starker realities of confrontation.

The Commission met first in Bonn during December 1977. In his foreword, Brandt says they regarded their task as: 'to study the grave global issues arising from the economic and social disparities of the world community'. The Report produces some impressive statistics (much quoted in subsequent debates). For example, one half of 1 per cent of 1 year's military expenditure would pay for all the farm equipment needed to increase food production and approach self-sufficiency in food-deficit, low-income countries by 1990, a statistic produced prior to 1980.

One of the most telling points made in the Report is the following: 'Mankind has never before had such ample technical and financial resources for coping with hunger and poverty. The immense task can be tackled once the necessary collective will is mobilized.' Unfortunately, reading through the Report, one realizes again and again that the collective will to mobilize these resources to combat poverty does not exist.

In Chapter Three – Mutual Interests – there is a section entitled 'An Opportunity for Partnership' which states: 'We are looking for a world based less on power and status, more on justice and contract; less discretionary, more governed by fair and open rules.' The report speaks of *moral imperatives* as opposed to power, yet while much lip-service is paid to the idea, countries continue to act in pursuit of power.

In Chapter Seven – Disarmament and Development – the huge disparity between military spending and ODA is highlighted: 'Total military expenditures (world) are approaching $450 billion a year, of which over half is spent by the Soviet Union and the United States, while annual spending on official development aid is only $20 billion.' This may have been so, but military expenditure in the eyes of even the smallest nations (including those of the Third World) represents national interest, while ODA is politically marginal.

The recommendations at the end of Chapter Nine – Commodity Trade and Development – begin: 'The commodity sector of developing countries should contribute more to economic development through the greater participation of these countries in the processing, marketing and distribution of their commodities.'

Again, the sentiment is fine. All Third World countries (or certainly the great majority), which are dependent largely upon the export of commodities, would agree. But as always the question remains: how can this improved state of affairs be brought about? It is true that the Report goes on to say that measures should include the removal of tariff and other trade barriers against processed goods from developing countries, which are at present operated by the industrialized countries of the North, but as to who makes the rich remove such barriers the Report is silent.

This criticism – or question – applies to all the

recommendations throughout the Report. The Brandt Report was hailed – especially by the western media – as statesmanlike and moral. Meetings to launch it were held in the countries of the North. Then, at least as far as governments were concerned, it was largely forgotten. To make sense, its recommendations have to be backed by mechanisms or pressure groups with 'teeth' to ensure that at least some of them are implemented. Yet by the time the Report was published, OPEC's teeth had largely been drawn or, if its teeth were not yet drawn, its members were by then more concerned with their own development problems than with acting as the bargaining front-runners for the already moribund North–South dialogue.

Chapter Seventeen of the Report – a Programme of Priorities – has a section 'Tasks for the 80s and 90s' which begins: 'All countries must be able to participate fully in the world economy in a way which assists genuine development. This will come about in the long run only in an economic environment which enables all developing countries to achieve self-sustaining growth.' These admirable sentiments are followed by paragraphs on 'Priority Needs for the Poorest', 'Abolition of Hunger', 'Commodities', 'Manufactures', 'Transnationals, Technology and Mineral Development', 'Reform of the Monetary System' and 'A New Approach to Development Finance'. The last paragraph is entitled 'Power Sharing'. This begins: 'While these specific tasks (referring to the list above) require major transfers of finance, we believe that the power and decision-making within monetary and financial institutions must also be shared more broadly, to give more responsibility to the developing world.' Once again it is pertinent to ask: 'who in the North is prepared to share more in such a fashion?'

Few would object to the sentiments expressed in the Brandt Report nor to most of its analysis of the problems besetting the South or those which enmesh North–South relations. But what must be understood is the fact that the Commission had no powers of implementation. In so far as governments paid heed to its findings at all, they did so politely because of the eminent people who had been involved. Then they shelved it.

On the other hand the Report became a useful tool for aid agencies, non-government organizations and others who wished to argue a case for greater interdependence. The expectations raised during its preparation – while the old political ploy that nothing should be done until this weighty report appeared was successfully employed – meant that 3 years were wasted. The Brandt Report was finished in December 1979 and became public in 1980. By then the world economy was moving into recession, splits in OPEC were widening, the West had largely recovered the initiative in relation to the South which it had lost in 1973–74, and politicians generally unsympathetic to the aspirations of the South – Ronald Reagan in the USA, Margaret Thatcher in Britain, Helmut Kohl in West Germany – were firmly in the saddle. Nothing was done, a result which could have been anticipated anyway.

If a lesson is to be learnt from the story of NIEO, the North–South dialogue and the Brandt Report it is that only when the Third World maintains complete solidarity and is prepared ruthlessly to use such power as it has against the North – in the form of oil power for example – will it have any hope of breaking the present pattern of North–South relations, certainly as far as economic exploitation of the South by the North is concerned. There was a brief chance of such a breakthrough in the mid-1970s. That opportunity has passed. In the troubled early 1990s there seems little likelihood of another such chance occurring before the end of the present century.

8 The Population Factor

In 1992 the world population stood at 5.4 billion and was projected to reach 6.2 billion by the year 2000. Of this 4.3 billion belonged to the countries of the Third World. China and India between them accounted for just under half the Third World total with 2 billion while a further nine countries – Bangladesh, Indonesia, Pakistan, the Philippines, Thailand and Vietnam in Asia, Mexico and Brazil in Latin America, and Nigeria in Africa – accounted for another 930 million. Thus 11 Third World countries share a population of 2930 million. The world's 5 billionth inhabitant was born during June 1987 and the 6 billionth is now expected to arrive before the year 2000 (in early 1998).

During the earlier part of the 1980s the world population increase averaged 78 million a year; by the 1990s it had leaped to 91 million a year and 90 per cent and more of this increase (despite moderate levelling of growth rates in some Third World countries) will continue to be in developing countries. At present about 40 per cent of the Third World population is aged below 30. But estimates of Third World population are complicated by highly unreliable statistical data as the variable calculations about Nigeria's population in the 1980s and early 1990s have demonstrated. Huge population increases render a great deal of development achievement little more than an exercise of running to stand still. This situation can be changed only when patterns of life are fundamentally altered.

In 1992 the world's 12 most populous countries were:

Country	Population
China	1,165,888,000
India	889,700,000
USA	255,414,000
Indonesia	184,796,000
Brazil	151,381,000
Russia	148,469,000
Pakistan	130,129,000
Japan	124,330,000
Bangladesh	110,602,000
Nigeria	89,666,000
Mexico	84,439,000
Germany	79,122,000

For example, in 1975-80, while developed countries averaged 16 births per 1000 a year, developing countries averaged 33 per 1000. Thus the countries which could least afford to cope with extra numbers had twice as large an increase as did the rich developed nations. UN figures show that average (world) life expectancy at birth for 1950-55 was 47.0 years; by 1975-80 it had increased to 57.5 years; and by 1992 it had increased again to 63 years for males and 67 years for females, so much progress has been achieved. But the variations are enormous. Thus, while Japan has the world's highest life expectancy of 76 years for men and 82.1 years for women, and an infant mortality rate which has been brought down to only 4.6 per 1000 live births, in Africa and parts of Asia the infant mortality rate is over 100 deaths per 1000 live births.

On present projections, approximately 84 per cent of the total world population will belong to the Third World in the year 2000. Africa continues to have the highest rates of increase with some countries well in excess of 3 per cent a year. This is partly the result of rapid falls in death rates, because of improved medical and health services, matched by better child care, which have led to some startling statistical rises in infant survival, a combination which produces rapid population increases.

Not many developing countries have detailed population control programmes (though the idea of such programmes has become more acceptable in recent years). There are a number of reasons for this. Resistance to population control may arise from religious, social, economic or political taboos. In effect population control means an average family size of two children; for most developing countries that target is simply not in sight. The worst mortality rates are in Africa and then, in descending order, Asia, the Pacific, Latin America and the Caribbean, the Middle East and Mediterranean. As long as high mortality rates persist (the result of poverty, poor health facilities, malnutrition), there will be little incentive to cut back the size of families. Thus population control is only likely to come when development has produced higher living standards.

Land degradation, soil erosion or a too rapid run-down of resources are usually the result of overpopulation, when there are not enough resources to meet even the basic needs of the people. Such a situation will place unacceptable strains upon the ecology. During the 1970s and 1980s, growing attention (especially in the North) has been paid to ecology and all aspects of conservation, including the disastrous destruction of savannah, the extinction of wildlife species, and pollution. Yet none of these concerns touches people desperate to survive. In a country such as Sudan, where wood is the basic fuel for most people, desertification will continue until a cheap alternative fuel to wood is available. In places, the Sahara is advancing southwards by 7 miles a year.

Not many development plans pay attention to the pressures exerted by poor populations on resources or the ecology, and then relate such pressures to future development prospects. Moreover, in some countries where the population increase is very rapid, resources are being depleted far faster than makes sense in terms of the future simply in order to deal with the additional mouths which have to be fed every year.

A number of results follow from the population explosion though they vary from country to country:

1. Over-use of fertilizers to accelerate agricultural production, although this can do long-term damage to the soil;
2. Overgrazing of pastoral land;
3. Deforestation for fuel;
4. The drift to urban areas is accelerated, yet work does not exist in the towns and a new series of urban problems are created;
5. Accelerated depletion of non-renewable resources.

Furthermore, too rapid population growth usually means there is not enough 'development' to go round: the education system cannot cope and illiteracy grows, and so on. Failure to control population, therefore, may prove fatal to development plans and yet control of population requires the incentive of better conditions at which people can aim. Like so many Third World problems we face a vicious circle.

The UN has been concerned with population problems since its inception and the role of UNFPA (see Chapter Two) is to assist governments to develop population goals and programmes. The major part of UNFPA's funds are allocated to family planning projects. The First World Population Conference was held at Bucharest in 1974 when a World Population Plan of Action was adopted. A second conference was held 10 years later in Mexico City.

Urban problems

The huge drift to the towns since 1950 has been one of the most important developments throughout the Third World. In part it is directly attributable to population pressures. The problems created by vast urban sprawls are especially difficult for developing countries to solve.

In 1950 there were 287 million urban dwellers in the Third World. By 1980 the figure had reached 1 billion. One estimate suggests that 2 billion people will live in urban areas of the developing countries by the year 2000. That represents a doubling of the figure over 20 years. Already in 1980 there were 16 cities in the Third World with populations in excess of 5 million. These huge cities present a range of problems that are all growing more acute: slums and health hazards; lack of social facilities, schools or other social services; an increase in crime through overcrowding, poverty and unemployment; political confrontation and urban violence – with governments unable to do more than resort to repression. Often the largest cities are the capitals, and governments may well find they are obliged through fear of revolution to deal with overpopulation in the cities by diverting to them an unfair proportion of resources. As a result they retard development everywhere.

In 1992, of the top 25 most populous urban areas in the world (each with populations in excess of 6 million), nine were in the North. Of the remainder, three were in China:

Shanghai	13,341,896
Beijing	10,819,407
Tianjin	8,785,402

Three were in India:

Bombay	12,571,720
Calcutta	10,916,272
Delhi	8,375,188

Four were in Latin America:

São Paulo	15,199,423
Mexico City	14,991,281
Buenos Aires	10,887,355
Rio de Janeiro	9,600,525

The other six were:

Seoul	17,588,000
Cairo	8,761,927
Jakarta	8,254,000
Manila	7,832,000
Karachi	7,702,000
Tehran	6,773,000

The growing problems associated with urban growth led the UN to call a conference on the subject. This was held in Vancouver in 1976: Habitat: United Nations Conference on Human Settlements. Growing from this the world body created the United Nations Centre for Human Settlements (Habitat) in 1978 with headquarters in Nairobi. Habitat is especially concerned to link urban and regional development programmes with national plans.

Third World populations by region

A breakdown of the Third World into regions, with 1991 population figures, is as follows:

Sub-Saharan Africa	488.9 million
Middle East and North Africa	244.1 million
East Asia and Pacific	1666.5 million
South Asia	1152.2 million
Latin America	445.3 million

Ten countries in Africa have populations in excess of 20 million:

Algeria	25.7 million
Egypt	53.6 million
Ethiopia	52.8 million
Kenya	25.0 million
Morocco	25.7 million
Nigeria	89.0 million
South Africa	38.9 million
Sudan	25.8 million
Tanzania	25.2 million
Zaïre	41.1 million

A further seven African countries have populations between 10 and 20 million:

Cameroon	11.9 million
Côte d'Ivoire	12.4 million
Ghana	15.3 million
Madagascar	12.0 million
Mozambique	16.1 million
Uganda	16.9 million
Zimbabwe	10.1 million

Such population figures must be related to the stage of a country's development, the distribution of wealth, the agricultural potential of the land, other resources, education and so on. They must also be related to political factors. Thus in South Africa, which is both potentially and actually one of the richest countries anywhere, a high proportion of the black population lives in deep poverty. They have an unacceptably high rate of population growth (above their capacity to deal adequately with the increase) as a direct result of the way the country has been run for the benefit of the white minority.

A tiny country may also face fundamental problems when its population is related to its resources. Thus, in 1986 for example, Cape Verde with a population of only 327,000 was again declared to be at risk of serious famine by the UN. Size of country and size of population must always be related to available resources.

Two countries in Latin America – Brazil and Mexico – are in the giant league of population:

Brazil	151.4 million
Mexico	83.3 million

Another factor to take into account is the rate of population increase: Brazil (on present trends) is expected to double its population in 38 years, Mexico in 27 years.

Seven other Latin American countries have populations in excess of 10 million:

Argentina	32.7 million
Chile	13.4 million
Colombia	32.8 million
Cuba	10.8 million
Ecuador	10.8 million
Peru	21.9 million
Venezuela	19.8 million

In the case of these seven countries there are interesting differences in the amount of time they will take (on present estimates) to double their populations, an indication of the extent to which either relative prosperity or family planning or both are operating to curtail too rapid a population explosion. Argentina and Cuba both now have a doubling time of 63 years, Chile 41, Colombia 36, Peru and Venezuela 28, and Ecuador only 25.

The Third World's two giants – China and India – are in Asia:

China	1,165,888,000
India	889,700,000

But whereas China, which has made strenuous efforts to control population, has a present estimated doubling time of 54 years, (a drop from 60 years since the mid-1980s), India (where in the 1970s an unsuccessful and highly publicized sterilization programme was attempted) will double in only 34 years.

Six other countries in Asia have populations between 50 and 190 million as follows:

Bangladesh	110,602,000
Indonesia	184,796,000
Pakistan	130,129,000
Philippines	63,609,000
Thailand	56,801,000
Vietnam	69,052,000

In these six high population countries one – Thailand – will take 50 years to double its population; Indonesia will take 34 years, Bangladesh 32, Vietnam and the Philippines 29, and Pakistan 23.

Conclusions

What almost all developing countries face in common in population terms – and this applies equally to countries at either end of the population scale – are huge pressures upon all aspects of their development and resources simply to provide more goods and services to care for the annual increase in numbers. This has to be done before the population as a whole can become absolutely better off. This constant pressure exerted by annual population growth repeatedly upsets development calculations. Such is not the case in the advanced countries of the North where, if anything, the national worry is likely to be about a stagnant population. Until population growth has levelled off, most Third World countries will see it as a major complication affecting all aspects of their development.

9 Resources and Exploitation

The extent of a country's resources does not necessarily or usually match its economic power. Both the USA and the USSR (prior to the end of the Cold War) had massive resources, yet the USA had mobilized its resources absolutely more effectively than had the USSR. China and Brazil possess vast resources yet both have a long way to go to catch up the advanced economies. Resources provide a basis of wealth that will be realized only when they have been combined with technological skills. Japan is not blessed with any abundance of resources, yet has raised itself to the position of second economy of the world and a formidable competitor for every other advanced nation. Japan's achievement is the result of technology and education combined with national discipline, particularly because the great majority of the resources it requires for its industry have to be imported.

The extent of Third World resources, therefore, has to be viewed with caution. Just because a country or region has an abundance of minerals (or one particular mineral) does not automatically ensure economic prosperity. Indeed and perversely, it may produce the reverse. Other factors have also to be taken into account. These include:

1. Operations by transnational corporations (TNCs). To what extent are they entrenched in a Third World country and how much power do they exercise?
2. Political pressures which force a developing country to use up resources for quick revenue, when it would make greater sense to preserve them for the future when the country itself can both develop and use them.
3. The politics of management. OPEC is a classic example of this, being a cartel which priced itself out of power in 10 years.
4. Agricultural commodity distortion. The production of such commodities as coffee, sugar or tea for export, but to the neglect of food for home consumption, with the result that half

the foreign exchange earned has to be spent to pay for imported food.

There are other reasons why the possession of an important mineral or the capacity to produce a major agricultural commodity is not in itself any guarantee of economic progress. The sugar producers of the Caribbean remained just that for 300 years and today are among the world's poorest nations. In the recent post-independence era, countries in possession of a major mineral, such as Zambia with copper, have found their efforts to progress to the next stages of production (semi-finished or finished products) thwarted or at least retarded by TNCs, by so-called market forces, and by the fact that most of the 'strings' which control world production are firmly in the hands of the North. OPEC in the mid-1970s made a brave effort to alter that balance and did have some impact. But one of the most important factors which divides North and South is simply that the North has (and is determined to retain) the technology which adds most of the value to any commodity. The 'value added' to a raw or semi-raw material is the source of most of the profits to be derived from the end product and it is the North which possesses the technology to do this. Wherever possible it prefers to keep the South as producer of raw materials to feed the industries of the North.

All Third World resources have to be related to what is required in the North. At present and for a long time to come, the South – or a majority of its members – will have to study what resources are wanted in the North and what proportion of these, if any, they are in a position to supply.

Nonetheless, in recent years some real progress has been made by the Third World. In the case of certain leading minerals the position of the South has improved over the last 25 years. Between 1965 and 1980, for example, Third World countries increased their world shares of production in copper, iron ore and nickel. They held their own with lead and zinc, although their share of total bauxite production fell. (When relating resource capacities of North and South, it has to be remembered that, apart from the USA and Russia, a number of other countries in the North such as Canada and Australia are extremely richly endowed with a wide range of minerals and export these to the main markets of the USA, Japan and Europe in competition with Third World exporters.)

Third World countries do have certain advantages over the North which they deploy when they are able. For example, wages are generally lower and governments, as a rule, have much tighter control over the unions. In addition, governments often control or have a majority interest in a high proportion of mining enterprises so that to some extent governments can control pricing and production policies. For example, about 70 per cent of Third World copper production is state controlled. These advantages, however, are fairly limited.

Transnational corporations

The TNCs have become one of the bogeymen of North–South relations. This is unsurprising, not just or necessarily in terms of what they actually do, but because of their perceived role. The power of the TNCs is very great and even when they do not attempt to manipulate Third World development to their advantage – which is rare – they are generally believed always to do so.

TNCs now control a third or more of all world production. In 1980 the top 380 TNCs had over 25,000 foreign affiliates, a high proportion of which were in the Third World. Moreover, 40 per cent of world trade now takes place within TNCs and about 9 per cent of trade in commodities is controlled by them.

Some TNCs, especially in mining, have a high profile in the Third World. These include the Anglo-American Corporation operating from South Africa, the giant Rio Tinto Zinc Corporation, and the oil companies such as Shell and BP, the role of whose affiliates in South Africa in supplying the illegal Rhodesian government with oil over 15 years of UDI provides an excellent example of how such companies are able to bypass political decisions with impunity. TNCs are a factor in most Third World economic policies. They are seen to play a vital role in ensuring continuing economic domination by the North.

Depletion and sometimes destruction of resources is often related to the operations of TNCs, but also to Third World government policies. In this respect the assault upon the world's dwindling rain forest reserves has attracted much attention in recent years. The great belt of rain forests runs across the world north and south of the equator so that, with the single exception of northern Australia, all the world's rain forests are in Third World countries. In Latin America, Brazil

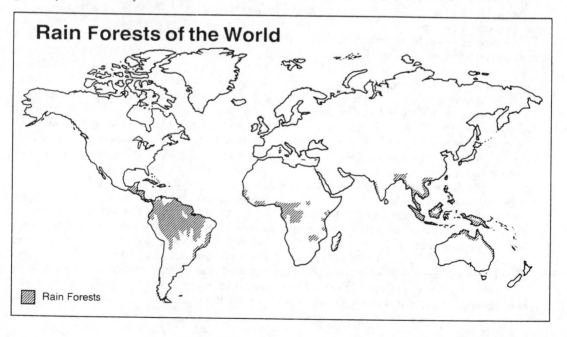

Rain Forests of the World

Rain Forests

possesses the most extensive rain forests of all; they are being depleted at an alarming rate. Elsewhere in Central America there are rain forests in Costa Rica, Colombia and Venezuela. In Africa the second great belt of rain forest begins in south-eastern Nigeria and extends through Cameroon, Congo, Gabon and across Zaïre; smaller areas are found along the Zambezi Valley and in Mozambique. The third region of rain forest lies in Asia, in parts of India, Burma, Thailand, southern China, Malaysia, Indonesia, the Philippines and New Guinea.

This vast ecological resource is now seen to be at risk. One estimate suggests that 30 acres (12 hectares) of rain forest fall to commercial developers in every minute of every day.* Sometimes this depletion may be due to company operations for wood; sometimes to clearance for agriculture; and sometimes for other purposes, such as government hydroelectric developments. Once the rain forest has gone it cannot be replaced.

Capacity of the land

The capacity of the land to bear food has to be related to the distribution of the population and the intensity of agricultural production. It must also be seen in terms of land use strategies and priorities. For example, in the late 1970s, 27 of 43 sub-Saharan African countries depended upon agricultural exports for 50 per cent or more of their foreign exchange earnings. Yet at the same time, some of these countries were experiencing food shortages at home and in certain cases were in receipt of World Food Programme (WFP) assistance because they could not feed themselves.

Nigeria has a total of 92.3 million hectares of land. Of this about a third is under cultivation. Altogether 71.2 million hectares of land is cultivable so that slightly less than half is under production. By the end of the 1970s and into the 1980s, Nigeria spent an increasing amount of foreign exchange (well over 1 billion naira a year) to pay for imports of food because it was no longer producing enough to feed its population. The land was available. The incentives or political priorities, however, were not sufficiently geared to agricultural production. In order to bring unused but cultivable land into use, substantial numbers of people would first have to be moved to new areas,

*In the Rainforest by Catherine Caulfield, Heinemann, 1985

with all the political and social upheavals such moves always entail. By contrast, China in the mid-1970s had 135 million hectares under cultivation. Yet China managed, by employing far more intensive methods of cultivation so that some areas produced two or even three crops in a year, to feed 1000 million people or about 12 times Nigeria's population, using only four times as much land.

Many Third World countries have the land on which to produce the food they require. For various political or economic reasons they have not exploited it properly for this purpose, namely:

1. It may require the mass movement of people.
2. It may require capital which is not available.
3. The government has concentrated upon the production of cash crops for export in order to obtain foreign exchange to finance other developments at the expense of growing food to meet national requirements.
4. There has grown up the easy, if expensive, habit of importing food in good economic times or appealing to the world community for food aid in bad economic times.

Northern dependence upon Third World exports

The major industrial countries of the North are dependent upon Third World countries for certain tropical agricultural commodities which grow only in the South. The most important are coffee, tea, cocoa, natural rubber, jute and hard fibres. In addition, some countries of the North, and most particularly those of the EC and Japan, are dependent upon the Third World for certain minerals such as copper, manganese, nickel and tin. The USA and Russia (now no longer a superpower) remain broadly self-sufficient in most major minerals, although the rate at which the USA is depleting some of its resources is altering this position at speed.

However, a number of countries of the North – Canada and Australia being the most important – have huge surpluses of a wide range of minerals which they export to other countries of the North. Only in a few cases does the Third World enjoy a semi-monopoly position with regard to particular minerals. These include South Africa for gold and the OPEC countries for oil, though that near monopoly in part disappeared between 1980 and

1985 with the advent of other non-OPEC oil fields, for example those in the North Sea.

In fact many Third World countries are more dependent upon exporting their minerals or commodities to the North than are the countries of the North dependent in any absolute sense upon importing such minerals or commodities from the South.

The Rio Earth Summit 1992

The United Nations Conference on Environment and Development (UNCED), popularly known as the Rio Earth Summit, was held from 3 to 14 June 1992 in Rio de Janeiro, Brazil. It was attended by over 100 heads of State and Government and representatives of 178 countries altogether. It was the largest ever world summit meeting. At a time of growing concern about the use – and misuse – of the earth's resources, the summit focused attention as never before upon the escalating depletion of world resources and the difference in approach to consumption and conservation by the North and the South. Essentially, the North wished to safeguard its right to consume and the South to exploit what resources it possesses.

In this light US President George Bush refused to sign the Convention on Protecting Species and Habitats (the bio-diversity convention) in order to protect US patents on products developed from materials obtained from overseas. At the same time, emphasizing the confrontational approach between North and South, Governor Gilberto Mestrinho from Brazil's state of Amazonas, said (of the North): 'The developed world sold $200 billion of products based on molecules from the tropical forests last year, yet not one cent came to the Amazon region.' Perhaps Malaysia's prime minister, Mahathir Mohamad, put the case of the South most succinctly (prior to the summit) when he argued: 'If the rich North expects the poor to foot the bill for a cleaner environment, Rio would become an exercise in futility.' He also said: 'There will be no development if the poor countries are not allowed to extract their natural wealth . . . fear by the North of environmental degradation provides the South with the leverage that did not exist before. If it is in the interest of the rich that we do not cut down our trees, then they must compensate us for the loss of income.'

When he opened the Conference, the UN Secretary-General, Boutros Boutros-Ghali, said

the planet was 'sick with over- and-under-development'. And Cuba's Fidel Castro, in a speech before US President George Bush, German Chancellor Helmut Kohl and British Prime Minister John Major said: 'With just 20 per cent of the world's population, (the developed world) consumes two-thirds of all its metals and three-quarters of all the energy produced.' Later in his ·speech, he said: 'We need less luxury and waste in a few countries so there can be less poverty and hunger in the greater part of the world.'

In the end the Conference produced two Conventions and an agenda – Agenda 21. The two conventions were the Framework Convention on Climate Change (aimed at stabilizing 'greenhouse' gases so as to prevent global warming) and the Convention on Biological Diversity (to curb the destruction of biological species, habitats and ecosystems). Agenda 21 outlines recommendations for action on a range of environmental problems which include climate change, depletion of the ozone layer, air and water pollution, desertification, deforestation, soil loss, toxic wastes, depletion of stocks of fish and other marine resources. How many of these decisions will be translated into firm practice remains to be seen. At least the Rio Earth Summit was the first occasion when the world as a whole – North and South – recognized in theory that problems relating to the world's resources are joint problems that must be tackled by everyone on a global basis.

Regional production

The spread of minerals or the capacity to produce commodity crops is unevenly distributed through the Third World.

Africa

Agriculture still accounts for about 30 per cent of Africa's total production (much more in some cases), earns about 60 per cent of foreign exchange and is the livelihood of 75 per cent of the population. Fisheries are an important aspect of food production for certain countries (though 15 of the world's landlocked countries are in Africa). South Africa accounts for a third of Africa's total fishing catch, while both Namibia and Mozambique in southern Africa have rich off-shore fisheries.

At least part of Africa's food problems (apart from natural disasters such as droughts or famines caused by wars) is the result of political decisions: to concentrate upon export crops or the mining-industrial sector at the expense of the rural areas. The land resources exist; they are not always put to the best use. Africa's main export crops are tea, coffee, cocoa, sugar, cotton, groundnuts and fruit.

Africa has an estimated 30 per cent of the world's (apart from the former Communist bloc countries) minerals, excluding oil, although it has about 20 per cent of traded oil. Algeria, Libya, Nigeria and Gabon are oil producers in OPEC. Angola, Congo, Egypt and Tunisia are also oil producers. In 1992 Egypt's output ran at 925,000 b/d while through the years (1975-1990) Angola largely financed its costly civil war from its oil revenues. Most African countries are engaged in an on-going search for oil.

Africa accounts for about 15 per cent of world copper production and 70 per cent of cobalt production. South Africa is the richest storehouse of all, producing 29 per cent of the world's gold as well as diamonds, uranium and chrome and a number of other rare metals. Zimbabwe has deposits of 40 valuable minerals and an abundance of chrome. South Africa, Zimbabwe and Botswana have large coal reserves. The list can be extended. But the abundance of certain minerals has not meant any rapid transformation of the economies of the continent which generally remains the world's poorest region.

Latin America and the Caribbean

About a third of all workers in this region are in agriculture. Latin America's share of the principal agricultural commodities is approximately as follows: coffee 66 per cent, cocoa 35 per cent, sugar cane 46 per cent, citrus fruits 15 per cent, hardwoods 15 per cent, beef 25 per cent, and wool 10 per cent.

Mexico, Trinidad, Venezuela, Colombia, Ecuador, Peru, Brazil, Chile and Argentina each have *some* oil. Mexico is a major world producer, but only Venezuela is in OPEC.

The region is rich in certain minerals, notably silver, gold, copper, lead and zinc. Brazil, Venezuela and Peru are major iron ore producers, with Brazil responsible for about 10 per cent of world output. A quarter of the world's bauxite comes from three Caribbean territories: Jamaica, Guyana and Surinam. Cuba, in addition to being a leading sugar producer, has substantial chrome and nickel deposits. The region possesses a quarter of the world's antimony, 27 per cent or more of its silver and 17 per cent of its tin.

Asia

China is a 'continent' on its own and though well endowed with a wide range of minerals needs most of its output for its own development. Though smaller and less well endowed, India, which has huge iron ore deposits, has a comparable population to absorb what it produces.

Asia is rich in oil, notably in the Middle East, China and Indonesia (though China does not export), and has been far more successful than Africa in matching agricultural output to the needs of a far larger population.

Mineral and commodity distribution and production in the Third World

An examination of international commodities reveals the extent to which in field after field they are controlled by the North. Not only does the North provide the main markets, but in a high proportion of cases also produces more of them quantitatively than does the South. In certain fields such as aeronautics, the North dominates production and trade completely; in others such as aluminium, the South produces a substantial proportion of the commodity for export, although consumption is overwhelmingly in the North. Only in a minority of cases such as tropical foodstuffs like coffee and cocoa is the South the only producer and even then its markets are virtually all in the North.

Aluminium

The main producing countries (where bauxite is processed to aluminium in the producing country) are the USA, Russia, Jamaica and Canada, and the main exporting countries are Jamaica, the USA, Canada, Brazil and Surinam (three out of five from the Third World). The main bauxite exporting countries (where no processing has taken place) are Jamaica, Guinea, Indonesia, China and Ghana.

Copper

Four Third World countries – Chile, Peru, Zaïre and Zambia – formed the copper cartel (CIPEC) which accounts for 55 per cent of output (apart from the former Communist bloc countries), although the USA and Canada rank as the world's first and third producers.

Diamonds

Apart from Australia and Russia almost all the important diamond producers are in Africa: Zaïre and Botswana (with Australia and Russia) are leading world producers while the other African producers are South Africa, Namibia, Ghana, the Central African Republic, Sierra Leone, Liberia, Angola and Guinea.

Iron ore

There are huge world resources of iron ore with China and Brazil as major Third World producers and India and Venezuela as main Third World exporting countries.

Lead and zinc

Lead and zinc are generally found together and of the world's top seven producers only two come from the Third World – Mexico and Peru.

Natural gas

Of the world's top seven producers of natural gas only two – Algeria and Indonesia – come from the Third World though huge resources of natural gas exist in a number of other Third World countries such as Iran.

Phosphorites

Phosphorites are the basis for fertilizers and a number of Third World countries are substantial producers including Morocco, Jordan and Tunisia on a major scale followed by Togo, Syria, Senegal and Algeria on a smaller scale, and for this commodity the South is a significant importer as well as exporter.

Chromite, platinum, silver, tin

Chromite is produced (on a substantial scale) by South Africa, Zimbabwe and Gabon in Africa; Brazil, Bolivia, Chile, Cuba and Mexico in Latin America. South Africa is the world's leading producer of platinum. Mexico and Peru are the main Third World producers of silver, while all the main sources of tin are in the South: Brazil, Malaysia, Indonesia, China, Thailand and Bolivia.

Tropical fruits, nuts and bananas

These commodities are only produced in the South and form a staple export for many Asian, African and Latin American countries. The main producers of bananas are Brazil, the Philippines, Ecuador, Honduras and Indonesia, although mini-states, for example a number of Caribbean islands, may be dependent for as much as 70 per cent of their foreign exchange earnings upon banana exports.

Cocoa

Cocoa is a principal tropical food commodity and is produced on a major scale by seven Third World countries: Brazil, Ecuador, Cameroon, Côte d'Ivoire, Ghana, Nigeria and Malaysia.

Coconuts

The production and trade of coconuts is confined to the South. Malaysia, the Dominican Republic, Sri Lanka and Guatemala are the main producers, while Singapore, Hong Kong and El Salvador import and process them for the copra.

Coffee

Coffee is the most valuable agricultural commodity and is produced only in the South, principally by

Brazil, Colombia, Indonesia, Mexico and Côte d'Ivoire, although for a number of small producers (in terms of quantity) it is crucial to their economies (for example it accounts for about 75 per cent of Burundi's exports).

Tea

The main producers and exporters of tea are China, India, Sri Lanka and Kenya; while, unusually, of the main importers – Britain, the USA, Egypt, Iraq and Pakistan – three of the five belong to the South.

An examination of other commodities would reveal much the same pattern: the major markets almost always lie in the North and though the South enjoys a monopoly in the production of a number of commodities – principally the tropical fruits – these do not provide it with a leverage comparable to that of oil in the 1970s. Thus, the South remains the producer of raw materials most of which are exported to the North, while the North also produces a large proportion of the same commodities.

Narcotics

The trade in narcotics, covering cocaine, heroin and marijuana, is now second only to that in arms and was worth an estimated $500,000 million in 1990. It comes from three main regions in the South: Latin America (Bolivia, Colombia, Ecuador and Peru for coca, and Mexico for marijuana); the golden crescent in South Asia (Afghanistan, Iran and Pakistan for opium); and the golden triangle (Myanmar, Laos and Thailand also for opium). Lebanon and Guatemala are lesser producers. The huge one-way traffic in drugs to the main markets of the North – the USA, Europe and increasingly Russia – might almost be seen as the South's revenge for other injustices.

Figures for world-wide trade reveal just how far the South has to go to catch up the North. In 1989 all the developing countries of the South only accounted for 19.3 per cent of world trade with the least developed countries accounting for a mere 0.4 per cent of this, while the North accounted for the remaining 80.7 per cent.

Dependence on one commodity

Many Third World countries depend for 50 per cent or more of their foreign earnings upon the export of one commodity group. In the list below the map on pages 168–9, the term 'petroleum products' includes crude as well as refined products and, in certain cases, associated natural gas as well. The precise percentage figures – which fluctuate from year to year – have been taken from the *Britannica World Data* figures for 1993 and in a majority of cases they refer to 1991 or 1992. (In the first edition of this handbook, published in 1989, 58 countries were included in this list. In this second edition 17 countries of that list have been removed – in the intervening years they have sufficiently diversified their economies so as not to be 50 per cent or more dependent upon one commodity for export – although they have been replaced by a different 15 countries which for one reason or another have now moved into the position of being so dependent.)

Of the 56 nations listed overleaf, 12 are 90 per cent or more dependent upon one commodity, seven for over 80 per cent of their foreign earnings, 11 for 70 per cent and above, 10 for 60 per cent and above, and 16 for over 50 per cent. Petroleum products are the one commodity in no fewer than 22 of the 56 nations. This is so for even quite modest oil producers such as Congo, while investment in refining capacity has clearly paid handsomely for small territories such as Bahamas and Seychelles. Ten countries depend upon other minerals such as diamonds (Botswana and Central African Republic), copper (Zambia), alumina (Jamaica) or uranium (Niger). The remaining 24 countries depend upon agricultural or forestry products.

Conclusions

Some developing countries have managed a good deal of development based upon the high prices they have obtained from one major commodity. However, those dependent for 50 per cent or more of foreign exchange earnings upon one product are, on the whole, far too vulnerable for comfort and generally subject – as the oil-exporting countries discovered in the 1980s – to huge fluctuations that upset development plans based upon higher prices.

Commodity Export Dependent Countries

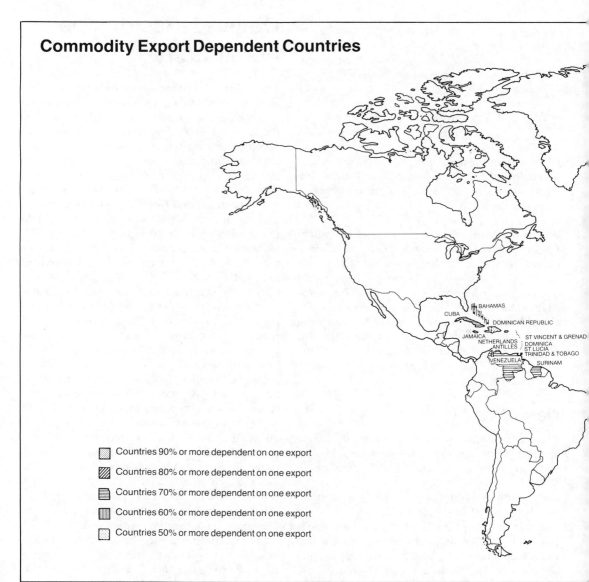

Countries 90% or more dependent on one export

Countries 80% or more dependent on one export

Countries 70% or more dependent on one export

Countries 60% or more dependent on one export

Countries 50% or more dependent on one export

Country	Product	%	Country	Product	%
Algeria	petroleum products	96.8	Cuba	sugar	73.2
Angola	petroleum products	89.8	Dominica	bananas	55.9
Bahamas	petroleum products*	64.6	Dominican Republic	sugar/honey	54.2
Bahrain	petroleum products	79.0	Egypt	petroleum products	50.7
Benin	cotton	55.6	Ethiopia	coffee	55.0
Botswana	diamonds	80.1	Gabon	petroleum products	70.8
Brunei	petroleum products	96.4	Ghana	cocoa	53.9
Burundi	coffee	81.0	Guinea	bauxite	56.9
Cambodia	rubber	82.9	Guinea-Bissau	cashews	52.8
Cameroon	petroleum products	54.2	Iran	petroleum products	91.3
Central African Republic	diamonds	66.2	Iraq	petroleum products	99.5
Chad	cotton	91.1	Jamaica	alumina/bauxite	57.3
Comoros	vanilla	63.8	Kuwait	petroleum products	92.2
Congo	petroleum products	76.7	Liberia	iron ore	55.1

Country	Product	%	Country	Product	%
Libya	petroleum products	96.8	St Lucia	bananas	58.1
Macau	textiles and garments	69.5	St Vincent & Grenadines	bananas	53.9
Malawi	tobacco	75.6	São Tomé & Príncipe	cocoa	95.4
Mauritania	fish	58.6	Saudi Arabia	petroleum products	100.0
Mauritius	clothing and textiles	51.7	Seychelles	petroleum products*	60.2
Netherlands Antilles	petroleum products	96.5	Somalia	live animals	56.7
New Caledonia	ferronickel/nickel matte	68.8	Surinam	alumina	71.9
Niger	uranium	71.5	Tonga	squash	60.2
Nigeria	petroleum products	96.2	Trinidad & Tobago	petroleum products	66.7
Oman	petroleum products	91.7	Tuvalu	copra	86.4
Papua New Guinea	copper (gold)	70.7	Uganda	coffee	79.6
Qatar	petroleum products	84.1	UAE	petroleum products	65.6
Réunion	sugar	74.7	Venezuela	petroleum products	79.7
Rwanda	coffee	66.7	Zambia	copper	85.2
				*based upon refinery activities	

Although a number of Third World countries are extremely well endowed with raw materials – minerals – or the capacity to produce one or more of the major agricultural commodities, such as tea, coffee, cocoa and sugar, in neither case does this mean that they have been able to overcome some of the fundamental problems of development-dependence upon the North. It is technology or its lack that determines which countries are at the head of the economic league.

Questions for the future and, increasingly it would seem, the fairly close future concern the untapped regions of resources: the Arctic, Antarctica and the ocean beds. Unless in the very immediate future the UN can work out a fair formula to prevent the most powerful countries seizing control of such resources – it is likely that in the race for these as yet unclaimed resources, a race which seems almost certain to take place within a generation, the countries of the Third World will once more be left behind.

Despite recognition (as in the Brandt Report of 1980, and then in the Report of the South Commission under the chairmanship of Julius Nyerere, in 1990) of the desirability for more South–South trade, the pattern remains overwhelmingly South to North. Thus intra-African trade is variously estimated at no more than 4 to 6 per cent. China and India are special cases, because of their size and the numbers of their huge populations.

A number of Third World countries have made substantial advances in industrialization, though in most cases the process has been fairly uneven. Sometimes referred to as the Newly Industrializing Countries (NICs), they are generally at the top end of the development scale. In Africa they include Algeria, Egypt, Nigeria, South Africa and Zimbabwe. In Asia countries in this category include China, India and four small territories – Hong Kong, Singapore, South Korea and Taiwan. In Latin America they include Argentina, Brazil, Mexico and Venezuela.

But though some Third World countries such as those listed above have achieved considerable breakthroughs and a degree of industrialization, this is still too rare an achievement. Generally the gap between the countries of the North and the bulk of Third World countries is increasing rapidly with no reversal of this situation in sight.

10 Biographical Notes

The following entries are selective: leading figures from Third World countries who have made a particular impact in the period since 1945.

Abdul Rahman, Tunku (1903–1990)

Tunku Abdul Rahman became Prime Minister and Minister of External Affairs of the Federation of Malaya in 1959. He was a principal architect of the Federation of Malaysia and when this was formed in 1963 he continued as its Prime Minister and Minister of External Affairs until 1970, when he handed over to his successor Tun Abdul Razak. At the 1961 Commonwealth Conference it was Tunku Abdul Rahman who raised the issue of South African membership while that country's government continued to practise apartheid, so forcing the Republic to withdraw from the association. During his rule in the 1960s, Malaysia had to face 'confrontation' with Indonesia and then in 1967 became a founder member of the Association of South East Asian Nations (ASEAN).

Allende Gossens, Salvador (1908–1973)

In 1933 Allende helped found the Chilean Socialist Party. When he became President in 1970 as leader of FRAP – Frente de Acción Popular – he was the first Marxist head of state to be democratically elected. A major programme of nationalization and reforms aimed at redistribution of wealth followed and a consequent political polarization led to increasing violence. By 1973 the rate of inflation had risen to 500 per cent, the economy appeared on the verge of collapse and the USA was openly hostile. Then the military, under General Pinochet, mounted a coup to overthrow the government: Allende is believed to have shot himself during the attack upon the presidential palace. Subsequently thousands of his supporters were killed or arrested.

Amin Dada, Idi (Field Marshall) (1925–)

A soldier who had received rapid promotion in the years following Uganda's independence, Amin came to power by coup in January 1971 when

President Obote was at the Singapore Commonwealth Conference. Some of his early measures such as the expulsion of the Asians or nationalization of foreign (British) assets were popular, but he soon revealed himself as a tyrant whose mass killings and brutalities became a byword which did great damage to Africa's world image. He invaded Tanzania in 1978 to distract attention from the rapidly deteriorating political and economic situation at home. The following year Tanzanian troops in support of exiled Ugandans invaded Uganda and by April Amin was forced to flee the country. He was granted asylum in Saudi Arabia.

Arafat, Yasir (1929–)

Chairman of the Palestine Liberation Organization (PLO) since 1969, Yasir Arafat was a co-founder of al-Fatah, the main military wing of the PLO. In 1971 he became commander-in-chief of the Palestinian Revolutionary Forces and in 1973 head of the political department of the PLO. He was the first-ever leader of a liberation organization to address a plenary session of the UN (1974). The long-drawn out nature of the PLO struggle in the Middle East has taken its toll of the leadership and in 1982 Arafat found himself the subject of attacks from increasingly fanatical groups in the PLO as well as from their principal backers, the Syrians. Following the Israeli invasion of Lebanon (1982) Arafat had to abandon his headquarters in Beirut and move to Tunisia. Often written off by his opponents, he has had the capacity to make many comebacks and, most notably, did so in 1993: after a series of secret negotiations with the Israelis the PLO agreed to recognize Israel and, as a first stage towards a Palestinian state, accept autonomy over the Gaza Strip and Jericho.

Bandaranaike, Sirimavo (1916–)

When her husband, who became Prime Minister in 1956, was assassinated in 1959, Sirimavo Bandaranaike became leader of the Sri Lanka Freedom Party (SLFP) and the world's first woman prime minister. She led her party in government from

1960 to 1965 and was returned to power again in 1970, this time at the head of a left-wing coalition. She was responsible for a number of left-wing populist policies: her language policy inflamed the Tamil minority; her secularization of education antagonized the Roman Catholics. Her insistence upon the political predominance of Sinhalese Buddhists made a confrontation between Sinhalese and Tamils inevitable. Her coalition government was decisively defeated in the elections of 1977.

Ben Bella, Ahmed (1916–)

After serving in the French army during World War II, Ben Bella joined the Algeria People's Party in 1945. He was one of the nine 'historic leaders' of the FLN who launched the Algerian rebellion in 1954. He was captured by the French in 1956 and only released in 1962 in the period before a final independence agreement had been reached. In the power struggle which followed the departure of the French, Ben Bella emerged as Prime Minister and then in September 1963 as President of Algeria. He was deposed by Boumedienne in a bloodless coup in 1965 on the grounds that he was too dictatorial. He is a classic example of a man who made a better revolutionary than post-independence ruler.

Boumedienne, Houari (1927–1978)

In 1965 Boumedienne seized power in a coup against Ahmed Ben Bella, Algeria's first president, after the two men disagreed over policy. He remained president of Algeria until his death in 1978. Although he lacked popular appeal, Boumedienne introduced a series of socialist economic measures and in 1971 brought to an end Algeria's special relationship with France, when he established state control over the oil and gas industries. He chaired the 1974 Special UN Session held in Algiers which popularized the idea of a New International Economic Order and came to be regarded as one of the leaders of the Non-Aligned Movement.

Castro Ruz, Dr Fidel (1926–)

On trial after his failed rebellion in 1953, Castro made the famous remark: 'History will absolve me.' Eventually he was to lead a successful rebellion to become Premier of Cuba in March 1959 on the fall of Batista. His socialist revolution has provided the people of his country with a better standard of living than ever before. Castro has always been regarded as a threat to the region by the United States whose attempts to overthrow him have enhanced his standing in the Third World. Under Castro, Cuba has provided vital military assistance to the left-wing governments in both Angola and Ethiopia. Havana was the site for the 1979 Non-Aligned Summit though some countries objected that Castro was in fact too committed to the Communist camp. Following the end of the Cold War and a withdrawal of Soviet support Castro, who insisted upon maintaining a largely Marxist orientation, faced severe financial and other pressures.

Gaddafi, Muammar al (1938–)

Gaddafi became president of Libya in 1969 following the coup which ousted King Idris. His determination to take effective control of the country's oil resources began the process which gave OPEC 'teeth' in the 1970s. Always controversial, Gaddafi has used Libya's oil wealth to support many nationalist and more dubious causes round the world. He is an advocate of Arab unity and a hardliner over Israel. His unpredictability has earned him many enemies in the Arab world and further afield although his defiance of the United States has been generally popular. His 'extreme' attitudes emerged at the 1986 Harare Non-Aligned Summit from which he stormed out after a speech branding a majority of the countries in attendance as being aligned to the West. Mounting western pressures for UN sanctions against Libya followed the bombing of Pan Am flight 103 over Lockerbie, Scotland, in 1988 with the loss of 259 lives, a terrorist act for which two Libyans were held responsible by the West.

Gandhi, Indira (1917–1984)

As the daughter of Pandit Nehru, Indira Gandhi had a long political apprenticeship. She became Prime Minister of India in 1966, a position she held until 1977. She won a huge election victory in 1971 and great prestige for her handling of the crisis and war with Pakistan. She was a pragmatist and emphasized the need to promote production so that she was criticized for deviating from socialism. In 1975 she imposed a state of emergency and continued to rule until her party was overwhelmingly defeated in the elections of 1977 by the Janata coalition. She returned to power after the 1980 elections and ruled India until her assassination by Sikh extremists in 1984. She dominated Indian politics for 18 years.

Gandhi, Mohandas Karamchand (Mahatma) (1869–1948)

This extraordinary man mounted an unique campaign against the British in India. Where other nationalists resorted to force he preached non-violence and urged civil disobedience and, more than anyone else, helped make British India ungovernable. When India became independent in 1947 Gandhi remained outside the government though he was regarded as the ultimate nationalist leader.

His fasts, his non-violent philosophy and his exaltation of individual conscience placed him on a different plane to all other nationalists and for millions of Indians he became a saint. For the subject peoples of other countries then struggling to emerge from the imperial age he became a symbol, unrivalled then or since.

Gowon, Yakubu (General) (1934–)

A Sandhurst-educated Nigerian army officer, Gowon was appointed Chief of Staff in January 1966 and following the July 1966 coup which overthrew General Aguiyi-Ironsi he became head of the Federal Government and Commander-in-Chief. He held these posts until 1975 when he was ousted in a bloodless coup while leading the Nigerian delegation to the OAU summit in Kampala. He then went to study at Warwick University in England. Gowon presided over Nigeria through its most dangerous post-independence crisis. When the civil war had been brought to an end and Nigerian unity had been preserved he was responsible, in the years 1970 to 1975, for the rehabilitation of the defeated Ibos, arguably his greatest achievement.

Guevara, Ernesto 'Che' (1928–1967)

One of the most romantic figures to emerge from the many struggles in the Third World since 1945, Che Guevara said of himself: 'I was born in Argentina, I fought in Cuba, and I began to be a revolutionary in Guatemala.' In Cuba he was a principal figure in the Castro revolution and for a time (1959-60), when perhaps as many as 700,000 middle-class Cubans fled the country, he became the directing force of the revolution. He was both a militant Communist, political philosopher and romantic (he was also a doctor). He remained at the centre of Cuban politics until 1965. Sartre described Che as 'The most complete man of his age'. He was shot after being captured wounded in the Bolivian jungle in 1967, fighting for a hopeless cause. He became the folk hero of a generation.

Hammarskjöld, Dag Hjalmar Agne Carl (1905–1961)

A Swedish economist, Dag Hammarskjöld became the second Secretary-General of the United Nations in 1953; by the time of his death 8 years later he had become recognized as a world statesman. He played a major part in finding a solution to the Suez Crisis of 1956 and again in the 1958 Middle East crisis in Lebanon and Jordan. In 1960, under his leadership, the UN sent a peace-keeping force to the newly independent Congo to suppress the civil strife. In September 1961 he was killed in an air crash near Ndola, Northern Rhodesia, in circumstances which have never been properly explained, while on a mission to see Moise Tshombe, the leader of the breakaway Katanga Province. He is best remembered for his efforts to find a solution in the Congo.

Ho Chi Minh (1890–1969)

Ho Chi Minh founded the Indochina Communist Party in 1930 and the Viet Minh in 1941. He led the nationalist movement of Vietnam for three decades and must rank as one of the leading anti-colonial figures of his age. In the difficult years of struggle he managed a balance between the USSR and China, obtaining support from both. In his later years (1959-1969) he moved into the political background but his popularity remained immense – to his people he was Uncle Ho – and for many throughout the Third World he became the symbol of a small backward nation struggling against great odds, in his case the power of the USA. His 1966 message to the people, 'Nothing is as dear to the heart of the Vietnamese people as independence and liberation', could be his epitaph.

Hussein, Ibn Talal (1936–)

Harrow- and Sandhurst-educated, King Hussein succeeded to the throne of Jordan as a minor in 1952 and took full control the following year. A moderate in the volatile politics of the Middle East ruling a poor state on the frontline with Israel, Hussein has survived precariously despite numerous assassination attempts and other Arab pressures against him. His attempt to control the Palestinians in the war of 1970-71 isolated him in the Arab world and yet by November 1987 he was able to host the Arab summit which decided that members could renew relations with Egypt, a triumph for Hussein's pragmatism. In 1988 he renounced Jordan's claims to the West Bank, a decision which recognized the existing reality but also strengthened the claims of the PLO.

Kaunda, Kenneth David (1924–)
A popular nationalist leader in Northern Rhodesia, Kaunda became President of the United National Independence Party (UNIP) in 1960 and led his country to independence as Zambia in October 1964, when he became its president. Following UDI in Rhodesia (November 1965) Kaunda became increasingly preoccupied with the growing problems of confrontation between the frontline states and the white-dominated territories of southern Africa: first Rhodesia under the Smith régime (it is claimed that Zambia suffered more from sanctions than did Smith's Rhodesia); and then South Africa. In 1979 at the Commonwealth Conference held in Lusaka, Kaunda played a leading role helping the Rhodesia peace talks which led to an independent Zimbabwe in 1980. In 1985 he succeeded Julius Nyerere as chairman of the frontline states and in 1987 he became chairman of the OAU. At the Vancouver Commonwealth Conference of 1987 he argued that Britain – standing alone on the issue of sanctions against South Africa – had the 'right to be wrong'. But in presidential elections in October 1991 Kaunda and his United National Independence Party (as well as the one-party system) were swept from power. Subsequently he retired from politics.

Kenyatta, Jomo (Mzee) (1893–1978)
One of the father figures of African nationalism, Kenyatta first came to prominence in the 1920s. He was arrested by the colonial authorities in 1952 and charged with managing the secret nationalist society, Mau Mau. He was sentenced to 7 years in prison after the last great stage-managed colonial trial but during the final years of his detention was increasingly consulted as to the political future of the country. Released in 1961, he became President of the Kenya African National Union (KANU). In 1963 he became the country's first prime minister and a year later its first president when Kenya became a republic, a position he held until his death in 1978.

Khomeini, Ruhollah (Ayatollah) (1900–1989)
A lifelong opponent of the Shah, Khomeini was a leader of the Shi'ah Sect. His many religious writings led to him being proclaimed an Ayatollah during the 1950s. His criticism of the Shah's reforms led to his imprisonment in 1963 and exile in 1964. He spent the years 1964 to 1978 in Iraq; then he was asked to leave and moved to Paris where he agitated for the overthrow of the Shah.

Massive unrest throughout Iran led to the collapse of the government in January 1979 when the Shah left the country. Khomeini returned to Iran on 1 February 1979 to become the religious leader of the revolution. In December 1979 Iran became an Islamic Republic and Khomeini was named political and religious leader for life. Under him the Shah's pro-western policies were reversed while Iran supported Islamic revolution throughout the Middle East.

Lee Kuan Yew (1923–)
In the 1950s Lee Kuan Yew acted as a defence lawyer to left-wing opponents of British rule in Singapore and in 1954 helped to found the People's Action Part (PAP). In 1959 PAP won the elections and Singapore became independent with Lee as Prime Minister. From that time he moved steadily to the political right. By 1966, for example, his increasingly repressive measures led all opposition MPs to resign. He led Singapore into the Federation of Malaysia in 1963 and out again in 1965. His policies were always strongly pro-western and he saw Singapore as the key to a western economic presence in South-east Asia. He took Singapore into ASEAN. Under Lee Singapore became a one-party state and his rule became increasingly authoritarian. He stepped down as Prime Minister in 1990.

Lumumba, Patrice (1925–1961)
As a leading trade unionist, Patrice Lumumba was a co-founder of the Mouvement National Congolais, an organization which advocated national unity in a country rent by tribal separatism. The MNC did not win an absolute majority in the post-independence elections and Lumumba became Prime Minister of a coalition with Joseph Kasavubu as the Congo's first president. Lumumba was prime minister for only 3 months; then in September 1960 Kasavubu dismissed him. In the subsequent factional turmoil that rent the Congo he was handed over to his political enemies in the breakaway Katanga Province where he was murdered. He became a political martyr.

Mahathir bin Mohamad, Datuk Seri (1925–)
One of Malaysia's most successful politicians, Mahathir bin Mohamad entered parliament in 1964. He became Deputy Prime Minister in 1976 and Prime Minister in 1981, a post he has held until the present time. During the late 1980s he emerged as an important spokesman for the Third World.

He acted as host for the 1989 Commonwealth Summit which was held in Kuala Lumpur. In 1992 he criticized the economic policies of the North during the run-up to the Rio Earth Summit, challenging the North to help the South with adequate aid if it expected it also to change its policies: 'There will be no development if the poor countries are not allowed to extract their natural wealth . . . fear by the North of environmental degradation provides the South with the leverage that did not exist before. If it is in the interest of the rich that we do not cut down our trees, then they must compensate us for the loss of income.'

Makarios III Mouskou (1913–1977)

The Archbishop of all Cyprus, Makarios became prominent in the 1950s as a nationalist demanding independence from the British and Enosis (union) with Greece. The British authorities deported him to the Seychelles in 1956 for collaborating with the terrorist Eoka organization but he was released in 1957. He became President of an independent Cyprus in 1960. He was briefly forced out of power in 1974 when Nikos Sampson became President but returned in December of that year to resume the presidency until his death in 1977. A narrow Greek Cypriot nationalist who became a symbol of opposition to British colonial rule, he failed to reconcile the Greeks and Turks of the island to make Cyprus a single nation.

Mandela, Nelson (Rohihlala) (1918–)

South Africa's most famous black nationalist, Nelson Mandela was condemned to life imprisonment in 1964 and spent the next 18 years on the notorious Robben Island before he was transferred to Pollsmoor prison. Regarded as its leader by the ANC throughout his period of more than a quarter of a century in prison, while not allowed to be quoted in his own country, Mandela became a symbol of the human spirit in adversity. His defence speech at his trial in 1964, justifying his actions against an unjust state, is famous. In the turmoil that beset South Africa from 1984 onwards Mandela remained in the public eye as international figures called for his release and the South African government debated whether he was a greater threat inside or outside prison. Mandela was released from prison on 11 February 1990. In South Africa's first all-race elections in April 1994, Mandela was elected as the country's first black president and was inaugurated on 10 May 1994.

Mao Zedong (1893–1976)

One of the world's great revolutionary figures, Mao Zedong emerged as the leader of the Chinese Communist Party during the 1920s. In 1934-35 he led his forces on the famous 'long march' from Kiangsi to Shensi. In 1949, after the Nationalists had been driven out of China, Mao was elected Chairman of the Republic, a position he retained unchallenged until his death in 1976.

Mao's great achievement was to create a strong united China for the first time in more than 150 years. As a political thinker he was preoccupied with how to maintain the momentum of revolution, hence his many experiments such as the year when he said 'Let a hundred flowers blossom and diverse schools of thought contend' or the licence he later gave to the Red Guards.

Mugabe, Robert Gabriel (1924–)

A radical and theoretical Marxist, Mugabe became a nationalist while at Fort Hare University in South Africa. He spent some years in Nkrumah's Ghana before returning to Rhodesia in 1960. In 1963 he helped the Reverend Ndabaningi Sithole break away from Nkomo's ZAPU to form the Zimbabwe African National Union (ZANU). He was arrested in 1964 and spent the next 10 years in prison where he studied law by correspondence. After his release in 1975 he waged guerilla war against the UDI government from bases in neighbouring Mozambique. He won a landslide victory in the 1980 independence elections which followed the Lancaster House talks of 1979, to become Zimbabwe's first prime minister. In 1986 he became chairman of the Non-Aligned Movement after its summit in Harare. At the end of 1987 Mugabe became the country's executive president.

Nasser, Gamal Abdel (1918–1970)

Colonel Nasser masterminded the 1952 coup which overthrew King Farouk of Egypt; by 1954 he had become undisputed leader of the revolution. His nationalization of the Suez Canal in 1956 was highly popular and after the abortive Anglo-French invasion Nasser achieved the height of his influence in the Middle East. His land reforms and industrialization measures did much to modernise Egypt while the Aswan High Dam became his greatest monument. A leading Arab nationalist and determined supporter of the concept of non-alignment his ambitions, nonetheless, caused his neighbours to be wary of him. After Egypt's defeat in the June War of 1967 he resigned but was called back to the presidency by popular acclaim. He died of a heart attack in 1970.

Nehru, Jawaharlal (1889–1964)
After a long apprenticeship in the Indian Congress Party as a nationalist opposing British rule – he spent a total of 13 years in prison for his nationalist activities – Pandit Nehru became the first prime minister of an independent India in 1947, a post he held until his death in 1964. It was due to his determination and leadership more than anything else that the idea of a third force or non-alignment was born. He became undisputed leader of the movement during his lifetime, in part because he ruled one of Asia's two giants. It was a fundamental aspect of his politics – at the height of the Cold War – that decisions about Asia had to be taken by Asians and not by the big powers.

Nkrumah, Dr Kwame (Osagyefu) (1909–1972)
In 1949 Kwame Nkrumah founded the Convention People's Party and in 1951 he became the Gold Coast's first prime minister. He led his country to independence in 1957 and ruled it until 1966 when he was ousted in a military coup. An ideas man as well as politician (he had a number of books published), Nkrumah used his great prestige as the first newly independent black leader to push for African unity but his ambition was distrusted by other African leaders. In the early days of African independence Nkrumah, with his powerful personality, became a symbol for the whole continent.

Nyerere, Julius Kambarage (Mwalimu) (1922–)
Julius Nyerere became Prime Minister of Tanganyika at independence in 1961 and President of the United Republic of Tanzania in 1964. He has achieved an international reputation as a political philosopher and his Arusha Declaration of 1967 is seen as a milestone in African political thinking. Being better with theory than practice, Nyerere's experiments in socialism and, most notably, the attempt to collectivize the people in *ujamaa* (self-help) villages were far from a success, and the experiment had to be modified. Nyerere resigned as President in 1985 though he was to remain chairman for a time of the Revolutionary Party of Tanzania (Chama Cha Mapinduzi). He chaired the South Commission which was formed in 1987 and reported in 1990.

Pahlavi, Mohammed Riza (Shah) (1919–1980)
Mohammed Riza succeeded to the throne of Persia (Iran) in 1941 following the forced abdication of his father. He briefly fled the country in 1953 when Mussadiq was Prime Minister but returned with American assistance. Always an autocrat, he nonetheless instituted a series of reforms and, following the huge boom in oil prices of the mid-1970s, said his aim was to make Iran the fifth most important country in the world by 1990. Seen by many as a puppet of the West his rule was made possible by ever greater authoritarianism and the use of the hated secret police (Savak). He created the conditions which led to his own downfall in 1979 in revolutionary circumstances that brought the Ayatollah Khomeini to power. The latter saw that Iran became an Islamic Republic.

Sadat, Anwar (1918–1981)
Sadat became President of Egypt on Nasser's death in 1970. He gained huge prestige and popularity following Egypt's military successes in the 1973 war against Israel. He made an historic breakthrough which led to turmoil in the Arab world when he visited Jerusalem in 1977 to address the Israeli Parliament in a bid to end the hostility which had dominated Middle East politics since the creation of the state of Israel. His meetings with the Israeli Prime Minister Menachim Begin at Camp David in the USA in 1978 and 1979 which led to a peace treaty between the two countries also led to the isolation of Egypt in the Arab world and its expulsion from the Arab League. Sadat was assassinated in 1981.

Sukarno, Ahmed (1901–)
A lifelong nationalist, in 1945 Sukarno proclaimed the independence of the Republic of Indonesia from the Dutch. In the fighting which followed he was taken prisoner by the Dutch in 1948 but in 1949 he was elected president of the new republic. He played host to the 1955 Bandung Conference which saw the launching of Non-Alignment. From 1957 to 1965 he ruled his huge country according to the principles of 'guided democracy' under which he remained the central figure. But his charisma began to wane following the 'confrontation' with Malaysia and the abortive coup of 1965. Thereafter he was deprived of his power and handed over the presidency to Suharto in 1967.

Tito, Josip Broz (1890–1980)
The communist leader of Yugoslavia who organized successful resistance to the Nazis during World War II, Tito refused to submit to dictation from Moscow and was expelled from the Comin-

form in 1948. He insisted that Yugoslavia should follow its own communist path and he survived many pressures and sanctions from the USSR to rule Yugoslavia until his death in 1980. He became a founder member of the Non-Aligned Movement. This was all the more significant because he brought to its membership a genuinely communist country which gave to the concept of non-alignment an added dimension. The first Non-Aligned Summit was held in Belgrade in 1961.

Touré, Ahmed Sekou (1922–1984)

President of the small West African state of Guinea from independence in 1958 to his death in 1984, Sekou Touré upset French plans for a Paris-controlled African community when in 1958 he opted for total independence. He then said: 'We prefer poverty in liberty to wealth in slavery'. As a result of his 'No' to the community France broke relations with Guinea and the breach was not healed until the mid-1970s. An influential figure in pan-African politics and Marxist-oriented, Sekou Touré first turned for assistance to the USSR but by 1961 had opted for a policy of non-alignment.

Williams, Eric (1911–1981)

A scholar and historian, Eric Williams founded the People's National Movement (PNM) in Trinidad in 1956 to become Chief Minister that year and Premier in 1959. He was an advocate of a federation of the British Caribbean islands but withdrew from the Federation in 1961 following Jamaica's withdrawal, as otherwise Trinidad would have been obliged to sustain the poorer territories of the Federation. He became the Prime Minister of Trinidad and Tobago when it became independent in 1962 and retained the office until his death in 1981. He was conservative, orthodox and pro-western in his politics. His best known book was *Capitalism and Slavery* (1964).

Yamani, Ahmad Zaki (Sheikh) (1930–)

Sheikh Yamani became one of the best known figures on the international scene during the 1970s when OPEC power was at its greatest. As Saudi Arabia's petroleum minister he represented the country with the largest oil reserves in the world. Saudi decisons at the OPEC conferences of the 1970s – its huge resources made it the 'swing' country of the organization with the capacity to increase or decrease production to an extent that could alter prices – gave to Yamani an unique position among oil ministers. In the early 1970s he was the first to suggest the use of the oil weapon against countries supporting Israel. Later he became a moderate, realizing that the continuing prosperity of the oil producers depended upon the strength of the US economy. He was dismissed as oil minister by King Fahd in October 1986.

Zhou Enlai (1898–1976)

Zhou Enlai joined the Communists in 1927 and was to be a close associate of Mao Zedong for the rest of his life. In 1949, after the overthrow of the Nationalists, he became Premier and Foreign Minister. He emerged as a major international figure during the 1954 Geneva Conference which ended the war in Indo-China. At the Bandung Conference the following year he persuaded the non-aligned countries to accept the concept of 'peaceful co-existence' even if they rejected China's Communism. This was a major triumph, particularly as China was then almost totally isolated and excluded from the UN. Zhou Enlai was especially concerned to build friendly relations with the new nations of Asia.

11 Country Gazetteer

The following gazetteer covering 157 countries provides basic statistical information. The choice of facts must in part be arbitrary and is also dictated by considerations of space.

The gazetteer includes all independent Third World countries (and since the first edition has also included certain new states including some of the successor states to the former USSR) and some of the larger, more important dependencies, such as French Guiana and Hong Kong. But a number of small dependencies, mainly those of Britain, Australia and New Zealand, have been omitted.

The gazetteer is divided into five sections: Africa, Asia (Middle East), Europe, Asia (East, Far East and Pacific), and Latin America and the Caribbean. Of these 157 countries, 55 come under Africa, and of these 52 are independent members of the OAU; two – Mayotte and Réunion – are overseas (island) departments of France; and South Africa (though in transition away from apartheid) remains a special case.

South Africa has not until now been considered as a member of the Third World. It has been included here for two reasons. First, with the ending of apartheid and the establishment of an equitable political system South Africa will shortly qualify as a Third World country in terms of the overall economic conditions of its people; while an independent South Africa will wish to join the OAU.

Some 16 countries are listed under Asia (Middle East) (since the first edition of this Handbook the former two Yemens have united to become a single state) which extends from the Mediterranean island of Cyprus to Afghanistan. As with South Africa, the case of Israel is complex. In terms of development it hardly qualifies as a Third World country, while its neighbours have long regarded it as an outpost of the West in the Arab world. In terms of the vast sums of aid it has been receiving annually from the USA, it is certainly a dependent nation but this aid – overwhelmingly – has been designed to maintain Israel's military capacity rather than promote its economic progress. The confrontation between Israel and its neighbours has long retarded progress in the region although the 1993 decision of the PLO to recognize Israel and the creation of autonomous regions in the Gaza Strip and Jericho might herald the beginning of a new era for the region. On balance, therefore, Israel should be seen as a member of the Third World.

The high per capita GNP figures for certain oil-rich Middle East nations highlights the fact that wealth alone is not a qualification for membership of the North. In 1993 three Middle East countries enjoyed per capita incomes above $15,000 – Kuwait, Qatar and the United Arab Emirates – as a result of oil. Yet high income is only part of the story. These same countries still require a range of development assistance so that such wealth may be translated into a reasonable standard of living for all their subjects.

Malta, the only entry listed under Europe, is like a number of other Third World countries poised uneasily between the Third World and the North. Is it a poor member of the rich North or a relatively advanced member of the Third World?

Part Four, Asia (East, Far East and Pacific) lists 46 countries, including the world's giants, China and India. (Since the first edition of this Handbook the break-up of the USSR has meant that eight of the former Soviet republics have qualified for membership of the Third World, certainly in terms of their relative lack of development.) Five of these 46 countries have special or colonial status: French Polynesia, Guam, Hong Kong, Macau and New Caledonia while the former Trust Territory of the Pacific Islands has split into the Marshall Islands and Micronesia. No other area shows such a range of size or stages of development. At one end of the scale are the Asian population giants, China, India, Indonesia, Pakistan, Bangladesh and Vietnam with populations ranging from 60 million to more than 1000 million. Among the remote Pacific territories on the other hand, 16 have populations of less than 1 million and two of them – Nauru and Tuvalu – less than 10,000.

Part Five, Latin America and the Caribbean, includes 39 states of which 21 are mainland and 18 are island territories, some very small as to both size and population. Five territories included in this region – Bermuda, French Guiana, Guadeloupe, Martinique and Netherlands Antilles – are still colonies.

Under each country the following information has been given: the political system, capital, area, population, a number of economic indicators. These are total GNP and per capita income; a brief description of the economy – a majority, for example, have been described as predominantly agricultural economies. 'Mixed economy' indicates at least a degree of industrialization, including mining. Commodities given in brackets (cocoa or bauxite) are major foreign exchange earners.

The spread of the economy can also be gauged to some extent from the breakdowns given under *labour force* which shows percentages of workers in agriculture, industry and services. Agriculture includes forestry and fishing; industry includes mining and construction; services covers everything else – government administration, army, tourist facilities and so on.

Finally, the percentage figures for urban development are included. This is a further guide to the extent of industrialization or diversification away from a rural society, but is also an indication of the extent of one of the Third World's greatest problems: urban growth which is unmatched by urban employment. (GNP figures for the new Asian countries of the former Soviet Union have not been given, as translation from roubles to US dollars makes little sense at the present stage of fluctuating economic fortunes in those countries.)

GNP comparisons

It is worth making a few GNP comparisons as between North and South in order to obtain a perspective. For example, in 1990 the combined GNPs of every country on the African continent including South Africa and the oil-rich nations of North Africa came to less than $399,000 million. In the same year the GNP of Britain was $927,959 million.

Also in 1990, the combined GNP of six of the largest Third World countries – Bangladesh, Brazil, China, India, Indonesia and Pakistan – only came to $1,279,867 million, while Japan with a GNP of $3,140,948 million exceeded their combined figure by $1,861,081 million, which itself is more than four times the GNP of China.

Finally, the GNP of the USA stood at $5,694,900 million in 1991. Such figures indicate just how wide is the gap between North and South.

Sources

Area figures have been taken from the *UN Demographic Yearbook*, while GNP and per capita income figures in US dollars are derived from the 1993 World Development Report. Most figures relate to the years 1989 or 1990.

Part 1 Africa

Algeria
Democratic and Popular Republic of Algeria
Political system: military administration
Capital: Algiers
Area: 919,595 sq miles (2,381,741 km²)
Population: 26,401,000
Economy: GNP $51,585m per capita $2060
   A mixed economy heavily dependent upon oil and natural gas
Labour force: agriculture 15.9% industry 23.7% services 60.4%
Urban population: 51.7%

Angola
People's Republic of Angola
Political system: multi-party republic (civil war)
Capital: Luanda
Area: 481,354 sq miles (1,246,700 km²)
Population: 10,609,000
Economy: GNP $6070m per capita $620
   A mainly agricultural economy, but some oil and diamonds
Labour force: agriculture 71.4% industry 10% services 18.6%
Urban population: 28.3%

Benin
People's Republic of Benin
Political system: multi-party republic
Capital: Porto-Novo
Area: 43,475 sq miles (112,600 km^2)
Population: 4,928,000
Economy: GNP $1716m per capita $369
  Mainly agricultural economy, exporting cocoa, palm
  kernels, cotton
Labour force: agriculture 61.1% industry 9.1% services
  29.8%
Urban population: 26.5%

Botswana
Republic of Botswana
Political system: multi-party republic
Capital: Gaborone
Area: 231,805 sq miles (600,372 km^2)
Population: 1,359,000
Economy: GNP $2561m per capita $2020
  Cattle farming and mining (diamonds and copper)
Labour force: agriculture about 70% industry and
  services 30%
Urban population: 24.1%

Burkina Faso
Political system: multi-party republic
Capital: Ouagadougou
Area: 105,869 sq miles (274,200 km^2)
Population: 9,515,000
Economy: GNP $2955m per capita $330
  Predominantly agricultural economy
Labour force: agriculture 92.3% industry 2.8% services
  4.9%
Urban population: 8.6%

Burundi
Republic of Burundi
Political system: multi-party republic
Capital: Bujumbura
Area: 10,747 sq miles (27,834 km^2)
Population: 5,657,000
Economy: GNP $1157m per capita $210
  Predominantly agricultural economy
Labour force: agriculture 93.1% industry 2.4% services
  4.1%
Urban population: 7.5%

Cameroon
United Republic of Cameroon
Political system: multi-party republic
Capital: Yaoundé
Area: 183,569 sq miles (475,442 km^2)
Population: 12,662,000
Economy: GNP $11,233m per capita $940
  Predominantly agricultural economy but some oil
Labour force: agriculture 74% industry 7.7% services
  21.3%
Urban population: 41.2%

Cape Verde
Republic of Cape Verde
Political system: multi-party republic
Capital: Praia
Area: 1557 sq miles (4033 km^2)

Population: 346,000
Economy: GNP $331m per capita $890
  Predominantly agricultural economy
Labour force: agriculture 33.2% industry 32.4%
  services 34.4%
Urban population: 29.7%

Central African Republic
Political system: multi-party republic
Capital: Bangui
Area: 240,535 sq miles (622,984 km^2)
Population: 2,930,000
Economy: GNP $1194m per capita $390
  Predominantly agricultural economy, some mining
  (diamonds)
Labour force: agriculture 65.8% industry 6.8% services
  27.4%
Urban population: 46.7%

Chad
Republic of Chad
Political system: transitional
Capital: N'Djaména
Area: 495,755 sq miles (1,284,000 km^2)
Population: 5,961,000
Economy: GNP $1074m per capita $190
  Predominantly agricultural economy (pastoralist)
Labour force: agriculture 77.4% industry 6.3% services
  16.3%
Urban population: 23.9%

Comoros
Federal Islamic Republic of the Comoros
Political system: federal Islamic republic
Capital: Moroni
Area: 838 sq miles (2171 km^2)
Population: 497,000
Economy: GNP $227m per capita $480
  Predominantly agricultural but some manufacturing
Labour force: agriculture 53.3% industry 7.5% services
  39.2%
Urban population: 27.8%

Congo
People's Republic of Congo
Political system: multi-party republic
Capital: Brazzaville
Area: 132,047 sq miles (342,000 km^2)
Population: 2,692,000
Economy: GNP $2296m per capita $1010
  Oil and agriculture, including wood products
Labour force: agriculture 51.7% industry 12.8%
  services 35.5%
Urban population: 40.5%

Côte d'Ivoire
Republic of Côte d'Ivoire
Political system: multi-party republic
Capital: Abidjan
Area: 124,504 sq miles (322,463 km^2)
Population: 12,951,000
Economy: GNP $8920m per capita $730
  Predominantly agricultural economy
Labour force: agriculture 60.5% industry 10.1%
  services 29.4%
Urban population: 40.4%

Djibouti
Republic of Djibouti
Political system: multi-party republic
Capital: Djibouti
Area: 8494 sq miles (22,000 km^2)
Population: 557,000
Economy: GNP $216m per capita $475
    Predominantly transit facilities (port and railway) with
    agriculture and mining (salt)
Labour force: agriculture 76.9% industry 8.5% services
    14.6%
Urban population: 80.7%

Egypt
Arab Republic of Egypt
Political system: multi-party republic
Capital: Cairo
Area: 386,662 sq miles (1,001,449 km^2)
Population: 55,979,000
Economy: GNP $31,381m per capita $680
    Mixed economy: agriculture, manufactures, oil
Labour force: agriculture 42.7% industry 21.5%
    services 35.8%
Urban population: 48.9%

Equatorial Guinea
Republic of Equatorial Guinea
Political system: transitional
Capital: Malabo
Area: 10,831 sq miles (28,051 km^2)
Population: 367,000
Economy: GNP $136m per capita $330
    Predominantly agricultural economy (cocoa)
Labour force: agriculture 57.9% industry 3.5% services
    38.6%
Urban population: 31%

Eritrea
Political system: transitional (post-independence)
    government
Capital: Asmara
Area: 36,160 sq miles (93,679 km^2)
Population: 3,500,000
Economy:
Labour force:
Urban population:
    (NB. At the time of going to press, shortly after
    Eritrea's independence from Ethiopia, insufficient data
    was available.)

Ethiopia
Political system: transitional government
Capital: Addis Ababa
Area: 471,778 sq miles (1,221,900 km^2)
Population: 53,845,000
Economy: GNP $6015m per capita $120
    Predominantly agricultural economy
Labour force: agriculture 78.1% industry 8.5% services
    13.4%
Urban population: 11.2%

Gabon
Gabonese Republic
Political system: multi-party republic
Capital: Libreville
Area: 103,347 sq miles (267,667 km^2)

Population: 1,253,000
Economy: GNP $3654m per capita $3220
    A mixed mining (including oil) and agricultural
    (including forest products) economy
Labour force: agriculture 10.2% industry 15.4%
    services 74.4%
Urban population: 45.7

Gambia, The
Republic of the Gambia
Political system: multi-party republic
Capital: Banjul
Area: 4361 sq miles (11,295 km^2)
Population: 921,000
Economy: GNP $229m per capita $260
    Predominantly agricultural economy
Labour force: agriculture 73.7% industry and services
    26.3%
Urban population: 21.5%

Ghana
Republic of Ghana
Political system: multi-party republic
Capital: Accra
Area: 92,100 sq miles (238,537 km^2)
Population: 15,237,000
Economy: GNP $5824m per capita $390
    Predominantly agricultural economy, some mining
Labour force: agriculture 59.4% industry 14.5%
    services 26.1%
Urban population: 33%

Guinea
Republic of Guinea
Political system: transitional
Capital: Conakry
Area: 94,900 sq miles (265,857 km^2)
Population: 7,232,000
Economy: GNP $2756m per capita $480
    Predominantly agricultural society
Labour force: agriculture 76.3% industry 11.1%
    services 12.6%
Urban population: 25.6%

Guinea-Bissau
Republic of Guinea-Bissau
Political system: transitional
Capital: Bissau
Area: 13,948 sq miles (36,125 km^2)
Population: 1,015,000
Economy: GNP $176m per capita $180
    Predominantly agricultural economy
Labour force: agriculture 71.9% industry 2.4% services
    25.7%
Urban population: 19.9%

Kenya
Republic of Kenya
Political system: multi-party republic
Capital: Nairobi
Area: 224,961 sq miles (582,646 km^2)
Population: 26,985,000
Economy: GNP $8958m per capita $370
    Mainly agricultural economy, some industry, strong
    tourist sector

Labour force: agriculture 18.9% industry 18.7%
    services 62.4%
Urban population: 25.3%

Lesotho
Kingdom of Lesotho
Political system: multi-party, monarchy
Capital: Maseru
Area: 11,720 sq miles (30,355 km^2)
Population: 1,854,000
Economy: GNP $832m per capita $470
    Predominantly agricultural economy, but heavily
    dependent upon remittances from migrant workers in
    neighbouring South Africa
Labour force: agriculture 66.2% industry 8% services
    25.8%
Urban population: 45.9%

Liberia
Republic of Liberia
Political system: civil war-ECOMOG intervention
Capital: Monrovia
Area: 43,000 sq miles (111,369 km^2)
Population: 2,780,000
Economy: GNP $975.2m per capita $400
    A mixed mining and agricultural economy heavily
    dependent upon iron ore
Labour force: agriculture 68.3% industry 4.6% services
    27.1%
Urban population: 45.9%

Libya
Socialist People's Libyan Arab Jamahiriya
Political system: socialist state run by General People's
    Congress
Capital: Tripoli
Area: 679,362 sq miles (1,759,540 km^2)
Population: 4,447,000
Economy: GNP $23,333m per capita $5310
    Overwhelming dependence upon oil
Labour force: agriculture 19.2% industry 27.4% services
    53.4%
Urban population: 70.2%

Madagascar
Democratic Republic of Madagascar
Political system: multi-party republic
Capital: Antananarivo
Area: 226,658 sq miles (587,041 km^2)
Population: 12,804,000
Economy: GNP $2710m per capita $230
    Predominantly agricultural economy
Labour force: agriculture 77.9% industry 9.9% services
    22.2%
Urban population: 21.9%

Malawi
Republic of Malawi
Political system: one-party republic
Capital: Lilongwe
Area: 45,747 sq miles (118,484 km^2)
Population: 9,484,000
Economy: GNP $1662m per capita $200
    Predominantly agricultural economy
Labour force: agriculture 81.8% industry 4.6% services
    13.6%
Urban population: 14.6%

Mali
Republic of Mali
Political system: multi-party republic
Capital: Bamako
Area: 478,767 sq miles (1,240,000 km^2)
Population: 8,464,000
Economy: GNP $2292m per capita $270
    Predominantly agricultural economy (pastoral)
Labour force: agriculture 82.4% industry 2.5% services
    15.1%
Urban population: 24.9%

Mauritania
Islamic Republic of Mauritania
Political system: transitional
Capital: Nouakchott
Area: 397,956 sq miles (1,030,700 km^2)
Population: 2,108,000
Economy: GNP $987m per capita $500
    Agriculture and mining (iron ore)
Labour force: agriculture 66% industry 10% services
    24%
Urban population: 39.1%

Mauritius
Political system: multi-party republic
Capital: Port Louis
Area: 790 sq miles (2045 km^2)
Population: 1,081,000
Economy: GNP $2422m per capita $2250
    Mixed economy, sugar, manufactures
Labour force: agriculture 16.2% industry 42.4%
    services 41.4%
Urban population: 40.7%

Mayotte
Territorial collectivity of Mayotte
Political system: French dependency with a status
    between an overseas department and an overseas
    territory
Capital: Dzaoudzi
Area: 114.1 sq miles (372.2 km^2)
Population: 76,000
Economy: Predominantly agriculture and fisheries

Morocco
Kingdom of Morocco
Political system: constitutional monarchy
Capital: Rabat
Area: 172,395 sq miles (446,500 km^2)
Population: 26,239,000
Economy: GNP $23,788m per capita $950
    Mixed economy, agriculture, mining, tourism,
    phosphates the main export
Labour force: agriculture 37.2% industry 26.6%
    services 36.2%
Urban population: 49.5%

Mozambique
Republic of Mozambique
Political system: transitional
Capital: Maputo
Area: 309,496 sq miles (801,590 km^2)
Population: 14,842,000
Economy: GNP $1208m per capita $80
    Predominantly agricultural economy, also country of
    transit

Labour force: agriculture 83.8% industry 6.8% services
   9.4%
Urban population: 13.2%

Namibia
Political system: multi-party republic
Capital: Windhoek
Area: 318,261 sq miles (824,292 km^2)
Population: 1,512,000
Economy: GNP $1350m per capita $1030
   Mining and agriculture
Labour force: agriculture 19.5% industry 17.4%
   services 63.1%
Urban population: 32.8%

Niger
Republic of Niger
Political system: multi-party republic
Capital: Niamey
Area: 489,191 sq miles (1,267,000 km^2)
Population: 8,281,000
Economy: GNP $2355m per capita $310
   Predominantly agricultural (pastoralist) economy
Labour force: agriculture 77.8% industry 3.7% services
   18.5%
Urban population: 15.3%

Nigeria
Federal Republic of Nigeria
Political system: transitional
Capital: Lagos
Area: 356,669 sq miles (923,768 km^2)
Population: 89,666,000
Economy: GNP $31,285m per capita $270
   Mixed economy, oil, agriculture, some industry
Labour force: agriculture 43.1% industry 6.4% services
   50.5%
Urban population: 35.2%

Réunion
Department of Reúnion
Political system: overseas department of France
Capital: Saint Denis
Area: 969 sq miles (2510 km^2)
Population: 623,000
Economy: GNP $1871m per capita $230
   Mixed economy heavily dependent upon sugar
Labour force: agriculture 4.8% industry 12% services
   83.2%
Urban population: 73.4%

Rwanda
Republic of Rwanda
Political system: transitional
Capital: Kigali
Area: 10,169 sq miles (26,338 km^2)
Population: 7,347,000
Economy: GNP $2214m per capita $310
   Predominantly agricultural economy
Labour force: agriculture 91.8% industry 3.3% services
   4.9%
Urban population: 5.4%

São Tomé & Príncipe
Democratic Republic of São Tomé & Príncipe
Political system: multi-party republic

Capital: São Tomé
Area: 372 sq miles (964 km^2)
Population: 126,000
Economy: GNP $47m per capita $380
   Predominantly agricultural economy (cocoa)
Labour force: agriculture 40.4% industry 8.9% services
   50.7%
Urban population: 40.5%

Senegal
Republic of Senegal
Political system: multi-party republic
Capital: Dakar
Area: 75,750 sq miles (196,192 km^2)
Population: 7,691,000
Economy: GNP $5260m per capita $710
   Predominantly agricultural economy (some oil)
Labour force: agriculture 9.1% industry 30.6% services
   60.3%
Urban population: 38.6%

Seychelles
Republic of Seychelles
Political system: multi-party republic
Capital: Victoria
Area: 108 sq miles (280 km^2)
Population: 71,000
Economy: GNP $285m per capita $4170
   Mixed economy, tourism, manufacturing
Labour force: agriculture 9.4% industry 18.3% services
   72.2%
Urban population: 59.3%

Sierra Leone
Republic of Sierra Leone
Political system: military régime
Capital: Freetown
Area: 27,699 sq miles (71,740 km^2)
Population: 4,373,000
Economy: GNP $981m per capita $240
   Mixed though mainly agricultural
Labour force: agriculture 10.4% industry 30.9%
   services 58.7%
Urban population: 32.2%

Somalia
Somali Democratic Republic
Political system: civil war (UN presence)
Capital: Mogadishu
Area: 246,201 sq miles (637,657 km^2)
Population: 7,872,000
Economy: GNP $940m per capita $150
   Predominantly agricultural (pastoralist) economy
Labour force: agriculture 71.8% industry 9.5% services
   18.7%
Urban population: 63.6%

South Africa
Republic of South Africa
Political system: multi-party democracy
Capital: Pretoria, Cape Town (seat of legislature)
Area: 471,445 sq miles (1,221,037 km^2)
Population: 32,063,000
Economy: GNP $90,410m per capita $2520
   Mixed economy, strong in mining (gold), agriculture,
   industry – Africa's most developed economy

Labour force: agriculture 9.8% industry 23.5% services 66.7%
Urban population: 60.3%

Sudan
Republic of Sudan
Political system: military régime
Capital: Khartoum
Area: 967,500 sq miles (2,505,813 km^2)
Population: 29,971,000
Economy: GNP $10,094 per capita $420
   Predominantly agricultural economy
Labour force: agriculture 63.5% industry 7.2% services 29.3%
Urban population: 22%

Swaziland
Kingdom of Swaziland
Political system: constitutional monarchy
Capital: Mbabane
Area: 6704 sq miles (17,363 km^2)
Population: 826,000
Economy: GNP $645m per capita $820
   Predominantly agricultural economy, some mining
Labour force: agriculture 18.8% industry 17.3% services 63.9%
Urban population: 30.4%

Tanzania
United Republic of Tanzania
Political system: transitional
Capital: Dodoma
Area: 364,900 sq miles (945,087 km^2)
Population: 25,809,000
Economy: GNP $2779m per capita $120
   Predominantly agricultural economy
Labour force: agriculture 82.4% industry 4.7% services 12.9%
Urban population: 32.8%

Togo
Republic of Togo
Political system: transitional
Capital: Lomé
Area: 21,925 sq miles (56,785 km^2)
Population: 3,701,000
Economy: GNP $1474m per capita $410
   Predominantly agricultural economy
Labour force: agriculture 70.6% industry 10.8% services 18.6%
Urban population: 25.7%

Tunisia
Republic of Tunisia
Political system: multi-party republic
Capital: Tunis
Area: 63,170 sq miles (163,610 km^2)
Population: 8,413,000

Economy: GNP $11,592m per capita $1420
   Mixed economy, oil, manufactures, mining, agriculture
Labour force: agriculture 23% industry 32% services 45%
Urban population: 53%

Uganda
Republic of Uganda
Political system: no party government
Capital: Kampala
Area: 91,134 sq miles (236,036 km^2)
Population: 17,194,000
Economy: GNP $3814m per capita $220
   Predominantly agricultural economy
Labour force: agriculture 82.6% industry 5.1% services 12.3%
Urban population: 11.3%

Zaïre
Republic of Zaïre
Political system: one-party republic
Capital: Kinshasa
Area: 905,568 sq miles (2,345,409 km^2)
Population: 41,151,000
Economy: GNP $8177m per capita $230
   Mixed economy – agriculture and mining, heavy dependence on copper and cobalt
Labour force: agriculture 67.4% industry 14.8% services 17.8%
Urban population: 44.2%

Zambia
Republic of Zambia
Political system: multi-party republic
Capital: Lusaka
Area: 290,586 sq miles (752,614 km^2)
Population: 8,303,000
Economy: GNP $3391m per capita $420
   Mixed economy – agriculture and mining (heavy dependence on copper)
Labour force: agriculture 68.9% industry 5.4% services 25.7%
Urban population: 42%

Zimbabwe
Republic of Zimbabwe
Political system: multi-party republic
Capital: Harare
Area: 150,804 sq miles (390,580 km^2)
Population: 9,871,000
Economy: GNP $6313m per capita $640
   Mixed economy, strong agricultural and mining sectors, growing manufacturing sector
Labour force: agriculture 24.3% industry 27.3% services 48.4%
Urban population: 26.4%

Part 2 Asia (Middle East)

Afghanistan
Republic of Afghanistan
Political system: coalition of political factions
Capital: Kabul
Area: 250,000 sq miles (647,497 km^2)
Population: 18,052,000
Economy: GNP $3100m per capita $220
  Predominantly agricultural economy, natural gas,
  handicrafts
Labour force: agriculture 57.3% industry 12.2%
  services 30.5%
Urban population: 18.2%

Bahrain
State of Bahrain
Political system: monarchy (cabinet appointed by Emir)
Capital: Manama
Area: 240 sq miles (622 km^2)
Population: 531,000
Economy: GNP $3120m per capita $6380
  Predominantly oil economy
Labour force: agriculture 2% industry 32.3% services
  65.7%
Urban population: 83%

Cyprus
Political system: the island has been effectively
  partitioned since 1974 between its predominantly
  Greek and predominantly Turkish areas
Area: 3572 sq miles (9251 km^2)

Republic of Cyprus (Greek)
Capital: Nicosia
Population: 580,000
Economy: GNP $5633m per capita $8040
  Mixed economy, tourism
Labour force: agriculture 12.3% industry 25.8%
  services 61.9%
Urban population: 68.5%

Turkish Republic of Northern Cyprus
Capital: Nicosia
Population: 176,000
Economy:
Labour force: agriculture 26.1% industry 21.2%
  services 52.3%
Urban population: 35%

Iran
Islamic Republic of Iran
Political system: Islamic republic
Capital: Tehran
Area: 636,296 sq miles (1,648,000 km^2)
Population: 59,570,000
Economy: GNP $139,120m per capita $2450
  Mixed economy; oil predominates but manufacturing
  and agriculture also strong
Labour force: agriculture 24.9% industry 21% services
  54.1%
Urban population: 56.7%

Iraq
Republic of Iraq
Political system: one-party republic
Capital: Baghdad
Area: 167,925 sq miles (434,924 km^2)
Population: 18,838,000
Economy: GNP $73,000m per capita $4110
  Mixed economy, oil predominating
Labour force: agriculture 12.4% industry 16.7%
  services 70.9%
Urban population: 70.4%

Israel
State of Israel
Political system: multi-party republic
Capital: Jerusalem
Area: 7992 sq miles (20,700 km^2)
Population: 5,239,000
Economy: GNP $50,866m per capita $10,970
  Mixed economy – agriculture, manufacturing, tourism
Labour force: agriculture 3.1% industry 25.5% services
  71.4%
Urban population: 89.9%

Jordan
Hashemite Kingdom of Jordan
Political system: constitutional monarchy
Capital: Amman
Area: 37,738 sq miles (97,740 km^2)
Population: 3,636,000
Economy: GNP $3924m per capita $1240
  Mixed economy
Labour force: agriculture 7.3% industry 20.1% services
  72.6%
Urban population: 68%

Kuwait
State of Kuwait
Political system: constitutional monarchy
Capital: Kuwait City
Area: 6880 sq miles (17,818 km^2)
Population: 1,190,000
Economy: GNP $33,089m per capita $16,150
  Oil-dominated economy
Labour force: agriculture 1.3% industry 23.5% services
  75.2%
Urban population: 95.6%

Lebanon
Republic of Lebanon
Political system: multi-party republic
Capital: Beirut
Area: 4015 sq miles (10,400 km^2)
Population: 2,803,000
Economy: no reliable figures
  Mixed economy – agricultural and services
Labour force: agriculture 19.1% industry 24.1%
  services 56.8%
Urban population: 83.7%

Oman
Sultanate of Oman
Political system: monarchy with consultative council
Capital: Muscat
Area: 82,030 sq miles (212,457 km²)
Population: 1,640,000
Economy: GNP $9503m per capita $6327
  Oil-dominated economy
Labour force: agriculture 27.7% industry 26.5%
  services 45.8%
Urban population: 10.6%

Qatar
State of Qatar
Political system: constitutional monarchy based on
  Islamic law
Capital: Doha
Area: 4247 sq miles (11,000 km²)
Population: 520,000
Economy: GNP $6962m per capita $15,860
  Oil economy
Labour force: agriculture 3.1% industry 29.4% services
  67.5%
Urban population: 89.5%

Saudi Arabia
Kingdom of Saudi Arabia
Political system: monarchy
Capital: Riyadh
Area: 830,000 sq miles (2,149,690 km²)
Population: 15,267,000
Economy: GNP $89,986 per capita $6230
  Oil economy
Labour force: agriculture 9.9% industry 23.8% services
  63.3%
Urban population: 77.3%

Syria
Syrian Arab Republic
Political system: multi-party republic
Capital: Damascus
Area: 71,498 sq miles (185,180 km²)

Population: 12,958,000
Economy: GNP $12,404m per capita $1020
  Mixed economy, some oil
Labour force: agriculture 22% industry 26.8% services
  51.2%
Urban population: 50.4%

Turkey
Republic of Turkey
Political system: multi-party republic
Capital: Ankara
Area: 301,382 sq miles (780,576 km²)
Population: 58,584,000
Economy: GNP $91,742m per capita $1630
  Mixed economy, heavy agricultural emphasis
Labour force: agriculture 46.4% industry 18% services
  35.6%
Urban population: 61.3%

United Arab Emirates
Political system: monarchy, federation of seven emirates
Capital: Abu Dhabi
Area: 32,278 sq miles (83,600 km²)
Population: 1,989,000
Economy: GNP $31,613m per capita $16,614
  Oil economy
Labour force: agriculture 5% industry 33.2% services
  61.8%
Urban population: 77.8%

Yemen
Republic of Yemen
Political system: transitional
Capital: San'a
Area: 205,356 sq miles (531,869 km²)
  (claims an area undemarcated on Saudi border)
Population: 12,147,000
Economy: GNP $7303m per capita $640
  Mainly agricultural economy
Labour force: agriculture 56.3% industry 13.1%
  services 30.3%
Urban population: 28.9%

Part 3   Europe

Armenia
Republic of Armenia
Political system: multi-party republic
Capital: Yerevan
Area: 11,506 sq miles (29,800 km²)
Population: 3,426,000
Economy: GNP – per capita –
  Mixed economy
Labour force: agriculture 5.7% industry 30% services
  64.3%
Urban population: 69.5%

Azerbaijan
Azerbaijan Republic
Political system: federal multi-party republic
Capital: Baku
Area: 33,400 sq miles (86,600 km²)
Population: 7,237,000
Economy: GNP – per capita –
  Mixed economy
Labour force: agriculture 32.3% industry and services
  67.7%
Urban population: 53.5%

Georgia
Republic of Georgia
Political system: multi-party republic
Capital: Tbilisi
Area: 26,900 sq miles (69,700 km^2)
Population: 5,482,000
Economy: GNP – per capita –
    Mixed economy
Labour force: agriculture 26% industry 30% services
    44%
Urban population: 56.2%

Malta
Republic of Malta
Political system: multi-party republic
Capital: Valletta
Area: 122 sq miles (316 km^2)
Population: 360,000
Economy: GNP $2342m per capita $6630
    Mixed economy – tourism
Labour force: agriculture 2.5% industry 31.8%
    services 65.7%
Urban population: 85.3%

Part 4 Asia (East, Far East and Pacific)

Bangladesh
People's Republic of Bangladesh
Political system: multi-party republic
Capital: Dhaka
Area: 55,598 sq miles (143,998 km^2)
Population: 110,602,000
Economy: GNP $22,579m per capita $200
    Predominantly agricultural economy
Labour force: agriculture 57.2% industry 12% services
    40.8%
Urban population: 24.4%

Bhutan
Kingdom of Bhutan
Political system: constitutional monarchy
Capital: Thimphu
Area: 18,147 sq miles (47,000 km^2)
Population: 1,511,000
Economy: GNP $273m per capita $190
    Predominantly agricultural economy
Labour force: agriculture 87.2% industry and services
    12.8%
Urban population: 13.1%

Brunei
State of Brunei
Political system: monarchy
Capital: Bandar Seri Begawan
Area: 2226 sq miles (5765 km^2)
Population: 268,000
Economy: GNP $3302m per capita $13,250
    Oil economy
Labour force: agriculture 3.5% industry 17.9% services
    78.6%
Urban population: 63.6%

Cambodia
State of Cambodia
Political system: UN-supervised transitional government
Capital: Phnom Penh
Area: 69,898 sq miles (181,035 km^2)
Population: 8,974,000

Economy: GNP $1066m per capita $130
    Predominantly agricultural economy
Labour force: agriculture 70.4% industry and services
    29.6%
Urban population: 12%

China
People's Republic of China
Political system: one-party republic
Capital: Beijing
Area: 3,705,408 sq miles (9,596,961 km^2)
Population: 1,165,888,000
Economy: GNP $415,884m per capita $370
    Mixed economy
Labour force: agriculture 60.2% industry 21.6%
    services 18.2%
Urban population: 26.2%

Fiji
Sovereign Democratic Republic of Fiji
Political system: republic
Capital: Suva
Area: 7056 sq miles (18,274 km^2)
Population: 748,000
Economy: GNP $1316m per capita $1770
    Mixed economy – agriculture, tourism, light industry
Labour force: agriculture 44.1% industry 12.9%
    services 43%
Urban population: 38.7%

French Polynesia
Political system: French overseas territory
Capital: Papeete
Area: 1544 sq miles (4000 km^2)
Population: 202,000
Economy: GNP – per capita –
    Mixed economy, tourism

Guam
Political system: self-governing 'unincorporated territory'
    of the USA
Capital: Agana
Area: 212 sq miles (549 km^2)
Population: 145,000

Economy: GNP – per capita –
  Mixed economy
Labour force: agriculture – industry – services –
Urban population: –

Hong Kong
Political system: British colony
Capital: Victoria
Area: 403.5 sq miles (1045 km^2)
Population: 5,799,000
Economy: GNP $71,303m per capita $12,500
  Mixed (entrepreneurial) economy
Labour force: agriculture 0.9% industry 36.7% services
  62.4%
Urban population: 100%

India
Republic of India
Political system: multi-party federal republic
Capital: New Delhi
Area: 1,269,346 sq miles (3,287,590 km^2)
Population: 889,700,000
Economy: GNP $294,816m per capita $350
  Mixed economy
Labour force: agriculture 66.4% industry 12.2%
  services 21.4%
Urban population: 25.7%

Indonesia
Republic of Indonesia
Political system: unitary multi-party republic
Capital: Jakarta
Area: 741,101 sq miles (1,919,443 km^2)
Population: 184,796,000
Economy: GNP $101,151m per capita $560
  Mixed economy – oil
Labour force: agriculture 54% industry 8.5% services
  37.5%
Urban population: 31.4%

Kazakhstan
Republic of Kazakhstan
Political system: unitary multi-party republic
Capital: Alma-Ata
Area: 1,049,200 sq miles (2,717,300 km^2)
Population: 17,008,000
Economy: GNP – per capita –
  Mixed economy
Labour force: agriculture 18.8% industry 33.2%
  services 48%
Urban population: 57.6%

Kiribati
Republic of Kiribati
Political system: democratic republic
Capital: Bairiki on Tarawa atoll
Area: 281 sq miles (728 km^2)
Population: 74,700
Economy: GNP $54m per capita $760
  Agriculture and fishing
Labour force: agriculture 71% industry 2.9% services
  26.1%
Urban population: 34.8%

Korea, North
Democratic People's Republic of Korea
Political system: one-party republic
Capital: P'yongyang
Area: 46,540 sq miles (120,538 km^2)
Population: 22,227,000
Economy: GNP $23,100m per capita $1079
  Mixed economy
Labour force: agriculture 44.1% industry 33% services
  22.9%
Urban population: 59.8%

Korea, South
Republic of Korea
Political system: multi-party republic
Capital: Seoul
Area: 38,035 sq miles (98,484 km^2)
Population: 43,663,000
Economy: GNP $231,132m per capita $5400
  Mixed economy
Labour force: agriculture 17.8% industry 33.8%
  services 48.4%
Urban population: 74.4%

Kyrgyzstan
Republic of Kyrgyzstan
Political system: multi-party republic
Capital: Bishkek
Area: 76,600 sq miles (198,500 km^2)
Population: 4,533,000
Economy: GNP – per capita –
  Mixed economy
Labour force: agriculture 33.2% industry 28% services
  38.8%
Urban population: 38.1%

Laos
Lao People's Democratic Republic
Political system: one-party republic
Capital: Vientiane
Area: 91,429 sq miles (236,800 km^2)
Population: 4,409,000
Economy: GNP $848m per capita $200
  Predominantly agricultural economy
Labour force: agriculture 72% industry and services
  28%
Urban population: 19%

Macau
Province of Macau
Political system: territory under Portuguese
  administration
Capital: Macau
Area: 5.99 sq miles (15.51 km^2)
Population: 367,000
Economy: $3685m per capita $8000
Labour force: industry 41.3% services 58.7%
Urban population: 100%

Malaysia
Political system: federal constitutional monarchy
Capital: Kuala Lumpur
Area: 127,317 sq miles (329,749 km^2)
Population: 18,630,000
Economy: GNP $44,944m per capita $2470
  Mixed economy – oil, rubber

Labour force: agriculture 27.8% industry 26.5%
 services 45.7%
Urban population: 38.2%

Maldives
Republic of Maldives
Political system: republic
Capital: Malé
Area: 115 sq miles (298 km²)
Population: 230,000
Economy: GNP $96m per capita $440
 Fishing, agriculture
Labour force: agriculture 25% industry 15.9% services
 59.1%
Urban population: 25.9%

Marshall Islands
Republic of the Marshall Islands
Political system: republic
Capital: Majuro
Area: 70.07 sq miles (181.48 km²)
Population: 50,000
Economy: GNP $63m per capita $1500
 Predominantly agricultural, fishing
Labour force: agriculture 18.7% industry 8.2% services
 73.1%
Urban population: 64.5%

Micronesia
Federated States of Micronesia
Political system: federal republic in free association with
 the United States
Capital: Palikir
Area: 270.8 sq miles (701.3 km²)
Population: 114,000
Economy: GNP $150m per capita $1500
 Mixed (copra)
Labour force: agriculture 2% industry 10.8% services
 87.2%
Urban population: 19.4%

Mongolia
Political system: multi-party republic
Capital: Ulan Bator
Area: 604,250 sq miles (1,565,000 km²)
Population: 2,182,000
Economy: GNP $240.7m per capita $112
 Mixed economy
Labour force: agriculture 29.4% industry 25.5%
 services 45.1%
Urban population: 58%

Myanmar
Union of Myanmar
Political system: military régime
Capital: Rangoon
Area: 261,218 sq miles (676,552 km²)
Population: 43,466,000
Economy: GNP $16,330m per capita $400
 Predominantly agricultural economy
Labour force: agriculture 67.6% industry 8.8% services
 23.6%
Urban population: 25%

Nauru
Republic of Nauru
Political system: republic
Capital: Yaren (seat of government)
Area: 8.2 sq miles (21.2 km²)
Population: 8,200
Economy: GNP – per capita –
 Phosphates – local industries developing

Nepal
Kingdom of Nepal
Political system: constitutional monarchy
Capital: Kathmandu
Area: 54,362 sq miles (140,797 km²)
Population: 19,795,000
Economy: GNP $3289m per capita $170
 Predominantly agricultural economy
Labour force: agriculture 79% industry 3.6% services
 17.4%
Urban population: 59.4%

New Caledonia
Territory of New Caledonia and Dependencies
Political system: French overseas territory
Capital: Nouméa
Area: 7358 sq miles (19,058 km²)
Population: 174,000
Economy: GNP $1606m per capita $10,140
 Mixed economy (ferronickel)
Labour force: agriculture 11.8% industry 15.3%
 services 72.9%
Urban population: 59.4%

Pakistan
Islamic Republic of Pakistan
Political system: multi-party federal republic
Capital: Islamabad
Area: 310,404 sq miles (803,943 km²)
Population: 130,129,000
Economy: GNP $42,629m per capita $380
 Mixed economy
Labour force: agriculture 49.6% industry 18.6%
 services 31.8%
Urban population: 32%

Papua New Guinea
Political system: multi-party monarchy (the British
 monarch is Head of State)
Capital: Port Moresby
Area: 178,260 sq miles (461,691 km²)
Population: 3,834,000
Economy: GNP $3372m per capita $860
 Predominantly agricultural – some mining
Labour force: agriculture 77% industry 5.4% services
 17.6%
Urban population: 15.2%

Philippines
Republic of Philippines
Political system: unitary republic
Capital: Manila
Area: 115,831 sq miles (300,000 km²)
Population: 63,609,000
Economy: GNP $43,954m per capita $730
 Mixed economy

Labour force: agriculture 41.5% industry 13.4%
  services 45.1%
Urban population: 43.2%

Singapore
Republic of Singapore
Political system: multi-party republic
Capital: Singapore
Area: 224 sq miles (581 km^2)
Population: 2,792,000
Economy: GNP $33,512m per capita $12,310
  Mixed (entrepreneurial) economy
Labour force: agriculture 0.3% industry 34.7% services
  65%
Urban population: 100%

Solomon Is.
Political system: parliamentary monarchy (the British
  monarch is Head of State)
Capital: Honiara
Area: 10,983 sq miles (28,446 km^2)
Population: 339,000
Economy: GNP $187m per capita $580
  Mixed (mining) economy
Labour force: agriculture 28.9% industry 10% services
  61.1%
Urban population: 15.7%

Sri Lanka
Democratic Socialist Republic of Sri Lanka
Political system: multi-party republic
Capital: Colombo
Area: 25,332 sq miles (65,610 km^2)
Population: 17,464,000
Economy: GNP $7988m per capita $470
  Predominantly agricultural – some manufacturing
Labour force: agriculture 40.9% industry 17.4%
  services 41.7%
Urban population: 21.6%

Taiwan
Republic of China
Political system: multi-party republic
Capital: Taipei
Area: 13,900 sq miles (36,002 km^2)
Population: 20,727,000
Economy: GNP $180,162m per capita $8790
  Mixed economy
Labour force: agriculture 12.8% industry 39.1%
  services 48.1%
Urban population: 74.5%

Tajikistan
Republic of Tajikistan
Political system: republic (transitional)
Capital: Dushanbe
Area: 55,300 sq miles (143,100 km^2)
Population: 5,568,000
Economy: GNP – per capita –
Labour force: agriculture 42.9% industry 13.5%
  services 43.6%
Urban population: 31.4%

Thailand
Kingdom of Thailand
Political system: constitutional monarchy
Capital: Bangkok
Area: 198,456 sq miles (514,000 km^2)
Population: 56,801,000
Economy: GNP $79,044m per capita $1420
  Predominantly agricultural
Labour force: agriculture 56% industry 14.4% services
  • 29.6%
Urban population: 18.7%

Tonga
Kingdom of Tonga
Political system: constitutional monarchy
Capital: Nuku'alofa
Area: 258 sq miles (699 km^2)
Population: 97,300
Economy: GNP $100m per capita $1010
  Predominantly agricultural economy
Labour force: agriculture 42.9% industry 9.9% services
  47.2%
Urban population: 30.7%

Turkmenistan
Republic of Turkmenistan
Political system: republic
Capital: Ashkhabad
Area: 188,500 sq miles (488,100 km^2)
Population: 3,859,000
Economy: GNP – per capita –
Labour force: agriculture 42.6% industry 10.6%
  services 46.8%
Urban population: 45.4%

Tuvalu
Political system: constitutional monarchy (the British
  monarch is Head of State)
Capital: Funafuti
Area: 61 sq miles (158 km^2)
Population: 9500
Economy: GNP $8750m per capita $967
  Predominantly agricultural economy
Labour force: agriculture 1% industry 7.2% services
  91.8%
Urban population: 34.2%

Uzbekistan
Republic of Uzbekistan
Political system: multi-party republic
Capital: Tashkent
Area: 172,700 sq miles (447,400 km^2)
Population: 21,363,000
Economy: GNP – per capita –
  Mixed economy
Labour force: agriculture 29.1% industry 17.6%
  services 53.3%
Urban population: 40.3%

Vanuatu
Republic of Vanuatu
Political system: republic
Capital: Vila
Area: 5700 sq miles (14,763 km^2)
Population: 154,000

Economy: GNP $167m per capita $1060
  Predominantly agricultural economy
Labour force: agriculture 61.1% industry 3.2% services
  35.7%
Urban population: 18.4%

Vietnam
Socialist Republic of Vietnam
Political system: one-party republic
Capital: Hanoi
Area: 127,242 sq miles (329,556 km²)
Population: 69,052,000
Economy: GNP $15,200m per capita $230
  Predominantly agricultural economy

Labour force: agriculture 72.7% industry 13.5%
  services 13.8%
Urban population: 20.1%

Western Samoa
Independent State of Western Samoa
Political system: constitutional monarchy
Capital: Apia
Area: 1097 sq miles (2842 km²)
Population: 160,000
Economy: GNP $121m per capita $730
  Predominantly agricultural economy
Labour force: agriculture 63.6% industry 3.6% services
  32.8%
Urban population: 20.5%

Part 5 Latin America and the Caribbean

Antigua and Barbuda
Political system: parliamentary monarchy (the British
  monarch is Head of State)
Capital: St John's
Area: 171 sq miles (442 km²)
Population: 64,000
Economy: GNP $363m per capita $4600
  Mixed economy
Labour force: agriculture 9% industry 18.8% services
  72.2%
Urban population: 32%

Argentina
Argentine Republic
Political system: federal republic
Capital: Buenos Aires
Area: 1,068,302 sq miles (2,766,889 km²)
Population: 33,070,000
Economy: GNP $76,491m per capita $2370
  Mixed economy
Labour force: agriculture 12% industry 30.5% services
  57.5%
Urban population: 86.2%

Bahamas
The Commonwealth of the Bahamas
Political system: parliamentary democracy (British
  monarch is Head of State)
Capital: Nassau
Area: 5380 sq miles (13,935 km²)
Population: 264,000
Economy: GNP $2913m per capita $11,510
  Mixed economy, tourism
Labour force: agriculture 3.9% industry 12.6% services
  83.5%
Urban population: 64.3%

Barbados
Political system: parliamentary democracy (the British
  monarch is Head of State)

Capital: Bridgetown
Area: 166 sq miles (431 km²)
Population: 259,000
Economy: GNP $1680m per capita $6540
  Mixed economy
Labour force: agriculture 5.4% industry 19% services
  75.6%
Urban population: 37.9%

Belize
Political system: parliamentary democracy (the British
  monarch is Head of State)
Capital: Belmopan
Area: 8867 sq miles (22,965 km²)
Population: 196,000
Economy: GNP $373m per capita $1970
  Mixed economy – mainly agricultural
Labour force: agriculture 27.6% industry 13.3%
  services 59.1%
Urban population: 51.6%

Bermuda
Political system: British colony
Capital: Hamilton
Area: 20.5 sq miles (53 km²)
Population: 61,000
Economy: GNP – per capita – (high level)
  Mixed economy – tourism
Urban population: 100%

Bolivia
Republic of Bolivia
Political system: multi-party republic
Capital: La Paz (seat of government), Sucre (legal
  capital)
Area: 424,164 sq miles (1,098,581 km²)
Population: 7,739,000
Economy: GNP $4526m per capita $620
  Mixed economy – mining

Labour force: agriculture 42.3% industry 17.2%
services 40.5%
Urban population: 51.4%

Brazil
Federative Republic of Brazil
Political system: multi-party federal republic
Capital: Brasilia
Area: 3,286,488 sq miles (8,511,965 km^2)
Population: 151,381,000
Economy: GNP $402,788m per capita $2680
Mixed economy
Labour force: agriculture 22.5% industry 21.5%
services 56%
Urban population: 74.9%

Chile
Republic of Chile
Political system: multi-party republic
Capital: Santiago
Area: 292,258 sq miles (756,945 km^2)
Population: 13,599,000
Economy: GNP $25,504m per capita $1940
Mixed economy
Labour force: agriculture 17.8% industry 24.1%
services 58.1%
Urban population: 84.6%

Colombia
Republic of Colombia
Political system: multi-party republic
Capital: Bogotá
Area: 439,737 sq miles (1,138,914 km^2)
Population: 33,392,000
Economy: GNP $40,805m per capita $1240
Mixed economy
Labour force: agriculture 28.5% industry 16.9%
services 54.6%
Urban population: 67.2%

Costa Rica
Republic of Costa Rica
Political system: multi-party republic
Capital: San José
Area: 19,575 sq miles (50,700 km^2)
Population: 3,161,000
Economy: GNP $5342m per capita $1910
Mixed economy
Labour force: agriculture 24.4% industry 24% services
51.6%
Urban population: 54%

Cuba
Republic of Cuba
Political system: socialist republic
Capital: Havana
Area: 44,218 sq miles (114,524 km^2)
Population: 10,848,000
Economy: GNP $20,900m per capita $2000
Mixed economy – sugar
Labour force: agriculture 20.4% industry 21.8%
services 57.6%
Urban population: 72.8%

Dominica
Commonwealth of Dominica
Political system: multi-party republic
Capital: Roseau
Area: 290 sq miles (751 km^2)
Population: 71,500
Economy: GNP $160m per capita $1940
Predominantly agricultural economy
Labour force: agriculture 25.8% industry 20.3%
services 53.9%
Urban population: 17%

Dominican Republic
Political system: multi-party republic
Capital: Santo Domingo
Area: 18,816 sq miles (48,734 km^2)
Population: 7,471,000
Economy: GNP $5847m per capita $820
Mixed economy
Labour force: agriculture 22% industry 16.2% services
61.8%
Urban population: 60.4%

Ecuador
Republic of Ecuador
Political system: multi-party republic
Capital: Quito
Area: 109,484 sq miles (283,561 km^2)
Population: 10,607,000
Economy: GNP $10,112m per capita $960
Mixed economy
Labour force: agriculture 30.8% industry 17.5%
services 51.7%
Urban population: 55.4%

El Salvador
Republic of El Salvador
Political system: republic
Capital: San Salvador
Area: 8124 sq miles (21,041 km^2)
Population: 5,460,000
Economy: GNP $5767m per capita $1100
Predominantly agricultural economy
Labour force: agriculture 8.1% industry 28.3% services
63.6%
Urban population: 44.4%

French Guiana
Department of French Guiana
Political system: overseas department of France
Capital: Cayenne
Area: 35,135 sq miles (91,000 km^2)
Population: 123,000
Economy: GNP – per capita –
Mixed economy

Grenada
Political system: parliamentary democracy (the British
monarch is Head of State)
Capital: St George's
Area: 133 sq miles (344 km^2)
Population: 90,900
Economy: GNP $199m per capita $2120
Agriculture, tourism
Labour force: agriculture 14.3% industry 16.7%
services 69%
Urban population: 32.2%

Guadeloupe
Department of Guadeloupe
Political system: overseas department of France
Capital: Basse-Terre
Area: 687 sq miles (1779 km²)
Population: 400,000
Economy: GNP $1170m per capita $3200
   Mixed economy
Labour force: agriculture 7.2% industry 11.5% services
   81.3
Urban population: 48.4%

Guatemala
Republic of Guatemala
Political system: republic
Capital: Guatemala City
Area: 42,042 sq miles (108,889 km²)
Population: 9,442,000
Economy: GNP $8309m per capita $900
   Predominantly agricultural economy
Labour force: agriculture 48.9% industry 17.5%
   services 33.6%
Urban population: 38.3%

Guyana
Co-operative Republic of Guyana
Political system: multi-party republic
Capital: Georgetown
Area: 83,000 sq miles (214,969 km²)
Population: 748,000
Economy: GNP $293m per capita $370
   Mixed economy – mining
Labour force: agriculture 20.4% industry 18.5%
   services 61.1%
Urban population: 34.5%

Haiti
Republic of Haiti
Political system: military
Capital: Port-au-Prince
Area: 10,714 sq miles (27,750 km²)
Population: 6,764,000
Economy: GNP $2400m per capita $370
   Predominantly agricultural economy
Labour force: agriculture 57.5% industry 7.5% services
   35.2%
Urban population: 29.6%

Honduras
Republic of Honduras
Political system: multi-party republic
Capital: Tegucigalpa
Area: 43,277 sq miles (112,088 km²)
Population: 4,996,000
Economy: GNP $3023m per capita $590
   Predominantly agricultural economy
Labour force: agriculture 46.1% industry 17.9%
   services 36%
Urban population: 41.1%

Jamaica
Political system: constitutional monarchy (the British
   monarch is Head of State)
Capital: Kingston
Area: 4244 sq miles (10,991 km²)

Population: 2,445,000
Economy: GNP $3606m per capita $1510
   Mixed economy (bauxite)
Labour force: agriculture 23% industry 14.5% services
   62.5%
Urban population: 52.3%

Martinique
Department of Martinique
Political system: overseas department of France
Capital: Fort-de-France
Area: 425.5 sq miles (1102 km²)
Population: 369,000
Economy: GNP $1429m per capita $4100
   Mixed economy
Labour force: agriculture 7.1% industry 8.7% services
   84.2%
Urban population: 80.5%

Mexico
United Mexican States
Political system: federal republic
Capital: Mexico City
Area: 761,605 sq miles (1,972,547 km²)
Population: 84,439,000
Economy: GNP $214,500m per capita $2490
   Mixed economy – oil
Labour force: agriculture 22% industry 26.4% services
   51.6%
Urban population: 71.3%

Netherlands Antilles
Political system: non-metropolitan territory of the Nether-
   lands
Capital: Willemstad
Area: 371 sq miles (961 km²)
Population: 191,000
Economy: GNP $1490m per capita $7800
   Mixed economy – petroleum products, tourism
Labour force: agriculture 0.7% industry 13.6% services
   85.7%
Urban population: 92.4%

Nicaragua
Republic of Nicaragua
Political system: multi-party republic
Capital: Managua
Area: 50,193 sq miles (130,000 km²)
Population: 4,131,000
Economy: GNP $1661m per capita $460
   Mixed (mainly agricultural) economy
Labour force: agriculture 32.4% industry 9.8% services
   57.6%
Urban population: 59.8%

Panama
Republic of Panama
Political system: multi-party republic
Capital: Panama City
Area: 29,762 sq miles (77,082 km²)
Population: 2,515,000
Economy: GNP $4414m per capita $1830
   Agricultural economy, the chief resource being the
   Panama Canal
Labour force: agriculture 25.4% industry 13.7%
   services 60.9%
Urban population: 52.9%

Paraguay
Republic of Paraguay
Political system: republic
Capital: Asunción
Area: 157,048 sq miles (406,752 km²)
Population: 4,519,000
Economy: GNP $4796m per capita $1110
  Predominantly agricultural economy
Labour force: agriculture 42.9% industry 18.8%
  services 38.3%
Urban population: 47.5%

Peru
Republic of Peru
Political system: multi-party republic
Capital: Lima
Area: 496,225 sq miles (1,285,216 km²)
Population: 22,404,000
Economy: GNP $25,149m per capita $1160
  Mixed economy – mining
Labour force: agriculture 34% industry 16.6% services
  49.4%
Urban population: 71.3%

Puerto Rico
Commonwealth of Puerto Rico
Political system: self-governing commonwealth
  associated with the USA
Capital: San Juan
Area: 3435 sq miles (8897 km²)
Population: 581,000
Economy: GNP $22,831m per capita $6429
  Mixed economy
Labour force: agriculture 2.9% industry 19% services
  78.1%
Urban population: 70.7%

St Christopher-Nevis
State of St Christopher-Nevis
Political system: federal constitutional monarchy (the
  British monarch is Head of State)
Capital: Basseterre
Area: 101 sq miles (261 km²)
Population: 43,100
Economy: GNP $133m per capita $3330
  Mixed economy
Labour force: agriculture 29.6% industry 17.4%
  services 53%
Urban population: 48.9%

St Lucia
Political system: constitutional monarchy (the British
  monarch is Head of State)
Capital: Castries
Area: 238 sq miles (616 km²)
Population: 135,000
Economy: GNP $286m per capita $1900
  Mixed economy
Labour force: agriculture 33.9% industry 13.8%
  services 52.3%
Urban population: 46.4%

St Vincent and the Grenadines
Political system: constitutional monarchy (the British
  monarch is Head of State)
Capital: Kingstown
Area: 150 sq miles (388 km²)
Population: 109,000
Economy: GNP $184m per capita $1610
  Mixed economy
Labour force: agriculture 25.7% industry 15.6%
  services 58.7%
Urban population: 24.7%

Surinam
Republic of Surinam
Political system: multi-party republic
Capital: Paramaribo
Area: 63,037 sq miles (163,265 km²)
Population: 404,000
Economy: GNP $1365m per capita $3050
  Mixed economy – alumina and bauxite
Labour force: agriculture 16.8% industry 18.6%
  services 64.6%
Urban population: 65.2%

Trinidad & Tobago
Republic of Trinidad and Tobago
Political system: multi-party republic
Capital: Port-of-Spain
Area: 1981 sq miles (5130 km²)
Population: 1,261,000
Economy: GNP $4458m per capita $3470
  Mixed economy – oil
Labour force: agriculture 10.8% industry 28.5%
  services 60.7%
Urban population: 69.1%

Uruguay
Republic of Uruguay
Political system: republic
Capital: Montevideo
Area: 68,037 sq miles (176,215 km²)
Population: 3,130,000
Economy: GNP $7929m per capita $2560
  Mixed economy
Labour force: agriculture 14.5% industry 23.8%
  services 61.7%
Urban population: 85.5%

Venezuela
Republic of Venezuela
Political system: multi-party republic
Capital: Caracas
Area: 353,144 sq miles (912,040 km²)
Population: 20,184,000
Economy: GNP $50,574m per capita $2560
  Mixed economy – oil
Labour force: agriculture 11.9% industry 25.9%
  services 62.2%
Urban population: 84%

Index

The numbers in italic type refer to maps and charts; numbers in bold type refer to entries in the Country Gazetteer and Biographical Notes.

and Commonwealth   107, 108, 114
    debts   96
    as donor nation   146–7
    independence   3, 8, 45
    industrialization   170
    and New International Economic Order   153
    as oil producer   139, 143, 144, 146, 165
    population   157, 159
    resources and trade   163, 165, 169, 170
Nigerian Trust Fund (NTF)   50
Nimeiri, President   64, 74
Niue   9, 88
Nixon, Richard   83, 85
Nkomo, Joshua   7
Nkrumah, Dr Kwame   12, 43, 45–6, 46, 47, **176**
Non-Aligned Movement   xi, 30–42, *41*
    attitudes to Third World   32–6
    in Latin America   30, 35, 40, 92–3
    membership   30–2
    summit conferences   38–42, 92–3
    see also Nehru, Jawaharlal
non-government organizations (NGOs)   137–8
Norfolk Is.   9
Noriega, Manuel   94–5
North Atlantic Treaty Organization (NATO)   *34–5*
North Cyprus   108
North Korea   18, 125, **188**
North Vietnam   10, 12, 76, 83
North Yemen   60
    see also Yemen Arab Republic
North–South Dialogue   viii, xi, 4, 32, 62, 74, 115,
        130–1, 140, 144, 145, 148, 152–3, 153, 156
    see also Brandt Report
Northeastern New Guinea   21
Northern Rhodesia   114
Norway   34, 69, 122, 124, 131, 131–2
    New International Economic Order   153
NOVIB   136
nuclear weapons   vii, 6, 13, 81, 88
nuts   168
Nyasaland   7, 114
    see also Malawi
Nyerere, Julius Kambarage   53, 113–14, 115, 170,
        176

ocean beds   170
Oceania, Commonwealth countries   108
official development assistance (ODA)   124, 131
O'Higgins, Bernardo   89
oil   60, 62, 98, 139–49, *142*, 154, 156, 165
Okanagan Statement and Programme of Action on
        Southern Africa (1987)   111
Oman   60–1, 65, 66, 71, 72, **186**
    resources   169
OPEC Fund (OPEC Special Fund)   148–9
Opium Wars   10

Organisation commune africaine et malgache
        (OCAM)   52
Organisation pour la Mise en Valeur du Fleuve
        Sénégal (OMVS)   55
Organization of African Unity (OAU)   4, 39, 43,
        47–50, *48*, 58, 154
    Charter   47–50
Organization of American States (OAS)   87, 104,
        106
Organization of Arab Petroleum Exporting
        Countries (OAPEC)   72, 73, 140
Organization for the Development of the Senegal
        River (OMVS)   55
Organization of Eastern Caribbean States
        (OECS)   100
Organization for Economic Co-operation and
        Development (OECD)   109, 118–19, 121,
        122, 126–7, 128–30, 130, 131, 147
Organization of the Islamic Conference
        (OIC)   65, 88
Organization of Petroleum Exporting Countries
        (OPEC)   59, 62, 71, 73, 87, *139, 147*
    aid   51, 101, 120, 125, *128, 130*, 136, 137,
        146–9
    and New International Economic Order   150,
        151, 152, 152–3, 154, 155, 156
    production   161, 163–4, 165
    threat to Western capitalism   32
Overseas Development Administration
        (ODA)   132, 137, 152
OXFAM   136

Pacific   31, 87–8, 108, 157–8, 159
Pahlavi, Mohammed Riza, *see* Shah of Persia/Iran
PAIGC (resistance movement in Guinea-
        Bissau)   6–7
Pakistan   34, 35, *79*, **189**
    aid to   123, 124, 132, 148
    and Commonwealth   110, 111, 113, 114, 119–20
    debts   96
    as importer   167
    independence   1, 8, 9, 76–7, 85
    population   157, 160
    as pro-western   37, 84
    refugees   23
    see also Bangladesh
Palestine   40, 66, 67, 74
    refugees   *70*, 70
Palestine Liberation Army (PLA)   70
Palestine Liberation Organization (PLO)   xi, 40,
        65, 68–70, 71, 74, 75
Palestine National Council (PNC)   70
Palme, Olof   155
Pan-African Movement for East, Central and
        Southern Africa (PAFMECSA)   47
Pan-Africanism   43, 46–7